The Wild Man Within

THE WILD MAN

WITHIN *⌇ An Image in*
Western Thought from the Renaissance
to Romanticism ⌇ EDITED BY

EDWARD DUDLEY and
MAXIMILLIAN E. NOVAK

UNIVERSITY OF PITTSBURGH PRESS

Library of Congress Catalog Card Number 72-77191
ISBN 0-8229-3246-6
Copyright © 1972, University of Pittsburgh Press
All rights reserved
Henry M. Snyder & Co., Inc., London
Manufactured in the United States of America

The illustration on page iii is from *Valentine and Orson: The Two Sonnes of the Emperour of Greece* (London, 1649).

"The Image of the Indian in the Southern Colonial Mind" by Gary B. Nash appeared originally in *The William and Mary Quarterly*, 29 (April 1972).

"Leviathan Triumphant: Thomas Hobbes and the Politics of Wild Men" by Richard Ashcraft appeared originally in slightly different form under the title "Hobbes's Natural Man: A Study in Ideology Formation" in *The Journal of Politics*, 33 (November 1971). Used by permission.

Grateful acknowledgment is made to the following for permission to quote material that appears in this book:

Faber and Faber Ltd, for lines from the poem "The Allegory of the Wolf Boy" from *The Sense of Movement* by Thom Gunn. Used by permission.

Alfred A. Knopf, Inc., for lines from the poem "Sunday Morning" from *The Collected Poems of Wallace Stevens*. Copyright 1954 by Wallace Stevens. Used by permission.

G. Schirmer, Inc., for lines from *The Magic Flute* by Mozart, translated by Ruth and Thomas Martin. Copyright 1941, 1951, by G. Schirmer, Inc. Used by permission.

Contents

Illustrations

Introduction

More than thirty-five years ago Arthur O. Lovejoy and George Boas brought out the first volume of what was to be, as its title stated, *A Documentary History of Primitivism and Related Ideas*. The series, which never went beyond this first volume, an exploration of the problems of primitivism in antiquity, announced that it would explore "the record . . . of man's misgivings about his performances, about his prospects and about himself." Whatever the reason for failing to complete this project, it is clear that the subject was broader in its ramifications than its authors realized in setting out. And just as Lovejoy, Boas, and Lois Whitney, with their sophisticated approach to the history of ideas, were to show the limitations of a work like Hoxie Neale Fairchild's *The Noble Savage* (1928), so it may be said that, as an intellectual construct, primitivism was too complex for the methodology employed by Lovejoy and his co-workers.

The present volume, with essays from scholars in a number of disciplines, deliberately avoids a unified approach to so protean a subject as primitivism. Instead it focuses on the importance of wildness and the Wild Man during a period of Western thought which came to hold up ideals of cultures and civilization as its finest accomplishment. Because the idealization of the culture that came to flower in the Baroque and the Rococo palaces of Europe contained its inner contradictions, noble and ignoble savages abound in the writings of this period. As economists came to accept luxury as a virtue and moralists came to appreciate the ways in which manners had improved man's ethical nature, there rose other voices questioning the effects of civilization on man's essential humanity. Much of this may be summed up in the assertion of Tombo-Chiqui, an archetypal American Indian who appeared in a play by John Cleland in 1758. After observing the institutions of "Enlightened England" for some time, Tombo-Chiqui tells his master, "In short, you are Men in nothing, but so far as you resemble us, whom you call savages."

To Tombo-Chiqui, "civilization" is merely an aspect of madness, a reversal of everything truly reasonable and natural. And from this standpoint, the subject matter of this collection of essays is far more central to the thought, and indeed the psyche, of the seventeenth and eighteenth centuries than the theme of insanity which Michel Foucault has so brilliantly delineated in his *Madness and Civilization,* for as Foucault demonstrates, madness at this time was something alien, something to be cast out and separated from the body. The life of the savage, on the other hand, was something in every man, something to come to terms with—not so much a mirror for Western civilization as a fluoroscope, revealing the organs and bones below the clothing and flesh. Some writers used the Wild Man as a stick to beat Western civilization, others rejected him as debased, in some cases, as nonhuman. But they did not treat him as an abstract "idea." He was very much a reality for a period absorbing the meaning of the discoveries made by those terrestrial explorers who followed Columbus and by those philosophical explorers who followed Montaigne, Hobbes, and Rousseau in their voyages into the human mind.

As the contributors to this volume suggest, the savage was usually seen in terms of a complex set of attitudes that had been created around the Wild Man in the ancient world and in the Middle Ages. This mythic being, reared by bears or wolves, living in isolation, possessed of enormous physical strength and sexual potency, covered with hair, and often without any language, survived the realities of the voyages of discovery and lived on not only in the Western psyche but also in its official taxonomy as developed by Linnaeus. Transformed by Monboddo, Rousseau, and the Romantics, he entered modern thought and survives in a debased form in the abominable snowman of modern journalism or in that ferocious-sentimental Wild Man of the cinema, King Kong.

For the purposes of Western thought, the Wild Man and the savage served many of the same purposes. Both belonged to the region of the mind that treasured freedom over control, nature over art, passion over abstract reason. The Wild Man played a role in politics, education, linguistics, anthropology, philosophy, and literature, and all of these subjects are treated, some in terms of individual writers and works, others in essays covering a wide range of works and issues.

The editors wish to express particular thanks to Professor Alan Deyermond of the University of London. His lecture at the University of California, Los Angeles, on the wild men and wild women of the Spanish Middle Ages served as a catalyst for the present volume. His interest in the topic dates from an earlier study ("El hombre selvage in la novela sentimental," *Filología,* 10 [1964], 97–111).

The editors are also grateful to Steven Sharp of UCLA for his help in checking elusive references and in proofreading, and to Mary Van Dyke and Louise Craft at the University of Pittsburgh Press for their skill and patience in preparation of the manuscript. And finally we thank the Research Committee at the University of California, Los Angeles, for a grant that made this work possible.

The Wild Man Within

The Forms of Wildness: Archaeology of an Idea

 HAYDEN WHITE

But those things which have no significance of their own are inter-
woven for the sake of the things which are significant.

Saint Augustine, *The City of God*

The subject of these essays is the Wild Man during his age of triumph, the seventeenth and eighteenth centuries, when he was viewed as "the Noble Savage" and served as a model of all that was admirable and uncorrupted in human nature. My task in this introductory essay is to say something about this Wild Man's pedigree, to reconstruct the genealogy of the Wild Man myth, and to indicate the function of the notion of wildness in premodern thought. In order to provide the background required, I shall have to divide the cultural history of Western civilization into rather large, and perhaps indigestible, chunks, arrange them in clusters of possible significance, and serve them up in such a crude form as to obscure completely the great variety of opinions concerning the notion of wildness which is to be found in ancient and medieval literature. What I shall finally offer, therefore, will look more like an archaeologist's cabinet of artifacts than the flowing narrative of the historian; and we shall probably come to rest with a sense of structural stasis rather than with a sense of the developmental process by which various ideas came together and coalesced to produce the "Noble Savage" of the eighteenth century. Other essays in this collection will, however, provide the materials for a history of the idea of the Wild Man during his period of triumph. In this introductory chapter I can provide little more than the historian's equivalent of a field archaeologist's notes, reflections on a search for archetypal forms rather than an account of their varia-

3

tions, combinations, and permutations during the late medieval and early modern ages.

The notion of "wildness" (or in its Latinate form, "savagery") belongs to a set of culturally self-authenticating devices which includes, among many others, the ideas of "madness" and "heresy" as well. These terms are used not merely to designate a specific condition or state of being but also to confirm the value of their dialectical antitheses: "civilization," "sanity," and "orthodoxy" respectively. Thus, they do not so much refer to a specific thing, place, or condition as dictate a particular attitude governing a relationship between a lived reality and some area of problematical existence that cannot be accommodated easily to conventional conceptions of the normal or familiar. For example, the apostle Paul opposes heresy to orthodoxy (or division to unity) as the undesirable to the desirable condition of the Christian community, but in such a way as to make the undesirable condition subserve the needs of the desirable one. Thus he writes: "There must be also heresies among you, that they which are approved may be made manifest among you" (1 Cor. 11:19). And Augustine, in the passage from *The City of God* which serves as the epigraph of this essay, distinguishes between those subjects in his history which are significant for themselves and those which have no significance but exist merely as counterexamples or illuminative counterinstances of the operations of grace in the midst of sin.[1] Just as in his own *Confessions,* Augustine found it necessary to dwell upon the phenomena of sin in order to disclose the noumenal workings of grace, so too in his "prophetic history" of mankind he was compelled to focus on the sinful, heretical, insane, and damned in order to limn the area of virtue occupied by the pure, the orthodox, the sane, and the elect. Like the Puritans who came after him, Augustine found that one way of establishing the "meaning" of his own life was to deny meaning to anything radically different from it, except as antitype or negative instance.

The philosopher W. B. Gallie has characterized such notions as "democracy," "art," and the "Christian way of life" as "essentially contested concepts," because their definition involves not merely the clarity but also the self-esteem of the groups that use them in cultural polemics.[2] The terms "civilization" and "humanity" might be similarly characterized. They lend themselves to definition by stipulation rather than by empirical observation and induction. And the same can be said of their conceptual antitheses, "wildness" and "animality." In times of socio-cultural stress, when the need for positive self-definition asserts itself but no compelling criterion of self-identification appears, it is always possible to say something like: "I may not know the precise content of my own felt humanity, but I am most certainly *not* like that," and simply point to something in the landscape that is manifestly different from oneself. This might be called the technique of ostensive self-definition by negation, and it is certainly much more generally practiced in cultural polemic than any other form of definition, except perhaps a priori stipulations. It appears as a kind of reflex action in conflicts between nations, classes, and political parties, and is not unknown among scholars and intellectuals seeking to establish their claims to elite status against the vulgus mobile. It is a technique that is especially useful for groups whose dissatisfactions are easier to recognize than their programs are to justify, as when the disaffected elements in our own society use the term "pig" to signal a specific attitude with respect to the symbols of conventional authority. If we do not know what we think "civilization" *is*, we can always find an example of what it is not. If we are unsure of what sanity is, we can at least identify madness when we see it. Similarly, in the past, when men were uncertain as to the precise quality of their sensed humanity, they appealed to the concept of wildness to designate an area of subhumanity that was characterized by everything they hoped they were not.

So much for the general cultural function of those concepts that arise out of the need for men to dignify their specific mode of existence by contrasting it with those of other men, real or imagined, who merely differed from themselves. There is another point that should be registered here before proceeding. It has to do with the historical career of such concepts as wildness, savagery, madness, heresy, and the like, in Western thought and literature. When in the thought and literature of ancient higher civilizations these concepts make their appearance in a culturally significant way, they function as signs that point to or refer to putative essences incarnated in specific human groups. They are treated neither as provisional designators, that is, hypotheses for directing further inquiry into specific areas of human experience, nor as fictions with limited heuristic utility for generating possible ways of conceiving the human world. They are, rather, complexes of symbols, the referents of which shift and change in response to the changing patterns of human behavior which they are meant to sustain.

Thus, for example, as Michel Foucault has shown in his study of the idea of madness during the age of reason, the term "insanity" has been filled with a religious content during periods of religious enthusiasm, with a political content during times of intensive political integration, and with an economic content during ages of economic stress or expansion.[3]

More importantly, Foucault has shown that, whatever the specifically medical definition of insanity, the way societies *treat* those designated as insane and the place and nature of their confinement and treatment vary in accordance with the more general forms of social praxis in the public sphere. This is especially true of those forms of insanity which medical science is unable to analyze adequately. The case of schizophrenia in our own age comes to mind. R. D. Laing has argued that although it passes for a medical term, in reality the concept schizophrenia is used in a political way; in spite of medical science's ambiguities about the nature and causes of schizophrenia, the idea is still used to deprive people presumed to be suffering from it of their civil and even human rights in courts of law.[4]

All this points to the fact that societies feel the need to fill areas of consciousness not yet colonized by scientific knowledge with conceptual designators affirmative of their own existentially contrived values and norms. No cultural endowment is totally adequate to the solution of all the problems with which it might be faced; yet the vitality of any culture hinges upon its power to convince the majority of its devotees that it is the sole possible way to satisfy their needs and to realize their aspirations. A given culture is only as strong as its power to convince its least dedicated member that its fictions are truths. When myths are revealed for the fictions they are, then, as Hegel says, they become "a shape of life grown old." First nature, then God, and finally man himself have been subjected to the demythologizing scrutiny of science. The result has been that those concepts which in an earlier time functioned as components of sustaining cultural myths and as parts of the game of civilizational identification by negative definition, have one by one passed into the category of the fictitious; they are identified as manifestations of cultural neurosis, and often relegated to the status of mere prejudices, the consequences of which have as often been destructive as they have been beneficial. The unmasking of such myths as the Wild Man has not always been followed by the banishment of their component concepts, but rather by their interiorization. For the dissolution by scientific knowledge of the ignorance which led earlier men to locate their imagined wild men in specific times and places does not necessarily touch the levels of psychic anxiety where such images have their origins.

In part, the gradual demythologization of concepts like "wildness," "savagery," and "barbarism" has been due to the extension of knowledge into those parts of the world which, though known about (but not actually known), had originally served as the physical stages onto which the "civilized" imagination could project its fantasies and anxieties. From biblical times to the present, the notion of the Wild Man was associated with the idea of the wilderness—the desert, forest, jungle, and mountains —those parts of the physical world that had not yet been domesticated or marked out for domestication in any significant way. As one after another of these wildernesses was brought under control, the idea of the Wild Man was progressively despatialized. This despatialization was attended by a compensatory process of psychic interiorization. And the result has been that modern cultural anthropology has conceptualized the idea of wildness as the repressed content of *both* civilized *and* primitive humanity. So that, instead of the relatively comforting thought that the Wild Man may exist *out there* and can be contained by some kind of physical action, it is now thought (except by those contemporary ideologues on both sides of the iron curtain who think they can save "civilization" if only they can succeed in destroying enough "wild" human beings) that the Wild Man is lurking within every man, is clamoring for release within us all, and will be denied only at the cost of life itself.

The Freudian model of the psyche, conceived as an ego occupying a fortress under siege by a double enemy, the superego and the id, both of which represent the pressures of mechanisms with ultimately aggressive motor forces, is perhaps the best-known pseudoscientific example of this process of remythification.[5] But it is not the only one. The theories of C. G. Jung and many post-Freudians, including Melanie Klein and her American disciple, Norman O. Brown, represent the same process, as do those other contemporary culture critics who, like Lévi-Strauss, lament the triumph of technology over civilized man and dream of the release of the lost child or the Noble Savage within us.

I call this interiorization of the wilderness and of its traditional occupant, the Wild Man, a *re*mythification, because it functions in precisely the same way that the myth of the Wild Man did in ancient cultures, that is, as a projection of repressed desires and anxieties, as an example of a mode of thought in which the distinction between the physical and the mental worlds has been dissolved and in which fictions (such as wildness, barbarism, savagery) are treated, not as *conceptual instruments* for designating an area of inquiry or for constructing a catalog of human possibilities, or as *symbols* representing a relationship between two areas of experience, but as *signs* designating the existence of things or entities whose attributes bear just those qualities that the imagination, for whatever reasons, insists they must bear. What I am suggesting is that in the history of Western thought the idea of the Wild Man describes a transition from myth to fiction to myth again, with the modern form of the myth assuming a pseudoscientific aspect in the various theories of the psyche currently clamoring for our attention. I shall elaborate on this process of remythification at the end of this essay. For the moment I want to explain what I mean by the process of the original demythification of the Wild Man myth, its translation into, and use as, a fiction, in modern times, as a prelude to my characterization of its history in the Middle Ages.

Fictive, or provisional, characterization of radical differences between what is only a superficially diverse humanity appears to be alien to what Paul Tillich has conveniently called the "theonomic" civilizations.[6] Without the secularization or humanization of culture itself, without a profound feeling that whatever sense we make out of the world, it is the *human* mind that is at work in the business of sense-giving, and not some transcendental power or Deity that makes sense *for* us, the distinction between fiction and myth would be literally unthinkable. In the theonomic thought of ancient Egypt, for example, as in the thought world of most primitive tribes, the sensed difference between the "we" and the "they" is translated into a difference between an achieved and an imperfect humanity. Insofar as a unified *humanity* is imaginable, it is conceived to be the possession of a single group.

Among the ancient Hebrews, of course, ethical monotheism and the doctrine of the single creation tended to force thought to the consideration of the potential *re*unification of a humanity that had become fractured and fragmented *in time,* as a result of human actions and as part of the Deity's purpose in first creating mankind whole and then letting it fall apart into contending factions. And in medieval Christian theology, especially in its dominant Augustinian variety, by virtue of its Neoplatonic inclinations, the idea of a *vertical* unification of the whole of creation in a comprehensive chain of being, which embraced not only the Creator himself but the whole of his creation, was combined with the notion of a potential *horizontal* movement in time toward a final unification at the end of time, when the saved would be returned to the direct communion with God which Adam had surrendered in the Fall.[7] But even here the idea of a *historical* division of mankind prevails as a cultural force. The Hebrews experience a division of humanity into Jew and Gentile even though they are forced to imagine, by virtue of their conception of God's power and justice, a humanity that is finally integrated through the Hebraization of the world. Similarly, medieval Christians experienced a division of humanity, and indeed of the cosmos itself, into hierarchies of grace, which translated into a division between the saved and the damned, even though their conception of the power of divine love forced them constantly to the contemplation of a time when historical division would dissolve in the blinding fire of the final unification of man with himself, with his fellowman, and with God. As long as men appeared different from one another, their division into higher and lower forms of humanity had to be admitted; for, in a theonomic world, variation—class or generic—had to be taken as evidence of species corruption. For if there was one, all-powerful, and just God ordering the whole, how could the differences between men be explained, save by some principle which postulated a more perfect and a less perfect approximation to the ideal form of humanity contained in the mind of God as the paradigm of the species? Similarly, in a universe that was thought to be ordered in its essential relations by moral norms rather than by immanent physical causal forces, how could radical differences between men be accounted for, save by the assumption that the different was in some sense inferior to what passed for the normal, that is to say, the characteristics of the group from which the perception of differentness was made?

This is not to say that the conception of a divided humanity, and a humanity in which differentness was conceived to reflect a qualitative rather than merely a quantitative variation, was absent in those sectors of classical pagan civilization where a genuine secularism and an attendant humanistic pluralism in thought had been achieved. The "humanistic" Greek writers and thinkers, no less than their modern, secularized counterparts, found it easy to divide the world into their own equivalents for the Christian "saved" and "damned." But just as the Greeks tended to diversify their gods on the basis of external attributes, functions, and powers, so too they tended toward a conception of an internally diversified humanity. Even in Roman law, which begins with a rigid distinction between Roman and non-Roman—and even within the Roman community itself between partrician and plebeian—in such a way as to suggest a distinction between a whole and a partial man, the general tendency, in response no doubt to the exigencies of empire, inclined toward inclusion in the community of the elect rather than exclusion from it.

There is, therefore, an important difference between the form that the total humanity is imagined to have by Greek and Roman thinkers and that which it is imagined to have by Hebrew and Christian thinkers. To put it crudely, in the former, humanity is experienced as diversified in fact though unifiable in principle. In the latter, humanity is experienced as unifiable in principle though radically divided in fact. This means that perceived differences between men had less significance for Greeks and Romans than they had for Hebrews and Christians. For the former, differentness was perceived as physical and cultural; for the latter, as moral and metaphysical. Therefore, the ideas of differentness in the two cultural traditions define the two archetypes that flow into medieval Western civilization to form the myth of the Wild Man. To anticipate my final judgment on the matter, let me say that the two traditions in general reflect the emotional concerns of cultural patterns that can conveniently be called—following Ruth Benedict—"shame oriented" and "guilt oriented," respectively.[8] The result is that the image of the Wild Man sent down by the Middle Ages into the early modern period tends to make him the incarnation of "desire" on the one side and of "anxiety" on the other.

These represent the general (and I believe dominant) aspects of the myth of the Wild Man before its identification as a myth and its translation into a fiction in the early modern period. To be sure, just as there is a "guilt" strain in classical paganism, so too there is a "shame" strain in Judeo-Christian culture. And later on I shall refer to the idea of the "barbarian" as a concept in which these two strains converge in a single image at times of cultural stress and decline, as in the late Hellenic and late Roman epochs. For the time being, however, I am merely trying to block out the grounds on which the different conceptions of wildness which Richard Bernheimer, in his excellent book *Wild Men in the Middle Ages*,[9] has discovered in medieval fable, folklore, and art. It is on these grounds that the different archetypes of wildness met with in medieval Western culture take root. It is the dissolution of these grounds through modern scientific and humanistic study that permits us to distinguish between wildness as a myth and as a fiction, as an ontological state and as a historical stage of human development, as a moral condition and as an analytical category of cultural anthropology, and, finally, to recognize in the notion of the Wild Man an instrument of cultural projection that is as anomalous in conception as it is vicious in application.

I

I shall now turn to some examples of the concept of wildness as they appear in Hebrew, Greek, and early Christian thought. These examples are not exhaustive even of the *types* of wildness that the premodern imagination conceived. Moreover, I do not intend to try to characterize the complex differences between the various kinds of submen presumed to exist within each of the traditions dealt with. My purpose is rather to stress the components of wildness conceived to exist by the Hebrew, Greek, and early Christian imaginations that contrast with one another as distinctive cultural artifacts. I am quite aware, for example, that those images of the Wild Man which appear in Hebrew thought as incarnations of accursedness have their counterpart in Greek thought as projections of the fear of demonic possession, and that the descriptions of the mental attributes of wild men, conceived as what we would call mad or insane or depraved, are quite similar in the two cultures. I want, however, to identify the ontological bases which underlie the designations of men as wild in Hebrew, Greek, and early Christian thought respectively, in order to illuminate the differing moral attitudes with which men so designated were regarded in the different cultures. Only by distinguishing among the moral postures with which Jew, Greek, and Christian confronted the image of wildness can we gain a hold on how the idea of wildness was used in cultural polemic in the late Middle Ages and achieve some understanding of how the myth of wildness got translated into a fiction in the early modern period.

To begin with, it should be noted that the difference between Hebrew and Greek conceptions of wildness reflects dissimilar tendencies in the anthropological presuppositions underlying their respective traditions of social commentary. This difference may have had its origin in a tendency of Hebrew thought to dissolve physical into moral states in contrast to the Greek tendency to do the reverse. Greek anthropological theory tends to objectify, or physicalize, what we would call internal, spiritual, or psychological states. Hebrew thought consistently inclines toward the reduction of external attributes to the status of manifestations of a spiritual condition. The literary and anthropological implications of these crucial differences and the dynamics of their fusion in later Western thought and literature are fully explored in Erich Auerbach's book *Mimesis*, especially in its deservedly famous first chapter.[10] The cultural-historical bases of these different tendencies are analyzed in two works to which I am especially indebted: E. R. Dodds, *The Greeks and the Irrational*, and Johannes Pedersen's magisterial *Israel*, especially the brilliant chapter on the soul in ancient Hebrew thought.[11] The important point is that, although the distinction between an internal spiritual or psychological state and an external or physical condition was a very difficult distinction to arrive at in both Greek and Hebrew thought, the descriptive syntax used to represent human states in general tended to subordinate what we would recognize as internal to external factors in Greek thought, whereas the reverse was the case in Hebrew thought. This accounts in part for the different roles played by the images of the Wild Man deriving from the Bible on the one side and from classical paganism on the other.

The problematical nature of a *wild* humanity arises in Hebrew thought in large part as a function of the unique Hebrew conception of God. In the Hebrew creation myth, an omnipotent, omniscient, and perfectly just Deity creates the natural world and populates it with the various species of the physical, plant, and animal kingdoms—each perfect of its kind; and He then sets man, in the full perfection of *his* kind, at the world's moral center, to rule over it. In the Edenic state, the universe is conceived to be perfectly ordered and harmonious in its parts. Confusion and sin are introduced into this state by Adam's sin, and man is expelled from Eden and sent out into a world that suddenly appears hostile and hard. Nature assumes the aspect of a chaotic and violent enemy against which man must struggle to win back his proper humanity or godlike nature.

Of course, Adam's fall does not play the same role in Hebrew that it does in Christian thought. For the ancient Hebrews, the myth of the Fall had an essentially etiological function: it explained how men had arrived at their current general condition in the world and why, although some were chosen and some were not, even the chosen still had to labor to win their reward. The Fall was not, as it subsequently became for the apostle Paul, the cause of a kind of species taint that is transmitted from Adam to all humanity and that prevents all men from living according to God's law without the aid afforded by a special grace. The Fall is merely that event which explains the human condition in spite of the fact that man was created by a perfectly just and all-powerful God; it does not create an ontological flaw at the heart of humanity. And the Hebrew people—the descendants of Adam through Abraham—viewed themselves as a strain of humanity which, even in its natural condition, could, by adhering to the terms of the covenant, flourish before God, win the blessing (*Berâkâh*), and achieve a kind of peace and security on earth not too dissimilar to that enjoyed by Adam and Eve in Eden. Thus, the Old Testament does not present all men as having been made "wild" by Adam's fall, not even all Gentiles. In fact, the Gentiles actually serve as a paradigm of "natural" humanity, just as the Hebrews, the people of the covenant, serve as a paradigm of a morally redeemable humanity, a kind of potential superhumanity. Over against both the natural man and the superman, however, there is set a third alternative, the "wild man," the man from whom no blessing flows because God has withdrawn the blessing from him. When God withdraws the blessing from a man, an animal, a people, or the land in general, the result is a fall into a state of degeneracy below that of "nature" itself, a peculiarly horrible state in which the possibility of redemption is all but completely precluded.

Let me be more specific. The distinction between man and animal, though fundamental to Hebrew thinking, is less significant than the distinction between those things which enjoy the blessing and those which do not. Animal nature is not in itself "wild," it is merely not human. Wildness is a peculiarly moral condition, a manifestation of a specific relationship to God, a cause and at the same time a consequence of being under God's curse. But it is also—or rather it is indiscriminately—a *place;* that is to say, it is not only the *what* of a sin, but the *where* as well. For example, the biblical concordances tell us that the Hebrew word for "wilderness" (*sh*ᵉ*mâmâh*), used in the sense of "desolation," appears in 2 Sam. 13:20 to characterize the condition of the violated woman Tamar; but the *place* of the curse (the desert, the void, the wasteland) is also described as a wilderness. So too the place of the dead (*sh*ᵉ*ôl*) is described in Job 17:14 as a place of corruption and decay. These states and places of corruption or violation are distinguished from the "void" (*bôhûw*)[12] which exists before God creates the heavens and the earth and which is the only morally neutral state mentioned in the Bible. All other states are either states of blessedness or of accursedness. In short, it appears quite difficult to distinguish between a moral condition, a relationship, a place, and a thing in all those instances in the Bible where words that might be translated as wild or wilderness appear.[13]

This conflation of a physical with a moral condition is one of the sources of the prophets' power. It lies at the heart of the terror conveyed by Job in his lament, when in his characterization of his affliction, he refers to God's dissolution of his "substance," and (in Job 30:26–31) says:

When I looked for good, then evil came *unto me:* and when I waited for light, there came darkness. My bowels boiled, and rested not: the days of affliction prevented me. I went mourning without the sun: I stood up, *and* I cried in the congregation. I am a brother to dragons, and a companion to owls. My skin is black upon me, and my bones are burned with heat. My harp also is *turned* to mourning, and my organ into the voice of them that weep.

Job in his suffering has descended to the condition to which he originally (Job 30:3) consigned his enemies ("they were solitary; fleeing into the wilderness in former times desolate and waste"). The wilderness is the chaos lying at the heart of darkness, a void into which the soul is sent in its degradation, a barren place from which few if any return.

To be sure, the withdrawal of the prophet into the countryside is a common theme in the Old Testament. The prophet is sometimes pictured as coming out of the countryside, like Amos, or withdrawing to it in preference to concourse with a sinful Israel, like Jeremiah. But the countryside is one thing; the wilderness is quite another. The countryside is still the place of the blessing; the wilderness stands at the opposite side of being, as the place where God's destructive power manifests itself most dramatically. This is why wilderness can appear in the very heart of a human being, as insanity, sin, evil—any condition that reflects a falling away of man from God.

Those conditions which we would designate by the terms wildness, insanity, or savagery were all conceived by the ancient Hebrews to be aspects of the same evil moral condition. The relation between the condition of blessedness and that of wildness is therefore perfectly symmetrical: the blessed prosper and their blessedness is reflected in their wealth and health, the number of their sons, their longevity, and their ability to make things grow. The accursed wither and wander aimlessly on the earth—fearful, ugly, violent; and their fearfulness, ugliness, and violence are evidence of their accursedness.

The archetypal wild men of the Old Testament are the great rebels against the Lord, the God-challengers, the antiprophets, giants, nomads—men like Cain, Ham, and Ishmael, the very kinds of "heroes" who, in Greek mythology and legend, might have enjoyed a place of honor beside Prometheus, Odysseus, and Oedipus. Like the angels who rebelled against the Lord and were hurled down from heaven, these human rebels against the Lord continue—compulsively, we would say—to commit Adam's sin. And even though they often sin out of ignorance, their punishment is not less severe for it. They are depicted as wild men inhabiting a wild land, above all as hunters, sowers of confusion, damned, and generative of races that live in irredeemable ignorance or outright violation of the laws that God has laid down for the governance of the cosmos. Their offspring are the children of Babel, of Sodom and Gomorrah, a progeny that is known by its pollution. They are men who have fallen below the condition of animality itself; every man's face is turned against them, and in general (Cain is a notable exception) they can be slain with impunity.

Now, the *form* that the wildness of this degraded breed takes is described in terms of *species corruption*. Since at the Creation God fashioned the world and placed in it the various species, each perfect of its kind, the ideal natural order would therefore be characterized by a perfect species purity. Natural disorder, by contrast, has its extreme form in species corruption, the mixing of the kinds (*mýn*)—the joining together of what God in his wisdom had, at the beginning, decreed should remain asunder. The mixing of the kinds is, therefore, much worse than any struggle, even to the death, between or among them. The struggle is natural; the mixing is unnatural and destructive of a condition of species isolation that is a moral as well as natural necessity. To mix the kinds is taboo. Thus men who had copulated with animals had to be exiled from the community, just as animals of different kinds which had been sexually joined had to be slaughtered (Lev. 18:23–30). The horror of species pollution is carried to such extreme lengths in the Deuteronomic Code that it is there forbidden, not only to yoke different animals to the same plow (Deut. 22:10), but even to sow different kinds of seeds in the same field (Lev. 19:19).[14]

One example of a humanity gone wild by species mixture is provided in the book of Genesis, in that famous but ambiguous passage which records the effects of the mating of "the sons of God" with "the daughters of men" (ch. 6). This instance of species mixture brought forth a breed of men possessing an almost universally credited attribute of wildness: gigantism. The nature of these giants is even less clear than their ancestry. Biblical philologists link the word for giant (*nᵉphiyl* or *nᵉphîl*), which connotes the ideas of bully and tyrant, with the root for the verb *nâphal*, which means to fall, to be cast down, but which has secondary associations with the notions of dying, division, failure, being judged, perishing, rotting, and being slain. The appearance of these giants is offered as the immediate cause of God's decision to destroy the world in the Flood, except of course for Noah, his family, and two each of the kinds of animals.

After the Flood, however, evil and (therefore) wildness returned to the world, especially in the descendants of Noah's youngest son, Ham, who was cursed for revealing his father's nakedness. From Ham was descended, later biblical genealogists decided, that breed of "wild men" who combined Cain's rebelliousness with the size of the primal giants. They must also have been black, since, through etymological conflation, the Hebrews ran together word roots used to indicate the color black, the land of Egypt (i.e., of bondage), the land of Canaan (i.e., of pagan idolatry), the condition of accursedness (and, ironically, apparently the notion of fertility), with the proper name of Ham and its adjectival variations. Later on, Christian biblical commentators insisted that Nimrod, the son of Cush, must have been descended from Ham, which would have meant that he was not only black, but that he shared the attributes of the primal giants: grossness and rebelliousness.

In *The City of God,* for example, Augustine insists on reading the passage which describes Nimrod as "a mighty hunter *before* the Lord" as "a mighty hunter *against* the Lord."[15] And he goes on to identify Nimrod as the founder of the city of Babel, whose people had tried to raise a tower against the heavens and brought down upon mankind the confusion of tongues which has afflicted it ever since. In the linkage of Nimrod with Babel (or Babylon) and the further linkage of these with the account of how the different races were formed and the different language families constituted, we have almost completed our catalog of the main components of the Wild Man myth as it comes down from the Bible into medieval thought. Cursedness, or wildness, is identified with the wandering life of the hunter (as against the stable life of the shepherd and farmer), the desert (which is the Wild Man's habitat), linguistic confusion (which is the Wild Man's as well as the barbarian's principal attribute), sin, and physical abberation in both color (blackness) and size. As Augustine says: "And what is meant by the term 'hunter' but deceiver, oppressor, and destroyer of the animals of the earth?"[16] As for the Wild Man's inability to speak, which is part of the Wild Man myth wherever we meet it throughout the Middle Ages, Augustine says, "As the tongue is the instrument of domination, in it pride was punished."[17] The equation is all but complete: in a morally ordered world, to be wild is to be incoherent or mute, deceptive, oppressive, and destructive; sinful and accursed; and, finally, a monster, one whose physical attributes are in themselves evidence of one's evil nature.

All of this suggests the ways in which the conception of wildness found in the Old Testament gets transformed in the wake of the progressive spiritualization of the Hebrew conception of God through the work of the prophets and through the simultaneous physicalization of nature as the result of the union of Greek thought with Judaic thought in late biblical times. In ancient Hebrew thought, when a man or a woman or place or group lost the blessing and fell into a condition of accursedness, that spiritual condition was manifested in the form and attributes of wildness. At that point the relationship of the community to the accursed thing was unambiguous: it was to be exiled, isolated, and avoided at all costs, at least until such time as the curse was removed and the state of blessedness was restored.[18] But only God could remove the curse that he had placed on a thing. And since, at least in the more archaic part of the Old Testament, it was God's righteousness rather than his mercy that was stressed in thought about him, the tendency was to regard accursedness (and therefore wildness or desolation) as an all but insuperable condition, once it had been fallen into.

The Christian doctrine of redemption through grace, and of grace as a *medicina* that could be dispensed through the ministration of the Sacraments by the Church, encouraged a much more charitable attitude among the faithful toward the sinner who had fallen from grace into a state of wildness than the originally puritanical conception of the Deity in the Old Testament permitted. At least, such was the theory. Actually, Christian universalism was not notably less egocentric, in a confessional sense, than its ancient Hebrew prototype. Universalistic in principle, the Church was communally inclusive in practice only of those who accepted membership on its own terms. This meant that although anyone could be admitted to the Church on principle, the potential member of the Church had to be willing to put off the old man and put on the new. And although it was granted that lapses from grace might be forgiven, the lapsed sinner seeking readmission to the community of the faithful had to display evidence of his intention to accept the Church's authority and discipline in the future, and not seek to import alien doctrines and practices into the community from the state of sin into which, in his pride, he had fallen. All this had been involved in the struggles with the heresies of Donatus on the one side and of Pelagius on the other, during the fourth and fifth centuries.[19]

Still, Christian thinkers insisted that a man might sin and not lapse into a condition from which there was no redemption at all. After the Incarnation all men were salvageable in principle, and this meant that whatever the state of *physical* degeneracy into which a man fell, the soul remained in a state of potential grace. Sin, Augustine insists, is less a positive condition than a negation of an original goodness, a condition of removal from communion with God, which is at once the cause and the consequence of pride.[20] And it may or may not be attended by signs of physical degradation. Since only God himself knows precisely who belongs and who does not belong to his city, it remains for the faithful to work for the inclusion of everyone within the community of the Church. This meant that even the most repugnant of men—barbarian, heathen, pagan, and heretic—had to be regarded as objects of Christian proselytization, to be seen as possible converts rather than as enemies or sources of corruption, to be exiled, isolated, and destroyed. In the final analysis, Augustine says, even the most monstrous of men were still *men,* and even those races of wild men reported by ancient and contemporary travelers had to be regarded as potentially capable of partaking of that grace which bestowed membership in the City of God.

Commenting on the different kinds of monstrous races reported by ancient travelers—races of men with one eye in the middle of the forehead, feet turned backward, a double sex, men without mouths, pygmies, headless men with eyes in their shoulders, and doglike men who bark rather than speak—all of which, incidentally, appear in medieval iconography as representations of wild men—Augustine insists that these should not be denied possession of an essential humanity. They must all be conceived to have sprung from "the one protoplast," he says; and he argues that "it ought not to seem absurd to us, that as in individual races there are monstrous births, so in the whole race there are monstrous races."[21] To be sure, he believes that these monstrous races must have descended from Ham and Japheth, Noah's sons, the former regarded by medieval theologians as the archetypal heretic, and the latter as the archetypal Gentile, as against Shem, who was believed to be the archetypal Hebrew, the ancestor of Abraham, and of Christ himself. Their descent from the archetypal sinner—as against the Gentile races' descent from the archetypal heretic—accounts for these monstrous races' inability to speak (since confusion of language is regarded as a reflection of a confusion of thought) and for their devotion to monstrous gods. Nonetheless, Augustine insists, they are potentially salvageable, as salvageable as any Christian child that may have been born with four rather than five fingers on a hand. The difference between these monsters and the normal Christian or the normal variant (pagan) humanity is one of degree rather than of kind, of physical appearance alone rather than of moral substance manifested in physical appearance.

The superaddition of Greek, and especially of Neoplatonic, concepts to Judaic ideas in Christianity tended to encourage the distinction between essences and attributes rather than their conflation. Medieval theologians discussed the problem of the Wild Man not in terms of physical characteristics conceived as manifestations of spiritual degradation but in terms of the possibility of God's endowing a man with the soul of an animal, or an animal with the soul of a man. It was difficult to envisage the notion of a *Wild* Man because it suggested either a misfire of God's creative powers or a kind of malevolence for man on the part of God that the doctrine of Christian charity expressly denied. It made sense to speak of a degraded nature, a nature fallen into corruption and decay. And one could speak of a fallen humanity, the state from which Christ had come to release those enthralled by Adam's sin. But to speak of a *Wild* Man was to speak of a man with the soul of an animal, a man so degraded that he could not be saved even by God's grace itself.

Thomas Aquinas discusses at length the differences between the animal soul and the human soul. The animal soul, he says, is pure desire undisci-

plined by reason; it desires, but knows not *that* it desires. The animal
soul made living a ceaseless quest, a life of lust without satisfaction, of
will without direction, a wandering that ended only with death. It was
because animals possessed such a soul that they had been consigned to
the service of man and to his governance. And because they possessed
such a soul, man could do with animals what he would: domesticate them
and use them, or, if necessary, destroy them without sin.[22] If such was the
fate of animals, then wild men, men possessed of animal souls, had to be
treated by normal men in similar ways. But this ran counter to the message of the Gospels, which offered salvation to anyone possessed of a
human soul, whatever his physical condition. It was because man possessed a human soul that he was able to rise above the aimless desire that
characterized the merely animal state, and to realize that his sole purpose
in life was to seek reunion with his Maker, and to work for it, with God's
help and the Church's, throughout all his days. The state of wildness
into which the popular legend insisted that a man *might* fall expressed
a deep anxiety, less about the way of salvation than about the possibility
that one might regress to a condition in which the very *chance* of salvation might be lost. Medieval Christian thought did not permit the contemplation of that contingency. In *The Divine Comedy* Dante places the
closest thing to the possessors of an animal soul that he can imagine,
carnal sinners, those who "submit reason to lust," in the second circle of
hell. Their punishment is to be eternally buffeted by a dark, tempestuous
wind.[23] If these sinners had been *wild men*, lacking a human soul, they
would not have been punished in hell, but like the pagan monsters in
Dante's poem, set up as guardians of hell or torturers of the sinners
consigned to hell.

The Wild Man's supposed dumbness reminds us that for many Greek
thinkers a *barbaros* (a term whose English derivative, barbarian, we are
inclined to use to indicate wildness) was anyone who did not speak Greek,
one who babbled, and who therefore lacked the one power by which the
political life could be achieved and a true humanity realized. It is not
surprising that the images of the barbarian and the Wild Man become
confused with each other in many medieval, as in many ancient, writers.
Especially in times of war or revolution, ancient writers tended to
attribute wildness and barbarism to anyone holding views different from
their own. But in general, just as the Hebrews distinguished between
Jews, Gentiles, *and* wild men, so too did the Greeks and Romans distinguish between civilized men, barbarians, and wild men.

The distinction, in both cases, hinged upon the difference between those men who lived under *some law* (even a false law) and those who lived under *no law at all*. Although Aristotle, in a famous passage in the *Politics*, characterized barbarians as "natural outcasts," as being "tribeless, lawless, heartless," and agreed with Homer that "it is right that Greeks should rule over barbarians,"[24] most classical writers recognized that because barbarian tribes at least honored the institution of the family, they must live under *some kind* of law, and therefore were capable of *some kind* of order. This recognition is probably a way of signaling awareness of the uncomfortable fact that the barbarian tribes were able to organize themselves, at least temporarily, into groups large enough to constitute a threat to "civilization" itself. Medieval, like ancient Roman, thinkers conceived barbarians and wild men to be enslaved to nature, to be, like animals, slaves to desire and unable to control their passions; as mobile, shifting, confused, chaotic; as incapable of sedentary existence, of self-discipline, and of sustained labor; as passionate, bewildered, and hostile to "normal" humanity—all of which are suggested in the Latin words for wild and wildness.[25] Although both barbarians and wild men were supposed to share these qualities, one important difference remained unresolved between them: *the Wild Man always lived alone,* or at the most with a mate. According to the myth that takes shape in the Middle Ages, the *Wild Man is incapable of assuming the responsibilities of a father;* and if his mate has children, she drops them where they are born, to survive or perish as they will.[26]

This meant that the Wild Man and the barbarian represented different kinds of threats to "normal" men. Whereas the barbarian represented a threat *to society in general,* to civilization, to racial purity, to moral excellence, whatever the ingroup's pride happened to be vested in, the Wild Man represented a threat to the *individual,* both as nemesis and as a possible destiny, both as enemy and as representative of a condition into which an individual man, having fallen out of grace or having been driven from his city, might degenerate. Accordingly, the temporal and spatial relationship of the Wild Man to normal humanity differs from that of the barbarian to the civilized man. The home of the barbarian is conventionally conceived to lie far away in space, and the time of his coming onto the confines of civilization is conceived to be fraught with apocalyptical possibilities for the whole of civilized humanity. When the barbarian hordes appear, the foundations of the world appear to be cracking, and prophets announce the death of the old and the advent of the new age.[27]

By contrast, the Wild Man is conventionally represented as being always present, inhabiting the immediate confines of the community. He is just out of sight, over the horizon, in the nearby forest, desert, mountains, or hills. He sleeps in crevices, under great trees, or in the caves of wild animals, to which he carries off helpless children, or women, there to do unspeakable things to them. And he is also sly: he steals the sheep from the fold, the chicken from the coop, tricks the shepherd, and befuddles the gamekeeper. In medieval myth especially, the Wild Man is conceived to be covered with hair and to be black and deformed. He may be a giant or a dwarf, or he may be merely horribly disfigured, rather like Charles Laughton in the American movie version of *The Hunchback of Notre Dame*. But in whatever way he is envisaged, the Wild Man almost always represents the image of the man released from social control, the man in whom the libidinal impulses have gained full ascendancy.

In the Christian Middle Ages, then, the Wild Man is the distillation of the specific anxieties underlying the three securities supposedly provided by the specifically Christian institutions of civilized life: the securities of *sex* (as organized by the institution of the family), *sustenance* (as provided by the political, social, and economic institutions), and *salvation* (as provided by the Church). The Wild Man enjoys none of the advantages of civilized sex, regularized social existence, or institutionalized grace. But, it must be stressed, neither does he—in the imagination of medieval man—suffer any of the restraints imposed by membership in these institutions. He is desire incarnate, possessing the strength, wit, and cunning to give full expression to all his lusts. His life is correspondingly unstable in character. He is a glutton, eating to satiety one day and starving the next; he is lascivious and promiscuous, without even consciousness of sin or perversion (and therefore of course deprived of the pleasures of the more sophisticated vices). And his physical power and agility are conceived to increase in direct ratio to the diminution of his conscience.

In most accounts of the Wild Man in the Middle Ages, he is as strong as Hercules, fast as the wind, cunning as the wolf, and devious as the fox. In some stories this cunning is transmuted into a kind of natural wisdom which makes him into a magician or at least a master of disguise.[28] This was especially true of the wild *woman* of medieval legend: she was supposed to be surpassingly ugly, covered with hair except for her gross pendant breasts which she threw over her shoulders when she ran. This wild woman, however, was supposed to be obsessed by a desire for ordinary men. In order to seduce the unwary knight or shepherd, she could appear as the most enticing of women, revealing her abiding ugliness only during sexual intercourse.[29]

Here of course the idea of the wild woman as seductress, like that of the Wild Man as magician, begins to merge with medieval notions of the demon, the devil, and the witch. But again formal thought distinguishes between the Wild Man and the demon. The Wild Man (or woman) was generally believed to be an instance of human regression to an animal state; the demon, devil, and witch are evil spirits or human beings endowed with evil spiritual powers, servants of Satan, with capacities for evil that the Wild Man could never match. Since the Wild Man had no rational faculties, he could not self-consciously perform an evil action. Therefore, he could be conceived to be free of all feelings of guilt or conscience. Wildness is what a normal human being takes on as a result of losing his humanity, not something possessed as a positive force, as the power of the devil was.

The incapacity of official thought to conceive of a wild humanity did not, of course, destroy the power the conception exercised over the popular imagination. But it may have tempered it somewhat. For if, during the Middle Ages, the Wild Man was an object of disgust and loathing, of fear and religious anxiety, the quintessence of possible human degradation, he was not conceived in general to be an example of *spiritual* corruption. This position was reserved for Satan and the fallen angels. After all, the Wild Man was one who had lost his reason, and who, in his madness, sinned ceaselessly against God. Unlike the rebel angels, the Wild Man did not *know* that he lived in a state of sin, or even *that* he sinned, or even what a "sin" might be. This meant that he possessed, along with his degradation, a kind of innocence—not the moral neutrality of the beast, to be sure, but a position rather "beyond good and evil." Sin he might, but he sinned through ignorance rather than design. This gave to his expressions of lust, violence, perversion, and deceit a kind of freedom that might be envied by normal men, men caught in the web of repression and sublimation that made up the basis of ordinary life. It is not strange, then, that, in the fourteenth and fifteenth centuries, when the social bonds of medieval culture began to disintegrate, the Wild Man became gradually transformed from an object of loathing and fear (and only secret envy) into an object of open envy and even admiration. It is not surprising that, in an age of general cultural revolution, the popular antitype of the officially defined "normal" humanity, the Wild Man, should be transformed into the ideal or model of a free humanity, his presumed attributes made the essence of a lost humanity, and his idealized image used as justification for rebellion against civilization itself.

This redemption of the image of the Wild Man began simultaneously with the recovery of classical culture, the revival of humanist values, and the improvisation of a new conception of nature more classical than Judeo-Christian in inspiration. Classical ideas about nature and pagan nature legends survived throughout the Middle Ages. But, until the twelfth century, they had lived a kind of underground existence among intellectuals on the one side and the incompletely Christianized peasantry of the countryside on the other. According to Bernheimer, during the twelfth century wild men began to appear in folklore as protectors of animals and forests and as teachers of a wisdom that was more useful to the peasant than the "magic" of the Christian priest.[30] This conception of the Wild Man may reflect a more bucolic view of nature, itself in part a reflection of a new experience of the countryside. By the twelfth century new agricultural tools and techniques were bringing vast areas of Europe under cultivation, as forests were cleared and broken, and the back country turned into sheep runs. Or it may reflect a kind of pagan peasant resistance to Christian missionaries who were once more taking up the task of Christianizing Europe, started in earlier times but interrupted by the Viking invasions, Muslim assaults, and feudal warfare. Whatever the reason, the appearance of the beneficent Wild Man, the protector and teacher of peasants, is attended by his identification with the satyrs, fauns, nymphs, and sileni of ancient times. And this identification complements, on a popular level, the vindication of nature by intellectuals through the revival of classical thought, and especially of Aristotelianism, that was occurring at the same time.

II

I have already noted that classical thinkers regarded the Wild Man in a way different from that of their Hebrew counterparts. And I have pointed out that this was not because Greeks or Romans were less afraid of the wilderness than the Hebrews were. Like the Jews, the Greeks set the life of men who lived under some law over against that of men without the law, the order (cosmos) of the city over against the turbulence (chaos) of the countryside. Those who were capable of living outside the city, beyond the rule of law, Aristotle insisted, had to be either animals or gods. In short, for him, as for most Greek thinkers, humanity was conceived primarily as designating a special kind of *relationship* that might exist between men; not as an essence or a substance that might definitely distinguish men from gods on the one side and from animals on the other—

at least such is Aristotle's opinion in his discussions of social and cultural, as against metaphysical, questions.

Thus, although the Greeks divided humanity into the civilized and the barbarous, they did not obsessively defend the notion of a rigid distinction between animal and human nature. In part, this was because most Greeks subscribed to the notion of a simple, universal substance from which all things were made, or to the notion of a universal principle of which all things were manifestations.[31] The "normal" man was merely one who had been fortunate enough to be born into a city-state; "normal" man, Aristotle says, is "zoon politikon," a political *animal*. Only those men who had attained to the condition of politicality could hope to realize a *full* humanity. Not *all* within the city could hope to become fully human: women, slaves, and businessmen are specifically denied that possibility by Aristotle in his *Ethics*.[32] But *no one outside* the city had the slightest chance at all of *fully* realizing his humanity: the conditions of a life unregulated by law precluded it. Anyone who lived outside the human world might become an *object* of curiosity or a *subject* of study, but he could never serve as a model of what men ought to strive to be. Thus, what a Greek would have understood by our notion of a Wild Man would have appeared to be almost as much a contradiction in terms as it would be, later on, for Christian theologians.

Actually, the Greeks had no need of the concept of a Wild Man as a projective image of their fantasy life. Their imagination populated the entire universe with a host of species mixtures, products of sexual unions of gods with men, men with animals, animals with gods, and so on.[33] If species pollution was a fear among the early Greeks as strong in its own way as anything felt about it by the Hebrews, the Greek imagination still took a certain delight in the contemplation of the possible consequences of such pollution. Thus, over against, and balancing, the lives of gods and heroes, who differed from ordinary men only by the *magnitude* of their power or talent, there stood such creatures as satyrs, fauns, nymphs, and sileni; beneficent monsters such as the centaurs, and malignant ones such as the Minotaur, born of a union of a woman, Pasiphaë, and a bull. These creatures played much the same role for the classical imagination that the Wild Man did for the medieval Christian. Above all, they served as imagistic representations of those libidinal impulses which, for social more than for purely religious reasons, could not be expressed or released directly. Some of these creatures—fauns, satyrs, and sileni— are pure pleasure-seekers; the object of their desire is physical pleasure itself; and they are little more than ambulatory genitalia. Sensual, lascivious, promiscuous, the main activity of these creatures can be adequately characterized only by recourse to the vernacular. Endowed like rams, bulls, stallions, or possessing the fulsome breasts and buttocks of the eternal feminine, or, as in the case of Hermaphrodite, possessing both sets of sexual attributes, these creatures lived for little else than sexual intercourse—without conscience, self-consciousness, or remorse.

Characteristically these erotic creatures do not inhabit the desert or wilderness; they are usually represented as inhabiting the relatively more peaceful mountain meadows or pools. They are as undisciplined as the accursed ones of Hebrew lore, but they seek out any place in which to satisfy their (generally enviable) erotic capacities. It is the monsters born of a union of a human with an animal who inhabit the desert places, or, as in the case of the Minotaur, occupy an artificial environment, the Labyrinth, which, it has been suggested, is the archetypal representation of a savage or a wild city.[34] These monsters represent the dark side of the classical pagan imagination, the thanatotic, as against the erotic, fantasies of pagan man. Here wildness in its malignant aspect appeared as the counterpart of the Hebrew fear of the loss of the blessing from God.

Now, medieval man had no need to revive the dark side, the Cyclops or Minotaur side, of the classical conception of wildness; this side was already present in the very conception of the *Wild* Man held up as the ultimate monstrosity to the believing Christian. What he did need, when the time was ripe, was the other, erotic representation of the pleasure-seeking but conscienceless libido. And so when the impulses that led men to ventilate their minds by exposure to classical thought began to quicken in the twelfth century, Western man subliminally began to liberate his emotions as well. This at least may be one significance of the attribution to the Wild Man of the characteristics of satyrs, fauns, nymphs, and certain of the good monsters, such as the centaur teachers. This association of the Wild Man with pagan images of libidinal, and especially of erotic, freedom created the imaginative reserves necessary for the cultivation of a socially revolutionary *primitivism* in the early modern era.

Let me pause here to draw a distinction between primitivism and archaism to help clarify the relationship between the image of the Wild Man and social radicalism in modern culture. Primitivism seeks to idealize *any group* as yet unbroken to civilizational discipline; archaism, by contrast, tends toward the idealization of real or legendary *remote ancestors*, either wild or civilized. Both kinds of idealization appear to be eternal moments in human culture, representing a desire felt from time to time by all of us to escape the obligations laid upon us by involvement in current social enterprises. However, archaism appears to be the more constant, since it can be appealed to in ways that are socially reinforcing as well as ways that are socially disruptive. The notion that "once upon a time" man was uncorrupted by greed, egotism, envy, and the like—a condition from which the current generation has fallen—can serve conservative as well as radical social forces. It can be used to justify conventional values as well as to justify departure from conventional behavior. Archaism produces enabling myths which may serve to inspire pride in group membership (as in Virgil's *Aeneid* or Livy's *History of Rome*), or may be used in traditional society to help present a revolution (such as Luther's) as a *revival* or *reformation* rather than as an innovation. Among the Greeks, Hesiod used the myth of a golden age in the remote past, when men lived in harmony with nature and one another, as an antithesis of his own current age, the age of iron, when force alone prevailed, possibly in the hope of inspiring men to undertake social reform. But—as in the case of Hesiod—archaism usually contains within it a recognition that the men of the idealized early age were inherently superior to the men of the present, that they were made of *finer stuff*.[35] And thus the appeal to a golden age in the past can serve just as often to reconcile men to the hardships of the present as to inspire revolt in the interest of a better future.

It is quite otherwise with primitivism. Although used as an instrument of social criticism in much the same way as archaism, primitivism is quintessentially a radical doctrine. For basic to it is the conviction that men are really the same throughout all time and space but have been made evil in certain times and places by the imposition of social restraints upon them. Primitivists set the savage, both past and present, over against civilized man as a model and ideal; but instead of stressing the qualitative differences between them, they make of these differences a purely quantitative matter, a difference in degree of corruption rather than in kind. The result is that in primitivist thought reform is envisaged rather as a throwing off a burden that has become too ponderous than as a *recon*stitution or *re*construction of an original, but subsequently lost, human perfection. Primitivism simply invites men to be themselves, to give vent to their original, natural, but subsequently repressed, desires; to throw off the restraints of civilization and thereby enter into a kingdom that is *naturally* theirs. Like archaism, then, primitivism holds up a vision of a lost world; but unlike archaism, it insists that this lost world is still latently present in modern, corrupt, and civilized man—and is there for the taking.

One more point on this difference: archaists usually differ from primitivists in the way they conceive of that nature-in-general which serves as the background for their imagined heroes' exertions or as the antagonist against which their heroes act to construct a precious human endowment. The archaist's image of nature is shot through with violence and turbulence; it is the nature of the jungle, *animal* nature, nature "red in tooth and claw," of conflict and struggle, where only the strongest survive. It is the "dark wood" of Lucretius, of Machiavelli, of Hobbes, and of Vico, the horrible formless forest which serves Dante as the base line of his Christian pilgrim's journey. It is the nature of the hunt, as portrayed by Piero di Cosimo, or of the mystery, as in Leonardo da Vinci.[36]

The primitivists' nature is, by contrast, Arcadian, peaceful, a place where the lion lies down with the lamb, where shepherdesses lie down with shepherds, innocently and frivolously; it is the world of the enclosed garden, where the virgin tames the unicorn—the world of the picnic. Only in this second kind of nature can the Wild Man take on the aspect of the Noble Savage—the gentle savage of Spenser's *Faerie Queen* and of Hans Sachs's *Lament of the Wild Men about the Unfaithful World*.[37]

In Sachs's poem, written in the sixteenth century, the Wild Man lives in a state of Edenic purity, without any taint of original sin, as an *antitype* of the corrupt world of the court and the city. Bernheimer dates the appearance of the Wild Man as Noble Savage and renewed interest in a presumed lost golden age in western Europe from the fourteenth century; and he links both developments to the phenomena of cultural crisis. During times of cultural breakdown, he says, men feel the need to return to simpler ways of life, holier times, a need to start the fashioning of humanity over again. Following Huizinga, whose great book on the breakdown of medieval civilization appears to have inspired his study, Bernheimer attributes the flowering during this age of what I have called primitivism (to distinguish it from the archaism that appears simultaneously with it) to the fact that official culture, both secular and religious, had become excessively oppressive, while the available forms of sublimation had been preempted by a superannuated and psychotic chivalric nobility.[38] Writers and artists began to survey history, myth, and legend for figures that would at once express their innermost desires for liberation and still give expression to their respect for tradition, the old, and the familiar. Thus the appeal of the primeval nature of Piero di Cosimo, the oneiric landscapes of Leonardo, the simple Romans of Machiavelli, the plain apostles of Luther, Erasmus's fools, and Rabelais's vulgar and high living giants, Gargantua and Pantagruel. In an age of universal rejection of the conventional image of "normal" humanity, a notion of

humanity shot through with contradictions between its ideal and its reality, radicalism lay in the adoption of any antitype to that image that
would show its schizoid dedication to mutually exclusive concepts of
man's nature to be the sickness that it was. And, as Bernheimer says,
"Nothing could have been more radical than the attitude of sympathizing
or identifying oneself with the Wild Man, whose *way of life* was the
repudiation of all the accumulated *values* of civilization."[39]

III

Thus, by the end of the Middle Ages, the Wild Man has become
endowed with two distinct personalities, each consonant with one of the
possible attitudes men might assume with respect to society and nature.
If one looked upon nature as a horrible world of struggle, as *animal*
nature; and society as a condition which, for all its shortcomings, was
still preferable to the natural state, then he would continue to view the
Wild Man as the antitype of the *desirable humanity*, as a warning of
what men would fall into if they definitively rejected society and its
norms. If, on the other hand, one took his vision of nature from the cultivated countryside, from what might be called *herbal* nature, and saw
society, with all its struggle, as a fall away from natural perfection, then
he might be inclined to populate that nature with wild men whose function was to serve as antitypes of *social* existence. The former attitude
prevails in a tradition of thought which extends from Machiavelli through
Hobbes and Vico down to Freud and Jean-Paul Sartre. The latter attitude
is represented by Locke and Spenser, Montesquieu and Rousseau, and
has recent champions in Albert Camus and Claude Lévi-Strauss.

Significantly, during the transitional period between the medieval and
the modern ages, many thinkers took a more ambivalent position, on
both the desirability of idealizing the Wild Man and the possibility of
escaping civilization. In his famous essay on cannibalism, Montaigne uses
reports of primitive peoples in Brazil in much the same way that the
Roman historian Tacitus used reports of the German tribes: to bring the
provincialism and ethnocentrism of his own people under attack, to undermine conventions thoughtlessly honored by his own generation, to explode
prejudice, and to ridicule the barbarities of his own age.[40] But even in
his most depressed moments, Montaigne does not suggest that his readers
ought to release the beast or cannibal within themselves.[41]

Similarly, Shakespeare, even in what is regarded as his most pessimistic
play, *The Tempest*, remains ambiguous as to the relative value of the

natural and the social world. Thus Shakespeare sets Caliban, the incarnation of libido and possessed of an unquenchable desire for freedom, over against Prospero the magician, the quintessence of civilized man, all ego and superego, learned and powerful, but jaded and captive of his own sophistication. And the contest between them is resolved in a way definitively advantageous to neither ideal. Each gets what he wants in the end, but only by giving up something of what, at the beginning of the play, he had valued most highly, and taking on some of the attributes of his enemy. Caliban is restored to rule over his island, but only at the cost of his savage innocence. Prospero throws away his magic stuff, leaves the island, and resolves to live as a man among men, without superhuman advantage but also without illusion, which may be a higher kind of innocence.[42]

Shakespeare, like most of his contemporaries, is still the poet of order and civilization, whatever his insights into the repressive and oppressive natures of both. It is only that, like Montaigne, whom he admired, he was reluctant to see in the forces that opposed order and civilization the workings of a distinctively inhuman power.

And of course other factors were at work in the rehabilitation of the Wild Man. Reports of travelers and explorers about the nature of the savages they encountered in remote places could be read in whatever way the reader at home desired. In any event, the Wild Man was being distanced, put off in places sufficiently obscure to allow him to appear as whatever thinkers wanted to make out of him, while still locating him in some place beyond the confines of civilization.

This spatialization of the Wild Man myth was being attended by his temporalization in the most sophisticated historical thought of the time. Vico, the Neapolitan philosopher who spans the gap between Baroque and Enlightenment civilization, insisted that savagery was both the original and the necessary stage of every form of achieved humanity. In his *New Science*, originally published in 1725, Vico portrayed the savage as a natural poet, as the source of the imaginative faculties still present in modern, civilized man, as possessor of an aesthetic or form-giving capacity in which civilization had its origins—at least among the pagans.[43] It was primitive man's ability to poetize his existence, to impose a form upon it out of aesthetic rather than moral impulses, that allowed the pagan peoples to construct a uniquely human world of society *against* their own most deeply felt animal instincts. For Vico, the savage was one who *naturally* felt and thought *poetically*, the ancestor of modern man who had begun by *living* poetry and ended by *becoming* all prose. Vico main-

tained that the original barbarism of the savage state was less inhuman
than the sophisticated barbarism of technically advanced but morally corrupt civilizations in their late stages. Moreover, he maintained that perhaps the only cure for civilizations that had entered into decline lay in a
return to a condition of barbarism, a revival of the poetic powers of the
savage—not the Noble Savage of the philosophe (the savage as custodian
of untainted natural reason and common sense), but the possessor of pure
will that would later be held up as an alternative to civilized man by the
Romantics. However, the transformation of the Noble Savage into the
poetic beast in the late eighteenth century will be dealt with by other
contributors to this volume. I merely note it here for purposes of orientation. More important to us at the moment is the process of fictionalization
of the Wild Man myth which preceded the transformation of the Wild
Man into the Noble Savage sometime during the late seventeenth century.

IV

Whatever else a myth may be—a verbal equivalent of a ritual, a poetic
account of origins, a projection of possible last things—it is also, as
Northrop Frye tells us, an example of thought working at the extremities
of human possibility, a projection of a vision of human fulfillment and
of the obstacles that stand in the way of that fulfillment.[44] Accordingly,
myths are oriented with respect to the ideal of perfect freedom, or
redemption, on the one side, and the possibility of complete oppression,
or damnation, on the other. Since men are indentured to live their lives
somewhere *between* perfect order and total disorder, between freedom
and necessity, life and death, pleasure and pain, the two extreme situations in which these conditions might be imagined to have triumphed are
a source of constant speculation in all cultures, archaic as well as modern:
whence the universal fascination of utopian speculations of both the
apocalyptic and the demonic sort, the dream of satiated desire on the one
side and the nightmare of complete frustration on the other. Myths provide imaginative justifications of our desires and at the same time hold
up before us images of the cosmic forces that preclude the possibility of
any perfect gratification of them.

The myth of the Wild Man served a twofold function in the late Middle Ages. As Bernheimer has shown, in the Middle Ages the notion of
wildness is consistently projected in images of desire released from the
trammels of all convention and at the same time images of the punishment which submission to desire brings down upon us.[45] The Wild Man

myth is what the medieval imagination conceives life would be like *if* men gave direct expression to libidinal impulses, both in terms of the pleasures that such a liberation might afford and in terms of the pain that might result from it.

Bernheimer speaks in the Freudian language of repression and sublimation, and he is no doubt justified in doing so.[46] But the tensions reflected in medieval conceptions of the Wild Man are understandable as a distinctively *medieval* phenomenon for the reason that the two images of wildness—the one as desire, the other as punishment—derive from different, and essentially incompatible, cultural traditions. Bernheimer himself traces the benign imagery of wildness back to classical archetypes and the malignant imagery back to biblical ones.[47] The two sets of images apparently became fused (and confused) during the High Middle Ages, thereby creating that anomalous conception of the state of wildness that we find in the iconography of the thirteenth and fourteenth centuries, of a Wild Man that is both good and evil, both envied and feared, both admired and calumniated. Formal Christian thought sought to dispel the anomalous conception of wildness by appeal to the Christian philosophy of nature contained in Scholasticism. The effort was wasted on the peasantry, if Bernheimer's evidence of the survival of medieval Wild Man motifs in contemporary folklore can be taken at face value. But it did succeed in the sphere of high culture, where the idea of nature was progressively purged of all theoretical imputations of evil. As a result of this theoretical redemption of nature, as well as of more general cultural factors, sometime during the fifteenth century the benign conception of the Wild Man was disengaged from the malignant one, and writers and thinkers began to recognize the fruitful uses in culture criticism to which a demythologized version of the benign imagery could be put. In short, sometime in the early modern period, no doubt as part of a general movement of secularization and as a function of humanism, the image of wildness was "fictionalized," that is, separated from an imagined "essence" of wildness and turned to limited use as an instrument of intracultural criticism.

Let me illustrate what I mean by the translation of the myth of wildness into a fiction by reference to Montaigne, who here, as in so many other matters, gives us a clear indication of the way that a distinctively modern attitude will develop. In his essay "Of Cannibals," Montaigne observes that "each man calls barbarism whatever is not his own practice." Then, after commenting on some of the more shocking practices of primitive peoples as reported in the accounts of ancient and modern travelers, he goes on to note that we ought to call such peoples "wild," only in the way that "we call wild the fruits that Nature has produced by herself and in her normal course." Actually, he says, "it is those that we have changed artificially and led astray from the common order, that we should rather call wild." For whereas we might legitimately call savage peoples barbarian "in respect to the rules of reason," we are not justified in so calling them "in respect of ourselves," and this because we "surpass them in every kind of barbarity."[48]

Here Montaigne plays with the notion of wildness in order to draw attention to a distinction that lies at the heart of his scepticism, the distinction that turns, not on the divine-natural antithesis, as in Christian theology, but on that of natural-artificial. For him the natural is not necessarily the good, but it is certainly preferable to the artificial, especially inasmuch as artificially induced barbarity is much more reprehensible in his eyes than its natural counterpart among savages. Montaigne wants his readers to identify the artificiality in themselves, to recognize the extent to which their superficial "civilization" masks a deeper "barbarism," thereby preparing them for the release, not of their souls to heaven, but of their bodies and minds to nature. By his use of the concept of wildness as a fiction, Montaigne "brackets" the myth of "civilization" that anchors it to a debilitating parochialism. His purpose is not to turn all men into savages or to destroy civilization, but to give them critical distance on their artificiality, which both prohibits the attainment of true civilization and frustrates the expression of their legitimate natural impulses.

Montaigne's fictive use of the notion of wildness is a characteristically ironical tactic. In Roman times the historian Tacitus used the concept of the barbarian, in his *Germania*, in precisely the same way, consciously stressing the presumed virtues of the savage tribes to the north so as to force his readers to contemplate the vices of the civilized Romans in the south. The same tactic appears in much of the work of the modern cultural anthropologist Claude Lévi-Strauss on primitive peoples and "the savage mind." Lévi-Strauss suggests that what civilized men conventionally call "the savage mind" is a repository of a particularly powerful imaginative faculty that has all but disappeared from its "civilized" counterpart under the impact of modernization. The savage mind, he maintains, is the product of a unique kind of relation to the cosmos that we exterminate at the peril of our own humanity.

Tacitus, Montaigne, and Lévi-Strauss are linked by the "fictive" uses they make of the concepts of "barbarism," "wildness," and "savagery."

In their works they telegraph their awareness that the antitheses they have set up between a "natural" humanity on the one side and an "artificial" humanity on the other are not to be taken literally, but used only as the conceptual limits necessary for gaining critical focus on the conditions of our own civilized existence. By joining them in acting as if we believed mankind could be so radically differentiated, put into two mutually exclusive classes, the "natural" and the "artificial," we are drawn, by the dialectic of thought itself, toward the center of our own complex existence as members of civilized communities. By playing with the extremes, we are forced to the mean; by torturing one concept with its antithesis, we are driven to closer attention to our own perceptions; by manipulating the fictions of artificiality and naturalness, we gradually approximate a truth about a world that is as complex and changing as our possible ways of comprehending that world.

The lack of this fictive capability, the inability to "play" with images and ideas as instruments for investigating the world of appearances, characterizes the unsophisticated mind wherever it shows itself, whether in the superstitious peasant, the convention-bound bourgeois, or the nature-dominated primitive. It is certainly a distinguishing characteristic of mythical thinking, which, whatever else it may be, is always inclined to take signs and symbols for the things they represent, to take metaphors literally, and to let the fluid world indicated by the use of analogy and simile slip its grasp. When a fiction, such as a novel or a poem, is taken literally, as a *report* of reality rather than as a verbal structure with more or less direct reference to the world of experience, it becomes mythologized. Yet what Frank Kermode calls the degeneration of fictions into myths[49] is discernible only from the vantage point of a culture whose characteristic critical operation is to expose the myth lying at the heart of every fiction. During the Christian Middle Ages a similar critical tactic was used to distinguish "false" from "true" religious doctrines. But with this difference from modern criticism: there thought remained locked within the confines of the root metaphor that referred the true meaning of everything to its transcendental origin and goal—the metaphor that literally equated human life with a quest for transcendental redemption. Within the limits of such an enabling mythological strategy, the concept of the Wild Man had very little chance of being exposed as the useful fiction that is has since become in the hands of sceptics and radicals from Montaigne and Rousseau to Marx and Lévi-Strauss. For although Christian thinkers and writers excelled in exposing the "mythological" character of every pagan, non-Christian, or heretical idea, the fact remained that, for them, thought was intended to help men escape from time and history rather than to understand them and turn them to earthly uses. As long as the ideal remained a kind of holy superman, in which none of the flaws of actual humanity was present, then the ultimate horror, the condition that had to be avoided at all costs, had to remain that subman which the imagination constructed out of its own repressed desires and to which thought had given, in classical and in Old Testament times, the designation of "wild."

V

I shall close by sketching out some aspects of the Wild Man's career after the eighteenth century and suggesting some of the implications of his career for our time. During the nineteenth century and in spite of Romanticism, primitive man came to be regarded less as an ideal than as an example of *arrested* humanity, as that part of the species which had failed to raise itself above dependency upon nature, as atavism, as that from which civilized man, thanks to science, industry, Christianity, and racial excellence, had finally (and definitively) raised himself. In the Victorian imagination primitive peoples were viewed with that mixture of fascination and loathing that Conrad examines in *Heart of Darkness*— as examples of what Western man might have been at one time and what he might become once more if he failed to cultivate the virtues that had allowed him to escape from nature.

During the late nineteenth century, to be sure, the new science of anthropology was already working to soften this harsh judgment; and in the twentieth century it has worked hard to destroy it, along with the racial prejudice that has invariably accompanied it. For most modern social scientists, primitive man is no longer either an ideal on which we ought to model ourselves or a reminder of what we might become if we betrayed our achieved humanity. Rather, primitive cultures are seen as different manifestations of man's power to respond differently to environmental challenges, as a control on inflated concepts of Western man's presumed cosmic election, and as a negation of various forms of cultural provincialism.

Accordingly, in modern times, the notion of a "wild man" has become almost exclusively a psychological category rather than an anthropological one, as it was in the seventeenth and eighteenth centuries. I am speaking, of course, of *popular* psychological categories, not scientific ones. What was once thought of as representing a peculiar *form of humanity,* a presocial state or a supersocial state, as the case might be, has become a category designating those who, for psychological or purely physical reasons, are unable to participate in the life of *any* society, whether primitive or civilized. In modern times the concept of wildness, when applied to a human group or an individual human being, tends to be conflated with the popular notion of psychosis, to be seen therefore as a form of sickness and to reflect a personality malfunction in the individual's relation with society, rather than as a species variation or ontological differentiation.

Thus, in our time, the concept of "wildness" has suffered much the same fate as that suffered by the concept of "barbarism." Just as there are no barbarians any more, except in a sociopsychological sense, as in the case of the Nazis, so too there are no wild men any more, except in the sociopsychological sense, as when we use the term to characterize street gangs, rioters, or the like. Wildness and barbarism are now used primarily to designate areas of the individual's psychological landscape, not whole cultures or species of humanity. Value-neutral terms, like "primitive," which designate a particular technological stage or social structure, have taken their place. Wildness and barbarism are regarded, in general, as potentialities lurking in the heart of every individual, whether primitive or civilized, as his possible incapacity to come to terms with his socially provided world. They are not viewed as essences or substances peculiar to a particular portion of humanity *out there* in space or *back there* in time. At least, they ought not to be so regarded.

Earlier I said that thought about the Wild Man has always centered upon the three great and abiding human problems that society and civilization claim to solve: those of sustenance, sex, and salvation. I think it is no accident that the three most revolutionary thinkers of the nineteenth century—Marx, Freud, and Nietzsche—respectively take these themes as their special subject matter. Similarly, the *radicalism* of each is in part a function of a thoroughgoing atheism and, more specifically, hostility to Judeo-Christian religiosity. For each of these great radicals, the problem of salvation is a *human* problem, having its solution solely in a reexamination of the *creative* forms of *human* vitality. Each is therefore compelled to recur to primitive times as best he can in order to imagine what primal man, precivilized man, the *Wild Man* which existed before history—i.e., outside the social state—might have been like.

Like Rousseau, each of these thinkers interprets primitive man as the possessor of an enviable freedom, but unlike those followers of Rousseau who misread him and insisted on treating primitive man as an ideal,

Marx, Freud, and Nietzsche recognized, as Rousseau did, that primitive man's existence must have been inherently flawed. Each of them argues that man's "fall" into society was necessary, the result of a crucial scarcity (in goods, women, or power, as the case may have been). And although each sees the fall as producing a uniquely human form of oppression, they all see it as an *ultimately* providential contribution to the construction of that whole humanity which it is history's purpose to realize. In short, for them man had to *transcend* his inherent primitive wildness—which is both a relationship and a state—in order to win his kingdom. Marx's primitive food gatherers, Freud's primal horde, and Nietzsche's barbarians are seen as solving the problem of scarcity in essentially the same way: through the alienation and oppression of other men. And this process and alienation are seen by all of them to result in the creation of a false consciousness, or self-alienation, necessary to the myth that a fragment of mankind might incarnate the *essence* of all humanity.

All three viewed history as a struggle to liberate men from the oppression of a society originally created as a way of liberating man from nature. It was the oppressed, exploited, alienated, or repressed part of humanity that kept on reappearing in the imagination of Western man—as the Wild Man, as the monster, and as the devil—to haunt or entice him thereafter. Sometimes this oppressed or repressed humanity appeared as a threat and a nightmare, at other times as a goal and a dream; sometimes as an abyss into which mankind might fall, and again as a summit to be scaled; but always as a criticism of whatever security and peace of mind one group of men in society had purchased at the cost of the suffering of another.

NOTES

1. Augustine, *The City of God,* in *Works,* trans. Marcus Dods (Edinburgh, 1934), II, 108.

2. W. B. Gallie, *Philosophy and the Historical Understanding* (London, 1964), pp. 157–91.

3. Michel Foucault, *Madness and Civilization: A History of Insanity in the Age of Reason,* trans. Richard Howard (New York, 1965).

4. R. D. Laing, *The Politics of Experience* (New York, 1967), ch. 5.

5. I have in mind here specifically the famous map of the psyche drawn by Freud in *The Ego and the Id,* trans. Joan Riviere (London, 1950), chs. 2, 3. For an account of the revision of this map, see J. A. C. Brown, *Freud and the Post-Freudians* (London, 1963), chs. 5, 6. See also Claude Lévi-Strauss, *The Savage Mind* (Chicago, 1966), ch. 9; and Norman O. Brown, *Love's Body* (New York, 1966), ch. 2.

6. Paul Tillich, *The Protestant Era,* trans. James Luther Adams (Chicago, 1948), ch. 4.

7. Arthur O. Lovejoy, *The Great Chain of Being: A Study of the History of an Idea* (Cambridge, Mass., 1936), ch. 9.

8. Ruth Benedict, *The Chrysanthemum and the Sword: Patterns of Japanese Culture* (Boston, 1946).

9. Richard Bernheimer, *Wild Men in the Middle Ages* (Cambridge, Mass., 1952).

10. Erich Auerbach, *Mimesis: The Representation of Reality in Western Literature,* trans. Willard R. Trask (Princeton, 1953).

11. E. R. Dodds, *The Greeks and the Irrational* (Berkeley, 1951), chs. 2, 5; Johannes Pedersen, *Israel: Its Life and Culture* (London, 1954), I, 182–212.

12. Another word which is translated into English as "void" ($m^eb\hat{u}wq\hat{a}h$) is used in apposition to "waste" (*bâlaq*) in Nahum 2:10 to characterize a devastated city, as when the prophet says of Nineveh: "She is empty, and void, and waste."

13. Pedersen, *Israel,* II, 453–96.

14. Pedersen, *Israel,* II, 485–86.

15. Augustine, *City of God,* II, 112.

16. Augustine, *City of God,* pp. 112–13.

17. Augustine, *City of God,* p. 113.

18. Pedersen, *Israel,* II, 455.

19. See Charles Norris Cochrane, *Christianity and Classical Culture: A Study of Thought and Action from Augustus to Augustine* (London, 1957), pp. 206, 209, 452.

20. Augustine, *Of True Religion,* in *Augustine: Earlier Writings,* trans. J. H. S. Burleigh (London, 1953), pp. 235–39 (vi, 21–xv, 29).

21. Augustine, *City of God,* II, 118.

22. "The Summa Theologica," in *Introduction to St. Thomas Aquinas,* ed. Anton C. Pegis (New York, 1948), pp. 483–86 (quest. 6, arts. 2–4).

23. Dante, "The Inferno," in *The Divine Comedy,* canto V.

24. Aristotle, *Politics,* bk. I, ch. 2.

25. The Latin word for "wildness" is *ferus* (which connotes that which grows in a field), but also *silvester* (inhabiting the woods), *indomitus* (untamed), *rudis* (raw), *incultus* (untilled), *ferox* (savage), *immanis* (huge, cruel), *saevus* (ferocious), *insanus* (mad), *lascivus* (playful); and etymologists suggest that *ferus* has the same root as *ferrum* (iron); see Bernheimer, *Wild Men in the Middle Ages,* ch. 1. Bernheimer's work is the source of most of the information offered in this paper on the lore of the Wild Man; it is an indispensable work for anyone seeking to correlate the official thought on the subject of wildness with its popular counterparts.

26. Bernheimer, *Wild Men,* pp. 45–46.

27. See Denis Sinor, "The Barbarians," *Diogenes,* 18 (Summer, 1957), 47–60.

28. Bernheimer, *Wild Men,* pp. 38 f.

29. Bernheimer, *Wild Men,* p. 33.

30. Bernheimer, *Wild Men,* pp. 24–25.

31. See Harold Cherniss, "The Characteristics and Effects of Presocratic Philosophy," *JHI,* 12 (1951), 319–45; and R. G. Collingwood, *The Idea of Nature* (Oxford, 1945), pp. 29 f.

32. See Aristotle, *Nichomachean Ethics,* bk. X, ch. 8; *Politics,* bk. I.

33. Bernheimer catalogs the types of submen found in classical literature and folk-lore, pp. 86–101.

34. See Northrop Frye, "Archetypal Criticism: Theory of Myths," in *Anatomy of Criticism: Four Essays* (Princeton, 1957), esp. pp. 190 f. For a history of the image of the labyrinth in modern art and literature, see Gustav René Hocke, *Die Welt als Labyrinth: Manier und Manie in der europäischen Kunst* (Hamburg, 1957).

35. For an example of the political ambivalence of archaism, see Sir Ronald Syme, *The Roman Revolution* (Oxford, 1939), pp. 459–75, which analyzes "The Organization of Opinion" following upon the triumph of Augustus over Marc Antony, and the contribution made to it by Virgil and Livy.

36. For a discussion of contending images of the natural world as manifested in early modern art, see Kenneth M. Clark, *Landscape Into Art* (London, 1949), chs. 1–4.

37. On the image of the Wild Man in Spenser and Sachs, see Bernheimer, *Wild Men*, pp. 113 f.

38. Compare Bernheimer, *Wild Men*, pp. 144 f., and Johann Huizinga, *The Waning of the Middle Ages: A Study of the Forms of Life, Thought and Art in France and the Netherlands in the XIVth and XVth Centuries*, trans. F. Hopman (London, 1967), chs. 17, 18.

39. Bernheimer, *Wild Men*, pp. 144–45. Italics added.

40. Tacitus, *De Germania*, p. 19.

41. Michel de Montaigne, "Of Cannibals," in *The Complete Works of Montaigne*, trans. Donald M. Frame (Stanford, 1958), p. 152.

42. See Jan Kott, "Prospero's Staff," in *Shakespeare: Our Contemporary*, trans. Boleslaw Taborski (Garden City, N.Y., 1964), pp. 237–85.

43. See Edmund Leach, "Vico and Lévi-Strauss on the Origins of Humanity," in *Giambattista Vico: An International Symposium*, eds. Giorgio Tagliacozzo and Hayden White (Baltimore, 1969), pp. 309–18.

44. See Frye, "Archetypal Criticism," pp. 131–62, and "Varieties of Literary Utopias," in *Utopias and Utopian Thought*, ed. Frank E. Manuel (Boston, 1967), pp. 25–49.

45. Bernheimer, *Wild Men*, p. 2.

46. Bernheimer, *Wild Men*, p. 2.

47. Bernheimer, *Wild Men*, p. 120.

48. Montaigne, "Of Cannibals," pp. 152–53.

49. Frank Kermode, *The Sense of an Ending: Studies in the Theory of Fiction* (New York, 1967), p. 39.

Wild Men and Spain's Brave New World

 STANLEY L. ROBE

In cultural terms, Spain's role in Europe has long been that of a window, or perhaps more appropriately a door. For seven centuries, throughout all the Middle Ages and until somewhat later, the Iberian Peninsula was one of the major points at which Middle Eastern and even Oriental learning and oral tradition were funneled into western Europe. Spain was a vantage point from which Europe viewed the material manifestations of Islamic culture, absorbed the advances of its mathematics and medicine, and took in its philosophy, literature, and even its folklore. Thus, from a European base, Spain looked toward the east, but the year 1492, a landmark in many respects for the emerging nation, turned things around. The expulsion of the Moors, finally achieved with the surrender of Granada to the forces of Ferdinand and Isabella in January of that year, marked the interruption of this vision, which was to be replaced almost immediately by another.

The outlook now was toward the west and was characterized by a feverish period of voyages of exploration, conquest, and settlement of vast new lands in America. Whereas Spain's knowledge of a more or less exotic culture had come previously from occupation of her own soil by outsiders, now it was her turn to take the initiative and occupy distant territories inhabited by creatures hitherto unseen by Western eyes. The opportunity presented here was twofold. The first was to make known to these creatures the mysteries of Christianity and to secure their sincere belief in it. The second was to secure all available information concerning these ultramarine beings, in part to bring about their religious conversion but also out of a genuine curiosity that clearly was characteristic of the times, at both the popular and intellectual levels. The first of these opportunities loomed larger in the eyes of the Spanish, but the second has been the source of a wide range of knowledge that in various ways has affected

European thought in succeeding centuries, including the varying, shifting concepts of the Wild Man. It is with the second activity, or opportunity, as I have expressed it above, that I am concerned, realizing at the
same time that the influences of Spanish activities in the New World on
the life of modern man have not been limited to these two aspects.

What took place in America was essentially a collision between a
Western culture and a variety of nonwestern societies in various stages
of development. It is not my intent here to explore these societies from
the point of view of the anthropologist. It is sufficient to say that Spaniards and Europeans of the late fifteenth century were well aware that
the inhabitants of the newly discovered lands to the west and any societies that might exist there could differ considerably from themselves and
their own manner of living. Exoticism was to be expected, and the imagination need not necessarily be curbed. I have avoided purposely the terms
"men" and "humans" in reference to the Americans of this early contact
period. The situation brings to mind the speculation that currently exists
in regard to the existence and nature of any higher forms of extraterres-
trial life, as reflected in our contemporary entertainment, literature, and
even cartoons.

In its initial stages, the search to know man in the new lands had to
be guided by Old World standards, on the basis of man's experience with
peoples and places that at that time seemed remote and exotic, largely in
the Near East and Africa. Man's accumulated knowledge and lore were
his only available tools, however inappropriate they may now seem in
their application to the natives of fifteenth- and sixteenth-century America.

In this body of accumulated experience, the Wild Man has figured
prominently at both the popular and the learned levels. His presence is
documented only imperfectly during the Middle Ages and the Renaissance, yet Hispanic oral tradition gives evidence of continuing interest in
such a being. He may be born from the union of an animal and a woman
or because of the wish of human parents for an inordinately strong son.[1]
Thus is born the protagonist of a Spanish version of "Strong John," who
leaves home when his parents have no more food to satisfy his voracious
appetite. After the strong man kills all the king's knights in battle, the
king has him disposed of by a stratagem.[2] Far better known is "John
the Bear's Son,"[3] in which the protagonist conforms still more closely to
the concept of the Wild Man. When a man and his wife go hunting, a
bear steals the woman and takes her to his cave in the mountains, where
he keeps her captive. A most unusual child is born to them, half-bear and

half-human, and covered with hair over his entire body. When he is several years old he helps his mother to escape from the cave and in doing so kills his father. The strong, unruly youth is taken to a village to live, but when children at school tease him about his hairy coat, he kills them. He is then forced to leave school and seek his fortune. His great strength and cunning allow him to vanquish a series of supernatural opponents, and in the end his hirsuteness is no hindrance to his marrying a princess. At least a dozen versions have been reported from Spain and well over thirty from Spanish-speaking countries of America.[4] Both narratives have a wide distribution in western Europe and reflect a broad tradition of considerable time depth. Their transmission to the New World is a reminder that the Wild Man of Europe has held as great an appeal for Americans as their exotic humans have had for Europeans.

A similar migration is possible in the case of what may be considered a "wild woman," who figures prominently in the *Libro de buen amor*, a fourteenth-century work of Juan Ruiz, archpriest of the Spanish town of Hita. She is a *serrana*, a mountain shepherdess who recurs in popular verse, although the archpriest's description of her stresses the grotesque.[5] Her head is overly large, with ears like those of a year-old ass, deepset eyes, topping a short neck covered with hair. Her mouth is like a hound's, with long horselike teeth and a nose in the shape of a pickax. She is rawboned, her long breasts dangle below her waist, and when she walks she leaves a track larger than a bear's. The *llorona*, a spirit who wanders at night along the streams and watercourses of Mexico and Central America, cannot approach the *serrana* of Juan Ruiz in horrendous qualities, yet she has several of them: long, matted hair that reaches to her waist, completely covering her eyes; a face that inspires horror, perhaps because it is that of an ass; and in some cases feet whose position is reversed, that is, the heel is forward and the toes are to the back, so that her footprints make her appear to be walking backward.[6] Her physical characteristics and her broad geographical distribution argue for Hispanic rather than an indigenous American origin. Spanish colonists from the lower classes, of whom there were many, carried a variety of popular legends concerning wild men and women to America, where these tales have taken root and thrived.

The picture at the intellectual or learned level is somewhat different. The Wild Man's nature is no less fanciful than that held by the folk, perhaps even more so, but it is more frequently documented and is more discernible in later events. In the late Middle Ages and the early Renaissance, travel literature was eagerly sought after in western Europe,

especially accounts of real or imaginary voyages to Asia and Africa that
were pleasant reading and at the same time served as treatises on geography and natural history. The writers seemingly felt an obligation to
their reading public to provide not merely a straightforward narrative of
those places visited but to stress the exotic, particularly in the description of inhabitants of the more remote areas. Some were relatively reliable, considering when they were written, such as those of Odoric, William
of Boldensele, the Armenian monk Hatoume, John of Pian del Carpini,
and the more famous Marco Polo. The first four of these served as the
basis for a volume whose effect on the discovery and exploration of
America is clearly discernible. This is the book of Sir John Mandeville
(d. 1372), which Columbus must have read.[7]

Mandeville reported the presence of dog-headed folk, some who had
but one eye and that in the middle of the forehead, others who had no
heads and with eyes in their shoulders, still others with the face all flat
without nose or mouth—all of these in the vicinity of Java; he depicted
men with horns and hooves who lived in the kingdom of Prester John,
and in Ethiopia a folk that had but one foot, and it so large that when
they lay down to rest it served as a shade from the sun.[8] Mandeville
possessed a lively imagination. The reading public of the fifteenth century found it difficult to evaluate critically such a work, which is a mixture
of direct observation, hearsay, the author's own invention, and the assertions of authors from the classical period, such as Herodotus and Pliny.

Such was the assortment of ideas concerning man (or should I say
Wild Man?) held by the first Europeans who encountered the native
peoples of America. The entry in the diary of Christopher Columbus for
October 12, 1492, does not reveal any explicit expression of disappoint-
ment. True, the native population was hardly what he had expected, nor
did it consist of wild men. In line with the teachings of Aristotle, he had
thought that he would find Negroes similar to those of Guinea. Neither
could he be sure that he was in the Indies, an incertitude he attempted
to dispel during the rest of his life. Fortunately, the first meeting between
Europeans and the gentle inhabitants of the West Indies is remarkably
well documented. As the *Santa María* approached the island of Guana-
hání, Columbus and his crew spied naked people ashore. The Europeans
took to their ships' boats:

I . . . gave to some among them some red caps and some glass beads, which
they hung round their necks, and many other things of little value. At this they
were greatly pleased and became so entirely our friends that it was a wonder

to see. Afterwards they came swimming to the ships' boats, where we were, and brought us parrots and cotton thread in balls, and spears and many other things, and we exchanged for them other things, such as small glass beads and hawks' bells, which we gave to them. In fact, they took all and gave all, such as they had. . . . They all go naked as their mothers bore them, and the women also, although I saw only one very young girl. And all those whom I did see were youths, so that I did not see one who was over thirty years of age; they were very well built, with very handsome bodies and very good faces. Their hair is coarse and short, almost like the hairs of a horse's tail; they wear their hair down over their eyebrows, except for a few strands behind which they wear long and never cut. Some of them are painted black, and they are the colour of the people of the Canaries, neither black nor white, and some of them are painted white and some red and some in any colour that they find. . . . They are all generally fairly tall, good looking and well proportioned. I saw some who bore marks of wounds on their bodies, and I made signs to them to ask how this came about, and they indicated to me that people had come from other islands, which are near, and wished to capture them, and they had defended themselves. . . . They should be good servants and of quick intelligence.[9]

Entries for succeeding days are even more optimistic. The natives knew little or nothing about arms and warfare. They held few concepts about religion and could easily be converted to the Christian faith. Their material wants were few, and a bounteous nature provided these with only a modicum of effort necessary. They wore little if any clothing and lived in ingeniously constructed houses which were neat and clean. Columbus is impressed by the beauty of the natural setting and comments repeatedly about the lush vegetation, the trees that are green like those of Andalusia in April and May, and the perfume of the blossoms that is wafted from land over the sea. He closes his entry for Wednesday, October 17, with this statement: "Your highnesses may believe that this land is the best and most fertile and temperate and level and good that there is in the world."[10]

It is likely that Columbus is writing here for Ferdinand and Isabella, his monarchs, to impress them with the importance of his discovery. Later he visited Cuba and Haiti, and his remarks concerning those islands and their inhabitants are even more favorable. The first impact, however, often makes the strongest impression. These reports spread rapidly over Europe and were followed immediately by the *Decades of the New World* of Peter Martyr d'Anghera, who recounts Spanish activities in the New World from 1492 until approximately 1515.[11] The most frequent impression given by writers during this feverish period of discovery is that America was an earthly paradise. The effect is observable at varying levels of society; first in the scramble of the common man to leave Spain for America, there to bask in a tropical clime with exotic natives to attend to all his needs, and somewhat later among philosophers and men of literature, whose interest was piqued by the depiction of man in a society that called to mind their own of a millennium or so earlier, one outwardly simple, unspoiled, and free of many of the inconveniences of a more modern manner of life.

Samuel Eliot Morison, who is concerned primarily with nautical matters when writing of the voyages of Columbus, nevertheless provides a philosophical dimension to the admiral's discoveries:

But to the intellectuals of Europe it seemed that Columbus had stepped back several millennia, and encountered people living in the Golden Age, that bright morning of humanity which existed only in the imagination of poets. Columbus's discovery enabled Europeans to see their own ancestors, as it were, in a "state of nature," before Pandora's box was opened. The "virtuous savage" myth, which reached its height in the eighteenth century, began at Guanahaní on October 12, 1492.[12]

Despite his relatively straightforward observation of the native people of the West Indies, Columbus is alert for the exotic man. Apparently he asks the native population whenever he goes ashore, and the obliging Arawaks confirm the presence, always in a distant land, of other men with strange features. On the north coast of Cuba he learns of "men with one eye, and others with dogs' noses, who ate men, and that when they took a man, they cut off his head and drank his blood and castrated him."[13] Again in Haiti he is informed of "people who had one eye in the forehead,"[14] and of the island of Martinio, where there are only women and no men, reminiscent of the legend of the Amazons.[15] This type of information was confirmed by Peter Martyr, who interviewed Columbus and his crewmen upon their return to Spain in 1493, and strengthened and gave new life to concepts already existing in Europe. The excitement and stimulation wrought by the voyages of discovery merely gave these beliefs an American rather than an Old World habitat. At first the transfer of these strange creatures to America found a reception only in Spain, but before long they had spread to the rest of Europe. John of Holywood in his *Sphaera Mundi* of 1498 describes inhabitants of the New World as being "blue in colour and with square heads."[16] Such notions were persistent in northern Europe long after more level-headed reports from Spanish sources had laid them to rest in the peninsula. French, Dutch, and German writers kept them alive and provided illustrations to their texts to back up their assertions.

One report, however, did stand up under scrutiny. It dealt with cannibalism, encountered early in the period of discovery, from Columbus and Peter Martyr on. The gentle Arawaks of the Bahamas, Cuba, and Haiti expressed constant fear of fierce, warlike people who lived on islands to the southeast. They made known to Columbus that these vicious people ate human flesh and ate or enslaved their prisoners. They gave various names to these people. Columbus and Peter Martyr refer to their land as Caniba or Canibata and the people as *caníbales*. From a variant form, *Caribata*, the modern term Carib is derived.

The depraved nature of man eaters captured the imagination of Europeans. These were truly wild men of the lowest order, clearly beyond the pale of civilization and in a remote geographical setting whose exotic nature contrasted sharply with that of temperate Europe. The contrast in moral standards and in geography, the juxtaposition of the civilized known with the barbarian little known, were to be grist for philosophers, observers of the social scene, and writers in general throughout succeeding centuries. These reports gave new vigor to the concept of the Wild Man. The fires under the kettles of human flesh were rekindled through engravings depicting scenes from the New World (although rarely taken from life), through the uncritical acceptance of reports from America, and through the dissemination of these throughout Europe. But probably more significant is the accusation of the practice of cannibalism leveled against certain native groups as a pretext for their enslavement to swell the labor supply in the new Spanish colonies. As a result, the literature dealing with the Caribs is extensive and confusing. Lewis Hanke sought the opinion of an anthropologist, John Rowe, who has long studied the indigenous peoples of America. His evaluation is as follows:

There is no question that the Spaniards attributed cannibalism to many Indians who did not practice it in order to enslave them, but there nevertheless seems to be a good basis in fact for the attribution of cannibalism to *some* Caribs.[17]

The chronicles of the sixteenth century reveal a certain envy and admiration by the Europeans for this Wild Man. Despite his fierce countenance and the beastly grisly practices attributed to him, the Carib commanded respect and grudging admiration for his bravery, his physical prowess, and his ability and fearlessness as a warrior. The Carib, whom Europeans did not come to know personally until the second voyage of Columbus, presented in his nature a sharp contrast with the Arawak of

the Greater Antilles, depicted by the early chroniclers as living in a terrestrial paradise. Both are wild men, in different senses of the expression,
but the Carib has heightened the more horrendous connotations of the
term. Of the two indigenous groups, the Carib is the only one that has
survived at all. The Arawaks of the Greater Antilles have been extinct
since the middle of the sixteenth century.

The above considerations concerning man and wild men in America
have dealt mainly with physical and social features of these people and
date from the earliest years of European presence in the New World. As
time passed and the scope of involvement with the overseas territories
became apparent, Spain found it necessary to consider and resolve a
thorny philosophical question concerning the spiritual status of the
native peoples. In large part the problem arose because of Spain's concern with the legalistic aspects of the conquest—all undertakings required
legal backing and sanction—but combined with this spirit was the human-
itarian concern of a few sixteenth-century figures for the spiritual and
physical welfare of the considerable native population. The most prominent as well as the most vocal of these was Fray Bartolomé de las Casas,
who became incensed over treatment given to the natives of Haiti, relin-
quished his grant of land and the Indians who worked it, and became
a Dominican monk.

The philosophical question of the spiritual status of the American
peoples is germane to the idea of the Wild Man in a number of ways.
The myriad of greater and lesser tribes found in the New World lived
beyond the pale of known civilizations of the sixteenth century. Many of
their practices, particularly those of cannibalism and human sacrifice,
were barbarous in the eyes of the Europeans. Their geographical remote-
ness, the lack of a cultural frame of reference, and the repugnant things
they did sowed doubts in the minds of many Spaniards as to whether
these people were really human. Were they not subhumans without souls
and thus fit only to be enslaved?

There was an urgency to the problem that is not always apparent
today. Father Las Casas witnessed the rapid disappearance of the native
population of Cuba and Haiti, partly because the natives could not with-
stand the rigorous work standards imposed by Spanish planters and partly
from a kind of suicide born of desperation. The spiritual salvation of millions of potential human souls here and elsewhere was at stake, and the
responsibility for their disposition lay with the clergy. The latter found
it difficult to agree, and their differences of opinion were evident in the
bitter controversy that raged well into the sixteenth century. In the mean-

time, however, Indians in the new dominions were baptized, instructed in Christian doctrine, and administered the Sacraments.

In 1537 Pope Paul III issued a bull, *Sublimus Deus,* which provided a long-awaited decision. Indians were not to be considered "dumb brutes created for our service." Rather they were "truly men . . . capable of understanding the Catholic faith." The Pope made it clear that "the said Indians and all other people who may later be discovered by Christians, are by no means to be deprived of their property, even though they may be outside the faith of Jesus Christ . . . nor should they in any way be enslaved."[18]

The dispute continued in Spain, however, over the process of baptizing the Indians and their treatment by the Spaniards, but more crucially over whether or not the Indian was rational. A number of theologians still held to Aristotle's doctrine of natural slavery and argued that it should be applied to the Indian. In 1541 the emperor Charles V called upon the eminent theologian and philosopher Francisco de Vitoria for an opinion. His verdict was:

The Indian aborigines . . . are not of unsound mind . . . but have, according to their kind, the use of reason. This is clear, because there is a certain method in their affairs; they have politics which are carefully arranged and they have definite marriage and magistrates, overlords, laws, and workshops, and a system of exchange, all of which call for the use of reason; they also have a kind of religion.[19]

The controversy reached an acrimonious climax at Valladolid during 1550 and 1551 with the series of confrontations between Father Las Casas and Juan Ginés de Sepúlveda, a scholar and humanist who enjoyed considerable prestige at the Spanish court. The series of debates between these two men, decreed by Charles V, was not followed by an announced decision favoring the one or the other. The Aristotelian argument, supported by Sepúlveda and others, hereafter lost formal adherents and no longer influenced the formation of governmental policy relating to the spiritual state of the Indian in Spanish domains. The Indian was no longer a Wild Man in the official view.

No other colonial power undertook such an examination of the relationship of the conqueror to the conquered in its overseas territories. In the tumult of sixteenth-century international politics, the philosophical basis of the controversy has been lost from sight in countries outside Spain. Her northern European rivals of the period largely determined Spain's contribution to the concept of the Wild Man outside her own sphere of influ-

ence. Their interest lay in two areas: the first, the life of savages in an
exotic setting, a life sometimes idyllic and sometimes fantastic; and the
second, the cruelties perpetrated by men of an apparently civilized Western nation upon an innocent and frequently noble people, thus fortifying
the idea of the *leyenda negra*, or black legend, that apologists for Spain's
activities in the New World still combat vigorously.

It is time to consider another type of Wild Man who was present in
America during the sixteenth century. He was not an Indian but a Spaniard, who, for one reason or another, was removed against his will from
his own people and forced to live for an extended period either in complete solitude or as the captive of a native group. Such cases were not
uncommon in Spanish America, and they have clear parallels in the
colonial and nineteenth-century history of the United States. The experiences of the Spaniards, several of which are rather well documented, are
in the realm of adventure and in the colonial era are probably the nearest approach to the novel, a genre which did not appear in Hispanic
America until the period of independence. Unfortunately, the testimony
of these Europeans is relatively unknown to the large reading public
that cannot handle Spanish.

In 1511 fifteen men and two women who were en route from the
colony of Darién to Hispaniola were driven ashore on the eastern coast
of the Peninsula of Yucatan. The group was captured by a Mayan chieftain who ruled in the area, and its members suffered diverse fates. The
women among the prisoners were enslaved and set to doing menial tasks
for the Indians. The poor souls soon died of overwork. Six of the remaining men were imprisoned in cages by the chieftain and except for their
imprisonment led an easy life and were provided with abundant food.
They were not long in learning the reason for their treatment, for one
night the Indians removed one of the captives from his cage. Later the
five who remained heard in the jungle preparations for festivities by the
natives. These were punctuated by the shrieks and blood-curdling yells
of their former companion, who was to be the *pièce de résistance* of
the evening.

The five survivors, with courage and strength inspired by desperation,
managed to break the bars of their cages and escape into the forest. The
fate of three of these was never recorded and can only be the subject of
conjecture, but the subsequent roles of the other two are well known and
afford a fascinating contrast with what a European could do, or would
do, in order to survive in unfamiliar physical surroundings and among
frequently hostile natives.

In 1519, eight years after the castaways reached Yucatan, the expedition of Hernán Cortés anchored off the island of Cozumel. As he and his men were preparing their vessels for their westward journey toward the Gulf of Mexico, an Indian dugout drew alongside. Several bronzed men came aboard the ship of Cortés, and one of them, shedding tears, uttered a few halting words in Spanish. He embraced Cortés and identified himself as Jerónimo de Aguilar, a native of Ecija in Andalusia. Aguilar's rent and tattered clothing did such a poor job of covering his nakedness that Cortés quickly hustled him below and had him provided with a complete outfit of European clothing.

Once again in the presence of Cortés, Aguilar proceeded to relate the details of his stay among the Mayas. Following his escape from the flesh-eating tribe, he made his way to the village of another chieftain. There he was made a captive again, but not for the purpose of being eaten. The chieftain assigned to him the most menial type of labor, which Aguilar performed readily, although he gives the impression that because he had already taken orders as a lay friar it was below his dignity. Aguilar became fluent in the language of the Mayas, but on the basis of his own testimony he does not appear to have participated to any extent in other than domestic or household activities of the Indians. His constant companion during all this time was his Book of Hours, which he had saved from the shipwreck and was still carrying at the time of his reunion with his fellow countrymen, although its pages were worn and loose from constant use. Aguilar was overjoyed at being with men from Spain and willingly joined Cortés and his soldiers, to whom he later gave invaluable service an an interpreter. Aguilar was an unwilling Wild Man, and when the opportunity came to forsake other wild men he readily took advantage of it.

During his narrative, Aguilar remarked to Cortés that one of the original castaways was still alive and lived in a village not far from Aguilar's recent residence. Moved by the tale of the shipwreck and the hardships that these Spaniards had suffered, Cortés sent Aguilar to find this companion, named Gonzalo Guerrero, with the thought of rescuing him from the savages. Armed with a letter from Cortés and accompanied by several friendly Mayas, Aguilar set out. He soon found Guerrero and read the letter to him. He reasoned with Guerrero to return with him to the company of Cortés and eventually to Spain. Guerrero's answer was clearly "no." He explained that he now occupied a respected position among the natives of his village. He had taken the chieftain's daughter as his wife, and they now had several children. He had distinguished

himself in battle against neighboring tribes and now in case of war was
the trusted leader of his father-in-law's warriors. For these reasons, and
perhaps others that the chroniclers do not state, Guerrero refused to
accompany Aguilar. His lot was cast with the natives who had befriended
and honored him. His identification now was with them, in outward manners such as garb and perhaps paint on his face, as well as in spirit and
feeling. Guerrero, when faced with the choice of being a European or
a Wild Man, resolutely decided for the latter. Aguilar returned and
reported his failure to Cortés.[20]

The Indians of Spanish America did not always capture Spaniards for
the purpose of eating or enslaving them, even when the two groups
were engaged in warfare. In May 1629 a force of Araucanians captured
Álvaro Francisco Núñez de Pineda y Bascuñán, the handsome son of
one of the Spanish commanders in Chile. For six months the youth was
the prisoner of an Araucanian chief, living in the fashion of the Indians,
witnessing their rites and customs, eating their food, wearing their clothing, and participating, although reluctantly, in their dances and festivities. Núñez de Pineda some years later composed a chronicle in which
he relates these experiences, and in view of the title which he gave it,
they were not entirely unpleasant. He named it *Feliz cautiverio*, which
can be expressed in English as "The Happy Period of Captivity."[21]

The title is an appropriate one. The young captive narrates certain
handicaps and inconveniences to which he was subjected, such as the
forced marches of the Indians and their prolonged drinking bouts, but
sandwiched between these were periods that would make the most
civilized man leave home and country and take up the Indian manner of
life. Quilalebo, one of his captors, was taken with the young man, as were
other Araucanian chieftains, and these constantly offer their daughters
to the young Spaniard, in marriage or for the pleasure of the moment.

Núñez de Pineda recounts these amorous experiences, but he has
learned to tease his reader, to offer a tempting situation, leading the
reader on toward a juicy climax, but letting him down before that moment
is reached. During certain festivities of the Indians, a chieftain named
Ancanamon offers his daughter to the youth, and the girl makes advances
to him. Núñez de Pineda elaborates:

On such occasions no one is concerned with anything except drinking, dancing, and also each one's joining up with whatever woman he can find or for
whom he has desire. I decided that the chief did this to tempt me and to determine which direction my sensual appetite might take but I answered, explain-

ing that I was highly appreciative of the amorous attitude of the young lady but that he should pardon my inability to return her affection in a clumsy or indecent fashion.[22]

Her father tries to reassure the youthful captive after the latter's refusal:

If you do so out of shame or of fear, the chief answered me, you need not worry because that girl has no husband to look after her and she is the master of her own will, without there being anyone to inhibit her or hold her back. Take her, for I am going to take care of this companion of hers but I'll be back soon.[23]

The chief is well aware of the usual sexual proclivities of the Spaniards in his country:

But why, answered the chief, aren't you interested in such matters the way other Spaniards are? Because many of them have been among us and have gone to excess and even felt free to take up with other men's wives, and as for those women who are single there is no one to call them to account.[24]

Núñez de Pineda undergoes a series of such experiences during his captivity, but in the face of temptation he hides, or slips away, or prays, so he tells us. This is not the kind of fellow who will succumb and become a Wild Man. He is not of the same stuff as Gonzalo Guerrero.

I should like to speak of one more Spaniard who in the New World was forced by circumstances to lead a life of solitude, removed from his fellowmen and under trying circumstances. The experiences of Pedro Serrano so appealed to the Inca Garcilaso de la Vega that the Peruvian writer interpolated them into his *Comentarios reales de los Incas* in the midst of a geographical description of Peru. Garcilaso cannot resist the temptation of spinning a good tale. In the mid-sixteenth century, Serrano was shipwrecked in the Caribbean but managed to swim to the safety of a tiny island off the northern shore of Colombia. There he survived for three years, living precariously on shellfish and sea tortoises and drinking rain water that he was able to collect. Garcilaso notes that Serrano's clothing rotted away in the frequent rain and hot sun: "Because of the inclemency of the heavens, hair grew over his entire body to such a degree that it looked as if he had the hide of an animal, and not just that of any kind but that of a wild boar. His beard and his hair reached below his waist."[25]

Serrano was joined after three years by a companion, also shipwrecked, and the two spent four more years on the island before they were finally rescued by a passing vessel. Because of their lack of clothing and hairy body covering, both men by this time resembled "John the Bear's Son." Serrano's companion died aboard ship before they reached Spain.

The narrative that Serrano told concerning his experience on the desert island was so unusual and his experience so bizarre that he resolved to capitalize on them. Upon reaching Spain, he retained his beard and long hair and set out for Germany, where Charles V was holding court. By telling the story of his hardships and exhibiting his hairy body as proof, Serrano passed as a Wild Man in towns along the way, where the curious were willing to pay him money for his expenses. Garcilaso reports: "Gentlemen and knights, who enjoyed gazing upon his countenance, provided him with funds for his trip, and his imperial majesty, having seen and heard him, granted him four thousand pesos income, which are four thousand ducats in Peru." Having achieved this end, Serrano cut off part of his beard, in order to sleep more comfortably, and set off for Peru, there to enjoy his wealth, but he died at Panama before reaching his destination.

In his appearance Serrano possessed the necessary characteristics of a Wild Man. His hairy body, face, and head were those of a beast rather than of a human and fulfilled the requirements of the prevalent concept of a Wild Man. Of these four Spaniards who spent time in the wilds of America, only Serrano became known to any extent among his countrymen. The least known, of course, is Gonzalo Guerrero, and understandably so, because no renegade to his native culture can expect to be honored in his homeland.

Despite the stirring events that accompanied the discovery and conquest of America, it first aroused little interest in Europe. Throughout the sixteenth century there is little reflection in Spanish literature and art of the great accomplishments of Spaniards overseas. The realization of their magnitude was to come later. During this time Spain carried the concept of the Wild Man to America, particularly at the level of the folk, and simultaneously her intellectuals attempted to project upon the peoples of the new lands notions, frequently fanciful, long prevalent in Europe. From America, Spain and the Western world acquired a fresh vision of humans different in appearance and habits from themselves. With this vision, which comes to be based upon direct observation rather than fanciful conjecture from afar, the Wild Man begins to acquire a new character. No longer is he shunned. Now he has even a soul.

NOTES

1. Antti Aarne, *The Types of the Folktale: A Classification and Bibliography*, trans. and enl. Stith Thompson, 2d rev. (Helsinki, 1961), type 650A.

2. Aurelio M. Espinosa, *Cuentos populares españoles*, 2d ed. (Madrid, 1946–47), I, 65–66 (no. 35).

3. Aarne, *Types of Folktale*, type 301.

4. Espinosa, *Cuentos populares españoles*, II, 498.

5. (Madrid, 1941), pp. 55–60 (sts. 1008–21).

6. Ralph S. Boggs, "Mapa preliminar de las regiones folklóricas de México," *Folklore Americas*, 9, nos. 1–2 (1949), 1–4.

7. Jacques W. Redway, in Sir John Mandeville, *Voyages and Travels* (New York, 1901), pp. iii–xi.

8. Mandeville, *Voyages and Travels*, pp. 123, 127, 174, 97.

9. Christopher Columbus, *The Voyages of Christopher Columbus*, ed. Cecil Jane (London, 1930), pp. 148–49.

10. *Voyages of Columbus*, p. 157.

11. Peter Martyr d'Anghera, *De Orbe Novo*, trans. Francis MacNutt (New York, 1912).

12. Samuel Eliot Morison, *Admiral of the Ocean Sea: A Life of Christopher Columbus* (Boston, 1942), p. 231.

13. *Voyages of Columbus*, p. 169.

14. *Voyages of Columbus*, p. 180.

15. *Voyages of Columbus*, pp. 236, 238.

16. E. P. Goldschmidt, "Not in Harrisse," in *Essays Honoring Lawrence C. Wroth* (Portland, Maine, 1940), p. 140; cited by Lewis Hanke, *Aristotle and the American Indians: A Study of Race Prejudice in the Modern World* (London, 1959), p. 4.

17. Hanke, *Aristotle and the American Indians*, p. 131.

18. Hanke, *Aristotle and the American Indians*, p. 19.

19. Hanke, *Aristotle and the American Indians*, pp. 22–23.

20. The experiences of Aguilar and Guerrero are summarized in Fernando Benítez, *La ruta de Hernán Cortés*, 2d ed. (Mexico City, 1956), pp. 80–82. I have consulted also the works of Bernal Díaz and Francisco López de Gómara.

21. *Cautiverio feliz del Maestre de Campo Jeneral don Francisco Núñez de Pineda y Bascuñán y razón individual de las guerras dilatadas del Reino de Chile, compuesto por el mismo* . . . (Santiago de Chile, 1863).

22. Núñez de Pineda, *Cautiverio*, pp. 136–37.

23. Núñez de Pineda, *Cautiverio*, pp. 136–37.

24. Núñez de Pineda, *Cautiverio*, p. 138.

25. *Los comentarios reales de los Incas* (Lima, 1967), I, 83–87.

The Image of the Indian
in the Southern Colonial Mind

✒ GARY B. NASH

The changing image of the native inhabitants of North America
provides a penetrating glimpse into the fears, desires, and
intentions of Englishmen in colonial America. From the guileless primitive of certain sixteenth-century writers, to the savage beast of colonial
frontiersman, to the Noble Savage of eighteenth-century social critics, the
image of the Indian has furnished the social, intellectual, and cultural
historian with an important analytical tool. Just as Europeans saw in
Africa and Africans not what actually existed but what their prior experience and present needs dictated, so in America the image of the Indian
was molded by the nature of colonization and the inner requirements of
adventuring Englishmen.[1]

Understanding the English image of the Indian not only reveals the
conscious and unconscious workings of the Anglo-American mind, but
also gives meaning to English relations with the Indian and to English
policies directed at controlling, "civilizing," and exterminating him.
Images of the Indian were indicators of attitudes toward him. Attitudes,
in turn, were closely linked to intentions and desires. These intentions
and desires, acted out systematically over a period of time and often
provoking responses from the natives which tended to confirm and rein-
force first impressions, became the basis of an "Indian policy." Thus,
images of the Indians in colonial America are of both explanatory and
causative importance. They help us penetrate the innermost thoughts and
psychic needs of Englishmen confronting a distant, unknown, and terrifying land; and they provide a basis for understanding English interaction
with the native inhabitants over a period of close but abrasive contact
which lasted for more than 150 years.[2]

The early 1580s mark a convenient point to begin a study of the images
of the Indian refracted through the prism of the English mind. It was

then that Elizabethan England, already a century behind Spain and Portugal in exploiting the potentialities of the New World, took the first significant steps toward extending her power across the Atlantic. Two attempts at settlement in North America, in 1583 and 1584, one by Sir Humphrey Gilbert, among the most active promoters of English colonization, and the other by his half brother, Walter Raleigh, the best known and most romantic of the early adventurers, were undertaken. Gilbert sailed the northern route and made a landfall in Newfoundland with five ships and 260 men. He then turned west and disappeared at sea, leaving the other ships to return to England. Raleigh, plying the familiar southern route, touched land on the upper Carolina coast, left a small contingent on what was to be called Roanoke Island—located at the mouth of Albemarle Sound—and returned to England with two natives of the region. Thus began an era of English participation in the great race for colonial possessions that was to occupy—at times preoccupy—Europe for the next two centuries.[3]

What images of the Indians were lodged in the minds of men like Gilbert and Raleigh as they approached the forbidding coast of North America? One can be sure that they experienced the uncertainty and apprehension that regardless of time or place fill the minds of those who are attempting to penetrate the unknown. But in all likelihood they also had well-formed ideas about the indigenous people of the New World. Legends concerning other worlds beyond the sunset had reverberated in the European mind for centuries.[4] And, beginning with Columbus's report on the New World, published in several European capitals in 1493 and 1494, a mass of reports and stories had been circulating among sailors, merchants, and geographers who were participating in voyages of discovery, trade, and settlement.[5]

From this considerable literature, men like Gilbert and Raleigh were likely to derive a split image of the natives of North America. On the one hand, they had reason to believe that the Indians were savage, hostile, beastlike men, whose proximity in appearance and behavior was closer to the animal kingdom than to the kingdom of men, as western Europeans employed that term to describe themselves. As early as the first decade of the sixteenth century, Sebastian Cabot had paraded in England three Eskimos, taken captive on his voyage to the Arctic in 1502.[6] A contemporary described the natives as flesh-eating, primitive specimens who "spake such speech that no man coulde understand them, and in their demeanour like to bruite beastes."[7] In 1556 curious Englishmen could read an account of Giovanni da Verrazano's voyage of 1524 to North America, including descriptions of the natives which could have been little cause for optimism concerning the reception which Europeans would receive in the New World.[8] Other accounts were filtering back to England from fishermen operating off the Newfoundland Banks or from explorers such as Martin Frobisher, whose three attempts to find the Northwest Passage in the 1570s led to the publication of a number of descriptions of the northern reaches of the lands across the Atlantic.[9] The accounts from the Frobisher voyages were filled with descriptions of crafty, brutal, loathsome half men whose cannibalistic instincts were revealed, as Dionyse Settle wrote in 1578, by the fact that "there is no flesh or fishe, which they finde dead, (smell it never so filthily) but they will eate it, as they finde it, without any other dressing."[10]

Other unsettling accounts also became available through the translation of Spanish and Portuguese writers. Sebastian Munster's *A Treatyse of the newe India* was published in English in 1553; Peter Martyr's *The Decades of the newe worlde or west India* two years later; Jean Ribault's *The whole and true discoverye of Terra Florida* in 1563; Nicholas Le Challeux's *A true and perfect . . . description, of the last voyage . . . into Terra Florida . . .* in 1566; and André Thevet's *The Newe founde worlde, or Antarcticke* in 1568.[11] In all these works Englishmen of the day could read accounts which suggested that the people of the New World were not only primitive—simply by not being English one was that—but bestial, cannibalistic, sexually abandoned, and, in general, moved entirely by passion rather than by reason.

But another vision of the native was simultaneously entering the English consciousness. Columbus had written of the "great amity towards us" which he encountered in San Salvador in 1492 and described a generous, pastoral people living in childlike innocence.[12] Thenceforth, the accounts which Englishmen read were tinged with a romantic image of the New World, as if, Howard Mumford Jones has written, to fill some psychic need of a dreary, tired Europe.[13] Just a few years before the Gilbert and Raleigh voyages, Englishmen could read in translation Nicolas Monardes' *Joyfull Newes out of the New Founde World*, which limned America as a horn of plenty, an earthly paradise where nature's bounty allowed men to live for centuries in sensual leisure. To some extent this positive side of the image of the New World was based on the friendly reception which Europeans had apparently received in Newfoundland, parts of Florida, and elsewhere on the continent. Gilbert, for example, was familiar with the testimony of David Ingram, one of about a hundred sailors set ashore on the northern coast of the Gulf of Mexico by John Hawkins in 1568. Upon his return to England, Ingram wrote of the tractable and generous nature of the natives who provided food and were "naturally very courteous, if you do not abuse them."[14] Other accounts confirmed the notion that the natives as well as the climate in some parts of the New World would be hospitable.[15]

Three books published in the early 1580s, as the Roanoke voyages were being launched, provide a clearer insight into this split vision of English writers as they pondered the nature of the people inhabiting the lands of the New World. Two were written by the Richard Hakluyts, uncle and nephew—the greatest colonial publicizers and promoters of their age.[16] With pen rather than sword the Hakluyts inspired Elizabethan courtiers, adventurous sons of the lesser nobility, and merchants with venture capital to enter the colonial sweepstakes before Spain and Portugal, already firmly established in South America and the West Indies, laid claim to the whole of the New World. The third was penned by Sir George Peckham, who had accompanied Sir Humphrey Gilbert on the Newfoundland voyage of 1583 and left his impressions, *A True Reporte, of the late discoveries . . . of the Newfound Landes . . .*, as the latest guide to Englishmen eager to unravel the mysteries of North America.

In all these tracts the ambivalence and confusion in the English mind is readily apparent. The elder Hakluyt could write of the New World as "a Country no less fruitful and pleasant in al respects than is England, Fraunce or Germany, the people, though simple and rude in manners, and destitute of the knowledge of God or any good lawes, yet of nature gentle and tractable, and most apt to receive the Christian Religion, and to subject themselves to some good government."[17] In the same vein, the younger Hakluyt wrote in 1584 of a "goodd clymate, healthfull, and of goodd temperature, marvelous pleasaunte, the people goodd and of a gentle and amyable nature, which willingly will obey, yea be contented to serve those that shall with gentlenes and humanitie goo aboute to allure them."[18] These were useful promotional statements. And yet the Hakluyts could not banish the thought that planting English civilization in the New World would not be all gentleness and amiability. Festering in their minds was knowledge of the Spanish experience in America. They had read carefully every account of the Spanish conquest of Mexico, especially Bartholemé de las Casas' *Spanish Colonie, or Brief Chronicle of the acts and gestes of the Spaniards in the West Indies,* translated in 1583. Las Casas deplored the reign of death and terror which the Spanish had brought to aboriginal culture in the name of Christianity. In his own propaganda for colonization Hakluyt felt moved to quote several Spanish authors who labeled their countrymen "helhoundes and wolves"—men who claimed they had conquered and pacified the Indians, but who in reality had engaged in a policy bordering on genocide. The Indians, according to Hakluyt's source, "not havinge studied Logicke, concluded very pertinently and categorically that the Spaniardes which spoiled their Contrie, were more dangerous then wilde beastes, more furious then Lyons, more fearefull and terrible then fire and water."[19]

Did the same experience await the English? Few doubted that they enjoyed the same technological superiority as the Spanish. If they desired, they could thus lay waste to the country they were entering. Moreover, English experience with the Irish, in whose country military officers like Gilbert and Raleigh had been gaining experience in the subjugation of "lesser breeds" for several decades, suggested that the English were fully capable of every cruelty contrived by the Spanish. Thus, as the elder Hakluyt pointed out, if the English were not well received, they might be obliged to employ force to show the Indians the advantages of participating in the benefits of English civilization. "If we finde the countrey populous," he wrote in 1584, "and desirous to expel us, and injuriously to offend us, that seeke but just and lawfull trafficke, then by reason that we are lords of navigation, and they not so, we are the better able to defend our selves by reason of those great rivers, & to annoy them in many places." Hakluyt concluded that the English might find it necessary to "proceed with extremitie, conquer, fortifie, and plant in soiles most sweet, most pleasant, most strong, and most fertile, and in the end bring them all in subjection and to civilitie."[20] So the bitter would be mixed with the sweet.

George Peckham, writing contemporaneously with the Hakluyts, gave an even clearer expression of the emerging formula for colonization: exterior expressions of goodwill and explanations of mutual benefits to be derived from the contact of two cultures, but lurking beneath the surface the anticipation of violence. In his promotional pamphlet, *A True Reporte, of the late discoveries . . . of the Newfound Landes . . . ,* Peckham began with elaborate defenses of the rights of maritime nations to "trade and traficke" with "savage" nations and assured Englishmen that such enterprises would be "profitable to the adventurers in perticuler, beneficial to the Savages, and a matter to be attained without any great daunger or difficultie." Some of the natives, Peckham allowed, would be "fearful by nature" and disquieted by the "straunge apparrell, Armour, and weapon" of the English, but "courtesie and myldness" along with a generous bounty of "prittie merchaundizes and trifles: As looking Glasses, Bells, Beades, Braceletts, Chaines, or Collers of Bewgle, Christall, Amber, Jett, or Glasse" would soon win them over and "induce theyr Barbarous natures to a likeing and a mutuall society with us."[21]

Having explained how he hoped the English *might* act, and how the natives *might* respond, Peckham went on to reveal what he must have considered the more likely course of events: "But if after these good and fayre meanes used, the Savages nevertheles will not be heerewithall satisfied, but barbarously wyll goe about to practise violence either in repelling the Christians from theyr Portes and safe Landinges or in withstanding them afterwardes to enjoye the rights for which both painfully and lawfully they have adventured themselves thether; then in such a case I holde it no breache of equitye for the Christians to defende themselves, to pursue revenge with force, and to doo whatsoever is necessary for attayning of theyr safety: For it is allowable by all Lawes in such distresses, to resist violence with violence."[22]

With earlier statements of the gentle and receptive qualities of the Indians almost beyond recall, Peckham reminded his countrymen of their responsibility to employ all necessary means to bring the natives "from falsehood to truth, from darknes to lyght, from the hieway of death, to the path of life, from superstitious idolatry, to sincere Christianity, from the devill to Christ, from hell to Heaven." Even more revealing of his essentially negative image of the Indian, he wrote that the English, in planting their civilization, would aid the Indians by causing them to change "from unseemly customes, to honest maners, from disordred riotous rowtes and companies, to a wel governed common wealth."[23]

Thus, two conflicting images of the Indian were wrestling for ascendance in the English mind as the first attempts to colonize in the New World got underway. At times the English tended to see the native as a backward but receptive man with whom amicable and profitable relations might be established. The image originated not only in the utopian anticipation of the New World but in the desire to trade with the Indians. The early voyages were not intended primarily for the purpose of large-scale settlement and agricultural production. A careful reading of the promotional literature of this period will show that the English were interested primarily in a mercantile relationship. Trade with the Indians, the search for gold and silver, and discovery of the Northwest Passage were the keys to overseas development. Trade was expected to be a major source of profit. Not only would the natives provide a new outlet for English woolens, but all the rich and varied commodities of the New

World would flow back to England in ample measure. Since trade was the key to success in these bold, new adventures, a special incentive existed for seeing the Indian as something more than an intractable savage. For the Spanish and Portuguese colonizers in the New World (and for the English in Ireland) land had been the key. But land conquest did not figure importantly in Elizabethan planning. In fact, it would undermine attempts to establish a mercantile relationship. Instead, well-fortified trading posts would be established at the heads of rivers where the natives would come to trade. In this mercantile approach to overseas adventuring the English promoters were strongly influenced by English participation in the Levantine and Muscovy trade which English merchants had operated profitably for half a century, not invading the land of foreign peoples and driving them from it, but "trafficking" among them without challenging their possession of land. In Hakluyt's *Notes on Colonisation,* written five years prior to the Roanoke voyages, the recommendations for approaching the natives are almost identical to those given for adventurers seeking the Northwest Passage in 1580.[24]

Thus, one side of the image of the native had its source not only in the idyllic visions of the New World but in the intentions of the Elizabethan adventurers. It was only a friendly Indian who *could* be a trading Indian. If trade was the key to overseas development, then it is not surprising that English promoters suggested that the Indian might be receptive and generous—a man who could be wooed and won to the advantages of trade.

But the creation of a tractable Indian, amenable to trade, could never blot from the English mind the image of the hostile savage who awaited Christian adventurers. Most of the Elizabethan adventurers had been involved in the English invasions of Ireland and the Netherlands, where they had learned that indigenous peoples do not ordinarily accept graciously those who come to dominate them. They had special reasons for anticipating the darker side of the Indian's nature because they were familiar with the literature on the "savages" of the New World and were well acquainted with the Spanish and Portuguese overseas experience. With hostility on their minds, it was impossible to picture the Indian as a purely benign creature. Regardless of the natural temperament of the New World man, his contact with Europeans thus far had rarely been pacific. To imagine the Indian as a savage beast was a way of predicting the future and preparing for it and of justifying what one would do, even before one caused it to happen.

The experience at Roanoke Island between 1584 and 1587 illustrates how preconceptions affected the initial Anglo-Indian contacts. For Englishmen it was their first settlement in the New World. Initially, several hundred men attempted to maintain themselves on the island while making exploratory trips into the mainland wilderness. For three years the settlement struggled for existence, kept alive by fresh infusions of men and supplies from England. But left to its own resources when the Spanish Armada prevented provisioning ships from leaving England in 1588, the tiny colony perished.[25]

Three accounts of the Roanoke experience survive.[26] Because they were written at least partially as promotional pamphlets intended to inspire further attempts at settlement, they must be used cautiously as a source of information. Though differing in detail, all the accounts agree that the Indians of the Carolina region were receptive to the English. Arthur Barlow, a member of the first expedition, wrote that "we were entertained with all love and kindness, and with as much bountie, after their manner, as they could possibly devise. Wee found the people most gentle, loving, and faithfull, void of all guile, and treason," and noted that the Indians were "much grieved" when their hospitality was shunned by the suspicious English.[27] Other accounts, though less roseate, also suggest that the natives were eager to learn about the artifacts of the Europeans and, though wary, extended their hospitality.[28] Since the English came in small numbers, the Indians probably did not regard them as much of a threat. They were probably as curious about the English as the English were about them.[29] So far as one can tell from the surviving evidence, no conflict occurred until the English, upon discovering a silver cup missing, dispatched a punitive expedition to a nearby Indian village. When the Indians denied taking the cup, the English, determined to make a show of force, burned the village to the ground and destroyed the Indians' supply of corn. After that, relations deteriorated.[30] Aware of their numerical disadvantage and the precariousness of their position, the English used force in large doses to convince the natives of their invulnerability. As one member of the voyage admitted: "Some of our companie towardes the ende of the yeare shewed themselves too fierce, in slaying some of the people, in some towns, upon causes that on our part might easily enough have bene borne withall."[31]

In spite of these difficulties the principal members of the Roanoke colony who returned to England entertained considerable respect for Indian culture. Thomas Hariot wrote that "although they have no such tooles, nor any such craftes, sciences and artes as wee; yet, in those things they doe, they shewe excellencie of wit."[32] John White, a painter of some skill, who had accompanied the Roanoke expedition, brought back more explicit testimony of the Indians' culture, in the form of scores of sketches and water colors which show the Indians at various aspects of work and play. White's art reveals a genuine appreciation of the Indians' ability to control their environment through their methods of hunting and agriculture, their family and communal life, and other aspects of their culture.[33]

For two decades after the failure at Roanoke, Englishmen launched no new colonial adventures. Although a few English ship captains, who represented merchants dabbling in the West Indies trade, looked in on the coast of North America in hopes of bartering with the natives, and reported that their relations with them were generally friendly,[34] the next attempt at colonization did not come until the Virginia Company of London completed its plans in December 1606. The arrival of the first Virginia expedition in April 1607, with more than one hundred men in three ships, marked the beginning of permanent English presence in North America. Henceforward, Indians and Englishmen would be in continuous contact.

The crucial difference between the Roanoke colony of the 1580s and the settlement at Jamestown in 1607 was that the latter, after the first few years, was planned as a permanent community. From this point onward, Englishmen came to America not merely to trade with the natives or to extract the riches of the land but to build an enduring society—an extension of England overseas. It was this shift in intention that reshaped the nature of the contacts between English and Indians and consequently altered the English image of the native as well as the Indian perception of the Englishman. Permanent settlement required extensive acquisition by whites of land—land which was in possession of the Indian. That single fact was the beginning of a chain of events which governed the entire sociology of red-white relations.

For Englishmen the Indians' occupation of the land presented a problem of both law and morality. Even in the 1580s, George Peckham, an early promoter of colonization, had admitted that many Englishmen doubted their right to take possession of the land of others.[35] In 1609 the thought was amplified by Robert Gray, who asked, rhetorically, "By what right or warrant can we enter into the land of these Savages, take away their rightfull inheritance from them, and plant ourselves in their places, being unwronged or unprovoked by them."[36] It was a logical question to ask, for Englishmen, like other Europeans, had organized their society around the concept of private ownership of land and regarded this as an important characteristic of their superior culture. They were not blind to the fact that they were entering the land of another people, who by prior possession could lay sole claim to all the territory of mainland America. To some extent the problem was resolved by arguing that the English did not intend to take the Indians' land but wanted only to share with them the resources of the New World where there was land enough for all. In return, they would extend to the Indians the advantages of a richer culture, a more advanced civilization, and most importantly, the Christian religion. Thus, in 1610 the governing council in Virginia advertised to those at home that the English "by way of merchandizing and trade, doe buy of them [the Indians] the pearles of earth, and sell to them the pearles of heaven." A few decades later, Samuel Purchas, who took up the Hakluyts' work of promoting colonization in the seventeenth century, gave classic expression to this explanation: "God in wisedome having enriched the Savage Countries, that those riches might be attractives for Christian suters, which there may sowe spirituals and reape temporals."[37] Spirituals to be sown, of course, meant Christian doctrines; temporals to be reaped meant land.

A second and far more portentous way of resolving the problem of land possession was to deny the humanity of the Indians. Thus, Robert Gray, who had asked if Englishmen were entitled to "plant ourselves in their places," answered by arguing that the Indians' inhumanity disqualified them from the right to possess land. "Although the Lord hath given the earth to children of men, . . . the greater part of it [is] possessed & wrongfully usurped by wild beasts, and unreasonable creatures, or by brutish savages, which by reason of their godles ignorance & blasphemous idolatrie, are worse then those beasts which are of most wilde & savage nature."[38] This was an argument fraught with danger for the Indian, for whereas other Englishmen, such as William Strachey, secretary of the resident council in Virginia at this time, were arguing that "every foote of land which we shall take unto our use, we will bargaine and buy of them,"[39] Gray was suggesting that present and future acts of godlessness or savagery, as defined by the English, would entitle the colonists unilaterally to seize or occupy land. This notion that the "savages" by their nature had forfeited their right to the land was only occasionally mentioned in the early years. But in the 1620s, after a major war had been fought, the idea would gain greater acceptance.

Little evidence exists on which to base unequivocal assertions about English attitudes toward the Indians in 1607, at the moment of initial contact. But it seems likely that, given their belief that the Roanoke colony had been reduced to a pile of bones by the Indians a generation earlier, the English were not very optimistic about the receptiveness of the indigenous people. This pessimistic view must have been greatly intensified when the Jamestown expedition was attacked near Cape Henry, following their first debarkation in the New World. Hereafter the English would proceed with extreme caution, as well they might, given the size of their expedition. Violence was anticipated, and when Indians approached the English in outwardly friendly ways, the worst was suspected. Thus, when Christopher Newport led the first exploratory trip up the newly named James River, just weeks after a tiny settlement had been planted at Jamestown, he was confused by what he encountered. The Indians, a member of his group wrote, "are naturally given to trechery, howbeit we could not finde it in our travell up the river, but rather a most kind and loving people."[40] This account reveals that the English were wined and dined by the Indians, who explained that they were "at oddes" with other tribes, including the Chesapeake tribe that had attacked the English at Cape Henry, and were willing to ally with the English against their enemies.[41] It is clear from ethnological research that the Indians of the Chesapeake region, composing some thirty different tribes, were not monolithic in cultural characteristics and were undergoing internal reorganization. The most powerful tribe, the Pamunkey, of which Powhatan was chief, had been attempting for some time before the arrival of the English to consolidate its hold on lesser tribes in the area, while at the same time warding off the threats of westerly tribes of the Piedmont area. From the available ethnographic evidence, it appears that Powhatan saw an alliance with the English as a means of extending his power in the tidewater area while neutralizing the power of his western enemies.[42]

But the English, who were quick to comprehend the intertribal tensions as well as the linguistic differences among the Indians of the region, apparently could not convince themselves that some tribal leaders regarded the English as threatening whereas others found their arrival potentially to their advantage. Perhaps because they viewed their position as so precarious (the Jamestown settlement was in a state of internal crisis almost from the moment of landfall), they could only afford to regard all Indians as threatening. Thus, hostile and friendly Indians seemed different from each other only in their outward behavior. Inwardly they were identical. The hostile Indian revealed his true nature, whereas the friendly Indian feigned friendship while waiting for an opportunity to attack, thus proving even more than his openly warlike brother the treacherous nature he possessed.

Over the first few years of contact, during which time the Jamestown settlement was reprovisioned from England with men and supplies, the confusion in the English mind was revealed again and again. In the summer of 1607, when food supplies were running perilously low and all but a handful of the Jamestown settlers had fallen too ill to work, the colony was saved by the Indians who brought sufficient food to keep the struggling settlement alive until the sick recovered. This, too, was seen by many as an example of Powhatan's covert hostility rather than an attempt to serve his own interests through an alliance with the English. "It pleased God (in our extremity)," wrote Smith, "to move the Indians to bring us Corne, ere it was halfe ripe, to refresh us, when we rather expected . . . they would destroy us."[43] As a man of military experience among "barbarian" people in all parts of the world, Smith was not willing to believe that the Indians, in aiding the colony, might have found the survival of the English in their own interest. Hostility was on his mind, sporadic hostility had already been experienced, and thus all acts, friendly or foul, were perceived as further evidence of the natives' irreversible hostility and innate savagery.

The records left by the English would be couched hereafter in these terms. Outright conflict was taken as the norm because it represented the logical result of contact with a people who were hostile and treacherous by nature. Friendly overtures by Powhatan and other tribal leaders, who hoped to use the English to consolidate their own position, were seen as further examples of the dissembling nature of the Indians. One reads of "these cunning tricks of their Emperour of Powhatan," or "their slippery designes," or "perfidious savages," or "I know their faining love is towards me not without a deadly hatred."[44] Increasingly, of course, this was true, as Powhatan, finding his efforts to build a mutually profitable relationship fading, withheld trading privileges and assumed an uncooperative stance.

It was John Smith who, more than any other figure, wrought the most significant change in English attitudes and policy toward Powhatan. As the Jamestown settlement struggled for existence in 1607 and 1608, plagued by hunger, disease, dissension, and a remarkable refusal of most of its participants to work for their own survival, Smith emerged as the "strong man." Experienced in military exploits, skilled in cartography, and seemingly indestructible, Smith initiated an aggressive Indian policy based on the burning of Indian canoes, fields, and villages, in order to extort food supplies and to cow Powhatan and other tribal leaders. "The patient Councell that nothing would move to warre with the Salvages" was replaced by a policy of terrorization, which "brought them [the

Indians] in such feare and obedience, as his very name would sufficiently affright them."[45] It is not easy to fathom Smith's perception of the situation, especially since so much of the information available for this period must be gleaned from his own accounts. But certainly important in Smith's assessment of the Indians' intentions was the petty theft of English implements by Indians who circulated in the English settlements in the first year; the confession of two Indians in May 1608 (under duress, if not torture) that Powhatan was the recipient of the stolen objects and was secretly plotting to wipe out the colony;[46] and Smith's worldwide military experience, which convinced him that with "heathen" people the best defense was a good offense. On the last point Smith wrote that "the Warres in *Europe, Asia,* and *Affrica,* taught me how to subdue the wilde Salvages in *Virginia* and *New-England* in *America.*"[47]

In the short run, most of the colonists thought that Smith's policy of intimidation paid off. As it was later written, "Where before, wee had sometimes peace and warre twice in a day, and very seldome a weeke but we had some trecherous villany or other," now the Indians, both the openly hostile and the professedly friendly, were tamed.[48] But Smith's ruthless and indiscriminate approach disturbed some Virginia leaders who thought that on several occasions he mercilessly killed and attacked Indians who had done the English no harm and thus destroyed chances of profitable trade with the Indians while sowing the seeds for future discord. But Smith convinced most in the colony as well as the managers of the London-based Virginia Company of the efficacy of his strategy. The new attitude toward the Indians is apparent in the orders for Sir Thomas Gates, who sailed from England in 1609 to take command of the colony. Whereas in 1606 the company had instructed, "In all your passages you must have great care not to offend the naturals if you can eschew it," Gates was ordered to effect a military occupation of the Chesapeake region, to make all tribes tributary to him rather than to Powhatan, to extract corn, furs, dye, and labor from each tribe in proportion to its number, and, if possible, to mold the native into an agricultural labor force as the Spanish had attempted in their colonies.[49] As the English settlement gained in strength following the arrival of six hundred colonists in 1610, Gates continued Smith's policy of intimidation, as did his successor, Sir Thomas Dale. In 1610 and 1611, following sporadic violence by both sides, three attacks by the English took the lives of a significant portion of the population of three tribes and also destroyed the tribal centers of Appomattucks and Kecoughtan.[50] In 1613 the English kidnapped Powhatan's favorite daughter, Pocahontas, who had acted as intervening savior in 1608 when Powhatan conducted a mock execution of the captured John Smith. Pocahontas immediately won the love of John Rolfe, a leader in the colony, and Powhatan was reluctantly persuaded of the political advantages of allowing the first and perhaps the only Anglo-Indian marriage in Virginia's early history. A period of peace followed; and this, one suspects, further confirmed many in their view that the English policy, as it had evolved, was the best that could be devised.[51]

In spite of this tendency to read hostility and savagery into the Indians' character, the early leaders of the Virginia colony manifested a strong curiosity about native culture and in their writings did not suppress their respect for it. John Smith, as has been indicated, was the foremost proponent in the early years of cowing the Indians through repeated demonstrations of the English martial spirit and superiority in weapons. But in his descriptions of Indian culture Smith revealed a genuine respect for the native way of life. He marveled at the Indians' strength and agility, their talent for hunting and fishing, their music and entertainment. He noted that civil government was practiced by them, that they adhered to religious traditions, and that many of their customs and institutions were not unlike those of the Europeans. Smith's statement that "although the countrie people be very barbarous, yet have they amongst them such government, as that their Magistrats for good commanding, and their people for du subjection, and obeying, excell in many places that would be counted very civill"[52] illustrates the tendency to define the native as a hostile savage but still to retain an avid interest in his way of life. William Strachey, who served as secretary to the colony from 1610 to 1611, and Henry Spelman, who lived among the Indians for four years, also wrote appreciatively about Indian life. Borrowing liberally from Smith and other authors, Strachey wondered how the Indians could have effected "so generall and grosse a defection from the true knowledg of God." But with this off his chest, he went on to portray the natives as "ingenious enough in their owne workes" and in possession of much of the apparatus of "civilized" society.[53] Alexander Whitaker, an Anglican minister who proselytized among the Indians, wrote that some men "are farre mistaken in the nature of these men, for besides the promise of God, which is without respect of persons, made as well to unwise men after the flesh, as to the wise &. let us not thinke that these men are so simple as some have supposed them: for they are of body lustie, strong, and very nimble: they are a very understanding generation, quicke of apprehension, suddaine in their dispatches, subtile in their dealings, exquisite in their inventions, and industrious in their labour."⁵⁴ Whitaker's comments indicate the division of opinion that may have been growing in Virginia, with some men beginning to blot from their minds some of the positive characteristics of Indian society they had observed earlier.

Notwithstanding misconceptions on both sides, the English and the Indians lived in close contact during the first years. Neither mutual distrust, intermittent conflict, nor casualties on both sides kept the English from trading with the Indians when they could, from sporadically conducting experiments in proselytizing and educating the Indians, and even from fleeing to Indian villages, where some of the settlers found life more agreeable than at Jamestown, where a military regimen prevailed after 1608. After the colony's ability to survive and overmatch the Indians was established, Indians were frequently admitted to the white settlements as day laborers. Though perhaps accepting hostility as the norm after the first few years, both sides were tacitly agreeing to exploit the dangerous presence of the other as best they could.⁵⁵

Although the documentary record becomes much thinner after 1612, it appears that it was in the decade following this date that a major change in Indian relations occurred in Virginia. The Virginia Company of London gave up its plans for reaping vast profits through Indian trade or the discovery of minerals and instead instituted a liberal land policy designed to build the population of the colony rapidly, and ultimately to make it an agricultural province of such productivity that land sales would enrich its investors. When the cultivation of tobacco was perfected, giving Virginia a money crop of great potential, and further promotional efforts were rewarded with a new influx of settlers after 1619, the availability of land became a critical question for the first time in the colony's existence. As more and more men began pushing up the James River and its tributaries in the second decade of settlement to carve tobacco plantations out of the wilderness, the Indians of the region perceived that what had heretofore been an abrasive and often violent relationship might now become a disastrous one. It was the tension of a rapidly growing—and spreading—population that provided the highly combustible atmosphere, which in 1622 was ignited by the murder of a greatly respected Indian of the Powhatan confederacy. The result was a well-coordinated, all-out attack on the white settlement in that year.

In studying the colonial image of the Indian, the details of the "massacre" of 1622 are less important than the effect it had on English perceptions of the natives. It was, of course, a genuine disaster for the Virginia Company of London, which was shortly to go bankrupt, and for the weary Virginia settlement, which lost about one-third of its inhabitants. But more importantly, it confirmed beyond a shadow of a doubt what most Englishmen had suspected from the beginning: that all Indians were inherently treacherous, cunning, and infinitely hostile. No longer would it be necessary to acknowledge an obligation to civilize and Christianize the native. Even though several leaders in the colony confided that the real cause of the Indian attack was "our owne perfidiousness in dealing with them,"[56] it was generally agreed that henceforward the English would be free to hunt down the native wherever he could be found. A no-holds-barred approach to "the Indian problem" was now adopted. Whereas before the colonists claimed (at least officially) that they followed the principle of retributive justice, only engaging in attacks against the natives when they had been assaulted, now they were entitled to put aside all restraint and take the offensive. As one leader wrote revealingly after the Indian attack: "Our hands, which before were tied with gentleness and fair usage, are now set at liberty by the treacherous violence of the savages. So that we, who hitherto have had possession of no more ground then their waste, and our purchase at a valuable consideration to theire owne contentment gained, may now by right of Warre, and law of Nations, invade the Country, and destroy them who sought to destroy us; whereby wee shall enjoy their cultivated places, turning the laborious Mattocke into the victorious Sword (wherein there is more both ease, benefit, and glory) and possessing the fruits of others labours. Now their cleared grounds in all their villages (which are situate in the fruitfullest places of the land) shall be inhabited by us, whereas heretofore the grubbing of woods was the greatest labour."[57] A note of grim satisfaction that the Indians had succeeded in wiping out one-third of the English settlement can be detected. Now the colonizers were entitled to devastate Indian villages and to take rather than buy the best land of the area. John Smith, writing two years after the attack, noted that some men held that the massacre "will be good for the Plantation, because now we have just cause to destroy them by all meanes possible."[58]

Another writer gave clear expression to his genocidal intent when he reasoned that the Indians had done the colonists a favor by sweeping away the previous English reluctance to annihilate the Indians. Now the colony would prosper. The author relished in enumerating the ways that the "savages" could be exterminated. "Victorie," he wrote, "may bee gained many waies; by force, by surprize, by famine in burning their Corne, by destroying and burning their Boats, Canoes, and Houses, by breaking their fishing Weares, by assailing them in their huntings, whereby they get the greatest part of their sustenance in Winter, by pursuing and chasing them with our horses and blood Hounds to draw after them, and Mastives to teare them."[59]

Once the thirst for revenge was slaked, the only debatable question was whether the extermination of the Indians would work to the benefit or disadvantage of the colony. John Martin, a prominent planter, offered several "Reasons why it is not fittinge utterlye to make an exterpation of the Savages yett," and then assured his readers that it was not genocide he was against but the destruction of a people who, if properly subjected, could enrich all the Virginians through their labor.[60] Martin's advice was ignored, and during each summer in the decade following the attack of 1622, the provincial government dispatched raiding parties to destroy Indians and their crops wherever they could be found. In 1629 a peace treaty was negotiated but then rejected because it was decided by the Virginia Council that a policy of "perpetual enmity" would serve the colony better.[61] Rather than interpret the massacre of 1622 as the culmination of conflicting interests and acts of violence on both sides, the Virginians sought its origins in the nature of the native man. Because of the attack he had launched, the Indian had defined himself in a way that justified any course of action which the English might devise.

In the aftermath of the massacre of 1622 an unambiguously negative image of the Indian appeared. It would be strengthened and confirmed by later Indian attacks in 1644 and 1675. Words such as "perfidious," "cunning," "barbarous," and "improvident" had been used heretofore in describing the native, but his culture still commanded considerable respect in English eyes. After 1622 the Indians' culture was seldom deemed worthy of consideration. More and more abusive words crept into English descriptions of the Indian. Negative qualities were projected onto him with increasing frequency. Words like "beastly," "brutish," and "deformed" can be found in descriptions of the Indians after 1622. Whereas John Smith and others had described them as "ingenious," "industrious," and "quick of apprehension," Edward Waterhouse, writing after the massacre, informed his readers that the Indians "are by nature sloathful and idle, vitious, melancholy, slovenly, of bad conditions, lyers, of small memory, of no constancy or trust, . . . by nature of all people the most lying and most inconstant in the world, sottish and sodaine, never looking what dangers may happen afterwards, lesse capable then children of six or seaven yeares old, and less apt and ingenious."[62] This vocabulary of abuse reflects not only the rage of the decimated colony but an inner need to provide a justification for colonial policy for generations to come. Hereafter, the elimination of the Indians could be rationalized far more easily, for they were seen as vicious, cultureless, unreconstructable savages rather than merely as hostile and primitive men, though men with an integral culture and a way of life worthy of notice.[63]

The psychological calculus by which intentions governed white attitudes can be seen more clearly by studying the views of Englishmen who genuinely desired amicable relations with the Indians. The Quakers of Pennsylvania and west New Jersey, who were the most important early practitioners of pacifism in the New World, threatened no violence to the Indians when they arrived in the Delaware River Valley in the last quarter of the seventeenth century. It was pacifism, not violence, that was on the minds of the Quakers. Eager to avoid the conflict which had beset other colonies, and committed ideologically to banishing violence and war, the Quakers viewed the Indian in a different light. Though regarding him as backward and "under a dark Night in things relating to Religion," they also saw him as physically attractive, generous, mild-tempered, and possessed of many admirable traits. William Penn, the proprietor of the colony, gave new expression to old speculations that the Indians were the "Jews of America," the descendants of the lost tribes of Israel. He found their language "lofty" and full of words "of more sweetness or greatness" than most European tongues.[64] Though Quaker relations with the Indians were not so benign as some historians have suggested, it is significant that not a single incident of organized violence between Indians and Quakers occurred during the colonial period. The deterioration of Indian relations in Pennsylvania can be traced primarily to the rapid influx after 1713 of German and Scotch-Irish settlers whose land hunger and indifference toward the Indians combined with the Anglo-French wars of the mid-eighteenth century to set the frontier in flames for a quarter century.

In the southern colonies the image of the Indian also began to change, once the resistance of the natives to the territorial encroachment of white settlers faded. In almost all the colonies, concerted attacks by the Indians lasted only into the third generation. Thereafter the Indians who had survived contact with European culture either moved beyond the reach of the colonizers, at least temporarily, or lived within white communities in a subservient status. Thus, in Virginia the last significant Indian attack came in 1675. In South Carolina, settled six decades later, the last major Indian offensives were mounted in the Tuscarora and Yamassee wars of the early eighteenth century. Later, in the eighteenth century, Indian tribes fought English settlers on numerous occasions, but always as adjuncts of their French or Spanish allies, who armed, directed, and controlled them, rather than as independent nations.[65]

When the precariousness of the English position was eliminated as a significant factor in Anglo-Indian relations and when large-scale attacks on white communities had subsided, the image of the Indian began to change, at least among the literate or reflective element of society. Because the social context of Indian-white relations was changing, the white community was far better disposed emotionally to see the Indians as another cultural group rather than simply as the enemy. In the first half of the eighteenth century a number of colonial observers began to develop a new image of the Indian. Unlike later writers, who from seaboard cities or European centers of culture sentimentalized the native into a Noble Savage, these men knew of Indian life. from firsthand experience as missionaries, provincial officials, and fur traders. Close to Indian culture, but not pitted against the native in a fight for land or survival, they developed clearer perspectives on aboriginal life. Not yet seized by the certainty that they were fulfilling a divine mission in North America, they were able to take a more anthropological approach to Indian society rather than assaying it only in terms of its proximity to English culture.[66]

All the components in the revised image of the Indian emerging in the eighteenth century were linked together by the basic assumption that the Indians' culture was worth examining on its own terms. This in itself was a significant change, since during the period of Indian attacks most colonists had regarded the Indians as cultureless. Samuel Purchas's charge of 1625 that the Indians were "bad people, having little of Humanitie but shape, ignorant of Civilitie, of Arts, of Religion; more brutish then the beasts they hunt, more wild and unmanly then that unmanned wild Countrey which they range rather than inhabite" was a classic statement of the earlier view of the worthlessness or absence of Indian culture.[67] But now Englishmen began to rediscover all the missing elements in the Indians' cultural makeup—government, social structure, religion, family organization, codes of justice and morality, crafts, and arts.

So far as can be ascertained from the surviving sources, an unpublished anonymous account of 1689, perhaps by the Anglican minister John Clayton, was the first attempt after John Smith's description of 1612 to take Indian culture seriously. This "Account of the Indians in Virginia . . ." assumed a reportorial tone and described Indian customs, though not the Indians' character, in a neutral way.[68] Far more significant was Robert Beverley's *History and Present State of Virginia*, published in 1705, almost a century after the planting of the Jamestown settlement and at a time when the Indian population of the settled regions of the colony had declined from an estimated 18,000 in 1607 to about 2,000.[69] Even in the chapter headings he used—"Religion and Worship," "Laws and Authority," "Learning and Language," "Marriages and Children," and "Crafts"— Beverley revealed a new attitude toward the native. Much of what he saw in Indian culture reminded him of classical Spartan life. Beverley used words like "strange" or "remarkable" to describe Indian customs, but completely absent from his account were those earlier adjectival indicators, such as "beastly," "savage," "primitive," "monstrous," and "idolatrous." In Beverley's description can be seen the beginning of a new genre of literature on the Indian—a genre which included a foretaste of the Noble Savage tradition, but which was more fundamentally rooted in a desire to describe the Indians' culture than to use it as a foil for demonstrating the decadence of Western civilization.

Four years later, John Lawson, a proprietary officeholder who traveled extensively among the tribes of South Carolina and Georgia, published a lengthier description of Indian culture. In *A New Voyage to Carolina,* Lawson attempted to describe the material culture of the southern tribes and to examine their social, political, and religious institutions. Lawson's account was not free of judgmental statements about the "imbecilities" of certain native customs or their "lazy idle" habits, but like Beverley he seems to have made a conscious attempt to step back from his own cultural standards when observing the music, dancing, games, marriage and family customs, medicine, religion, and government of the southeastern tribes among which he traveled for eight years.[70]

Some eighteenth-century writers were still employing words like "savage," "monstrous," and "idolatrous" to describe the Indians, however. William Stith's *History of the First Discovery and Settlement of Virginia,* published in 1747, pictured the Indians as inherently treacherous and barbarous. Relying heavily on the early accounts of Virginia by John Smith and Thomas Hariot, Stith insisted that the English had always treated the Indians "with the utmost Humanity and Kindness, out of the Hope and Desire, of thereby alluring and bringing them over, to the Knowledge of God and his true Religion." At Jamestown the Indians had been "fed at their Tables, and even lodged in their Bedchambers: so that they seemed entirely to have coalesced, and to live together, as one People." The Indians had repaid this generous treatment, Stith claimed, with perfidious attacks on the English settlement.[71] The Anglican minister Hugh Jones, writing in 1724, was equally prepared to assign blame for Anglo-Indian hostility to the natives and to describe them as savage and idolatrous. But Jones also found the Indians serious in debate and possessed of "tolerable good notions of natural justice, equity, honour, and honesty." Although he could not persuade himself that the Indians would ever rise to the level of Christianity, Jones was far more appreciative of native culture than his seventeenth-century predecessors.[72]

The most complete statement of the integrity of Indian culture came from James Adair in his *History of the American Indians . . .*, published in 1775, and based on forty years of experience as an Indian trader on the frontiers of South Carolina and Georgia. In an argument extending to more than two hundred pages, Adair labored to prove the descent of the American Indians from the ancient Jews. In matters as widely separated as adherence to theocratic government, genius for language and rhetoric, and manner of embalming the dead, Adair found links between Semitic and Indian culture. Like a number of others who were describing the Indians, Adair was impressed with the "plain and honest law of nature" which governed native society and by the strong sense of religion that gave meaning and coherence to native life.[73]

Just as a new view of native culture was appearing in the eighteenth century, ideas about the Indians' character traits—or what would come to be called personality—were undergoing a marked change. Widespread agreement cannot be found among colonial writers, of course, for each was influenced by his own background and by his special purposes in writing about the Indians. Moreover, the personality of the Indian was in the process of change as he struggled to adapt to the presence of more and more Europeans and African slaves in his ancestral lands. But despite significant differences, eighteenth-century colonial observers of Indian character were far more favorable than those of an earlier period, when the ultimate outcome of Anglo-Indian confrontation had still been in doubt.

On one point agreement was nearly unanimous: the Indians were extraordinarily brave. Both men and women were fired with the most unswerving loyalty to their tribe and endowed with incredible stoicism under torture and duress.[74] At the same time, most observers thought the Indians were revengeful, never forgetting an ill deed or an injustice. Agreement was general that this was a weakness in the Indian, though to identify this as a defect was ironic, inasmuch as colonial Indian policy was unambiguous on the need to administer swift and severe retribution for every Indian offense.[75]

Predictably, observers took a variety of positions on the honesty of the natives. The old image of the cunning, deceitful, treacherous Indian retained its currency.[76] But other observers insisted that the Indians were more straightforward and honorable in matters of trade and land exchange than the English. For example, Edmond Atkin, who was appointed southern superintendent of the Indians in 1756, was convinced that "in their publick Treaties no People on earth are more open explicit and Direct. Nor did any people excel them in strict observance of treaties, once made."[77]

In the more favorable image of the Indian that was emerging, an element of considerable importance, because it related to the origins of Anglo-Indian hostility, concerned the attitude of Indians toward strangers. After the first concerted Indian attacks of the seventeenth century, writers had characterized the native as brutish, vicious, and hostile by nature. But in the eighteenth century, men who traveled among or negotiated with the Indians discovered that hospitality and generosity were important in the Indians' structure of values.[78] Robert Beverley made the point explicitly by noting that the Indians had been "at first very fair and friendly" and provided the provisions that kept the struggling Jamestown colony alive during the first hard winter.[79] Edmond Atkin charged that the English had had "a very hospitable Reception" at Roanoke Island but were rewarded for their pains by the leader of the colony, Richard Grenville, who punished the Indians for the action of a native "who did not know the difference in value between [the silver cup] and a horn Spoon."[80] Missionaries of the Society for the Propagation of the Gospel, the evangelical arm of the Anglican Church also reported on the equable temperament and the generosity of the natives. In 1766, for example, Francis Le Jau's first impressions of the Yamassee Indians in South Carolina was of a "very quiet, sweet humored, and patient [people], content with little."[81]

Physical attractiveness also commanded the attention of eighteenth-century commentators. In the previous century the Indian had not been regarded as physically repulsive, as was the African in some cases, but neither had the Indian women been generally regarded as suitable for marriage. Now, early in the eighteenth century, it was proposed that the Indians had an uncommonly handsome physique, which commended them for racial intermixture. William Byrd, one of Virginia's largest plantation owners and a man who kept the pleasures of the flesh and the mind in exquisite balance, described the Indians as strong, handsome, and at least as attractive as the first English settlers. Byrd was sufficiently impressed by the Indians' outward features to suggest that intermarriage should offend the tastes of nobody. If practiced earlier, he argued, a century of bloodshed might have been avoided. Their fine bodies, wrote Byrd in a revealing comment, "may make full Amends for the Darkness of their Complexions." If the English had not been "so Squeamish" and imbued with a "false delicacy," they might have made a "prudent Alliance" with the Indians of the Chesapeake region, to everyone's benefit. Byrd believed the Indians had been offended by this rejection and could never "persuade themselves that the English were heartily their Friends, so long as they disdained to intermarry with them." He advised that a lost opportunity might still be reclaimed by intermarriage—the "Modern Policy" in French Canada and Louisiana.[82] Robert Beverley took a similar view. He described Indian males as "straight and well proportion'd, having the cleanest and most exact Limbs in the World." As for the native woman, she was "generally Beautiful, possessing an uncommon delicacy of Shape and Features, and wanting no Charm, but that of a fair Complexion." Like Byrd, Beverley regretted that intermarriage had not occurred.[83] Lawson was another who remarked on the admirable stature of the Indian men, commenting on their "full and manly" eyes, their "sedate and majestick" gait, and their strength and agility. Indian women were no less appealing. They were described as "fine shap'd Creatures . . . as any in the Universe" and their smiles "afford the finest Composure a Face can possess."[84]

Closely tied to physical attractiveness in the mind of white writers was the notion of cleanliness—of both body and mind. Earlier colonists, perhaps projecting their own feelings of embarrassment and guilt, had frequently remarked on the nakedness and open sexual relations of the Indians, concluding that the natives were dirty and lewd. Beverley, however, wrote that Indian marriage was "most sacred and inviolable" and that the women were relaxed, good humored, and full of dignity. Though white men charged unmarried Indian women with promiscuity, Beverley was convinced that this was only a projection of "the guilt of their own Consciences," and added that white men, who kept their women in tight rein, were "not very nice in distinguishing betwixt guilt, and harmless freedom" when they saw the familiarity and openness of young Indian girls.[85] Adair was in agreement. He found the native women "of a mild amiable soft disposition: exceedingly soft in their behaviour," and compared Indian marriage and divorce traditions with those of the ancient Hebrews. The tribes of southeastern America had high moral standards, inhabited "clean, neat dwelling houses," and were critical, with much cause, of the laxity of white morals.[86] The Anglican missionary Le Jau, after observing both white and red settlements in South Carolina for a year, concluded that the Indians "make us ashamed by their life, Conversation and Sense of Religion." Whereas English settlers talked about religion and morality, the Indians lived it.[87] Lawson, however, was offended by the Indian practice of fornication before marriage and the readiness of Indian women to prostitute themselves to fur traders. But in personal habits he found the natives clean and "sweet."[88]

The ability to take a more dispassionate view of the Indian allowed discussion of the effects of white society on the Indians' way of life. Earlier, when the Indian had been seen simply as a savage, it was logical to assume that the confrontation of cultures could only benefit the indigenous man. If Europeans were civilized and Indians were heathen, cultural interaction would necessarily improve the inferior group. But eighteenth-century observers, more wont to take Indian culture on its own terms, frequently concluded that colonizing Europeans had perverted rather than converted the Indian. The English had introduced drunkenness and covetousness, Beverley complained, and robbed the natives of much of their "Felicity, as well as their innocence."[89] Almost every pre-Revolutionary eighteenth-century writer agreed that the Indians had been debauched by rum, and educated in thievery, avariciousness, and immorality. The lowest elements of white society, in most frequent contact with the natives, gave the Indians cause to suspect the superiority of white Christian culture to which they were incessantly urged to aspire.[90] Fur traders were no better, constituting a "Wretched sort of Men," as one Anglican missionary put it.[91] Agreement was general among members of the Society for the Propagation of the Gospel that it was impossible to convert the native until the "white barbarians" of the frontier areas, as Benjamin Franklin called them, had been brought within the pale of civilization.[92]

Ironically, the new image of the Indian was emerging at a time when the native qualities most likely to gain the admiration or respect of white society were disappearing. Ravaged by alcohol and European diseases, decimated by wars in which they fought at a technological disadvantage, the tribes of the coastal area were losing many of the age-old skills and cultural attributes which commended them to eighteenth-century observers. Even while the new view of them formed, the indigenous Americans were in some areas slipping into a state of dependency that eroded white respect enormously. As the gun and knife replaced the bow and arrow, as the kettle and fishhook replaced hand-fashioned implements, and as rum became the great pain killer for those whose culture was undergoing rapid change, the grudging respect of white culture turned to contempt.[93] While the colonial intelligentsia was discovering the integrity of native culture in the eighteenth century, the ordinary farmer and frontiersman found less and less to admire in Indian life. For the Indian the limited respect of European colonizers had come too late to halt the process of cultural change which would leave his image impaired and his power to resist further cultural and territorial aggrandizement fatally weakened. For the colonist, the image of the native, so useful in the past, would continue to reflect the needs and intentions of a restless, ambitious people.

N O T E S

1. For the Elizabethan image of the African, see Winthrop D. Jordan, *White Over Black: American Attitudes Toward the Negro, 1550–1812* (Chapel Hill, N.C., 1968). Jordan's perceptive treatment of early English attitudes toward the African is suggestive of the wide range of questions which need to be asked concerning white attitudes toward the Indian. Jordan's pervading theme—that white attitudes toward the African reflected attempts of Englishmen to resolve their own problems of identity—parallels Roy Harvey Pearce's organizing thesis in *The Savages of America: A Study of the Indian and the Idea of Civilization* (Baltimore, 1953). Pearce's Indian, like Jordan's African, "became important for the English mind not for what he was in and of himself, but rather for what he showed civilized men they were not and must not become" (p. 5).

2. Although American historians have amassed a vast literature on the Indian, they seldom have seen the necessity of employing anthropological or sociological categories in studying Anglo-Indian contacts, and they have rarely viewed the interaction as a dynamic process in which both groups acted and were acted upon. For a review of the historical literature on Anglo-Indian relations, see Lyman H. Butterfield, Wilcomb E. Washburn, and William N. Fenton, *American Indian and White Relations to 1830: Needs and Opportunities for Study* (Chapel Hill, N.C., 1957); and Bernard W. Sheehan, "Indian-White Relations in Early America: A Review Essay," *William and Mary Quarterly*, 3d ser., 26 (1969), 267–86. I have focused this study on the southern colonies, especially Virginia, excluding from consideration Puritan New England and, for the most part, the Middle Atlantic colonies. A whole range of factors, including geography, prior experience with Europeans, the cultural characteristics of the Indians, Puritan theology, and the psychic life of the seventeenth-century Puritan community affected attitudes and relations in these areas. Although little is known about Puritan attitudes, those interested may gain an introduction to the subject from Chester E. Eisinger, "The Puritans' Justification for Taking the Land," *Essex Institute Historical Collections*, 84 (1948), 131–43; Roy Harvey Pearce, "The 'Ruines of Mankind': The Indian and the Puritan Mind," *Journal of the History of Ideas*, 13 (1952), 200–17; Alan Heimert, "Puritanism, the Wilderness, and the Frontier," *New England Quarterly*, 36 (1953), 361–82; and Alden T. Vaughan, *New England Frontier: Puritans and Indians, 1620–1675* (Boston, 1965).

3. For the exploits of Gilbert and Raleigh, see David B. Quinn, ed., *The Voyages*

and Colonising Enterprises of Sir Humphrey Gilbert (London, 1940); Quinn, *Raleigh and the British Empire* (London, 1947); and Quinn, ed., *The Roanoke Voyages, 1584–1590* (London, 1955).

4. Loren Baritz, "The Idea of the West," *American Historical Review*, 66 (1961), 618–40. See also William H. Babcock, *Legendary Islands of the Atlantic: A Study in Medieval Geography* (New York, 1922).

5. A general treatment of this literature, as literature, is given in Howard Mumford Jones, *O Strange New World; American Culture: The Formative Years* (New York, 1964), pp. 1–70. John B. Brebner, *The Explorers of North America, 1492–1806* (New York, 1933) provides a short treatment of European activity in the western Atlantic prior to the Roanoke voyages.

6. For a consideration of English reactions to the Indian at home, see Sidney Lee, "The American Indian in Elizabethan England," in *Elizabethan and Other Essays*, ed. Frederick S. Boas (Oxford, 1929), pp. 263–301; and Carolyn Foreman, *Indians Abroad, 1493–1938* (Norman, Okla., 1943).

7. Richard Hakluyt, *Divers voyages touching the discoverie of America, and the islands adjacent . . .* (London, 1582; rpt. London, 1850), p. 23.

8. "The Relation of John Verrazanus . . .," in Hakluyt, *Divers Voyages*, pp. 55–71. By this time three accounts of the New World were available in English. They are reprinted in Edward Arber, ed., *The First Three English Books on America . . .* (Birmingham, Eng., 1885).

9. The most important were George Best, *A True Discourse of the late voyages of discoverie, for the finding of a passage to Cathaya . . .* (London, 1578); Dionyse Settle, *A true reporte of the last voyage into the West and Northwest regions . . .* (London, 1577); and Thomas Ellis, *A true report of the third and last voyage into Meta Incognita* (London, 1578). All are republished in Vilhjalmur Stefansson, ed., *The Three Voyages of Martin Frobisher . . .* (London, 1938).

10. Stefansson, ed., *Voyages of Frobisher*, II, 23.

11. For a compilation of books in English describing the overseas world before 1600, see George B. Parks, *Richard Hakluyt and the English Voyages* (New York, 1928), pp. 270–76; and John Parker, *Books to Build an Empire: A Bibliographical History of English Overseas Interests to 1620* (Amsterdam, 1965).

12. *The Journal of Christopher Columbus*, ed. Cecil Jane (New York, 1960), pp. 23–24.

13. Jones, *Strange New World*, pp. 10–13.

14. Quinn, ed., *Voyages of Gilbert*, II, 285.

15. Jones, *Strange New World*, pp. 1–34.

16. *Divers voyages touching the discoverie of America* and *Discourse of Western Planting* (London, 1584). The latter is reprinted in E. G. R. Taylor, ed., *The Original Writings & Correspondence of the Two Richard Hakluyts* (London, 1935), II, 211–236.

17. *Writings & Correspondence of the Hakluyts*, I, 164–65.

18. *Writings & Correspondence of the Hakluyts*, II, 223. Hakluyt was quoting from Jean Ribault, *The whole and true discoverye of Terra Florida*.

19. *Discourse of Western Planting*, in *Writings & Correspondence of the Hakluyts*, II, 309–10, 257–65. The quotations are from pp. 309–10. Spanish cruelty toward the natives was a stock theme in the literature of English expansionists; see, for example,

II, 212, 223, 241, and Quinn, ed., *Roanoke Voyages*, I, 490–91. The influence of Spanish colonization on English expectations of the New World, including the key notion that the Indians could be employed as an agricultural labor force, is discussed by Edmund S. Morgan, "The Labor Problem at Jamestown, 1607–18," *American Historical Review*, 76 (1971), 597–600.

20. *Inducements to the Liking of the Voyage intended towards Virginia . . .* (1585), in *Writings & Correspondence of the Hakluyts*, II, 329–30.

21. Quinn, ed., *Voyages of Gilbert*, II, 450–52.

22. *Voyages of Gilbert*, II, 453.

23. *Voyages of Gilbert*, II, 467–68.

24. Compare *Notes on Colonisation* (1578), written for Gilbert's voyage; *Instructions for the North-East Passage* (1580); and *Pamphlet for the Virginia Enterprise* (1585); all reprinted in *Writings & Correspondence of the Hakluyts*, I, 116–22, 147–58; and II, 327–38.

25. The best accounts of the Roanoke colony, from an English point of view, are in Wesley Frank Craven, *The Southern Colonies in the Seventeenth Century, 1607–1689* (Baton Rouge, La., 1949), pp. 27–59; and David B. Quinn's introduction to *Roanoke Voyages*. For the history of the colony from an Indian perspective, consult Maurice A. Mook, "Algonkian Ethnohistory of the Carolina Sound," *Journal of The Washington Academy of Sciences*, 34 (1944), 181–97.

26. Thomas Hariot, *A briefe and true report of the new found land of Virginia . . .* (1588); Arthur Barlow, *Discourse of the First Voyage . . .* (1585); and Ralph Lane, *Discourse on the first colony . . .* [1586?]. All were first published in 1589 in Richard Hakluyt, *The Principall Navigations, Voyages, and Traffiques & Discoveries of the English Nation . . .* (Glasgow, 1903–05), and are reprinted in *Roanoke Voyages*, I, 317–87, 91–116, 255–94.

27. Quinn, ed., *Roanoke Voyages*, I, 108. Although at first glance one might dismiss such comments as colonizing propaganda, it must be understood that all the accounts had to come to terms with the fact that conflict did break out and ultimately led to the extinction of the English settlement. Given the unhappy ending of the story, it is less likely that the authors would falsify the Indians' initial reactions to the arrival of the English.

28. Quinn, ed., *Roanoke Voyages*, I, 368–72, 376.

29. Of the attempts by anthropologists to analyze the reaction of the tribes in the Chesapeake region to the arrival of the English, the best is Nancy Oestreich Lurie, "Indian Cultural Adjustment to European Civilization," in *Seventeenth-Century America: Essays in Colonial History*, ed. James Morton Smith (Chapel Hill, N.C., 1959), pp. 33–60. Lurie draws upon and extends the work of an earlier generation of anthropologists, including Maurice Mook, James Mooney, John R. Swanton, and Frank G. Speck.

30. Quinn, ed., *Roanoke Voyages*, I, 191–92, 246, 259, 265, 271, 286–88.

31. *Roanoke Voyages*, I, 381–82.

32. *Roanoke Voyages*, I, 371.

33. Paul H. Hulton and David B. Quinn, *The American Drawings of John White, 1577–1590* (Chapel Hill, N.C., 1964).

34. Edward Arber and A. G. Bradley, eds., *Travels and Works of Captain John Smith* (Edinburgh, 1910), I, 335–39.

35. *A True Reporte of the Late Discoveries* . . . (1583), in Quinn, ed., *Voyages of Gilbert*, II, 449–50.

36. *A Good Speed to Virginia* (London, 1609), quoted in Wesley Frank Craven, "Indian Policy in Early Virginia," *William and Mary Quarterly*, 3d ser., 1 (1944), 65. A useful essay on the subject is Wilcomb E. Washburn, "The Moral and Legal Justifications for Dispossessing the Indians," in Smith, ed., *Seventeenth-Century America*, pp. 15–32. For another early seventeenth-century rationale, see William Strachey, *The Historie of Travell into Virginia Britania* (1612), eds. Louis B. Wright and Virginia Freund (London, 1953), pp. 7–29.

37. *A True Declaration of the State of the Colonie in Virginia* . . . (London, 1610), in Peter Force, comp., *Tracts and Other Papers, Relating Principally to the Origin, Settlement, and Progress of the Colonies in North America* . . . (Washington, D.C., 1836–46), III, no. 1, p. 6. *Hakluytus Posthumus, or Purchas His Pilgrimes* . . . (Glasgow, 1905–07), XIX, 232.

38. *A Good Speed to Virginia*, ed. Wesley Frank Craven (London, 1609; rpt. New York, 1937).

39. *Historie of Travell into Virginia* . . . , p. 19.

40. [Gabriel Archer?], "A relatyon . . . written . . . by a gent. of ye Colony," in *The Jamestown Voyages Under the First Charter, 1606–1609*, ed. Philip L. Barbour (London, 1969), I, 103–04.

41. Barbour, ed., *Jamestown Voyages*, I, 82–86. Powhatan swiftly attacked the Chesapeake tribe, killing several of its leaders and replacing them with "trusted kinsmen." Lurie, "Indian Cultural Adjustment," p. 41.

42. Lurie, "Indian Cultural Adjustment," pp. 38–47; Wesley Frank Craven, the most careful student of the English Indian policy in the first half of the seventeenth century, takes the view that Powhatan, like his Indian enemies, never regarded an alliance with the English as advantageous and plotted their destruction from their first arrival; Craven, "Indian Policy in Early Virginia," pp. 68–70. Though there is evidence to dispute this interpretation of Indian motives, it is preferable to the older, naïve, and sentimental view of the Indian as hapless and helpless victims whose disinterested goodwill and hospitality toward the English was met with hostility and violence. To imagine that the Indians were unable to comprehend what was in their self-interest and incapable of perceiving English intentions is to give them less than their due and consign them to an essentially passive role in what surely must have been a dynamic process. The psychology of the colonizer and the colonized, though a subject of considerable interest among European and African historians, has played almost no role in the interpretation of early American history. For European treatments of the subject, see Henri Baudet, *Paradise on Earth: Some Thoughts on European Images of Non-European Man*, trans. Elizabeth Wenthold (New Haven, 1965); Albert Memmi, *The Colonizer and the Colonized*, trans. Howard Greenfield (New York, 1965); Dominique O. Mannoni, *Prospero and Caliban: The Psychology of Colonization*, trans. Pamela Powesland (London, 1956); Franz Fanon, *Black Skins, White Masks*, trans. Charles L. Markmann (New York, 1967); and Fanon, *The Wretched of the Earth*, trans. Constance Farrington (New York, 1963).

43. *A True relation* . . . , in *Works of John Smith*, eds., Arber and Bradley, I, 8–9. George Percy wrote of the same event: "If it had not pleased God to have put a ter-

rour in the Savage hearts, we had all perished by those vile and cruell Pagans, being in that weake estate as we were" (Barbour, ed., *Jamestown Voyages*, I, 144–45).

44. Arber and Bradley, eds., *Works of John Smith*, I, 38; Susan M. Kingsbury, ed., *The Records of the Virginia Company of London* (Washington, D.C., 1906–35), III, 175, 93; *Works of John Smith*, I, 35.

45. *Works of John Smith*, I, 107.

46. *Works of John Smith*, I, xiv, 24–27, 32–33, 35–38, 106–07.

47. *Advertisements for the unexperienced Planters of New-England, . . .* (London, 1631), in *Works of John Smith*, II, 925.

48. *Works of John Smith*, II, 411.

49. *Works of John Smith*, I, xxxv, 122–23; Kingsbury, ed., *Records of the Virginia Company*, III, 14–21. A few years later Governor Thomas Dale saw divine approval of this course of action. "Now may you judge Sir," he wrote, "if the God of battailes have not a helping hand in this, that having our swords drawn, killing their men, burning their houses, and taking their corne; yet they tendred us peace, and strive with all allacrity to keep us in good opinion of them; by which many benefits arise unto us" (Ralph Hamor, *A True Discourse of the Present State of Virginia*, ed. A. L. Rowse [1615; rpt. Richmond, Va., 1957], pp. 54–55).

50. Ben C. McCary, *Indians in Seventeenth-Century Virginia* (Williamsburg, Va., 1957), p. 78.

51. The Rolfe-Pocohantas union and its political implications are best told in the primary source material by Ralph Hamor, *A True Discourse;* and in the secondary literature by Bradford Smith, *Captain John Smith, His Life and Legend* (Philadelphia, 1953), and Philip L. Barbour, *Pocahontas and Her World* (Boston, 1970). The view of the Anglican missionary, Alexander Whitaker, that the dual policy of ruthless militarism and political intermarriage was the best policy, is expressed in a letter written in 1614 and reprinted in Hamor, *A True Discourse*, pp. 59–61.

52. *A Map of Virginia . . .* , in *Works of John Smith*, eds. Arber and Bradley, I, 43–84. Smith's statement on the civility of Indian society was copied almost verbatim by Strachey; see *Historie of Travell into Virginia*, p. 77.

53. Strachey, *History of Travell into Virginia*, pp. 53, 74–116. Spelman's account is in Arber and Bradley, eds., *Works of John Smith*, I, cv-cxiv.

54. Whitaker, *Good Newes from Virginia* (London, 1613), quoted in Pearce, *Savages of America*, p. 13.

55. Lurie, "Indian Cultural Adjustment," pp. 48–50.

56. Kingsbury, ed., *Records of the Virginia Company*, IV, 117–18, 89.

57. Edward Waterhouse, *A Declaration of the State of the Colony and . . . a Relation of the Barbarous Massacre* (1622), in Kingsbury, ed., *Records of the Virginia Company*, III, 556–57.

58. Arber and Bradley, eds., *Works of John Smith*, II, 578–79.

59. Kingsbury, ed., *Records of the Virginia Company*, III, 557.

60. *Records of the Virginia Company*, III, 705–07.

61. McCary, *Indians in Virginia*, p. 80; Craven, "Indian Policy," p. 73. See also William S. Powell, "Aftermath of the Massacre: The First Indian War, 1622–1632," *Virginia Magazine of History and Biography*, 66 (1958), 44–75.

62. Barbour, ed., *Jamestown Voyages*, I, 104; II, 354–55; Waterhouse, in Kingsbury, ed., *Records of the Virginia Company*, III, 562–63.

63. Promotional literature would continue to minimize Anglo-Indian hostility and reiterate the old notions of converting the natives to Christianity. This literature is included in P. Lee Phillips, "A List of Books Relating to America, in the Register of the London Company Stationers from 1562 to 1638," *American Historical Association Annual Report* (Washington, D.C., 1897), pp. 1251–61.

64. William Penn, *A Letter to the Free Society of Traders* . . . (1683), in Albert Cook Myers, ed., *Narratives of Early Pennsylvania, West New Jersey and Delaware, 1630–1707* (New York, 1912), pp. 230, 234. On Indian relations in early Pennsylvania, see also Francis Jennings, "Glory, Death, and Transfiguration: The Susquehannock Indians in the Seventeenth Century," *Proceedings of the American Philosophical Society,* 112 (1968), 15–53; "The Indian Trade of the Susquehanna Valley," *Proceedings of the American Philosophical Society,* 110 (1966), 406–24; "The Delaware Interregnum," *Pennsylvania Magazine of History and Biography,* 89 (1965), 174–98; William W. Newcomb, Jr., *The Culture and Acculturation of the Delaware Indians* (Ann Arbor, 1956); Anthony F. C. Wallace, *King of the Delawares: Teedyuscung, 1700–1763* (Philadelphia, 1949); and Donald A. Cadzow, *The Susquehannock Indians of Pennsylvania* (Harrisburg, 1936). A descriptive study of Indian origins, as viewed by colonizing Europeans, is Lee E. Huddleston, *Origins of the American Indians: European Concepts, 1492–1729* (Austin, Tex., 1967).

65. A general treatment of eighteenth-century Indian wars is provided in Howard H. Peckham, *The Colonial Wars, 1689–1762* (Chicago, 1965).

66. It is doubtful that a new view of the Indian ever made much progress below the upper stratum of society. Among frontiersmen, who still competed for land with the native and whose contacts with him remained abrasive, the old stereotypes remained basically unchanged throughout the eighteenth century. The same was true in the middle and lower classes of the seaboard cities and towns. Only when geographical and social distance separated the two groups could a new popular image emerge. For treatment of the frontier image of the Indian, see Lewis O. Saum, *The Fur Trader and the Indian* (Seattle, 1965).

67. *Hakluytus Posthumus,* XIX, 231.

68. Stanley Pargellis, ed., "An Account of the Indians in Virginia . . . 1689," *William and Mary Quarterly,* 3d ser., 16 (1959), 228–43.

69. Robert Beverley, *The History and Present State of Virginia,* ed. Louis B. Wright (1705; rpt. Chapel Hill, N.C., 1947), pp. 159–233 passim.

70. John Lawson, *A New Voyage to Carolina,* ed. Hugh T. Lefler (Chapel Hill, N.C., 1967), pp. 19, 38.

71. William Stith, *The History of the First Discovery and Settlement of Virginia* (Williamsburg, Va., 1747), p. 210.

72. Hugh Jones, *The Present State of Virginia* . . . , ed. Richard L. Morton (1724; rpt. Chapel Hill, N.C., 1956), pp. 54–58.

73. James Adair, *The History of the American Indians* . . . (London, 1775).

74. Adair, *History of the American Indians,* p. 413; Wilbur R. Jacobs, ed., *Indians of the Southern Colonial Frontier: The Edmond Atkin Report and Plan of 1775* (Columbia, S.C., 1954), pp. 62, 68; William K. Boyd, ed., *William Byrd's Histories of the Dividing Line Betwixt Virginia and North Carolina* (Raleigh, N.C., 1929), pp. 3, 222; Jones, *Present State of Virginia,* p. 56; Lawson, *New Voyage to Carolina,* pp. 207, 243.

75. Adair, *History of the American Indians,* p. 4; Jones, *Present State of Virginia,* pp. 56–57.

76. For example, Jones, *Present State of Virginia,* p. 57; Adair, *History of the American Indians,* pp. 4–5.

77. Atkin, *Report and Plan of 1755,* pp. 38–39. A century and a half earlier, George Percy, a member of the first settlement, had written: "It is a generall rule of these people, when they swere by their God, which is the Sunne, no Christian will keep their Oath better upon this promise" (*Observations gathered out of a Discourse of the Plantation . . . in Virginia . . . ,* in Barbour, ed., *Jamestown Voyages,* I, 143). Atkin, however, found the Choctaw Indians "subtle, Deceitful, Insolent" (*Report and Plan of 1755,* p. 7).

78. Adair, *History of the American Indians,* pp. 422–24; Atkin, *Report and Plan of 1755,* p. 38; Beverley, *History of Virginia,* pp. 188–89; Lawson, *New Voyage to Carolina,* pp. 23, 35, 243.

79. Beverley, *History of Virginia,* p. 29.

80. Atkin, *Report and Plan of 1755,* p. 39.

81. Frank J. Klingberg, *The Carolina Chronicle of Dr. Francis Le Jau, 1706–1717* (Berkeley, 1956), p. 19.

82. Boyd, ed., *Byrd's Histories,* pp. 3–4, 116–22, 222.

83. Beverley, *History of Virginia,* pp. 159, 38–39. The degree of miscegenation between white males and Indian women—the reverse was almost certainly rare—has been often disputed but rarely supported with convincing evidence. Wilbur R. Jacobs believes that mixed marriages were a rarity; "British-Colonial Attitudes and Policies Toward the Indian in the American Colonies," in Howard Peckham and Charles Gibson, eds., *Attitudes of Colonial Powers Toward the American Indian* (Salt Lake City, 1969), pp. 90–92. Herbert Moller has argued that demographic ratios, both male to female and white to nonwhite, have been the controlling factor in the incidence of interracial sexual relations; "Sex Composition and Correlated Culture Patterns of Colonial America," *William and Mary Quarterly,* 3d ser., 2 (1945), 113–53. Both Beverley and Byrd noted the contrast between English and French or Spanish attitudes toward intermarriage with the Indians. Governor Alexander Spottswood claimed in 1717 that he had never heard of an Anglo-Indian marriage during his seven years in Virginia; R. A. Brock, ed., *The Official Letters of Alexander Spottswood . . .* (Richmond, Va., 1882–85), II, 227. This statement should be taken with caution, since Lawson, only a few years earlier, took note of interracial mating; pp. 195–96. The English government encouraged racial intermarriage in Nova Scotia between 1719 and 1766; see J. B. Brebner, "Subsidized Intermarriage with the Indians: An Incident in British Colonial Policy," *Canadian Historical Review,* 6 (1925), 33–36. The entire subject of interracial contact, both Anglo-Indian and Afro-Indian, needs further investigation.

84. Lawson, *New Voyage to Carolina,* pp. 175, 189.

85. Beverley, *History of Virginia,* pp. 170–71.

86. Adair, *History of the American Indians,* pp. 413–16.

87. Klingberg, *Carolina Chronicle of Le Jau,* p. 24. One of Le Jau's associates in the Society for the Propagation of the Gospel, Gideon Johnson, drove the point home in 1708 when he wrote to his superiors in London of the colonists he had encountered: "The People here, generally speaking, are the Vilest race of Men upon the Earth they have neither honour, nor honesty nor Religion enough to entitle them to any tolerable

Character, being a perfect Medley or Hotch potch made up of Bank[r]upts, pirates, decayed Libertines, Sectaries and Enthusiasts of all sorts . . . and are the most factious and Seditious people in the whole World" (Frank J. Klingberg, ed., *Carolina Chronicle: The Papers of Commissary Gideon Johnson, 1707–1716* [Berkeley, 1946], p. 22).

88. Lawson, *New Voyage to Carolina*, pp. 40–41, 189–90, 180.

89. Beverley, *History of Virginia*, p. 233.

90. Adair, *History of the American Indians*, pp. 4–5; Atkin, *Report and Plan of 1755*, pp. 23–26; Boyd, ed., *Byrd's Histories*, pp. 116–20; Lawson, *New Voyage to Carolina*, pp. 18, 211, 239–46; Klingberg, *Carolina Chronicle of Le Jau*, p. 54.

91. Klingberg, *Papers of Gideon Johnson*, p. 53.

92. Klingberg, *Anglican Humanitarianism in Colonial New York* (Philadelphia, 1940), p. 54; Klingberg, *An Appraisal of the Negro in Colonial South Carolina: A Study in Americanization* (Washington, D.C., 1941), pp. 54, 68.

93. The process has been studied in various regions. See, for example, Wallace, *Teedyuscung;* Anthony F. C. Wallace, *The Death and Rebirth of the Seneca* (New York, 1970); Allen W. Trelease, *Indian Affairs in Colonial New York: The Seventeenth Century* (Ithaca, 1960); Alfred G. Bailey, *The Conflict of European and Eastern Algonkian Cultures, 1504–1700* (St. John, N.B., 1937); David H. Corkran, *The Creek Frontier, 1540–1783* (Norman, Okla., 1967); and J. H. Kennedy, *Jesuit and Savage in New France* (New Haven, 1950).

The Wild Man
Through the Looking Glass

 EARL MINER

Wilde men may dance wise measures.
Richard Brathwaite, *Natures Embassie*

It is a commonplace that from the Renaissance to about the nineteenth century the function of art was thought to be the mirroring of life.[1] Art, men said, held up a mirror to nature, or reality. Art imitated reality, what is, except that what is was often defined for artistic purposes in terms of an idealized reality. Art was expected to show that kings were kingly, heroes were heroic, lovers were distracted, and nature was ordered by a providential plan. Nature was, then, imitated in a guise understood by Europeans of the civilized, upper classes in a hierarchical society. Much as it offends our democratic principles, the mirror of art in those generations did not often reflect the lives of the great mass of men or reflect man outside his European representative. Increasingly, from the fifteenth century, however, interest accelerates in something other than upper-class European man. Exploration seemed to lead men, as it did Lewis Carroll's Alice, through the looking glass to a land of dreams or nightmare. In retrospect, we observe that usually they described something more nearly like European men than the Wild Man. Quite without knowing it, their study of the Wild Man began to tell them something about themselves; and what they learned about themselves helped them to understand people different from themselves. I am concerned with the double reflection chiefly as it was understood in the seventeenth century, and chiefly in England.

In literary as in other kinds of history, there is process but there are few definable beginnings and endings, except in the literary works themselves. The sense of beginning and ending is, in fact, one source of the comfort that literary works bring to us men and women immersed in the seemingly inscrutable flux of history. We look back on the encounters of Odysseus with the cruel, one-eyed Cyclops, Polyphemus. We remember the hazards of Aeneas in taking civilization to the Italian peninsula, of Beowulf in conquering mysterious, malign forces, or even of Dante in *The Inferno*. Such great works show that literary encounters with the Wild Man in many guises were not a novelty in 1600.

But if as historians we cannot begin at the beginning, we must perforce choose a starting point, and mine will be cantos XV and XVI of the *Gerusalemme Liberata* of Torquato Tasso. Tasso completed the poem in 1575. The excellent English translation by Edward Fairfax was published in 1600 and had, with its original, an immediate influence on European writers and other artists.[2] As the title indicates, the poem deals with that contact with outsiders which was uppermost in the minds of Christendom since the earlier Middle Ages—the crusade against the Turkish infidel in the hope of winning Jerusalem from the crescent to the cross, and of taking suitable plunder in doing so. In canto XIV the efforts of the crusaders are at a standstill, with the assistance of the redoubtable Rinaldo very much needed. He has been lured far away, however, to an Atlantic island by the enchantress Armida. In order to reclaim him, Charles and Ubaldo must journey by ship to Teneriffe, one of the Fortunate Isles. In this general situation alone we can see four of the major motifs dominating seventeenth-century versions of encounters with the Wild Man. Religion, heroic effort, and high passion are repeatedly involved. And what is above all necessary to get through art's looking glass is a sea voyage. Charles and Ubaldo are, like their destination, fortunate, because unlike real mariners in the seventeenth century they travel in an angelically directed vessel out into the wide Atlantic and safely on to the Fortunate Isles.

And what kind of men dwell in the many hazily conceived lands of the Atlantic? We raise the traveler's perennial question: What are they like? The answer from the guide is that they are savages.

> Some pray to beasts, some to a stone or tree,
> Some to the earth, the sunne, or morning starre;
> Their meates unwholsome, vile and hatefull bee,
> Some eate mans flesh, and captives tane in warre.[3]

Paganism and cannibalism are two of the stereotypes of the Wild Man.

But the people actually seen appear to be slightly different. Our travelers pass some hovels:

> In seven of them the people rude among
> The shadie trees, their sheds had built of clay,
>   The rest lay waste, unlesse wilde beastes unseene,
>   Or wanton Nymphes, roam'd on the moūtaines greene.[4]

There is no question but that such men were spoken about by real travelers returning from real places. Frobisher wrote of American Indians who "live in Caves of earth, and hunt for their dinners or praye, even as the beare or other wild beastes do."[5] But we must not think that such a picture necessarily came secondhand from travelers. Such miserable people were to be found even in the wealthiest, most powerful, and presumably most civilized country of Europe in the seventeenth century—France. As La Bruyère wrote so affectingly of the French countryside:

One sees certain sullen animals, male and female, scattered about the country, dark, livid, scorched by the sun, attached to the earth they dig up and turn over with invincible persistence; they have a kind of articulate speech, and when they rise to their feet, they show a human face, and, indeed, they are men. At night they retire to dens, where they live on black bread, water, and roots; they save others the toil of sowing, ploughing, and garnering in order to live, and thus deserve not to lack the bread they have sown.[6]

Certain images constantly recur in the naturalistic description of savages, whether abroad or at home: dirt and darkness,[7] bestial appearance, sexuality, and especially cannibalism.[8] In Europe cannibalism was considered a horror or a state of bestiality to which man was sometimes reduced by famine or siege. In his *Histoire de la Ligue*, Louis Maimbourg wrote of the cannibalism and savagery to which men were reduced by the siege of Paris late in 1590.[9]

What was thought to be a rare disaster within the pale of civilization was one of the marks of savagery, and most of Ireland was indeed thought to lie beyond the Pale in savagery. Repression, poverty, and anarchy brought centuries of misery to the country, and the English, who were chiefly responsible for such wretchedness, excused their actions by accounting the Irish savages and cannibals. Early in the seventeenth century English soldiers reported seeing

a most horrible spectacle of three children (whereof the eldest was not above ten yeeres old), all eating and knawing with their teeth the entrals of their dead mother, upon whose flesh they had fed twenty dayes past, and having eaten all from the feete upward to the bare bones, rosting it continually by a slow fire, were now come to the eating of her said entralls in like sort roasted, yet not divided from the body, being as yet raw.[10]

One aspect of the Wild Man was, then, the savagery into which civilization is always in danger of lapsing and which three hundred years ago was the intermittent and even ordinary lot of most of our human ancestors. In a famous phrase describing the lot of man in an uncivilized "state of nature," Thomas Hobbes said that it was "solitary, poor, nasty, brutish, and short."[11] Or, as the poet Samuel Butler put it in the 1680s,

> The whole World, without *Art*, and *Dress*,
> Would be but one great *Wilderness*
> And Mankind but a Savage Heard,
> For all that Nature has Conferd.[12]

A generation later, Jonathan Swift was to write that since the Irish were allowing themselves to be eaten up economically by the English, they might as well go the whole distance and breed their children for sale in the meatshops. "A Child will make two Dishes at an Entertainment for Friends, and when the Family dines alone, the fore or hind Quarter will make a reasonable Dish, and seasoned with a little Pepper or Salt will be very good Boiled on the fourth Day, especially in Winter."[13] That this is true, the proposer knew on the testimony of an acquaintance from another land symbolic of barbarism, America.[14]

European and distant savagery could meet in a common barbarism, but there were other voices to argue in other terms. After the slaughter of the Irish in 1641, one writer argued "that the massacres perpetrated on [them were] . . . as ferocious, as brutal, and as bloody, as the horrible feats of Cortes or Pizzaro, Attila or Genghis Khann."[15] And in his famous essay, "Of Canniballs," Michel de Montaigne argued toward the end of the sixteenth century that the cannibalism of savagery was less savage than so-called civilization. "I conceive, there is more Barbarity in Eating a Man Alive, than when he is Dead; in tearing a Body Limb from Limb, by Wracks and Torments, . . . causing it to be bit and worried by Dogs and Swine . . . than to Roast, and Eat him after he is Dead."[16] The elements of comparison imply that Montaigne's purpose is satiric in praising the habits and government of cannibals. His essay on "Canniballs" describes a utopia of savagery to deflate the pretensions of civilized man.[17] We are now aware that utopian writing may have satiric ends,[18] and the same may be said of those writers who painted a picture of distant lands in the mellow hues borrowed from the classical golden age.

The mingling of such primitivism and satire is very common. In *A Satyr touching Nobility* (1683), John Oldham expressed a familiar conception of true virtue:

> Curs'd be the day, when first this vanity
> Did primitive simplicity destroy,
> In the bless'd state of infant time, unknown,
> When Glory sprung from Innocence alone.[19]

Another English writer used the savages of America to criticize Roman Catholic Spain: "The ingenious discourse and Replies of these naked *Americans,* shew that their Honesty, Truth and Integrity have been the chief occasions of exposing them to the Slavery and Barbarity of these wicked Treacherous and Idolatrous *Spanish* Christians."[20] More explicitly, the Indians of Virginia were found to be "most gentle, loving and faithfull, voide of all guile and treason, and such as live after the manner of the golden age."[21] Such accounts differ from the ideal of the golden age in one major particular. Before the ages of exploration, the golden age of Saturn could be depicted only in the nostalgia usually described as chronological primitivism. With exploration, exoticism could locate its ideals in a contemporaneous but different culture, and this is similarly called cultural primitivism.[22] The difference is very important in the development of Western thought, but in practice the old terms were frequently employed to convey new or analogous kinds of experience. Naked innocence is a motif common to *Paradise Lost* and explorers' tales. And in both will be found another major motif—that of an almost spontaneous natural plenitude. In his "Bermudas," Andrew Marvell gave a picture of the luxuriant plenty granted by God to English settlers fleeing the oppression of the Anglican Church:

> [God] hangs in shades the Orange bright,
> Like golden Lamps in a green Night.
> And does in the Pomgranates close,
> Jewels more rich than *Ormus* show's.
> He makes the Figs our mouths to meet;
> And throws the Melons at our Feet. . . .
> He cast (of which we rather boast)
> The Gospels Pearl upon our Coast.[23]

The motif of spontaneous plenitude returns us to Tasso's *Gerusalemme Liberata.* In spite of the savagery the work depicts, the same passage offers a vision of the golden age glimpsed by Charles and Ubaldo:

> Th' isles fortunate these elder time did call,
> To which high heav'n they fain'd so kind and good,

And of his blessings ritch so liberall,
That without tillage earth gives corne for food,
   And grapes that swell with sweete and pretious wine,
   There without pruning yeelds the fertill vine.[24]

The new world of the Wild Man, or the new found land of the European, accommodated such contraries as savagery and the golden age, misery and abundance. The world included a great deal more. As we have noted, Tasso's plot has the religious implications of a crusade, and in the sixteenth century especially, and among Portuguese and Spaniards in particular, the cross traveled with the crown and sword in one heroic enterprise. Religious concern was not forgotten by the seventeenth-century explorers. We may recall that the oldest surviving building in California is the chapel of San Juan Capistrano, dating from 1778; and that across this continent religious beliefs affected the constitutional forms assumed by different American colonies. Religious impetus waned, however, as a factor of seventeenth-century exploration, and especially in Protestant countries.[25] Another important change, which indeed reflected serious economic problems for Spain and Portugal, was the disappearance of the fact and the symbol of gold and treasure in the New World.[26] During the century what became increasingly important was trade, the motive of the three Anglo-Dutch naval wars and the object of a three- or four-way struggle between Spain and the Netherlands, France, and England. To each country trade seemed an economic necessity—to Spain and the Netherlands for survival, and to England for that expansion which made her the greatest European power in the eighteenth century.

It may seem that trade offered little of the idealism and rationale that religion had given to imperalism. But without seeking to draw connections between Protestantism and the rise of capitalism, it is possible to see that trade was the basic justification for imperalism from the seventeenth century to this century, because trade was associated with the growth of knowledge, with civilization, and with worldwide relations between men. Something of this idealism can be found as early as Tasso's *Gerusalemme Liberata.*

The time shall come that saylers shall disdaine
To talke or argue of Alcides streat,
And landes and seas that namelesse yet remaine,
Shall well be knowne, their bounders, scite and seat,
The ships encompasse shall the sollid maine,
As farre as seas outstretch their waters great,

> And measure all the world, and with the sunne
> About this earth, this globe, this compasse, runne.   (XV, xxx)

The vision became a detailed myth by 1667, when John Dryden treated the progress of shipping in his poem, *Annus Mirabilis*. Knowledge, trade, and commercial utopianism combine.

> But what so long in vain, and yet unknown,
>   By poor man-kinds benighted wit is sought,
> Shall in this Age to *Britain* first be shown,
>   And hence be to admiring Nations taught.
>
> The Ebbs of Tydes, and their mysterious flow,
>   We, as Arts Elements shall understand:
> And as by Line upon the Ocean go,
>   Whose paths shall be familiar as the Land.
>
> Instructed ships shall sail to quick Commerce;
>   By which remotest Regions are alli'd:
> Which makes one City of the Universe,
>   Where some may gain, and all may be suppli'd.
>
> Then, we upon our Globes last verge shall go,
>   And view the Ocean leaning on the sky:
> From thence our rolling Neighbours we shall know,
>   And on the Lunar world securely pry.   (641–56)

Such a faith in knowledge and trade, combined with a vision of progress for the human race, gave England a rationale that was to prove more suitable to the next two centuries than did the union of cross and sword for Spain.

By going through the looking glass, Europeans beheld in the Wild Man a focus for many of their most important concerns. We have seen that he—or she—was a focus for the zeal of religion, for heroism, and for passion. On the one hand the Wild Man was a cannibal—the ultimate stage of human debasement—and on the other a primitivist model of perfection. If he knew what was good for him, the Wild Man would accept a role as very junior partner in European economic expansion, and he too had a place in the utopian forecast of what trade might bring about for human security and knowledge. It is a bewildering picture reflected in the mirror of art, and one all the more human for combining bright colors of idealism with the shadowing of cruelty and exploitation. As it happens, there was a seventeenth-century English radical political figure who embodies such a mixture in both his activities and his name. As a political Leveller, John Wildman was radical in advocating changes in suffrage that did not come in fact to England till after the second Victorian Reform Bill. And yet Wildman was outraged by the almost democratic principles of the yet more radical Diggers, and he resolutely set out on the civilized task of making a fortune by buying up the forfeited estates of Royalists. The lesson is not that we should be cynical about the seventeenth century, but that we should appreciate the complexity of human events.

In what has been said so far, the proof texts have been found in a canto or two of *Gerusalemme Liberata*, which brilliantly provides us with a full range of images for the topics I have mentioned. But the provision is overprodigal, and it serves my interest better to follow a few dominant motifs through major works, principally plays, produced in England in the seventeenth century. Shakespeare is clearly the writer with whom to begin. He was obviously interested in the contact of men of different origins. His two major outsiders are of course Shylock and Othello, who find themselves in a Christian, white society. For some reason, Venice is the scene of both plays. Othello had traveled, and he brought back some tall tales to relate to Desdemona. It is not certain just how tall, or how accurate, Shakespeare intends us to think such stories are, but among other things Othello speaks of "Hair-breadth 'scapes," "deserts idle,"

> And of the Cannibals, that each other eat;
> The Anthropophagi, and men whose heads
> Do grow beneath their shoulders.[27]

Other plays have settings that remind us somewhat of motifs we have seen. The Illyria of *Twelfth Night* has some such touches of remote places, and the Forest of Arden yet more in *As You Like It*. But it is *The Tempest* above the rest of his plays in which Shakespeare set forth his —and his century's—understanding of the terms of encounter between civilization and the Wild Man in a state of nature. It is *The Tempest* that conceived and transformed motifs of events, places, and characters that recur and alter in subsequent decades. It is such recurrence and alteration that will subsequently concern me.

One such image is an old one for perilous human life—shipwreck. On the basis of a passage in Petronius,[28] Dryden wrote of the sad human lot:

> Such are the proud designs of human kind,
>   And so we suffer Shipwrack every where!
> Alas, what Port can such a Pilot find,
>   Who in the night of Fate must blindly steer![29]

These lines provide the shading in *Annus Mirabilis* for Dryden's bright hopes for peace and prosperity. Similar shadings and glories distinguish in high measure the wondrously mellow colorings of *The Tempest*. The play opens with a storm at sea, leading to shipwreck on an island. Shakespeare had been reading (or hearing) about a wreck in the Bermudas.[30] But his own island is ambiguously placed within floating distance of Milan,[31] because to this island, before the landing of the shipwrecked men, have floated Prospero, rightful Duke of Milan, and his daughter, Miranda. Having then been a baby, she cannot remember the event and asks, "How came we ashore?" "By Providence divine," her father answers. As her names suggests, Miranda is a wonder—beautiful, innocent, implicitly fertile, and even, within limits, wise. She is made into this ideal of womanhood by her noble blood and her education away from the corruptions of society by a father whose learning is so prodigious that he is a magician. Knowledge and innocence, or those themes of art and nature which preoccupy seventeenth-century literature, are fused in Miranda as if to fulfill a dream felt by man wherever romance has had an appeal. She is also an ideal by which the shipwrecked newcomers are to be judged.

The newcomers possess knowledge and art, but they lack innocence and primitive purity. Ferdinand is something of an exception, and he will be reclaimed by betrothal to Miranda. The contrast between Miranda and the Italians is not the most interesting one in the play from our point of view, however. There are other creatures on the island, one of them the good spirit Ariel, who is so far a creature of the element of air that he has no human feelings,[32] and another is Caliban, who is so much a creature of earth that his passions are monstrous.[33] In him we see the Wild Man as savage, and it is no accident that his name itself, Caliban, may be arranged so easily by anagram into "can[n]ibal." At the same time, Caliban is a version of a centuries-old European model, the *wodehouse* or *wodewose*, the Wild Man, the savage.[34] A major characteristic of this figure is his primitive sexuality. The contrast between such animality and human custom sanctioned by grace is readily shown by the fact that Caliban had once tried to assault Miranda, whereas she and Ferdinand are united by "a contract of true love" in a marriage masque of classical deities, nymphs, and reapers.[35]

One may not simply say that Caliban is a Wild Man and have done with it. For one thing, some of the Neapolitan nobility show themselves as ready as he to kill.[36] For another, the drunken riot of the sailors is as far removed from the orderly ceremony of betrothal as is Caliban's attempt on Miranda. It is significant that in much of the play Caliban and the drunken mariners are together, because in their relation we can see a theme that was to grow steadily in importance with subsequent versions of *The Tempest* situation. This theme may be called social in Shakespeare's play, although it also possesses overtones of government and religion. It may be illustrated by the fact that Caliban is called a slave, and by his transferral of masters when he is drunk from Prospero to Trinculo, who has been elected king by the drunken mariners. We see that to Shakespeare's view even the most rudimentary state to which men may be reduced demands a stratified social system. If Caliban had his way, the masses would rebel and overthrow their rightful prince. But it is plain that to Shakespeare the most such men might hope for is a change of master.

> 'Ban, 'Ban Ca—Caliban . .
> Has a new master:—get a new man.
> Freedom, high-day! high-day, freedom!   (II, ii, 184–86)

In Caliban, then, Shakespeare combined in varying proportions the cannibal of unknown islands, the Wild Man of Europe, the exploited savage, and the masses of subjected European peasants. He is controlled by Prospero—by Prospero as a rightful prince and by Prospero as a magician given his powers by knowledge.

The more purely social concerns may be seen, if dimly, in Tasso's poem, emerging with greater clarity in *The Tempest* and becoming central to some later treatments of the Wild Man. Before leaving Shakespeare, however, we ought to observe that he resolves the many dualities, contrasts, and antagonisms of *The Tempest*. The resolution can be construed in human or divine terms, but perhaps is best taken to involve both. Those who have done wrong must repent. Those who have been wronged must forgive. And those who love must be joined by ceremony. Even Caliban will "seek for grace," and just as "Providence divine" had brought Prospero and Miranda safely to the island, so the more than ordinary human knowledge of Prospero effects the reconciliation. That knowledge, that magical art, will enable European man to return safely to his proper home, because with Providence the guide, man has found the Pilot who, in Dryden's phrase, will steer man to port "in the night of Fate."[37]

Shakespeare was but one of many English writers in his generation or later to depict European encounters with the Wild Man and to show that the modern civilized European was to some extent a mirror image of the savage. Important writers like Ben Jonson wrote, like Tasso, of the Fortunate Isles and of discoveries in territories as remote as the moon.[38] Shakespeare could not fully explore the significance of such encounters for new generations, but he could provide approaches to the subject very important to subsequent writers. Both the recurrence and the alteration of his approaches can provide us with some understanding of the ways in which writers in the remainder of the seventeeth century were to develop the images and themes that Shakespeare himself had taken from earlier writers.

John Fletcher's play, *The Sea Voyage*, is characteristic of one line of development of matters treated in *The Tempest*. *The Sea Voyage* is not indebted to Shakespeare for very much in the way of characters or plot. But it does begin with a storm at sea, and it does have, in Clarinda, a Miranda character who has never seen a man. What *The Sea Voyage* does not have is a Caliban or an Ariel, and we can see from this that seventeenth-century English writers, Shakespeare included, were really less concerned with the Wild Man in himself than with civilized man in the wilds, or in the Wild Man lurking somewhere in us all. One can see a certain tact in the approach taken by the playwrights of the century. Not having been to sea and never having seen a Wild Man, they dealt with what might be more readily imagined—the behavior of Europeans in the wilds—a matter which provided Defoe's *Robinson Crusoe* with its interest. We may recall that the first good look that Englishmen had at men racially different from themselves was not gained until the visit of the embassy from Bantam in Java to the court of Charles II in 1682. The popular excitement was prodigious, and years later poets were still referring to the outlandish visitors.[39] Most of us do not realize, or remember, how significant is first acquaintance with a foreigner, especially when it comes only after reaching adulthood. But television, which makes the remote near and the sensational humdrum, shows in its landings of cartoon men among strange creatures on distant planets that the experience of three centuries ago has a modern equivalent and that we have not altogether improved our terms of understanding.

Both now and in the seventeenth century, the aim has been not so much to understand the Wild Man as to understand oneself. It is appropriate that Fletcher goes so far as to depict, in part, the European as Wild Man. To understand how he does so, we must consider his curious division of foreign parts into two islands. One is utterly desolate: "No rivers, nor no pleasant groves, no beasts; / All that were made for man's use fly this desert."[40] Not surprisingly, the men shipwrecked on so inhospitable a shore are soon on the verge of starvation. The one woman among them, Aminta, is so weakened by hunger and so ill-advised as to fall asleep and excite cannibalistic thoughts in some of the men:

> Of such restoring meats we have examples,
> Thousand examples, and allow'd for excellent;
> Women that have eat their children, men
> Their slaves, nay, their brothers.[41]

As we have seen, cannibalism was thought basic to savagery, and yet writers like Montaigne had used the practice as a means to criticize European man. The two lines shade together in Fletcher's treatment. Another characteristic assigned to the Wild Man was inordinate sexuality, and Fletcher presented a very special version of this to parallel the cannibalism. Alongside the desert island there is another, which is as profusely stocked with all good things as Marvell's Bermudas and indeed as most of the islands in seventeenth-century accounts. This island is inhabited by a race of women living under an Amazonian regime. But most of the women hunger as much from a need for men as the men for food. The problem of governing either of these two societies is nearly impossible. As one woman says of their stiff ruler, Rosellia, "But, if she command unjust and cruel things, / We are not to obey it."[42] It is cruel and unusual punishment to refuse women the company of men. The hunger for men in the two versions given by cannibalism and sexual yearning provide versions of the savagery in which European man may find himself.

Fletcher's solution to the seemingly intractable problems he raises may appear somewhat contrived. Another ship comes to these islands, and on it is Sebastian, the husband of Rosellia and father of other characters. Yet that is what happened in many true stories of rescue from shipwreck. At all events, if Shakespeare arouses one kind of belief with his mingling of Providence and magic, Fletcher brings into being another by uniting the family under the authority of the husband and father. The restoration brings order, rescue, and the satisfaction of appetites. What seems contrived in the ending actually testifies to the very deeply held seventeenth-century belief that men naturally ruled, and that the paternal family was an image, or basis, of larger social wholes. The play's division of society into desert and pastoral islands, men and women, parents and children, is therefore suggestive of disorder. The naturalness of paternal rule and of conservative European theories of government is tested by Fletcher, as it was by other writers, by placing a little society on a remote island.

Fletcher manages to bring together what the political philosophers of the time can be shown to have treated separately. In his *Patriarcha,* Sir Robert Filmer argued for the authority of kings derived from the paternal authority of Adam.[43] Milton would have angrily rejected the idea that kings could derive such absolute authority from any source, but in *Paradise Lost* he distinguished between Adam's looks implying "Absolute rule" and Eve's implying "Subjection."[44] The appearance of Sebastian toward the end of *The Sea Voyage* is, then, not merely that of *pater ex machina* but also of a rightful authority that can bring order. Between Fletcher and Filmer there had appeared James Harrington's description of an ideal republican state, to which he gave the significant name, Oceana.[45] Fletcher set out, like Shakespeare, to prove his important values by giving them the threat of a symbolic sea voyage or tempest. Harrington's republicanism was held in stout measure by Henry Neville, who published in 1668 *The Isle of Pines,* which managed to deceive much of Europe for its authenticity. Although a forerunner of the short story, *The Isle of Pines* presents itself as the account by George Pine of life on a "fourth Island near *Terra Australis, Incognita,*" as the title page puts it. We have the usual cause: shipwreck in a tempest, and a system of government really more like Filmer's than Harrington's. The government of the little society is based upon the Christian religion and, more especially, polygamy presided over by paternal authority. The story is a remarkable sexual daydream, with George Pine populating his island with something like 1,785 people in forty years, but it also is a romance of paternal authority bringing a utopian state.

It probably is not clear to readers today why theories of government should have been referred to remote and desolate areas by seventeenth-century writers, and certainly the matter is very complicated. A common belief was that society was founded on a so-called social contract, prior to which man lived in a state of nature. At the same time, however, there was also believed to be a natural law (sometimes distinguishing *lex natural* and *jus natural*), which might or might not be identified with divine law and human laws. Some of these concerns run back to antiquity. Some were defined by the Middle Ages. Others took their characteristic expression in the seventeeth and eighteenth centuries.[46] The existence of a social contract seemed to presume a time before the contract was entered into, a time Hobbes designated as a state of nature. His version was pessimistic, but others, with memories of the golden age of Saturn or of an Edenic paradise, looked back upon an idealized state of nature. When such chronological primitivism came to be replaced by cultural primitivism, some writers saw an opportunity to raise questions about government, about a social contract, and about a state of nature by placing European man on an island or by bringing him into contact with non-Europeans. Old concepts were renewed in the context of a new nature revealed by explorations, and old ideas of the patriarchal family as a basis of government might be tested in terms of families broken by distant travel, by cannibalism, or by other extremities.[47] The fact that the political philosophers used the images of the poets suggests that the poets were treating the themes of the philosophers. And it is a tribute to Shakespeare's play *The Tempest* and to Fletcher's *Sea Voyage* that both were sufficiently relevant in the last four decades of the century to be revived, revised, and even parodied.

When commercial theaters opened at the Restoration of Charles II, after almost two decades of closure, the lack of practiced and available playwrights naturally led to the performance of earlier plays. As is well known, Ben Jonson, Shakespeare, and the team of Beaumont and Fletcher were the most popular.[48] The eighteen years of closure inevitably brought problems, opportunities, and the differing experience of a generation that had known regicide, civil wars, and a new form of oligarchy. There was real continuity, and there was real change. The lack of boy actors for female roles led to the introduction of actresses. The experience of the continental theatrical resources gained by a court in exile led to a variety of new forms, to a new sense of theater typified by more sophisticated sets, to a new relation between society and the theater, and to innovations with opera, spectacle, and farce. From such novelties amid the still very dominant native tradition we may choose two features that were gradually to affect presentations of the older dramatists: realism and spectacle, opposite though the two may seem to be.

Realism and spectacle are both to be found in Thomas D'Urfey's adaptation of *The Sea Voyage*. *A Common-Wealth of Women* (1686) is a title declaring a more downright interest in the problems of government in a society artificially composed of women alone. In keeping with this tendency, D'Urfey clarifies the rather arbitrary and not always intelligible relations between Fletcher's characters. He innovates to the extent that the opening scene is not a tempest—apparently he thought that device had become too hackneyed to be employed at the outset. Instead, he brings the issues of the play closer to the audience by having the first scene take place in London's Covent Garden, where sex antagonism and thirst for riches drive men to the mariner's life. The tempest comes at the beginning of the second act, when it seems rather fresh after the reality of Covent Garden. The two worlds of London and the desert island are connected by the sighs of the shipwrecked men for their wives. Such alterations also affect the serious plot. Rosellia is led to justify with explicit theory her Amazonian commonwealth. As if that were not enough, D'Urfey gives us a curious version of the social contract and of the idea that those who do not enter into it are savages. The sisterhood is founded on a contract or oath to regard all men as monsters; and men, for whom in practice ideas of social contract were usually devised, are excluded as if they were Hottentots.[49] There is, then, a tendency to take the dramatic hypotheses of Fletcher and the theories of the social philosophers as a combined reality worth testing. Along with this tendency, there goes the other—to spectacle. This is best typified in the songs which introduce a note of pastoralism or romance that tends to exoticize and render remote, just as the Covent Garden scene had rendered an earlier romance near. The scene in the last act of men doing women's work while the women post a somewhat uncertain guard with whips no doubt owes something to ancient legends of the service of Hercules to Omphale, Queen of Lydia.[50] But to the people of the audience it could only betoken a topsy-turvy world which is righted at last when the family is united and when male dominance and class distinctions are reinstated.[51] As so often with comedy, a threat is defined in realism and in display, and the same means otherwise combined finally reduce the threat and bring a reconciliation with the customary world of the audience.

Although revived and revised, Fletcher's play did not meet with the great success of *The Tempest* on the Restoration stage. People unfamiliar with the actual practice of the theater in every place where it flourishes are often shocked to learn that Shakespeare's handiwork was often tampered with in the Restoration, not realizing that it has been tampered with every time it has been performed, there being no commercial possibility of performing his plays as they were in his own time. All the same, the steady alteration of *The Tempest* is a very curious, sometimes puzzling, and also revealing phenomenon. It was presented more or less intact until 1667, when Dryden assisted Sir William Davenant in revising the play.[52] It seems that by that point in the century certain features of the play had come to seem hard to believe, and especially Miranda, Ariel, and Caliban. Davenant therefore followed, as it were, Shakespeare's principle in *King Lear:* if one female character of a certain kind would be incredible by herself, make two of her and a man of the same kind. Shakespeare's Miranda had not seen a man except her father and yet talks like a well-bred English gentlewoman. So Davenant added a sister,

Dorinda, on the model of the sexually eager Clarinda of Fletcher's *Sea Voyage*. He also added another character, Hippolito, a man who had never seen a woman, again modeled on a female character in Fletcher's play, Hippolita, who had uttered the stirring sentiment, "We must and will have men."[53] In addition, Davenant gave Caliban a sister, Sycorax, and Ariel a girl friend, Milcha, who speaks one word.[54] Most commentators have found this kind of geometry in the dramatis personae somewhat offensive, and the Davenant-Dryden version is certainly no improvement on the warm romance that Shakespeare had written. But it is also far from negligible, and it is a fair question to ask how it could be described as perhaps "the favourite play of the Restoration stage."[55] One reason is that the basic conception of the play was so sound, and the adaptations really so much indebted to that conception, that the play's original merits could still commend it. Another reason is that the revisions reshaped the experience provided by the play along lines favored by a new generation. The course of exploration, colonization, trade, and science had come to make Shakespeare's romance seem at once close to contemporary life and yet too incredible in its magic to be taken as it was. One way out was to make what seemed artificial into a game—to double the romantic characters. There may also have been some thought that, if there was a romantic character of each sex who had never seen his or her opposite, it was somehow understandable how nature could provide the species.[56]

Yet another reason for the success of the play is to be found in the broad comedy of its subplot. In fact, the balance of interest in the play shifts from the dominant pastoral romance with which Shakespeare displays his themes of nobility, justice, and art to a concern with the public aspects of human relations. The new emphasis does not forget Shakespeare's themes, nor had Shakespeare ignored altogether matters that now come to have greater importance: natural law, the formation of society, and the institution of government. To put it simply, the mariners in Shakespeare's version provide something of parody and something of threat to the order of justice that Prospero is so carefully fashioning; but the mariners come to play a larger role in the revised version of Davenant and Dryden, written after the experience of civil war, the execution of a king, and the establishment of what seemed to them a bogus form of government to control anarchy.

In fact, the broad subplot is at once immensely entertaining and altogether serious. The drunken men of the ship lapse into a "state of nature" or of primitive freedom from rule in landing on the island with their drink. Next they enter into a social contract and establish a duchy on the principle of mixed monarchy. When threatened by civil war, they expel the threatener to that state of nature from which they had staggered with their brandy five minutes before. Mustacho begins the game by revealing, through the usual trope of cannibalism, that they are now in a state of nature.

Must[acho]. Our Ship is sunk, and we can never get home agen: we must e'en turn Salvages, and the next that catches his fellow may eat him.

Vent[oso]. No, no, let us have a Government; for if we live well and orderly, Heav'n will drive the Shipwracks ashore to make us all rich, therefore let us carry good Consciences, and not eat one another.[57]

Stephano, the captain of the ship, establishes his authority over the newly discovered island just as European kings did: by analogy to their sovereignty elsewhere. They ruled kingdoms in Europe and so ruled what was discovered; Stephano was master of the ship, and so he is duke of the discovered isle.

Steph[ano]. Whoever eats any of my subjects, I'le break out his Teeth with my Scepter: for I was Master at Sea, and will be Duke on Land: you *Mustacho* have been my Mate, and shall by my Vice-Roy.

Ventoso rejects the analogy:

When you are Duke you may chuse your Vice-Roy; but I am a free Subject in a new Plantation, and will have no Duke without my voice. And so fill me the other soop.

Discussion of the issue of a constitutional monarchy is disrupted when Trincalo staggers in, far advanced in drinking sack. Stephano, as ruler, seeks to cure disorder in his duchy.

Steph[ano]. *Trincalo*, sleep and be sober; and make no more uproars in my Country.

Trinc[alo]. Why, what are you, Sir, what are you?

Steph[ano]. What I am, I am by free election, and you *Trincalo* are not your self; but we pardon your first fault,

Because it is the first day of our Reign.

Talk of free election by royalist writers like Davenant and Dryden implies that Stephano is a usurper. Legitimate kings need only plead their lawful blood; usurpers like William I, Henry IV, and Oliver Cromwell had to rely on such weak straws as election.

Trincalo's threat is so much taken for real that Mustacho pleads with him, laying before him the conservative case for order under law.

Must[acho]. Art thou mad, *Trincalo*, wilt thou disturb a settled Government? . . .
Trinc[alo]. I'll have no Laws.
Vent[oso]. Then Civil-War begins   *[Vent. Must.* draw
Steph[ano]. Hold, hold, I'le have no blood shed,
My subjects are but few: let him make a rebellion
By himself; and a Rebel, I Duke *Stephano* declare him . . .

One cannot see in this scene much of Shakespeare's "pastoral."[58] And in the high plot of the nobility, the introduction of characters pairing some of Shakespeare's characters has not a little of the effect of drawing-room comedy. The atmosphere is less that of the stiff formality of the reigns of Elizabeth I and James I, and more that of the sauntering of Charles II, with his spaniels before him and doffing his hat to his subjects. Just as the low plot, which is essentially a threat to the order of the high plot, had had its attempt to discover order in government, so does the high plot, which has so much order imposed on it by the pairing of characters and Prospero's power, admit to a threat which was associated with the Wild Man from the Middle Ages: sexuality. In Shakespeare's version, the sexual threat is that of Caliban against his superior, Miranda. In Davenant and Dryden's version the threat is among the higher characters themselves. Dorinda, the second daughter of Prospero "that never saw man," and Hippolito, a foil to Ferdinand but also "one that never saw woman," are particularly curious about sex. They are at once naïve and prurient. This side of the revised version develops partly out of another aspect of the tradition of the Wild Man, to be sure, but more particularly out of Fletcher's play, *The Sea Voyage*. In addition, Sycorax has a brief speech on polyandry, a practice that interested most seventeeth-century men less than polygamy, but which was nonetheless associated with savage customs, especially in the East Indies.[59] A perceptible difference comes with the introduction of sexual interest and rivalry as a disruptive force to be reconciled at the end by marriage and the affirmation of social bonds. Shakespeare's warm romance has become an earthy comedy.

The tendency to comedy was taken to extraordinary lengths by one of the funniest parodies in English literature, Thomas Duffett's play, *The Mock-Tempest: or the Enchanted Castle* (1675). The castle is Bridewell, the workhouse prison for apprehended prostitutes. Like all good parodies, it is interesting in its own right and for catching and distorting matters essential in the original. There is no need to follow the very funny plot, but we may observe that two of the traditionally best-known scenes of *The Tempest* are seized on for parody. The more famous is the noise-making that begins *The Tempest* to designate a storm. Duffett's first stage direction begins: "*A great noyse heard of beating Doors, and breaking Windowes, crying a Whore, a Whore, &c.*" The other symptom of Duffett's acquaintance with the tradition of the play is his amusing parody of Prospero's notoriously tedious relation to Miranda of their earlier life. Duffett begins:

> Pro[spero]. *Miranda*, where's your Sister?
> Mir[anda]. I left her on the Dust-Cart-top, gaping after the huge noyse that went by.[60]

After that, Prospero more and more amuses us as a dithering fool and Miranda as a wonderfully naïve slattern. These scenes, combined with operatic episodes of considerable charm, make Duffett's spoof a worthy precursor of Gay's *Beggar's Opera*. In fact, Duffett anticipates certain themes of Gay: concern with law as an instrument of government and with a father's responsibility to marry off daughters, even when they are, as it was put in those days, "damaged goods."

Numerous other plays, stories, and poems—not to mention treatises in cold prose—would need to be mentioned in any complete account of what happened when seventeenth-century European man stepped through the artistic looking glass in search of the Wild Man. A gloss of the numerous hints by Tasso reveals how many issues were raised by concern with the Wild Man, and attention to developments in one significant artistic line shows how the changing experience of the seventeenth century might subtly affect a single set of images. By turning now to three late seventeenth-century English works, we should be able to discern something of the range of experience conveyed by the Wild Man during that century and something of the attitude that would come to dominate the next age.

The first of these versions of the Wild Man depicts him as a romance hero and a mysterious stranger in civilized society. In Dryden's ten-act, double play, *The Conquest of Granada*, the fire-eating hero Almanzor appears amid Moorish civilization as a powerful, heroic stranger of uncertain disruptive or cohering effect. When taxed for having created this extraordinary character, Dryden defended himself by precedent in the Achilles of Homer, the Rinaldo of Tasso's *Jerusalem Delivered*, and the Artaban of Calprenède's *Cléopatre*.[61] But what makes Almanzor a figure in the lineage of the Wild Man is a significant difference. In classical,

Germanic, and romance epics alike, the mysterious stranger is conventionally mysterious, not to the reader, for whom he is an ethical norm, but to the society in which he arrives, like Odysseus washed ashore to the Phaeacians, or Beowulf by ship to the Danes. As a corollary, the society to which the hero seems mysterious holds much that is unknown or mysterious to us. Dryden's Almanzor, on the other hand, is as mysterious to us as to the Moors of Granada. Powerful, capricious, possessed of a moral code all his own, and given to changes of front that make summary impossible, Almanzor is at once an aid and a threat to any society. When the Moorish king Boabdelin in exasperation sentences Almanzor to death, the bravado of heroic defiance reveals the Wild Man in heroic guise:

> No man has more contempt than I, of breath;
> But whence hast thou the right to give me death?
> Obey'd as Soveraign by thy Subjects be,
> But know, that I alone am King of me.
> I am as free as Nature first made man ⎫
> 'Ere the base Laws of Servitude began ⎬
> When wild in woods the noble Savage ran. ⎭

This passage[62] apparently introduces into English a phrase that was to endure as a label for concepts often very different from Dryden's: the Noble Savage. It is a phrase revealing how mixed were the attitudes toward men outside the pale of ordinary society. Montaigne's reasonable cannibals provide an earlier example, as Dryden's heroic dissident, the Noble Savage Almanzor, furnishes a later example of the ambiguous feelings of Europeans discovering something about themselves while discovering men different from themselves. Dryden finds his mercurial hero admirable, especially among the tame and venal Moors. But in the course of ten acts set in the heroic context of the Spanish *reconquista* of about 1492, Almanzor is reconciled to society. He saves it, as it at last confers on his heroism a customary and civilized sanction. Dryden had a number of such heroes, and one can trace some literary descendants as well as ancestors.[63] But Almanzor and his kin in other heroic plays by Dryden seem to supply us with our last full-blooded versions of the hero of the romance epic.

There were versions of the Noble Savage contemporary with Almanzor that sometimes differed from him to an extraordinary degree. One of the most sensational versions of man free and wild is the Don John of Thomas Shadwell's tragedy, *The Libertine* (1676), a version of that Don Juan story which has provided audiences in several centuries with a sexual bogeyman and literary historians with some exotic philosophical fruit. Shadwell's Don John has no ordinary morality. "By Nature's order Sense should guide our Reason," he declares, pleading a naturalism and sensuality that were capable of philosophical justification. He declares that *"by Nature"* he *"is free to enjoy all he can."*[64] The doctrine has roots in classical philosophy and is plausible enough in terms of the *libertin* thought developed in France and espoused in England in the late seventeenth century by writers like the Earl of Rochester and Sir George Etherege.[65] But Shadwell has sensationalized to provide a very different kind of human tempest from that represented by Almanzor. Almanzor was a savage force whose wildness led to constructive achievement. Don John is a philosopher pleading nature as cause sufficient for a civilized man to turn savage. Many plays or stories in the Don Juan tradition begin with an exposition or background telling us what kind of characters we have to deal with and posing questions whether we can expect any greater enormities.[66] One of Don John's fellow naturalists, Don Lopez, is said to be guilty of fratricide to possess his brother's estates. Another, Don Antonio, is guilty of incest—with *both* his sisters. It is revealing of seventeenth-century paternal conceptions of government that Don John's own climactic crime in this rehearsal is patricide, although incest with his aunt is added to boot.[67] Such things are mere background. In the action proper, enormity follows enormity. Some nymphs of a pastoral age —visited, as we might expect, by a sea voyage—are casually ravished; and the three unfettered friends go on to such pranks as setting fire to a convent so that they may rape the nuns as they flee.[68] A certain garish bravado attends Don John, but the play is ultimately frustrating. Although Shadwell follows a line of writers who plead morality as an end to justify an ingeniously sensational action, the reader today scarcely knows whether his amusement or his nausea is likely to prevail. When he thinks of Mozart's incomparable tact and beauty in *Don Giovanni* or of the deftness of Shaw's touch in *Man and Superman,* he can only fit Shadwell into a mood of dark humor employing disgust. The arousal of disgust in this version of the Wild Man was certainly part of the playwright's purpose, but a puritanical prurience has so distorted the code of philosophic libertinism that the Wild Man has become a Gothic psychopath. Ahead of Don John lies Monk Lewis with his horrors and the Marquis de Sade with his perversions. The natural man had often been shown to be monstrous, but monstrous because he lived outside the benefits of education and civilization. In placing the Wild Man within society, Shadwell replaces Montaigne's civilized irony and Almanzor's awesomeness with a sexual shudder.

Such excess is very different from the heroic exaggeration of Almanzor, and it is therefore not surprising that a step parallel with sensationalism of that kind should be another, weaker form of excess—sentimentalism. Among the many works that might be chosen as forecasts of the rise of the sentimental version of the Wild Man in the next century and a half, one of the most suggestive is Aphra Behn's rudimentary novel, *Oroonoko: Or, the Royal Slave* (1688). We may translate "royal slave" as "noble savage" without much inaccuracy, but the translation describes a very different character from Almanzor. Oroonoko is a black prince sold into slavery in the Indies. He is a passive Almanzor, whose dignity consists in an emasculation of spirit and an endurance that is incredible. We are supposed to shed tears at every cliché. For example, the story is true: Mrs. Behn witnessed "a great part" of what she relates.[69] The black Indians are innocent and therefore naked, "like our first Parents before the Fall."[70] Sentimental sexuality enters within a few pages of the beginning, and we are not surprised to learn that the Indians "have Plurality of Wives" or that the arrangement pleases the women.[71] Oroonoko has of course his beloved, his Imoinda, his "fair Queen of Night," whom he woos, it must be confessed, like a sentimental football player.[72] There is a suitably salacious European whose advances Imoinda resists. Her hero is lost to her in the end, when he dies a stoic death though covered with dozens of wounds that have been sadistically inflamed by irritants.

It is difficult to take all that very seriously. How much more satisfactory the robust, unsentimental version of the Wild Man as epic hero seems to be! And yet we must remind ourselves that there had long been a sentimental version of the Wild Man as the contemporary equivalent of men in that ancient golden age of pastoral simplicity. There had been, as we noted earlier, a substitution of cultural for chronological primitivism. And it is not by any means a long step from cultural primitivism to exoticism and sentimentalism.[73] We should also remind ourselves that the robustness that we prize in the literature of the fifteenth, sixteenth, and seventeenth centuries was founded on assumptions that seem unjust today. Spain's exploitation of Indians in American mines and England's periodic massacre of the Irish are not pleasant to contemplate. Some of our greatest writers have written stirringly about actions that are indefensible by modern standards. The crusade against Jerusalem extolled by Tasso was a sorry business, as the massacre recounted in the final stanzas shows at once. Similarly, Spenser's account of Justice in the Irish context of the fifth book of *The Faerie Queene* may be theoretically sound, but given frail human nature and the actual motivation behind English justice-by-death, the story is morally repulsive. Tasso and Spenser are great poets, and Mrs. Behn is certainly not a great novelist. But again we can remind ourselves that the situation in her *Oroonoko* represented an evil —slavery—which countries like England exported to their great profit and countries like the United States imported to their lasting loss. It is no doubt true that more tears were shed in England for stories like that of Mrs. Behn, for Thomas Southerne's play of the same title (1695–96), and for sentimental successors than were shed for the injustices they recounted. But the tears on behalf of literary works of sometimes doubtful merit assisted in establishing a wider sense of universal social justice. Blake's persecuted chimney sweepers, Shelley's Indian, Harriet Beecher Stowe's Uncle Tom, and Dickens's poor people helped melt centuries of heartlessness with tears. Most of us would prefer that literary and social merits always coincide, and in almost all cases there is some deep sense in which they do. But it is also the case that we as well as the Marxists may appreciate the social value of certain kinds of writing.

Such developments out of the tradition of the Wild Man, like certain related popularizations of the ideas of Rousseau, are, however, matters lying ahead of my proper time. Looking back, we can see that Tasso's Rinaldo, Montaigne's "Canniballs," Shakespeare's Caliban, Dryden's Almanzor, and numerous lesser literary creations enabled the Wild Man to raise questions about the government of strong passions, of the individual, and of the state. Moreover, the conception of the Wild Man was also one that vibrated those two important strings of seventeenth-century harmony and discord, nature and art. The conception also assisted in definitions of man, law, and society. Finally, the idea of the Wild Man carried with it a charge of dissidence or challenge that required reconciliation by the grim justice of extermination, by divine grace, or by human love. It is as if in viewing himself in the looking glass of art, a cultivated European of the Renaissance or seventeenth century saw in himself the savagery he feared to encounter as he set out on his sea voyages. Such a double exposure led some of the best minds to turn voyager into themselves, as did Montaigne. Some others saw a chance to redeem the Wild Man and also to use his newly tamed strength as a way of redeeming civilized society. Indeed, by the nineteenth century, the usual literary version of the Wild Man is like that of Shadwell's libertine Don John— the Wild Man is bred within society and within it perverted by custom, by mysterious Gothic tendencies, or by monstrous psychological inclination. There is a process of taming the Wild Man stretching from at least Odysseus's encounter with Polyphemus to the descendants of Oroonoko, and that process of taming is in no small degree a process of learning on the one hand to see the Wild Man or savage in oneself, and on the other the gradual alteration of the Wild Man from a real outside terror into a metaphorical creation within apparently tame society. What vanished or took new expression was an older vision of life, combining magic, terror, mystery, heroism, and dreams of ideal states.

It seems altogether appropriate that so momentous a shift in European sensibility should be accompanied by a change in conceptions of art. By the nineteenth century, art was no longer the mirror of nature, and the poet was no longer thought to combine the roles of maker and imitator. The new symbols for art were the aeolian harp on which the wind of imaginative inspiration played its song, or the lamp illuminating the darkness, or the sensitive organic plant. The traditional looking glass of art had been broken, and if the conception was recalled by Lewis Carroll for his Alice, it was a conception for a child and at all events turns out to have been but a dream. The age of heroic discovery was past. Henceforth it was not Jerusalem that needed to be delivered from without, but America, Paris, Russia, or colonial peoples that needed to be delivered from within, by revolution. Single startling figures of large dimensions might emerge, but they were not the slogan or the norm. Henceforth revolutionary movements and inner psychological worlds were to be considered. But the shattered glass of older traditions still reflects, and perhaps it reflects—the more prismatically for being broken—those richer colors of an age of heroes and terrors.

NOTES

1. Meyer H. Abrams, *The Mirror and the Lamp* (New York, 1953), ch. 2, especially pp. 30–42.

2. Fairfax entitled his translation *Godfrey of Bulloigne, or the Recoverie of Jerusalem* (London, 1600). For aspects of the influence of Tasso in the original and translation, see note 61. See also John Dryden, preface to *Fables* (London, 1700), in which he distinguished the line of Fairfax and Waller within English poetry from that of Chaucer, Spenser, and Milton; *John Dryden: of Dramatic Poesy and Other Critical Essays*, ed. George Watson (London, 1962), II, 270–71 (hereafter cited as Dryden, *Essays*).

3. Fairfax, trans., *Godfrey of Bulloigne*, p. 272 (XV, xxviii).

4. Fairfax, trans., *Godfrey of Bulloigne*, p. 275 (XV, xli).

5. See Richard Hakluyt, *The Principal Navigations* (Glasgow, 1903–05), VII, 370; quoted by Roy Harvey Pearce in *The Savages of America* (Baltimore, 1953), p. 5.

Pearce's first chapter is very relevant for the idea of the Indian in seventeenth-century England.

6. Quoted by Jacques Boulenger, *The Seventeenth Century in France* (New York, 1963), p. 354. In mid-seventeenth-century England an agricultural laborer might get only about £4 10s. per year and expect to be tithed and taxed in one way or another on that; see Christopher Hill, *Puritanism and Revolution* (London, 1962), p. 181. But he was better off than his French and Spanish counterparts. In those countries the nobility or gentry were exempt from taxation, for although the French gabelle, or salt tax, was an excise, it was trivial to the nobility although an almost certain guarantor of continuing poverty to the poor. On the misery of the Spanish poor, see J. H. Elliott, *Imperial Spain, 1469–1716* (New York, 1964), p. 306.

7. See Edward Cooke, *A Voyage to the South Sea* (London, 1712), II, 70: the Hottentots are "the most filthy beastly People of any yet discover'd, and harden'd in their Brutality."

8. To the examples given later may be added this by Sir Thomas Herbert, *A Relation of Some Yeares Travaile* (London, 1634), p. 10, on the Anzigues: "They delight in eating mans flesh, more then other food. . . . They have shambles of men and womens flesh, ioynted and cut in severall morsels. . . ."

9. *The History of the League*, trans. John Dryden (London, 1684), p. 801.

10. Fynes Moryson, *An Itinerary . . . Containing His Ten Yeeres Travell* (London, 1617), pt. II, p. 271. There is more in a like vein. See also *The Rebels Turkish Tyranny* (London, 1641) for similar enormities a generation later; and Edmund Spenser, *View of the Present State of Ireland*, in *The Works of Edmund Spenser: Prose Works*, variorum ed. (Baltimore, 1949), pp. 90, 102, for the Elizabethan view, which dominated much subsequent thought. Spenser's *Faerie Queene*, book V, tells of the measures England employed to inflict a kind of justice on unhappy Ireland. Cromwell's measures after the Battle of Drogheda in 1651 have never seemed to the Irish to possess the logic attributed to them by some English historians.

11. Thomas Hobbes, *Leviathan*, ed. Michael Oakeshott (Oxford, 1960), p. 82 (I, xiii).

12. Samuel Butler, "The Ladies Answer to the Knight," ll. 233–36, in *Hudibras*, ed. John Wilders (Oxford, 1967), p. 317. The usual seventeenth-century polarity of art and nature is here evident in one of its numerous forms, opposition.

13. Jonathan Swift, *Satires and Personal Writings*, ed. William Alfred Eddy (New York, 1933), p. 24.

14. Swift, *Satires and Personal Writings*, p. 23.

15. Matthew Carey, *Vindiciae Hibernicae* (London, 1819), p. 11.

16. *The Essays of Michael Seigneur de Montaigne*, trans. Charles Cotton, 3 vols. (London, 1685–86), I, 375 (ch. 30). See also I, 366.

17. Similarly in his "Apology for Raymond Sebond," Montaigne had argued that beasts are superior to man, a paradoxical and ironic preference for nature over art. On this related topic, see George Boas, *The Happy Beast in French Thought of the Seventeenth Century* (Baltimore, 1933).

18. See A. R. Heiserman, "Satire in the *Utopia*," *PMLA*, 78 (1963), 163–74; and Robert C. Elliott, "The Shape of Utopia," *ELH*, 30 (1963), 317–34.

19. *Poems, and Translations* (London, 1683), p. 133.

20. [Nathaniel Crouch?], *The Extraordinary Adventures and Discoveries of Several Famous Men* (London, 1683), p. 12.

21. Hakluyt, *Principal Navigations*, VIII, 305–10. See also Sir Walter Raleigh's account of the inhabitants of Guinea; *Principal Navigations*, X, 338–431.

22. The distinction between chronological and cultural primitivism is one propagated by Arthur O. Lovejoy et al., *A Documentary History of Primitivism and Related Ideas*, vol. I (Baltimore, 1935), dealing with antiquity; see also George Boas, *Essays on Primitivism and Related Ideas in the Middle Ages* (New York, 1966), which continues the story. No such magisterial study appears to exist in English for modern times. I have suggested some connections between exoticism and primitivism in *The Japanese Tradition in British and American Literature* (Princeton, 1958), p. 29.

23. *The Poems and Letters of Andrew Marvell*, ed. H. M. Margoliouth (Oxford, 1927), I, 17 (ll. 17–22, 29–30). See also "The Garden," ll. 33–40; Dryden, *Threnodia Augustalis*, ll. 360–63; and Milton, *Paradise Lost*, IV, 215–68.

24. Fairfax, trans., *Godfrey of Bulloigne*, p. 273 (XV, xxxv). The description continues into the next stanza. The combination of plenitude and religion in this special context can be seen repeatedly in the travel writers. In his account of the island of Johanna, in *A New Account of East-India and Persia* (London, 1698), John Fryer wrote: "Here the flourishing Papaw, . . . Citrons, Limons, and many more, contend to indulge the Taste; the warbling Birds and Ear; and all things, as if the general Curse [original sin] were exampted, strive to gratify the Life of Man" (quoted in a very useful study, R. W. Frantz, *The English Traveller and the Movement of Ideas: 1660–1732* [Lincoln, Nebr., 1934], p. 89).

25. See Frantz, *English Traveller*, p. 7. In *The Hind and the Panther*, II, 548–75, Dryden contrasts Roman Catholic propagation of faith as part of explorations with English indifference: "Religion is the least of all our trade"; but the Dutch are designated the worst offenders, since they "sell all of Christian to the very name" in order to be the sole traders in Japan.

26. See Elliott, *Imperial Spain*, pp. 182–85, 331, 352.

27. *Othello*, ed. M. R. Ridley, 7th Arden ed. (London, 1958), p. 29 (I, iii, 143–45).

28. *Satyricon*, cap. 115, "Si bene caculum ponas, ubique naufragium est." Not to mention *The Odyssey*, there are numerous classical parallels, and Dryden could have found the formula in Edmund Waller's poem, "Of a War with Spain, and Fight at Sea," ll. 51–60. But it is also implicit in *The Tempest* and other works.

29. John Dryden, *Annus Mirabilis*, ll. 137–40.

30. See *The Tempest*, ed. Frank Kermode, 6th Arden ed. (Cambridge, Mass., 1958), pp. xxvi f. for details.

31. See I, ii, 44–45.

32. See V, i, 16–20.

33. The imagery is consistent. See, for example, Trinculo's comment in II, ii, 178: "A howling monster; a drunken monster!" The word or variants is significantly used in other contexts, e.g., III, iii, 95. Cf. also p. 89 above and note 7.

34. See *The Tempest*, p. xxxix, n. 2; and Richard Bernheimer, *Wild Men in the Middle Ages* (Cambridge, Mass., 1952). See also Donald Cheney, *Spenser's Image of Nature: Wild Man and Shepherd in the Faerie Queene* (New Haven, 1966).

35. See IV, i. "Grace" is a conception crucial to the play, and even Caliban seeks it at the play's end; V, i, 295.

36. Cf. II, ii or III, iii with III, ii, 65–66.

37. The guidance of Providence is crucial in many works of the time: in *Godfrey of Bulloigne*, XV; in Spenser, *The Faerie Queene*, passim; in Milton, *Paradise Lost*, XII; and in numerous poems by Dryden and other seventeenth-century writers before and after Milton.

38. See Ben Jonson's masques, *The Fortunate Isles* and *News from the New World Discovered in the Moon*.

39. On the visit, see John Evelyn, *Diary*, 19 June 1682; one later reference will be found in Dryden, *To Sir Godfrey Kneller* (1694), l. 54.

40. John Fletcher, *The Sea Voyage*, I, iii; *The Works of Beaumont and Fletcher*, ed. Rev. Alexander Dyce (London, 1843–46), VIII, 308.

41. *The Sea Voyage*, III, i; Dyce, ed., *Works of Beaumont and Fletcher*, VIII, 329.

42. *The Sea Voyage*, II, ii; Dyce, ed., *Works of Beaumont and Fletcher*, VIII, 321.

43. Filmer's *Patriarcha* was first published in 1680 and was thereafter reprinted.

44. Milton, *Paradise Lost*, IV, 301, 310; see also X, 145–56, which is in some ways yet more explicit in its political analogy.

45. Harrington's *Oceana*, first published in 1656, was soon reprinted.

46. Two studies of these matters that are useful to understanding the literature discussed in this essay are: Herschel Baker, *The Wars of Truth* (Cambridge, Mass., 1952), index, s.v. Social Contract; and Maximillian E. Novak, *Defoe and the Nature of Man* (Oxford, 1963), passim. In *Studies of Political Thought from Gerson to Grotius, 1414–1625* (Cambridge, 1916), J. N. Figgis still has useful things to say; see index, s.v. Law of Nature and Social Contract.

47. Pearce, *The Savages of America*, pt. 1.

48. Among the many studies of Restoration performance of earlier plays, one of the most recent and interesting is that of Gunnar Sorelius, *"The Giant Race before the Flood": Pre-Restoration Drama on the Stage and in the Criticism of the Restoration, Acta Universitatis Upsaliensis, Studia Anglistica Upsaliensia*, no. 4 (Uppsala, 1966); there is a useful bibliography on pp. 204–11.

49. Thomas D'Urfey, *A Common-Wealth of Women* (London, 1686), pp. 23–28.

50. See Ovid, *Heroides*, IX. The case for female government of men is made in Butler, *Hudibras*; see "The *Ladies* Answer," ll. 239–382.

51. D'Urfey, *Common-Wealth of Women*, pp. 46–47.

52. Davenant was but one of several links between the theatrical generations before and after the Civil Wars and interregnum; he even countenanced a story that he was Shakespeare's illegitimate son. As for bardolatry among scholars, it passes understanding that they should think he never wrote a wrong word and yet have left him the sole exception among our greatest English writers in not editing his works along modern textual principles.

53. *The Sea Voyage*, II, ii; Dyce, ed., *Works of Beaumont and Fletcher*, VIII, 324. Hippolita, queen of the Amazons, behaves so differently in Chaucer's Knight's Tale, in Shakespeare's *Midsummer Night's Dream*, and in other works that Fletcher's tongue must have been in cheek in giving his character her name.

54. In the later version of *The Tempest*, usually attributed to Thomas Shadwell, Milcha's role is somewhat more substantial. The relations between the Davenant-Dryden version and the "Shadwell" version (which are very similar) are extremely

complex; for discussion, see *The Works of John Dryden*, X, ed. Maximillian E. Novak and George R. Guffey (Berkeley, 1970).

55. The phrase is taken from the learned and frequently reliable Montague Summers, *The Complete Works of Thomas Shadwell* (London, 1927), I, civ. For a more temperate view, see William Van Lennep et al., ed., *The London Stage, 1660–1800; Part I: 1660–1700*, (Carbondale, Ill. 1965), p. clxxiv.

56. Such realism (though artificial like all else in art) was a motive, as we have seen in Fletcher, and led Davenant to introduce numerous nautical terms into the opening scene of *The Tempest*.

57. *The Tempest* (London, 1670), p. 19–20.

58. "Pastoral" is Kermode's description; see note 30.

59. *The Tempest* (London, 1670), p. 42. The speech is dropped, for some reason, from the "Shadwell" version (1674).

60. Duffett, *The Mock-Tempest* (London, 1675), p. 9.

61. "Of Heroic Plays: An Essay," Dryden, *Essays*, I, 163–64.

62. John Dryden, *The Conquest of Granada* (London, 1672), p. 7 (I, i, 203–09).

63. Among the descendants there is Richard Cumberland's hero a century later, *The West Indian* (1771), a sentimentalized version. Among the ancestors there is Armusia in Fletcher's play, *The Island Princess*, III, i: "Oh, that Armusia, that new thing, that stranger" (Dyce, ed., *Works of Beaumont and Fletcher*, VIII, 459).

64. Thomas Shadwell, *The Libertine* (London, 1676), pp. 2, 25.

65. Cf. Rochester, *A Satyr Against Mankind;* Etherege, *The Man of Mode*. On the philosophical background of *libertin* thought, see Dale Underwood, *Etherege and the Seventeenth-Century Comedy of Manners* (New Haven, 1957), pt. I, ch. 2.

66. In some ways the most useful of the many studies of the Don Juan story is that of Georges Gendarme de Bévotte, *La Légende de Don Juan* (Paris, 1906), which treats the growth of the story and various major examples, including Shadwell's; see pp. 338–51.

67. Shadwell, *The Libertine*, pp. 3–4.

68. *The Libertine*, pp. 64, 67, 74–80.

69. Aphra Behn, *Oroonoko* (London, 1688), p. 2.

70. *Oroonoko*, p. 7.

71. *Oroonoko*, p. 10.

72. *Oroonoko*, p. 24.

73. See note 22.

The Wild Man Goes Baroque

✍ EDWARD DUDLEY

The figure of the Wild Man is all too visible on the literary landscape of seventeenth-century Spain.[1] Like Goya's visions of giants and titans in the eighteenth century, the literary wild men of the Baroque tower above the horizon, dwarfing the entire scene. In poetry the metrical athlete of the age, Góngora himself, creates Polifemo, the Cyclops whose gigantic proportions embody the bigger-than-life passions of the Baroque. The pastoral harmonies of the Renaissance are invaded by the forgotten and egocentric lusts of a monster who destroys an idyllic vision of love. The tortured dissonance of Góngora's metrics and syntax are tuned to the violence of the new century and the approaching Thirty Years' War, Europe's most destructive conflict prior to our own times. Standing at the opening of the seventeenth century, the myopic passions of Polifemo seem to foreshadow the outbreak of uncontrollable savagery.

But it was in the theater that the Wild Man was to gain his greatest fame. In the opening scene of *El burlador de Sevilla* a duchess calls out in the darkness of a Neapolitan palace, "Who are you?" and a male voice answers: "Who am I? A man without a name." Thus, the most volatile character of European literature steps onto the stage and defines himself. Tirso's play was to give a name if not a habitation to Don Juan but, like the Wild Man he is, he escaped into the European imagination via Molière, Mozart, Byron, Shaw, and Freud. The forces embodied in Don Juan are in part at least a male resistance to the cult of courtly love and the prolonged period of masculine servitude to the feminine ideal. Maurice Valency has pointed out that Don Quijote, the man who waits indefinitely, and Don Juan, the man who doesn't wait at all, are at opposite ends of the European love gallery.[2]

But the greatest Wild Man of the Golden Age theater is Calderón's brooding Segismundo in *La vida es sueño*, the barbarian who rises from the prison of himself to the heights of ethical and metaphysical sublimity. His triumph, tinged with tragic resignation, is one of will and reason over the forces of passion and fortune. Thus, he is the prototype of the Baroque hero, just as Don Juan, the man who fails to rule his passion, is the Baroque son of a bitch. Both these figures are comprehensible only when seen against the background of Augustinian theology and the polemics of the Counter-Reformation. Viewed from a historical perspective, these plays are part of the epic struggle to save man's belief in his free will, and this intellectual crusade of the Church, with Spain and the Jesuits at the forefront, was successful. The Enlightenment's blind faith in reason was the secular child of the Baroque's faith in free will, just as the Wild Man-turned-monarch of Calderón's drama is the divine ancestor of the benevolent despot.[3]

In prose works of the era, coming closer to our own topic, two or three major instances of wild men immediately come to mind. Is the *pícaro*, for instance, also a Wild Man? He definitely shares a common ground outside the pale of society with the savage. He may represent an antisocial force which the author is criticizing or supporting, but his Wild Man traits often lack the freedom associated with a precivilized state. Rather, the *pícaro* is at the other end of the social spectrum; he is the postcivilized savage, the result of society's mismanagement of human potential. As such he is the voice of the new savagery generated by civilization, a fact which guaranteed his spectacular success in the newest art form, the novel. But along with Don Juan, the *pícaro* is a perennial, and his problems involve ideological expanses too great for treatment here.

A more apparent confrontation with the problem of savagery and civilization can be found in the enigmatic *Persiles*, Cervantes' final statement on the human condition. Curiously, or not so curiously, its publication date—1617—synchronizes with the appearance of the first volume of El Inca Garcilaso's *Comentarios reales*. Both works were immediate successes in Spain and the rest of Europe, an index of the numinous potency the savage held for civilized men. With Cervantes, however, the problem again involves the Counter-Reformation, for his novel begins with a terrifying picture of human sacrifices in a savage kingdom and closes amid the Baroque splendor of Rome. This reminds us that the glittering world of the Spanish Hapsburgs not only reached around the world but to the gates of heaven—where entry proved more difficult. In May 1521 Charles V issued the imperial edict in Worms condemning Luther, just as Cortés began the final siege of the Aztec capital in Mexico. Cervantes' novel, approximately one hundred years later, takes up the terrible problems of heresy and savagery signified by those two events. The *Persiles* remains today as one of the most ambitious intellectual feats ever attempted by a novelist. Certainly nothing until *Finnegans Wake* has seemed so resistant to critical explication, and T. S. Eliot was probably right when he complained that one such conundrum is enough for any language. Nevertheless, the pilgrimage from the wilderness to the Eternal City was attempted again later in the century by Gracián in the *Criticón*, this time utilizing a fable of natural intelligence awakening to truth.[4] But by this time the Enlightenment is already luminous on the horizon, and the Wild Man bears the letters patent concerning his nobility.

But the Wild Man within, the Wild Man threatening the intimate security of each of us, received his most profound and revealing analysis in another work, the best known of any considered here. This Wild Man is Cardenio, the soul brother of Don Quijote and, like him, a victim of madness. Their meeting in the Dark Sierra occurs in an atmosphere of unspoken attractions, and Don Quijote, already mad, is driven farther into the shadowed wilderness of his insanity. His subsequent imitation of Cardenio's madness is the high point of his lunacy. The rescue of Don Quijote effected by Cardenio, Dorotea, and the priest is the geographical and psychic turning point of his journey and his novel. The question of the rhetorical intent of this *aventura* is central to the creation of the entire book and to the meaning hidden in the madness of Don Quijote himself. Without this understanding of the role of Cardenio, the structure of Part One—and the ancient critical battle of the interpolated novels— remains enigmatic. The Wild Man is the narrative turning point of Part One, and an analysis of his role provides a crucial insight into the structure of the total novel.

A brief overview of Part One of the *Quijote* is necessary in order to place Cardenio into the fabric of the whole book. In particular, he must be seen against the background of the so-called interpolated novels,[5] those stories—some brief, some long—in which Don Quijote himself seems to participate only peripherally or not at all. The function of these stories, though the subject of debate since the time of Cervantes, is curiously a neglected area of analysis in our study of the novel as a genre. The question has always been why the interpolated novels are there at all, and the defense has remained apologetic. But their use by Cervantes is a matter of orchestration. The stories not only vastly expand the area of reality explored by the book, but they create a unity that focuses directly on the problem of Don Quijote himself. In no way can their meaning be realized if they are separated from the totality of the book. Thus even the novella of the "Curioso impertinente," the story most singled out for attack, is crucial for the situations and themes utilized by Cervantes. For instance, the "meaning" of Cardenio and Dorotea, including their relationship with Don Quijote himself, is incomplete without the mirror world of Camila and Anselmo. Anselmo, as much as Cardenio, is a Wild Man, and the example of his destruction is as meaningful to Cardenio as the fall of Camila is to the rise of Dorotea. (We remember that Cardenio and Dorotea hear the story of Anselmo and Camila.) Don Quijote sleeps through the story but interrupts it to announce he has killed the lustful giant Pandafilando de la Fosca Vista, thus foreshadowing the triumph of Dorotea in her struggle with the lustful desires of Fernando.

The entire fabric of the stories that interweave themselves with Don Quijote's are remindful of the wonderful unity of medieval tapestries where sequential scenes of a story form the pattern for the whole. If this type of unity has been forgotten since the triumphs of the rationalistic novels of the nineteenth century, it is because criticism has too long concentrated its attention on purely intellectual explications and forgotten that dreams, too, in spite of their superficial appearance of chaos, are as rigidly controlled unities as *Madame Bovary*. In this sense the criticism of literary arts in our own time has lagged far behind the evaluation of plastic forms. Critics have had no trouble understanding El Greco, while Cervantes has somehow been treated as a "primitive," an interesting forerunner of later and more sophisticated artists. The facts may very well be the opposite. Cervantes' techniques seem if anything to have outstripped the sophistication of both the critics and the novelistic successors of his genius, and this aspect of his work has remained misunderstood. No criticism can hope to explain the matter of his genius, but it can, by indicating the possibilities of the genre, facilitate the acceptance of a particular structure in a particular novel. Cervantes would seem to be, in fact, both more primitive and more modern than hitherto realized. In this sense, the role of Cardenio, the Wild Man of the Sierra, is an indication of the complexities of the novel as Cervantes conceived it.

Since Cardenio of all the interpolated protagonists is the closest to Don Quijote himself, both in his personal relationship to Don Quijote and in his approximation of the Don Quijote archetype, he is a fitting point of departure for the study. Along with Cardenio, the Wild Man, there is also Dorotea, the wood nymph and enchantress, a fitting wild woman found in a stream. Not surprisingly, she is to be the guiding spirit who leads the group out of the Sierra and works the transformations that occur in the Inn. The story of Cardenio and Dorotea, together with their counterparts Fernando and Luscinda, form the apex of the interpolated structure of the novel, and their story is intimately woven into the Don Quijote construct. To understand them is to begin to understand Don Quijote, for their adventures and salvation could not be effected without his intervention. They are the redeemed and he the redeemer, and thus by means of their problems Don Quijote finally becomes the true *caballero andante*. There is no salvation alone in the world of Cervantes. The entire tapestry of these stories is furthermore both the prototype and the approach to the structure of Part Two, in which Don Quijote must find his own salvation. Thus he can achieve his own fulfillment only through his early adventures. In other terms, *Don Quijote* Part One focuses on Don Quijote's role as savior, and his energies are directed outward. He becomes the *caballero andante* or messiah who saves the world. In Part Two we have the redemption of the messiah himself. The pattern is further paralleled in the structures of Parts One and Two. In Part One, chapter 23, Don Quijote meets Cardenio, the Wild Man, and begins a series of adventures leading to the salvation of Cardenio at the Inn, although Don Quijote himself remains mad. This is the first confrontation with madness. In Part Two, chapter 23, Don Quijote relates his descent into the Cave of Montesinos, where he meets his own madness. This begins a search for a means to disenchant Dulcinea, which forms the fictional vehicle of Part Two. Her enchantment, which comes to symbolize the basic dilemma of Don Quijote's existence, is resolved just before Don Quijote recovers his sanity and dies. Thus, these two episodes—Cardenio and the Cave of Montesinos—serve as the fictional and thematic turning points of the two parts of the novel.

Returning to the interpolated structure of Part One, a number of basic similarities among the stories help signal their rhetorical intent. First of all, they are love stories. The role of love in the *Quijote* is often overlooked in favor of more abstract considerations, but there is a valid case for the proposition that love, that is, the relationship between the sexes, is the basic concern of the entire book. The first part concentrates on a more romantic and physical love among the young, whereas the second part is concerned with the higher love that Don Quijote himself exemplifies. Questions of the nature of reality and idealism fit comfortably within the scope of love. Don Quijote is incapable of love at the beginning, and all his first adventures are failures. His initial success, though slight, is his intervention on behalf of the beauteous Marcela (chapter 14). This occurs only because he has been struck by the power of her physical beauty and the discretion of her language. Beauty and eloquence are two of the most powerful Renaissance ideals, and this victory, influenced by such forces, foreshadows his greater triumphs fighting beneath the banner of Dorotea. But in any case the love problems in the interpolated novels concern the various sexual permutations and combinations, including everything from chastity to adultery, homosexuality, sadism, donjuanism, and masochism. Don Quijote not only intervenes in all these affairs but echoes the problems in his own relationships with Dulcinea and the redoubtable Maritornes. In this way his love scene with the latter in the attic of the Inn becomes one of the most complex and hilarious actions in all literature.

Related to the Renaissance love theories examined are the literary prototypes and genres for each story. Sometimes there is a single antecedent being worked over—Grisóstomo, for instance, comes straight from the *novela sentimental* of the fifteenth century, whereas others combine several literary types. Dorotea has a complex ancestry in the various novelesque genres of the sixteenth century. She is a shepherdess, a wild woman, a princess, and a sorceress all at once and shows symptoms of belonging to the pastoral, sentimental, byzantine, folkloric, and chivalric modes. The question of genres relates not only to the love situations but to the concepts of personality and role as well. Don Quijote is only the most obvious example of a protagonist trying to live a novel. To a greater or lesser degree all the lovers are modeling their behavior on one genre or another. Everyone is the hero of his or her own novel, and his or her ultimate redemption is dependent on finding the right novel. The basic theme of art and life is thus infused into the ever-shifting configurations of love and personality. In this way Cervantes succeeds in converting esthetic considerations into the raw material of fiction.[6] Much of the richness of the novel is due to this aspect of his vision. What is banal in a love relationship becomes provocative when the heroine is found to be aware of her role and even more so when she decides to improvise. There is a joy in the conscious control of the life forces, and particularly when that control is playful. This artistry is the ultimate esthetic pleasure provided by a great matador with a great bull or a great pianist playing a Mozart sonata. The source of this joy in the *Quijote* is the brilliance of Cervantes' orchestration, his manipulation of the fictional modes, and his evocation of the human personality in conflict with itself and its surroundings. Realization of the self is man's greatest pleasure.

One final consideration before turning to Cardenio is the role of the Inn as the focus of Part One. Whatever is resolved in Part One finds its solution at the Inn.[7] There the entangled web of Cardenio, Dorotea, Fernando, and Luscinda is set right; there the Captive and Zoraida find their homecoming, and there the child lovers Don Luis and Doña Clara reach their magic city of innocent love. Only Don Quijote, who is old and who seeks another magic city, fails to find salvation at the Inn. A precarious resolution of his problem is left on the linguistic level of the *baci-yelmo*, Sancho's ritualistic title for Don Quijote's enchanted helmet. The question of redemption for Don Quijote is left until Part Two, where it is again Sancho who points the way with his enchantment of Dulcinea. This enchantment is Don Quijote's greatest challenge and its resolution his final victory. He ultimately breaks the spell and finds his true self before he dies.

It must be realized that enchantment is the metaphor, in both dreams and art, for change, transformation, growth. The nature of such events or processes is ultimately enigmatic, in that the intellect can only describe what has happened and what forces are operative in the change. But the event itself, like the opening of a flower, is ultimately mysterious. Man can foster growth or can destroy it, but by itself change is as unfathomable as the universe. Something of this sense of magic hovers over the Inn. Don Quijote is the first to perceive it when he describes it as an enchanted castle, and his famous love scene with Maritornes confirms his intuition and even convinces Sancho that some unseen potency is operative there. This realization is a prelude to what happens when Dorotea, playing the role of the Princess Micomicona, leads Don Quijote, Cardenio, Sancho, and the priest out of the Dark Sierra to the Inn. The movement is from chaos toward integration, and the figures of the procession seem to suggest the anima leading the shadow, the self, and the ego. Don Quijote and the priest divide the conscious ego between them, signifying madness. Cardenio is the destructive but also potentially positive forces of the shadow; Sancho is the unconscious but organized self from whom the ultimate solution will spring (when he enchants Dulcinea), and the discrete Dorotea is the feminine anima, the intuitive guide of the totality. As for the Inn itself, the pattern of happy or tragic resolution to the love situations is dependent on the lovers reaching the Inn. Marcela and Grisóstomo do not, nor do Sancho's folkloric lovers Torralba and Lope Ruiz. The fatal triangle of Camila, Lotario, and Anselmo, the most sensuous of Cervantes' lovers, do not. Finally the heroes of the last tale, the faithless Leandra, the deceptive Vicente de la Roca, and Eugenio, act out their story without going to the Inn, and their tragedy clashes violently with Don Quijote's just as Part One concludes. They, like Don Quijote himself, are excluded from the magic circle.

In contrast, the triumphant lovers all reach the Inn and form two configurations of four, the magic number of completion and integration.

The first set of four is Dorotea and Fernando, Luscinda and Cardenio. Their story is completed before the second set of four arrive. Then the Captive and Zoraida find room at the Inn, unlike Joseph and Mary, their archetypal antecedents; there they are joined by Don Luis and Doña Clara. Thus the Inn is where the four sets of lovers find their appropriate roles, and their problems are dissolved because each lover is put into communication with his or her proper counterpart. Both psychologically and mythically the forces motivating their stories are harmonized. In contrast, Don Quijote fails to achieve for himself what he achieves for the others; his personality is not integrated. Instead the anti-Dulcinea figure of Maritornes enchants him, and he is sent back to the village.

Thus Part One is organized on a myth of completion and disintegration that has its center of gravity at the Inn. Only those stories in which Don Quijote successfully intercedes can be resolved happily. Where he is excluded, the forces of evil prevail. There are four pairs of lovers in each category. Linguistically it should be added that this pattern is expressed in the verb tenses. Those stories told in the present or perfect tenses are resolved, but those placed into the past or imperfect tenses are unresolvable. The question of time is an obvious key here. We can only be saved in the present tense. Cardenio's tale is the third in order of appearance, and he begins by saying, "My name is Cardenio." The two stories that precede his have ended unhappily. This is important because, particularly in the case of Grisóstomo, who died for love, a trajectory of disaster has been traced. When Don Quijote meets Cardenio he seems fatally bound to the same pattern of love as death.

The meeting of Cardenio and Don Quijote is one of the most carefully prepared and fully realized events in the *Quijote*. It takes up an entire chapter by itself, signifying that this adventure is to be of considerable weight. In a work of such numerous episodes it is obvious that all of them cannot receive this much space. Cervantes' usual method is to present a new character with a few telltale adjectives, and often no physical description at all is included. But Cardenio's portrait is fully drawn twice before he ever speaks. More than that, the thematic groundwork for his apparently sudden appearance is carefully prepared as Cervantes gives an unusually complete picture of the wildness of the Sierra Morena. The approach to a Wild Man hidden in a threatening wilderness is an archetypal pattern familiar in world folklore and one utilized by artists again and again. Perhaps the most poetically intense realization of this myth is found in Conrad's *Heart of Darkness*. In all these stories the hero penetrates a symbolic "heart of darkness" and finds some sort of frightful demon figure, only to discover ultimately some truth about himself. The Wild Man is in essence some forgotten potency of his own personality. This is also true of Don Quijote, although the situation is more complex because Cervantes manages to create an autonomous character in Cardenio but without destroying the archetypal significance of the Wild Man for Don Quijote. As with many characters, Cardenio is himself, with his own salvation to secure, and at the same time he also symbolizes an aspect of Don Quijote's personality. Thus Cervantes is able to treat simultaneously two separate but related configurations. The first of these is his hero Don Quijote, with his broad spectrum of psychic mysteries, and the second is the entire love complex embodied in Cardenio's situation. This double approach is endemic in the *Quijote* and gives the interpolated stories a systemic function in the totality. They are psychic segments of Don Quijote's being as well as events in their own right. Just as in a dream a person may be someone known to the dreamer, say a friend or an enemy, but within the structure of the dream this person functions as part of the dreamer's personality. After all, *other* people, regardless of how autonomous they appear to the dreamer, do not really participate in the dream. The figure in the dream is a creature of the dreamer's imagination. This is part of the mystery of self and others that underlies the question of reality. This mystery also infuses the entire *Quijote* with its irresistible appeal and accounts, in part, for the phenomenon of its meaning. An awareness of this duality of self and nonself makes the meeting of Don Quijote and Cardenio all the more potent with hidden significance.

Likewise the two adventures just preceding his meeting with Cardenio have prepared Don Quijote for his new challenge. In chapter 21 Don Quijote acquires what he believes to be the helmet of Mambrino. The question of the helmet is germane to the problem of his chivalric incarnation. Most famous knights have been known for their remarkable swords—the Cid, Roland, King Arthur, Amadís—all possess swords that symbolize their roles. But Don Quijote's crucial armament is his helmet, because his head and not his arm is the source of his power. Thus the enchanted helmet of Mambrino must be his, but unfortunately for his sense of identity (and like his sense of identity), its existence remains problematic. The question of the helmet comes to the fore again at the Inn when the barber claims it is his stolen basin. This is all the work of a malign enchanter, according to Don Quijote, and Sancho resolves the matter linguistically by baptizing it as a *baci-yelmo* (basin-helmet). However, its appearance just before the meeting with Cardenio is a sign that Don

Quijote will now have his full knightly potencies and that other transformations are imminent.

In chapter 22, immediately preceding and in a curious way overlapping
the appearance of Cardenio, is the disastrous adventure of freeing the
galley slaves. This bit of madness sets into motion a series of forces
that Don Quijote cannot control. The most immediate of these consequences is the fact that Don Quijote and Sancho are themselves in trouble
with the feared *Santa Hermandad* (the highway police of the era) and
thus forced off their road into the hidden recesses of the Sierra Morena.
There they will meet those other refugees of their own actions, Cardenio
and Dorotea, who are also hiding in the wilderness. The Spanish past
participle *descaminado* (literally off-the-roaded) becomes the metaphor
for Don Quijote's condition and is applied in some way or other to all
the heroes and heroines of the interpolated novels. Everyone is the victim
of his own mistakes. Don Quijote's own act of madness with the galley
slaves drives him into the wilderness to explore the madness of Cardenio.

Don Quijote's journey into the innermost part of the Sierra is characterized by two motifs. First of all, the place itself is inaccessible, wild, and
remote, beyond the reach of normal human traffic. Cervantes cannot give
enough emphasis to this aspect:

That night they arrived to the middle of the inner Sierra.   (II, 235)[8]

Don Quijote's imagination is stimulated by the surroundings:

There came to his mind the marvellous happenings that beset knights errant
in such remote and wild places.   (II, 237)

And again:

But since in that inhospitable and rough place there was no one whom he
could ask, he thought of nothing but to proceed, without following any road
but that which Rocinante desired—which was where he could pick his way,
and always Don Quijote's imagination was fixed on the thought that in such a
wild place some strange adventure was bound to befall him.   (II, 245)

When they finally do come upon an old goatherd standing on a peak,
Don Quijote calls to him for directions.

He [the goatherd] shouted back asking who had brought them through that
pass, a place rarely or never tread upon except by the feet of goats or of wolves
and other wild animals that roamed through these parts.   (II, 248)

The last two quotes pick another strain of imagery also associated with
Cardenio—that of animals. The tradition of associating animals with the

bestial side of man's nature is an ancient one, dating back to the fauns and satyrs of the Greeks. Thus it is Rocinante who leads the way to Cardenio, and the will of Rocinante has already assumed two appropriate functions: First, Don Quijote leaves to Rocinante the choice of the road, because he believes in that way to cast himself into the hands of fortune. Secondly, the reader has learned through a previous misadventure (that of Rocinante and the mares) that Rocinante's will is sometimes associated with lust. Then the goatherd's subsequent reference to goats and wolves is even more to the point, since these two images suggest respectively the problems of sex and violence that haunted the seventeenth century.

Cardenio's personal appearance in no way belies the setting. His figure also evokes thoughts of sex and violence in human guise. But the humanity of Cardenio, with all the appeal of strength and youth, is found to be possessed by a strange demonic force.

Proceeding then with this thought [that some strange adventure was about to befall him] Don Quijote saw, at the top of a peak that rose before his eyes, a man leaping from crag to crag and from bush to bush with a strange rapidity. It seemed to him that the figure was naked—with a thick black beard, heavy and tangled hair, bare feet and bare legs; his thighs were covered with britches, it seemed of a tawny velvet, but so tattered that his flesh was visible in many places. His head was uncovered; and although he passed with the rapidity mentioned, the Caballero de la Triste Figura saw and noted all these details; and although he tried, he could not follow him, because it was not given to the weakness of Rocinante to cross such rough terrain.   (II, 245)

The wildness of the Wild Man is greater than that of animals, and Don Quijote loses sight of Cardenio for the moment, but his brief appearance is already significant. The animal movements, his nakedness, and great mane of disheveled hair make him seem like a character from our own contemporary theater, and then as now the overt sexuality of the portrait cannot be missed.

To Cervantes' audience, however, several other clues are found here which tell considerably more about the Wild Man's identity and condition. First of all, he is a recognizable literary type, with an ancestry reaching back to the Middle Ages. His most famous and most immediate prototype is of course Ariosto's Orlando in the *Orlando Furioso*, and this similarity is not lost on Don Quijote himself. In Spanish literature, perhaps the closest parallels are the hairy anchorites in the novels of Juan de Flores.[9] In either case we recognize the civilized man—he still wears tatters of velvet pants—gone wild. The cause of the wildness in these cases is of course love and, speaking more bluntly, lust. The sexual drive is conceived as having the power to overthrow the entire personality if it is permanently thwarted. This can occur in the courtly love syndrome only if the lover is loyal to one lady and she spurns him. Thus something of Cardenio's story is already clear. This madness may end in suicide, a possibility previously actualized in the story of Grisóstomo and further suggested here by the tawny-colored velvet. Tawny (Sp. *leonado*) signifies desperation (*desesperar*), the psychic *sine qua non* for Spanish love suicides.[10] In order further to intensify the image, Cardenio's animal movements specifically suggest the goat, the most lustful of beasts in the folklore of love. So the situation is already deep in crisis, but as yet death has not sealed off the interplay of chance and will.

We have found the Wild Man hidden in the landscape of the Sierra Morena and have been able to organize his problem around a focus of love, madness, violence, and death. But in order to realize fully all the problems that orbit around the figure of the Wild Man, we have to recognize also that he is placed in another less visible landscape which organizes his reality in a manner not yet perceived. This is the genre problem which underlies the entire *Quijote* and intimately fuses the question of psychic identity (literary persona) and the function of art. Don Quijote is more that just the hero of his own novel, that is, not only does he seek to impose an esthetic arrangement of reality upon reality itself, but he further seeks to intervene in other people's novels and ultimately convert them into literary types belonging to his own vision. Thus Cardenio, the hero of the sentimental genre, is gradually absorbed into Don Quijote's novel of chivalry. In the process he also suffers a sea change from the *amante desesperado* into a *caballero andante*. As such he cannot ignore the call to action and thus is saved. In this way Cervantes again transforms the material of art into the material of life, and what was a genre problem becomes an ethical and a psychological crisis.

Underlying the whole of this is the Counter-Reformation's concern with the role of free will in conflict with fortune or destiny. But the way in which Cervantes presents the problem it is also a problem of epistemology, with an emphasis on the validity of the senses. For Don Quijote in particular, nothing is real but his perception of reality, and that is the basis of his ethics.[11] This is clear in the passage just analyzed, for we recall that we only see the Wild Man through Don Quijote's vision of reality. Linguistically the entire scene is constructed on verbs of perception: Don Quijote "saw [*vio*], there rose before his eyes [*delante de sus ojos se le ofrecía*], it seemed to him [*figurósele*], he saw and noted all [*miró y notó.*]." In short, no action of Cardenio is presented except through Don Quijote's senses. Then, dependent on this perception is Don Quijote's decision to act: he tried to follow him. The free will can only act on what is presented to it by sense perception and the workings of fortune. Rocinante also comes into the event, because he has not the strength to follow Cardenio, thus limiting Don Quijote's action, but at the same time Don Quijote would not have caught sight of the Wild Man at all if Rocinante had not brought him to that place at that time. Rocinante, here as in other instances, is the means by which fortune has offered this adventure. In this complex system of perception, fortune, and will, Cervantes has synthesized the basic conundrums of sixteenth- and seventeenth-century thought.

We have said that Cardenio's literary prototype is the hero of a sentimental novel, and this is true enough when we regard his physical appearance. But characters of any stature in the *Quijote* tend to have more than one role to play and follow more than a single literary antecedent, and so it is with Cardenio. Before Don Quijote ever has his vision of the Wild Man leaping from rock to rock, he has found a series of abandoned possessions in the Sierra. The nature of these discoveries points to a violent occurrence having overtaken the former owner. These articles are a saddlebag and a small grip. Inside Don Quijote and Sancho find four clean linen shirts, a purse containing over a hundred gold coins, and a small notebook. These remains, so to speak, are the last vestiges of the original Cardenio, a well-born and sensitive young man from Andalucía.[12] The "librillo de memoria" (little notebook) is the most significant of these finds, because not only does it reveal the mental and emotional state of the former owner but it triggers a chain of events that reaches to the very end of Part Two. Among the verses and lover's complaints written in the book, Don Quijote also finds a letter addressed to the owner's beloved. This is the first reference to the existence of Luscinda, Cardenio's childhood sweetheart, and it appears she has dumped him for someone richer and more noble than Cardenio. In the letter he also speaks of her great beauty, which he claims is a false expression of her inner being. The situation couldn't be more conventional, and it echoes the Grisóstomo-Marcela story, particularly in reference to feminine beauty and the effect of feminine beauty on the beholder. The very commonplace quality of all this is gold in Cervantes' hands.

First the appearance of the letter foretells the nature of the story that is to follow, and on looking into the narration Cardenio tells, we find that all crucial events are triggered by letters. From the first letter of Fer-

nando's father, the Duke, to the last letter scribbled in the notebook Don
Quijote finds, we find the outline of an epistolary novel.[13] And this structure is perfectly suited to Cardenio's view of reality and to the nature of
his madness. For Cardenio's problem is that he cannot talk effectively,
that he cannot communicate by means of the spoken word. All the succession of failures in his pursuit of Luscinda could have been avoided if
he had only spoken out. The entire story is the result of his inability to
speak to his own father concerning the marriage, a significant clue in the
prognosis of his insanity. By the time Don Quijote finds him in the Sierra
his voice is almost gone. In effect, he can speak only to himself.

The letter, however, is even more important in the subsequent adventures of Don Quijote himself, for stimulated by Cardenio's example, Don
Quijote decides to send a letter to Dulcinea. This letter is the crucial link
to the subsequent adventures, for Sancho goes back to the Inn with the
letter and meets the priest, thus bringing him, and later Dorotea, to Don
Quijote. In Part Two of the *Quijote* the consequences are equally important. Since Sancho fails to deliver the letter, he is forced to lie to Don
Quijote about this matter. He even goes to the lengths of describing
Dulcinea's reactions while reading the letter in a delicious satire of the
sentimental novel. This deception traps him in Part Two, for there Don
Quijote calls upon Sancho to lead him to Dulcinea's palace in El Toboso.
Sancho secretly curses his earlier lies but because of them is inspired to
invent the matter of Dulcinea's transformation into an ugly village girl.
This in turn becomes the main concern of Part Two, and Don Quijote's
one goal becomes the disenchantment of his lady. In this way Cardenio's
"librillo de memoria," symbolizing Don Quijote's encounter with the
epistolary novel, leads first to Cardenio, and the entire cycle of stories
that focus on the Inn, and ultimately to the enchantment of Dulcinea
herself.

Cardenio's story itself is told in three installments. The first of these is
related by the old goatherd, who in effect describes the last stage of Cardenio's madness. Clinically Cardenio's condition has been diagnosed as
a case of zoanthropy (animal-man).[14] From a timid and *apocado* young
man, he is converted into a violent maniac who leads an animal existence. His madness seems to have three degrees of intensity. Generally he
wanders in his wild state such as we have seen, sleeping at night in trees.
Once the goatherds find him in the catatonic position, hidden inside a
cork tree. At certain times a second more sane condition prevails, when
he comes out of hiding and asks the goatherds politely for food. Although
his physical state is much deteriorated, his manner still shows him to be

gracious and well-bred. A third more violent phase seems to come upon him suddenly, perhaps while talking to the goatherds, in which he attacks them with a maniacal fury and steals their food. This occurs even though they offer him food freely. One such fit of violence erupts later when he is relating his story to Don Quijote and Sancho; this, however, has to do with the conflicting visions of Don Quijote and Cardenio. On the other hand, when they first meet, that is, when they first speak to each other, Cardenio is enjoying one of his saner intervals.

There is a curious accord between the interruptions in his madness and the interruptions in his literary genre. The matter and the mode proceed by fits and starts, and the appearance of letters at intervals presents the hero with a series of decisions or options. Cardenio's dilemma is the result of his wrong choices, though he constantly blames fate (*suerte*) for his own destruction. Thus Cardenio is, at the moment of his meeting Don Quijote, a Baroque failure. Like Don Juan, he has failed to direct his passions intelligently (and generously). But in fact he is an anti–Don Juan, a lover who has isolated himself from his beloved, and this is the basis of his neurotic attraction for Fernando, the real Don Juan. Both these young men are depicted by Cervantes as having serious sexual hang-ups, and their none-too-healthy attraction for one another stems from their weaknesses. Fernando goes from woman to woman because he cannot love the same woman twice. Cardenio is paralyzed by his attraction to Luscinda and at the same time is constantly placing barriers between the love object and himself. His state of wildness is the inevitable result of his actions. In this sense both men are "enchanted," to use the language of the novel of chivalry; that is, they are imprisoned by their respective neurotic structures. It is Dorotea, the wood nymph found in a stream, who disenchants them and releases their true potencies at the Inn. In generic terms she releases them from their wrong roles and leads them to their right roles in life. In the process she also releases herself from a state of enchantment that holds her imprisoned in the stream. Her own psychic disenchantment is aided by the priest and ultimately by Don Quijote, the magician at the eye of the storm. From this overview of the situation it will be easier to see what is operative at each stage in the following analysis.

First, the curious salutations between Cardenio and Don Quijote take on meaning if we see these two madmen from the viewpoint of their roles. Don Quijote, the *caballero andante,* the man bent on releasing people from evil spells, naturally concludes that, having seen Cardenio in his wild state, he must help him (an act of will). This decision is immediately followed by the arrival of Cardenio (an act of fortune), who comes out from a break in the rocks, muttering to himself. The nature of their greeting is an episode unparalleled in the *Quijote,* for it seems that some numinous attraction draws them together.

As the young man approached he greeted them in a hoarse and broken voice but with great courtesy. Don Quijote returned the greeting with no less courtesy and, dismounting from Rocinante, he went, in a graceful and noble manner, to embrace him, and he held him tightly in his arms for a goodly length of time, as if he had known him from long ago. The other . . . after having let himself be embraced, stepped back a bit from Don Quijote, and placing his hands on Don Quijote's shoulders, stood staring at him, as though trying to see if he knew him; no less surprised perhaps to see the figure, appearance and arms of Don Quijote than Don Quijote was to see him.   (II, 258)

It is a moment of mutual puzzlement and recognition. The figure of Cardenio seems to have a special meaning for Don Quijote, and the embrace signifies that Don Quijote has known Cardenio and Cardenio's condition in his own youth. We must remember that we are told virtually nothing of the man who becomes Don Quijote, but here we see that he has known what it is to be young and frustrated. Don Quijote too has lived the life of the *apocado,* the nobody who dreams everything and dares nothing. Likewise Cardenio can try to devise the condition of the old madman, the dreamer whose dreams have clouded his vision of reality. Ideologically the two figures represent two stages of Renaissance love theory: Cardenio, the young man turned into a beast by lust, and the old man capable of a more spiritual love because he is not driven by a youthful urgency. Both are extreme examples of their types, and it is clear that their psyches have met somewhere else—off on a distant landscape of love and madness.

The first words spoken by Cardenio are at the same time a declaration of his psychological malady and his ethical "sin." They are also a literary echo of a similar statement in similar circumstances made by Leriano, the hero of *Cárcel de amor.* In the case of Leriano, he is tied to the burning chair of desire in the prison of love and unable to respond to the narrator's offer of help because of the all-encompassing suffering caused by frustrated lust. Cardenio's situation is psychologically identical, and his words express the same idea. He speaks immediately after the mutual embracing just described.

Certainly, sir, whoever you may be, for I don't know you, I thank you for the signs of courtesy you have used with me, and I wish I were in a position to be able to return your reception with more than the good will you have shown you have for me; but my fate [*suerte*] doesn't leave me anything to correspond to the efforts you make on my behalf—other than the good wishes of satisfying them. (II, 260)

Cardenio's statement, like Leriano's before him, expresses the belief on the part of the hero that his "love" is so great that no other aspect of reality has any meaning for him, a psychological state common to the young in both life and literature.[15] But the two statements by Leriano and Cardenio have opposing rhetorical intents. Leriano's statement is "straight," that is, it is believed not only by Leriano but by the other personages in the novel, and by the reader. The entire meaning of the work is built upon the concept of love as suffering and death. This is the meaning of the prison of love allegorically presented at the opening of the novel. But in the *Quijote* the statement functions ironically. It is belived by Cardenio, and in effect is a description of his egocentric madness. However, within the framework of the novel, Cardenio's condition places him at the bottom of the ethical ladder. Cardenio cannot meaningfully relate to humankind and is thus "wild." The potential for his salvation, however, is present in the concept of the good wishes he claims he has but cannot put into effect. Theologically this is his sin. One is not saved by good intentions. From this "prison of love" Cardenio must evolve to the point of being able to help others. The model for this behavior is, of course, before him in the figure of Don Quijote, the *caballero andante*, and Don Quijote's response to Cardenio's statement perfectly expresses this ideal. To begin, Don Quijote assures Cardenio that he has no desire but to help him, finding the remedy for his (Cardenio's) great suffering if any such remedy can be found. But, Don Quijote goes on, if this proves impossible, he will aid Cardenio in his laments and weeping, because it is a consolation in suffering to find someone who weeps with you. These things Don Quijote swears to do because he is a *caballero andante,* and as such this is the fulfillment of his obligations and of his being ("I must serve you faithfully as I am obliged to do because of who I am" [II, 261]). Significantly, these same ideals are echoed five chapters later in the *Quijote* when Cardenio offers himself as *caballero andante* for Dorotea ("for I swear to you by the faith of a knight [*caballero*] and a Christian that I will not abandon you until I see you under the protection of Don Fernando" [III, 82]). In this act of generosity he not only foregoes his desires of vengeance on Fernando but seeks to restore Dorotea to him and thereby save Fernando as well. Cardenio has thus completed the journey from egocentric preoccupation with his own desires to the sacrificing of these desires to the cause of others, including his archenemy and former friend Fernando. The emphasis given by the phrase "as a Christian," an emphasis lacking in Don Quijote's original offer, suggests the new Baroque ideal of gentleman and Christian embodied in the figure of Calderón's Segismundo. Even the Wild Man can aspire to reach the full expression of his humanity and partake thereby in salvation. To be fully human, to be in possession of all one's faculties and potencies, and to direct them unselfishly to relieve the suffering of others, is the goal of the true gentleman. Conversely, to ignore these goals, to fail to express what is generous within us (Cardenio's condition when he meets Don Quijote), is to leave our lives unlived and, what's worse, to fall victim of these hidden potencies. For these energies, transformed into unhealthful compulsions, will possess us in a madness like Cardenio's, driving us into the dark sierra of loneliness, there to perish like animals.

This analysis of Cardenio's madness is actually made by Don Quijote and its cure is begun, also analytically, by Don Quijote when he begs Cardenio to tell who he is and what his story has been. This is not just idle curiosity on Don Quijote's part, but a desire to find the causes of the madness. Don Quijote's words to Cardenio made this abundantly clear:

And if my good intention [to help you] deserves to be thanked with some sort of courtesy, I beg you, sir, by the great amount of courtesy I see locked within you, and further I beg you in the name of the object in this life that you have most loved or love, to tell me who you are and the cause that has brought you to live and die in this wilderness like a brute animal, since you will die among them, far removed from the true self that your clothes and person show you to be.   (II, 261)

Don Quijote in this way anticipates the twentieth-century analyst who begins the cure by having the patient tell his story, and it is in the story that the cause of the madness is found, just as it is by means of Don Quijote's intervention that the cure is initiated.

The Wild Man, however, is not without defenses in his madness, and the road to the Inn is not without setbacks. First Cardenio attempts to forestall Don Quijote's intervention by placing a condition on his story-telling. He agrees to relate the matter only after he has been given food and only on the condition that no one will interrupt him. The reason given for this is that the story is too painful to dwell upon and he wants to pass over it as quickly as possible. But as he proceeds it becomes apparent that the real reason is that he is autistic and wants above all not to be challenged in his dubious interpretation of the events. Only in this way can he continue to blame fate (*suerte*) for what has happened. In reality the events were all of his own making. There was no obstacle to his marriage to Luscinda. He even states that both families had more or less accepted the fact that the inevitable outcome of their childhood romance was to be matrimony. Luscinda's father, the conventional ogre of the Spanish courtly love syndrome, has even agreed to the marriage. The only step left to be taken is for Cardenio to speak to his own father, and there is no indication given that he will disapprove. This is all the more significant since Cardenio is much given to blaming others when he is not blaming fate. Thus his other subterfuge is to blame Luscinda and Fernando for double-crossing him, when in fact it is made absolutely clear in his own words that he has failed them. So his failure to blame the father is all the more curious. Since the father never actually appears, the only clue we get is Cardenio's confession that he has always believed he would never get in life those things he wanted most. This belief is the obvious source of his problems, since it makes him passive rather than active in the pursuit of his goals, and indeed makes him unnecessarily dependent on the turns of fortune.

The role of fortune in the story is, of course, every bit as important as the role of will, and again the arrangement of reality is generically determined. Just as the manner of leaving the choice of the road to Rocinante is the means by which fortune is brought into play in the novel of chivalry, so it is the arrival of the letters that calls the turns in the epistolary novel. Nowhere in the *Quijote* is the mode so neatly available for Cervantes' view of the interplay of will and fortune. The crucial arrival of the first letter within Cardenio's narration clearly shows the power of fortune and the weakness of Cardenio's will.

Cardenio has just arranged the matrimony with Luscinda and her father, and there remains only the crucial talk with his own father. That Cardenio does have difficulties speaking out has already been made clear. He has confessed that the relationship between himself and Luscinda has reached its warmest level since they have communicated by letter, because he is tongue-tied in her presence. His verbal inhibitions have, nevertheless, not placed any barrier in the way of their physical communications, since it becomes clear later that Luscinda is not a virgin. However, he omits any reference to this is his own story. It is only one of the small but crucial dishonesties in his storytelling technique. A short passage will adequately illustrate the vision of reality of this complicated young man:

Right then and there I went to tell my father what I wanted, and at the very moment when I entered the room where he was, I found him with an open letter in his hand, which, before I could say a word, he handed to me and said:

"In this letter, Cardenio, you will see that Duke Ricardo has every intention
of doing you a great favor." This Duke Ricardo, as you gentlemen must know,
is a grandee of Spain who has his seat in the very best part of our Andalucía.
I took and read the letter, which was so insistent in tone that even to me it
seemed that it would be very bad if my father failed to do what he asked,
which was that he send me to him right away; for he wanted me to be a
companion and not a servant of his eldest son, and that he [the Duke] would
see to it that I was placed in a position equal to the great estimation he had
for me. I read the letter and became mute reading it, and even more so when
I heard my father say: "You will leave in two days, Cardenio, in compliance
with the Duke's request, and give thanks to God, for He has opened a road to
you by which you will achieve that which you deserve." He added to this
other advice suitable from a wise father. The date of my departure having
arrived, I spoke one night with Luscinda.   (II, 267)

If the style is the man, we already know a great deal about Cardenio. He
reveals himself not only by what he says but by what he doesn't say. For
instance, the lack of transition from one scene to another is evident in
the last sentence. What did he do in those two days? Was there no other
chance to talk to his father in that time? It doesn't seem that he is inaccessible, judging from Cardenio's presentation at the beginning of the
passage. Does Cardenio wait till the last minute to speak to Luscinda?
Do they talk only once about this serious departure? Wouldn't she have
some justification if she felt he was treating her rather offhandedly? The
father's words about God's offering Cardenio a road prove to be ironically
true.[16] He chooses here the wrong road and ultimately finds what he
deserves in his madness. Of course, this is only the first wrong road; he
repeats the mistake each time a moment of decision is presented to him.
In other words, he is following a psychological pattern of the type that is
most difficult to break.

    Other stylistic traits here confirm this analysis. He speaks headlong,
without any paragraph breaks. (The entire first installment told to Don
Quijote is one endless paragraph, broken only when Don Quijote interrupts.) In fact, Cardenio hardly breaks his thoughts into sentences. Every
statement is closely followed by at least one or two dependent clauses,
so that events move forward in a tortured but uninterrupted syntactical
flow. He leaves no linguistic opportunity for any possible intervention.
When Don Quijote finally does break in, he does so in midsentence. Furthermore, Cardenio lovingly expands his own personal reactions to every
detail but neglects to say what other people must have felt, and, in particular, the feelings of Luscinda are at no time mentioned. This is a curi-

ous omission for a young man madly in love. In short, the story is a hermetically sealed vision, focused entirely and egotistically on Cardenio's own feelings.

There is another even more serious flaw in his presentation of the events that we recognize as a further symptom of madness. Not only is the world of Cardenio a humorless and rigid movement from event to event, but the entire force of events comes from the outside. He only reacts to external stimuli. For instance, his decision to ask for Luscinda's hand only comes about because her father has forbidden him access to the house. No doubt the relationship might have gone on indefinitely had this obstacle not roused him to action. He never at any time initiates action without an external prod. Furthermore, his account has a brooding intensity that doesn't necessarily go with the rather uncomplicated events of his life. For instance, he constantly blames fate for having treated him more harshly than any mortal could be expected to endure. But nothing violent or untoward ever occurs in the story, except his own supercharged reactions to the most commonplace events.

It is perfectly clear that Cardenio has had more than his share of the good things of the world. He is young, handsome, healthy, noble, rich. He is the beloved of a beautiful, rich, and ultimately loyal girl of his own class. There is no obstacle to their marriage at the opening. Even the Duke's letter, which illustrates that Cardenio has a rather glittering array of opportunities in this life, would not have created difficulties if Cardenio had not seen everything as an either/or option. The marriage could have been arranged before he left, and the official engagement was as good as a legal contract in the Spain of his time. But Cardenio, like the rather disturbed person he is, sees everything as a crisis, and everything as a barrier to his happiness. He is spoiled, indolent, weak, and selfish. His real problem is that he has never had a real problem—except his own personality. Only by careful management does he succeed in turning the golden situation toward disaster. The worst of these errors is, of course, his subsequent utilization of Fernando, the Duke's second son, as an intermediary in the question of arranging the marriage. Nor is this done blindly, for he has shown in his own account that he did not trust Fernando and that he knew him to be a Don Juan.

When Don Quijote faces Cardenio in the Sierra, the problem seems insurmountable, but simply by being Don Quijote, as he has said, he initiates the cure of the Wild Man by interrupting the story. The moment of interruption occurs when Cardenio mentions *Amadís de Gaula*, and the moment is generically appropriate. For it is the novel of chivalry that intervenes in Cardenio's epistolary novel, just as Cardenio must drop his passive role as hero of his own novel and become, in the manner of Don Quijote, a *caballero andante*. That is, he moves from a passive to an active role, from the epistolary novel to the novel of chivalry; and what is more important, he learns to forget his own problems long enough to think of someone else's. In the performance of an unselfish gesture Cardenio himself initiates his own salvation. However, this simple but at the same time exceedingly difficult step is still in the future when Don Quijote interrupts Cardenio's story, but the very act of interrupting shatters Cardenio's narcissistic and masochistic mirror world. He reacts violently by falling into his most fanatic rage and physically attacking Don Quijote, who is barely saved by the peasant strength and determination of Sancho.

From this low point in Cardenio's madness he can be saved only by further interventions. These come in two stages: First, the priest, in search of Don Quijote in the Sierra, meets Cardenio and learns the rest of the story. However, Cardenio shows himself to be somewhat better. His story is not told in such a pell-mell rush of words, and he even allows the priest to interrupt without lapsing into madness. Secondly, we have a catalytic new element added to the situation with the sudden appearance of Dorotea. Her story provides the missing links to Cardenio's, since it is she who has been abandoned by Fernando or rather shunned by him after a night spent in her bedroom. Thus she too is wandering in the Sierra and isolated from humankind, though she shows far greater courage than Cardenio in confronting her situation. Her mind is clear and her beauty intact, but, like the plants that grow in her mountain stream, she belongs to no one, nor can she belong to anyone except Fernando, who has possessed her and then abandoned her to the social wilderness. The role she comes to play in Cardenio's story is as important as the role he plays in hers. Their meeting is thus the resolution of the forces of lust and selfishness that have dominated their respective lives. And their relationship fills out the spectrum of Renaissance love theories that form the ideological background of the novel.

The first sight Cardenio gets of Dorotea is from behind some rocks, where he observes her without being seen. She is alone and is washing her feet in the obligatory crystal stream of Renaissance countrysides. She is dressed as a shepherd boy, and only the bare feet of a dazzling whiteness can be seen. Then, in a carefully orchestrated gesture, she lifts her face to reveal a beauty that has already blinded Fernando. Cardenio's reaction is the key to his salvation. So far every man who has looked upon this face has attempted to ravish Dorotea. But Cardenio, already driven mad by lust, exclaims, "This beauty, since it is not Luscinda's, is not human but divine."

In essence his reaction is his salvation, because he reacts without lust to a vision of pure beauty. In the best Renaissance tradition, he is redeemed by unselfishly contemplating beauty. Thus he begins his ascent to a psychological salvation which culminates when he becomes her knight and serves her without expectation of reward, just as Don Quijote serves his Dulcinea. The adventures that follow really belong to Dorotea and her novel of chivalry, for she invents the captivating role of Princess Micomicona, by which she leads poor Don Quijote out of the wilderness and back to the Inn. There they encounter Fernando and Luscinda, and the stage is set for one of the best love games of Renaissance musical chairs, similar to the magic scenes of Shakespeare's *Midsummer Night's Dream*. It all ends in a triumphant finale, played definitively by Dorotea.

But all this is contingent on the adventures in the Sierra Morena and the meeting of Cardenio, whose name after all means red, the color of lust, and Dorotea, whose name is, most appropriately, "the Gift of God." And we are reminded of Cardenio's father's words of farewell. The road he saw opening before his son was to be a gift of God, an act of grace, that opened a door in an airtight room of youthful selfishness. Cardenio is saved because finally that store of generosity that Don Quijote saw locked within him was released by the beauty of an enchanted princess. The intellectual landscape of this adventure belongs to Saint Augustine; while the esthetic problems are part of Cervantes' vision of the novel. Cardenio abandons his epistolary madness and becomes the chivalric hero in his own right. And in this way Cervantes tells us that to be selfish is to be "wild" and that to be saved we must learn to love—unselfishly.

NOTES

1. The problem of the Wild Man in Spanish literature has not been broadly studied. Prof. Alan Deyermond gave it initial attention in his article, "El hombre salvaje en la novela sentimental," *Filología*, 10 (1964), 97–111, and again during a recent lecture tour of the United States in which he spoke at UCLA. It was this lecture which served as catalyst for this volume.

2. Maurice Valency, *In Praise of Love* (New York, 1961), p. 17.

3. Other wild men and wild women abound in golden age drama, functioning as symbols of social protest, moral decay, and even sexual ambivalence. In the latter category were the *bandoleras,* female transvestites who exercised a strong fascination for an audience where female roles were rigidly controlled; see a recent article by Melveena McKendrick, "The *Bandolera* of Golden-Age Drama: A Symbol of Feminist

Revolt," *Bulletin of Hispanic Studies,* 46 (January 1969), 1–20. See also Oleh Mazur, "Various Folkloric Impacts Upon the Salvaje in the Spanish *Comedia,*" *Hispanic Review,* 36 (July 1968), 207–35.

4. I am indebted to Prof. A. A. Parker for pointing out to me the parallel between *Persiles* and the *Criticón.*

5. The bibliography of this problem is extensive and has engaged the greatest minds to concern themselves with the *Quijote.* Opposing views were taken by F. Schlegel (for) and Unamuno (against). More recently critics such as Américo Castro, Joaquín Casalduero, Julián Marías, Bruce Wardropper, E. C. Riley, and J. B. Avalle-Arce have moved critical opinion toward a positive position. See J. B. Avalle-Arce, *Deslindes cervantinos* (Madrid, 1961), and Frank Pierce, ed., *Two Cervantes Short Novels* (Oxford, 1970), for further bibliography.

6. This device has been beautifully analyzed by E. C. Riley in his *Cervantes's Theory of the Novel* (London, 1962), pp. 35-48, and in an article reprinted in a recent collection of essays on Cervantes, E. C. Riley, "Literature and Life in *Don Quijote,*" *Cervantes, A Collection of Critical Essays,* ed. Lowry Nelson, Jr. (Englewood Cliffs, N.J., 1969), pp. 123–36.

7. The recognition of the focal role of the Inn was first signaled by Avalle-Arce in *La novela pastoril española* (Madrid, 1959), pp. 75–76. In that instance he pointed out the folkloric use of a magic place as the goal of a journey. He compares the Inn to the palace of the sabia Felicia in *La Diana* or to the magic city of Oz in the children's story, *The Wizard of Oz.*

8. Quotations from the *Quijote* refer to the Rodríguez Marín edition (Madrid, 1964) in eight volumes. The translations are my own and remain as literally faithful to the Spanish as possible.

9. The tradition of the hairy anchorite singled out by Barbara Matulka in *The Novels of Juan de Flores and Their European Diffusion* (New York, 1931), pp. 283–94, is a related phenomenon. The psychological "penance" that Cardenio is imposing on himself is particularly relevant here.

10. *Leonado* was used in *Cárcel de amor* to signify *tristeza;* see Diego de San Pedro, *Cárcel de amor,* in Obras (Madrid, 1958), p. 119. On the significance of *desesperar* see also Avalle-Arce, *Deslindes cervantinos,* pp. 97 ff.

11. The question of appearance and reality has been treated in numerous studies. See in particular Richard L. Predmore, *The World of Don Quijote* (Cambridge, 1967), ch. 4.

12. The parallel with Conrad's *Heart of Darkness* is very close here. Marlow keeps finding vestiges of the "original Kurtz" on his journey up the Congo. Just as with Cardenio here, the persona has been shattered and the original figure is already dead. When Cardenio reintegrates his personality during the adventures with Dorotea, he is no longer the person he used to be.

13. The generic antecedent here is, of course, Juan de Segura's *Processo de cartas de amores,* ed. Edwin B. Place, (Evanston, Ill., 1950), but exchange of letters as a means of triggering action dates back to the novels of chivalry and the early sentimental novels; see also Charles Kany, *Beginnings of the Epistolary Novel in France, Italy and Spain* (Berkeley, 1937).

14. Cf. *MD,* 6 (1963), 135 f. This issue is dedicated to Spanish medicine.

15. Compare Leriano's statement in *Cárcel de amor,* p. 121: "I would like to have

some part of my heart free from feeling, so that I would sympathize with you, as I should, and as you deserve; but you already see that in my tribulation I do not have the strength to feel any pain other than my own. I ask you to take as satisfaction, not what I do, but, rather, what I desire" (my translation).

16. This is the beginning of the road imagery related to Cardenio. From this point on he is *descaminado*. So he remains until the meeting with Dorotea offers him a last chance to find his way again. Thus, the "road" or "way" offered by God here ultimately leads to his redemption.

Leviathan Triumphant: Thomas Hobbes and the Politics of Wild Men

⟋ RICHARD ASHCRAFT

For three centuries Thomas Hobbes has roamed the intellectual forests of Western civilization, ravishing those who ventured forth to entrap him. Scarred and hounded, this bête noire has found refuge in those corners of our cultural unconscious where "nasty" and "brutish" are still enshrined as the rustic weapons of ideological combat against those whom we perceive to be a threat to our life-style.

Because few individuals, in his age or in ours, have openly professed themselves Hobbesians, we have tended to discount the influence of Hobbes' ideas. Yet it is a mistake to view Hobbes in purely negative terms, ignoring the compelling attractiveness of his argument which has insinuated itself into our thoughts and, more importantly, has helped to guide our actions, despite all the verbal protests raised against Hobbes' "pernicious" doctrines. Not until the full effects of Hobbes' sweeping assault on certain classical ideas within our intellectual heritage have been recognized will we be in a position to proclaim with confidence our rejection of Hobbist beliefs.

That recognition depends in large measure upon a reexamination of historical origins, and especially of that "crisis" period of Anglo-American history, the seventeenth century, when so many of our now commonplace assumptions found their first expression as challenging ideas. In this essay I propose to examine one such idea, viz., anarchy, and to devote some attention to the process by which it was assimilated into the ideological vocabulary of liberalism. Focusing upon Hobbes' political theory, I shall argue that two strands of thought, one deriving from the discourse of philosophy and theology, the other from writings on history and anthropology, were fused together in Hobbes' notion of the state of nature. Hobbes' perversion of the traditionally accepted beliefs in both areas produced an explosive concept, one which after the initial shock became a powerful weapon in the hands of a successfully established liberalism. In effect, through Hobbes, the Wild Man and the anarchist became synonymous labels to be applied to any enemy to the order and "civilization" of English society.

In developing this theme, three issues prominent in the secondary literature on Hobbes must be subjected to close scrutiny: first, the relationship between Hobbes and his contemporaries; secondly, the historicity of Hobbes' state of nature; and finally, the influence of Hobbesian ideas on later liberals. In most instances I accept the summary conclusion generally adopted by other scholars, but an effort will be made to pay greater attention to those elements which are usually "factored out" in the process of arriving at that conclusion, in order to indicate some of the complexities which inhere in the emergence and formulation of a political ideology.

I. Hobbes and His Contemporaries

From the opposition Hobbes provoked, one might conclude that, despite the fascination he holds for the twentieth century, his influence on his contemporaries was entirely negative. This is, in fact, the prevailing view among Hobbes scholars.[1] Recently, however, this position has been attacked, less because it is erroneous than because it is too simplistic.[2] It is an easy matter to tabulate the number of critics who visited their wrath upon Hobbes, but it is much more difficult to explain why, within such a short period, more than fifty volumes and countless sermons should have appeared in print attacking ideas which some would have us believe were so isolated from the concerns of seventeenth-century Englishmen. Robert Boyle, for example, explained that he was writing against Hobbes because "his *Leviathan,* and some other of his writings, [had] made too great impressions upon divers persons."[3] Similarly, Joseph Glanvill, in the dedication of his *Scepsis scientifica* (1664), justified his attack on Hobbes by pointing out that "divers of the brisker Geniuses . . . have been willing to accept Mechanism upon Hobbian conditions, and many others were in danger of following them into the precipice."[4]

We may point to the dramatic renunciation of Hobbist beliefs by one or two university students as negative evidence of their acceptance, but why did George Lawson feel with a certain degree of resignation that, only six years after the publication of the *Leviathan,* too many university students had already been converted to Hobbes' ideas?[5] The same attitude is expressed by the Earl of Clarendon, who complains that Hobbes' precepts have "prevailed over too many."[6] Even before the latter had added his distinguished name to the growing list of Hobbes' opponents, Bishop Tenison could assume that there was "certainly no man" who was then "unacquainted" with Hobbes' name or doctrines.[7] Of course, Hobbes' critics might be guilty of exaggeration, but the intensity and frequency of their attacks ought rather to make us wary of the fire than complacent about the smoke which they find encircling their audience.

This is not to say that great numbers of seventeenth-century Englishmen rushed to embrace Hobbes' political theory. But I do suggest that Hobbesian ideas played a powerful, though complex, role in shaping the intellectual life of Restoration England, and that we should therefore pay more careful attention to their relation to the ideology of liberalism that emerged from this cultural milieu.[8] How ideologies arise, as a general problem, is obviously a matter beyond the scope of this essay, but even a few cursory observations on the subject may prove helpful here in providing a framework for the specific discussion of Hobbes below.[9]

An ideology, as an articulated defense of certain political interests in society, arises from a recognition of the conflict between the aims and objectives, including material benefits, of two (or more) power groups. This recognition almost always occurs initially in a socially disadvantaged group which seeks by an unmasking process to undermine the superior position of the group(s) which it perceives as obstacles to the achievement of its objectives. One of the functions of an ideology, then, is the exposure of the contradictions between the opponent's rhetoric and his real interests, and the consequent mobilization of others who, seeing this conflict, might also find themselves opposed to the real interests of the ruling group(s).

The formulation of an ideology necessarily involves a genetic approach, since it seeks to uncover the origins of thought, and to relate its assessment of the present political conflict to the rediscovered origins of that conflict in the past. Political ideologies, therefore, raise questions concerning the origins of political society and attempt to relate some specific view about political origins (which itself may be very abstract, of course—e.g., consent, conquest, family, a constitution) to the present political discontent of one or more groups in society. And again, this process is initiated by the dissidents who thereby force the defenders of the status quo to define or reiterate their genetic theory of society.

Although it is possible to describe the debate on this level as a collision between opposing "world-views," as one writer has characterized the exchange between Hobbes and his contemporaries, it is certainly not true that what is at issue are two wholly different viewpoints.[10] There are assertions contained in a dissident ideology which prompt men to act so as to strive for a realignment of the group relationships within society through a power confrontation. Yet, these irreconcilable "shifts" from the status quo are embedded in an intricate framework which can only be described as orthodox or traditional. This is hardly surprising, since the quest for legitimacy is no less important to a revolutionary than an established ideology; both require a sense of "rootedness" in the past. Because the same past, and more important, the same event, document, or thinker is accepted by both sides as the legitimate source for a genetic account of society, much of the rhetoric in the debate will inescapably reflect the same social values.

Finally, even this skeletal account of ideology would be grossly misleading if most of our attention were focused—as it usually is in discussions of this subject—upon ideology as a *product* rather than upon the *process* by which an ideology emerges. Certain thinkers may be singled out as progenitors of an ideology (e.g., Locke, Marx), but an examination of their thought and its historical context becomes, in effect, a biographical illustration of the process of ideology formation taking place in society at large. Or, to put it in another way, to understand what they are saying it becomes extremely important to understand what their *opponents* are saying. Without Filmer and Hobbes, no Locke; without Hegel and Adam Smith, no Marx. This would be a sound rule of interpretation in writing intellectual history in any case, but where ideas are being related to political interests in a period when those political interests shift or clash in a recognizably significant way, indebtedness to one's opponent frequently becomes a casualty of the historian's emphasis of the intensity of the debate, the sharpness of the rhetoric, and the newness of the ideas in the ascendancy. It is also true, of course, that those engaged in the debate are not always generous (or conscious) enough to admit how much they owe to the opposing viewpoint. Precisely because definite and real political interests are at issue, such an explicit admission would blunt their effectiveness as ideologues. Later, after a shift in power has occurred, it will be noted how much the two viewpoints had in common, and some form of synthesis or assimilation of ideas will take place. I am suggesting, in other words, that to view Luther vis-à-vis the development of Roman Catholicism, or Adam Smith vis-à-vis the formation of Marxism, as purely negative influences is to miss the point and to fail to understand the *process* of ideology formation. Yet that is, in general, precisely how Hobbes has been viewed by those who address themselves to the political thought of Locke and the rise of liberalism as a political ideology.

Whatever the indifference of later commentators, the scope of the intellectual controversy of concern to us did not escape the notice of its participants. According to Bishop Bramhall, Hobbes had removed "all ancient landmarks" of authority with a single act of "ontological reductionism."[11] The "ancient landmarks" obliquely referred to by the bishop were to be found in the cosmology of a Christianized Aristotelianism. Though it had for some time suffered from erosion, this hierarchial world view retained a remarkably strong hold over men's minds throughout the seventeenth century.[12] Nevertheless, despite the prevalence of a *Weltanschauung* emphasizing the order, beauty, and symmetry of the world, there were crevices in the structure of which Hobbes might have availed himself, had he chosen to do so, in presenting his own ideas. That he did not identify his position, at least explicitly, with these dissident components of the intellectual milieu not only reveals something about Hobbes' obsessive insistence upon his own novelty, but also helps to explain why the ground of attack shifted from opponent to opponent, and why it is erroneous to assume that Hobbes' opponents were themselves in general agreement simply because they all singled him out for criticism.

There were, for example, theological precedents for something very close to the Hobbesian state of nature. Calvinism, with its emphasis on man's wickedness, could easily be phrased in language recognizable to Hobbes' readers. Without religion, Calvin declared, "men are in no wise superior to brute beasts, but are in many respects far more miserable. Subject, then, to so many forms of wickedness, they drag out their lives in ceaseless tumult and disquiet."[13] Like an animal, man "follows the inclination of his nature," and "so depraved is his nature that he can be moved or impelled only to evil."[14] Thus, "all man's faculties are, on account of the depravity of nature, so vitiated and corrupted that in all his actions persistent disorder and intemperance threaten because these inclinations cannot be separated from such lack of restraint. Accordingly, we contend that they are vicious."[15] And, Calvin concludes, because of the threatening "persistent disorder" among "natural" men, "no city or township can function without magistrate and polity." Hence, some form of political organization is necessary in order to secure peace among men.[16] A life of sin, John Sharp preached, "is a state of Disorder and Confusion; a perpetual violence and force upon our Natures." It is a state in which men cannot be distinguished from brute beasts.[17] Another influential minister portrayed men living in sin and ignorance as "brutish" creatures at war with each other. "There is nothing in our nature," he declared, "to limit its breaking out to evil. . . . These distempers of our Nature are boundless in themselves: No bottom, no stop, but *Grace* or *Death*."[18] In the 1559 *Primer* and in the 1578 *Book of Christian Prayers*, reference is made to the "great confusion" where there is "no love, no faith, no keeping of covenants, no reverence of laws, no awe of such as are in authority."[19] Those who espoused some such version of Calvinism, however, were virtually unanimous in believing that it was through the grace of Christianity that men were delivered from this state of sin and confusion.

In his early writings, Hobbes occasionally lapsed into the language of theology, using terms such as "wickedness" to describe the human condition. But this is probably due more to a reminiscence of his early education than to any desire on his part to associate his views with Calvinist doctrine.[20] In any event, he very quickly eliminated these expressions from his writings.[21] Moreover, Hobbes never accepted the most important part of Calvinism—its insistence that men were saved from their "brutish" condition solely through the grace of Christianity. Hobbes' emphasis on the primacy of the political order as the means of human deliverance assured him of opponents who might otherwise have identified themselves with the premises of his argument.

In philosophy, too, there were precedents for the "beastial" description of man.[22] But whereas the ancient thinkers had stressed the role of force, Hobbes makes consent the basis for political authority. Perhaps the author of *Vindiciae contra Tyrannos* was closer to the Hobbesian position in maintaining that without laws based on consent men would "be forced to live brutishly in caves and deserts like wild beasts." Yet his conclusion, that men were justified in resisting established political authority, was wholly unacceptable to Hobbes.[23] Another sixteenth-century writer expressed the idea in the form of biblical history, stating that from Adam to the Flood men had lived scattered on the earth, with no money, no place of abode, and "neither lawe nor equitie toward strangers," with "no officers of Justice" nor "any kinde of bonde knowen amongst them."[24]

The most striking anticipation of Hobbes' viewpoint I have found appears in an interesting essay by Sir Walter Raleigh, entitled "Of the Original and Fundamental Cause of Natural, Arbitrary, and Civil War," and one passage from it is worth quoting at length. Raleigh describes a civil war as "a state of War, which is the meer state of Nature of Men out of Community, where all have an equal right to all things, and I shall enjoy my Life, my Substance, or what is dear to me, no longer then he that has more Cunning, or is Stronger than I, will give me leave; for Natural Conscience is not a sufficient Curb to the violent Passions of Men out of the Laws of Society."[25]

In their accounts of the inhabitants of the New World, both Joseph de Acosta and Garcilaso de la Vega supply historical evidence for Hobbes' position, and their phraseology is also worth noting. The latter, for example, observes that in the beginning "the people lived like wild beasts without religion, nor government, nor town, nor houses, without cultivating the land, nor clothing their bodies."[26] Nor was this description of the savages of the New World atypical. Writing in 1575, one author portrayed them as "people living yet as the first men, without letters, without lawes, without Kings, without common wealthes, without arts; . . . not civil by nature, nor governed by discipline, . . . living without houses, townes, cities."[27] Borrowing from such travelers' reports, Montaigne, in his celebrated essay, "Of Cannibals," writes that they have "no manner of traffic; no knowledge of letters; no science of numbers; no name of magistrate or statesman; . . . no contracts; . . . no clothing; no agriculture; no metals."[28]

Even in that twilight zone between natural history and mythology, individuals in the seventeenth century were disposed to believe in satyrs who were "very brute beasts" although they outwardly resembled human beings. Satyrs, it was said, lived "in solitary places," usually "desert Islands," and were "wilde men" of "uncivil behaviour," engaged in fighting and in following their lusts.[29]

My point in citing these sources is not to detract from Hobbes' originality (as if, at this late date, that were possible), but rather to indicate that in theology, philosophy, political history, anthropology, and mythology there were fragments of a countercosmology sufficiently compatible with Hobbesian ideas to guarantee them a serious consideration. Nor is it necessary to demonstrate that Hobbes consciously borrowed from, or identified his views with, any or all of these dissident beliefs in order to point out the ideological purchase with his contemporaries which the rigor of Hobbes' logical mind could have had in systematically fusing together the disparate opinions they held in isolation.

Therefore, in formulating an assessment of the place of Hobbesian ideas within the total intellectual life of the seventeenth century, I am suggesting that greater attention and importance be paid to the fact that Hobbes' opponents regarded him as a formidable adversary, one who, in *their* opinion, exercised considerable influence over their contemporaries. I have also tried to indicate that there were beliefs, some of them widespread, which could with little difficulty be made compatible with Hobbes' description of the state of nature, regardless of whether or not those who held them also subscribed to any other part of Hobbes' thought. To these I might add the *ad hominem* observation that a number of Hobbes' critics recognized that they were addressing an individual who, setting aside his ideas, was one of the most attractive personalities and foremost minds of the age.[30]

II. Hobbes' State of Nature: History and Ideology

The second theme insisted upon in the secondary literature on Hobbes which we must consider is the designation of Hobbes' state of nature as an analytical and nonhistorical concept. It is certainly true that what is striking about the *Leviathan* as a work of political literature is the attempt by its author to build his argument on the solid foundation of "scientific" principles. Almost no one has looked upon the outcome of this bold venture as an unqualified success, but few who have examined Hobbes' writings have not been impressed with the brilliance that lay behind the undertaking. For reasons which have a great deal to do with the historical development and definition of what is, in our time, called philosophy, the logic of Hobbes' argument has become a matter of almost obsessive fascination.[31] This is not to deny that as a result of approaching Hobbes in this fashion we have gained a number of valuable insights into the workings of his mind. Nevertheless, some balance must be restored to our perspective if we are to grasp the *political* significance of Hobbes' ideas.

The state of nature for Hobbes, we are repeatedly told, is nothing more than a "logical abstraction," a "hypothetical construct," or a "methodological fiction."[32] It is "wholly independent of the historicity of a primitive state of nature," a matter which "had little interest for Hobbes."[33] It is "in no sense a product of realistic political observation" and has nothing to do with either history or anthropology.[34] That is the clear consensus among Hobbes scholars. Still, being scholars, they are cognizant of Hobbes' references to the Indians in America as examples offered by him of men who, in his time, were living proof that such a state of nature as he describes actually existed; some commentators even quote Hobbes on this point. But then, one might ask, to what end do they cite him if their evaluations of the concept are so exclusively phrased in analytic, logical, and ahistorical terms? One recent writer, for example, admits that "Hobbes writes at times as though this [the state of nature] were an his-

torical account of the condition of man before the State is established,"
and he concludes this sentence by saying, "but his State of Nature is a
logical rather than an historical postulate." Nor is this an untypically
confused treatment of Hobbes' position.[35]

Let me make it clear that I am not denying that Hobbes' approach to
politics was fundamentally analytical, that his model of science was
geometry, not biology, that he followed Galileo in employing the
"resolutive-compositive" method, and that his statement, "Experience con-
cludeth nothing universally," expressed his general attitude toward the
fact-gathering alternative to his own methodology. All of that, it seems
to me, is unchallengeably true.[36] I would also agree that Hobbes begins
his discussion of politics, as he began his physiological discussion of man,
by "feigning" the "annihilation" of the world, and that he therefore did
intend to produce a "fiction" to be used as the starting point for his
reconstruction of political society.[37]

The state of nature, then, is clearly an analytical construct, but if it is
judged to be only that, some of the substance and impact of Hobbes'
argument will be missed. For example, Hobbes has for too long suffered
from the misdirected accusation of atomism. Exclusive concentration on
Hobbes' commitment to logic may lead one to conclude, erroneously,
that Hobbesian men are merely "a sand-heap of separate organisms."[38]
Or it may lead to the view that a differentiation between the state and
society is of no importance to Hobbes.[39] Recently some effort has been
made to redirect our thinking about the Hobbesian state of nature. The
importance of Hobbes' acceptance of patriarchalism and of the family
as the "natural" unit of human existence has been pointed out.[40] At the
same time, we have been advised to view Hobbesian man in terms of the
historical sources from which the logical abstraction of the state of nature
was drawn.[41] Both of these are useful steps toward a fuller understanding
of Hobbes' thought and the historical context from which it emerged. I
shall draw upon both suggestions for support in developing my argument.
After first outlining the substantive issues in the debate between Hobbes
and his critics arising out of the former's description of the state of
nature, I shall examine in greater detail what might be called the cultural
framework of the debate itself.

We might begin by considering the comparative status of men, beasts,
devils, and Indians, because such a comparison will disclose some of the
connecting links between cosmology and natural history. In the clear
light of Aristotelianism, men stood above the beasts, and, Christians
added, devils were beneath the latter. The exact classification of Indians

posed something of a problem, however, since they were men who lived like beasts and, generally, worshiped the devil. Traditionally, it was assumed that beasts were distinguishable from men in the grand scheme of things, because, among other reasons, the former were "irrational" creatures and therefore not subject to the law of nature.[42] An obvious and relevant issue, then, concerned the relationship between the "wild" American and natural law. That was by no means an easily answerable question.

Seventeenth-century Englishmen were raised on the belief that without religion and a notion of the Deity, men would live like "savage beasts."[43] Naturally, this opinion easily shaded itself into the conviction that it was Christianity which rescued men from their "beastly" condition.[44] Or, to put it another way, on the religious plane, the choice lay between Christians and "brute beasts, Atheists, Devils incarnate."[45] "A man in his unconverted estate" might be regarded as "the slave and drudge of the Devill."[46] The accounts of travelers in the sixteenth and seventeenth centuries made men aware that most of the Indians were devil worshipers. America, therefore, came to represent the "last outpost" of Satan's kingdom.[47] This information was not, in itself, necessarily discouraging, and the example of the Indian was frequently used, polemically, as an antidote to atheism.[48] Yet, since they were unconverted, the tension between Christian and heathen remained; so long as the gospel had not reached into all corners of the world, the social distance between seventeenth-century Englishmen and the American Indians would never be bridged. However much they extolled natural reason, and even natural religion, most Englishmen simply were not willing to place themselves, enlightened as they were by the precepts of Christianity, on a par with these "beastlike" men as obedient subjects of the law of nature. The growing store of information about America, therefore, only served to blur the "ancient landmarks" of Aristotelianism.[49] Thus, at one end of the spectrum the inhabitants of the New World forced a reconsideration of the boundaries of natural history, while at the other end, their religion, or lack of it, provoked a defense of the faith which reinforced the existing divisions between Christian and non-Christian, civilized and savage man.

Suddenly, in the midst of this arena of confusion, Hobbes reached out and pulled down the pillars; the collapse of the Old World view was resounding. Almost no one had doubted that beasts living in a condition of absolute liberty existed in a state of war with each other. Now Hobbes made that the "natural condition of mankind." Men are naturally equal, said Hobbes, not because they are "reasonable" creatures, nor because they are the common offspring of a divine Creator, but because they are equal in their capacity to kill each other.[50] Outside the commonwealth, man to man *"is an arrant wolf."*[51] Hobbes boldly extended the scriptural authority granted men over beasts to include other men. By the "right of conquest," he wrote, men have a "lawful title to subdue or kill" any "irrational creatures" who are dangerous. Thus, "by the right of nature, we destroy, without being unjust, all that is noxious, both beasts and men."[52] Reacting to Hobbes' account of the state of nature, Bishop Bramhall declared that it was "as if man were like the colt of a wild ass in the wilderness, without any owner or obligation."[53] In fact, if there is one outcry from Hobbes' critics that strikes a chord of unison, it is that Hobbes has made men out to be "more *barbarous* and *beastly* then *Beasts* themselves"; and, in so doing, he has "villified" human nature.[54]

Although it was unquestionably Hobbes' redefinition of the state of nature which shocked his contemporaries, Hobbes' originality was not limited to his attack on Aristotelianism. As has been noted, the assumptions of anthropological history were in a state of flux as a result of a century of contact with the inhabitants of the New World. Hobbesian ideas had a similarly explosive effect within this tradition.

The European attitude of superiority to the Indian was part of the cultural baggage of any voyage to America. Hence, the metaphorical language of travelers' reports emphasizes the "beastial" nature of primitive life. These "new men," as Joseph de Acosta refers to them, were "like savage beasts."[55] Throughout his *Commentaries,* Garcilaso de la Vega associates the Indians with "wild beasts" who have to be "taught" how "to live like men."[56] Virginia, one Englishman reported in 1609, "is inhabited with wild and savage people, that live and lie up and down in troops like herds of deer in a forest."[57] "We look upon them [the Indians]," wrote another, "with Scorn and Disdain and think them little better than Beasts in Human Shape."[58] Indeed, others were prepared to "set aside" their human shape.[59] In short, the Indians were regarded as being "as wilde as . . . any other wilde beast" and were only grudgingly admitted into the ranks of humanity.[60]

It would be a mistake to infer from these remarks, however, that Englishmen bore any real hatred for the Indians. Whatever contempt they may have inwardly felt for these "beastial" men, their relations with the savages are best described, generally, as paternalistic. In the pre–Civil War period especially, seventeenth-century travel literature echoed with the image of the Indian as a "poor innocent beast," to be treated charitably.[61] It was no contradiction, therefore, to label the Americans "brutish and beastly," and, at the same time, to insist that they were "naturally very courteous if you do not abuse them."[62] As Montaigne had observed:

We call barbarism that which does not fit in with our usages. And indeed we have no other level of truth and reason but the example and model of the opinions and usages of the country we live in. . . . Those people [Indians] are wild in the sense in which we call wild the fruits that Nature has produced by herself.

And, he concluded, their society resembled that described by the ancient poets who spoke of a "golden age."[63]

Montaigne certainly expressed what most seventeenth-century Englishmen felt. On the one hand, the inhabitants of America were "wild," "savage," "barbarous," and "beastial"; but, at the same time, they were simple, peaceful, innocent, and uncorrupted by the evils of civilization. "We found the people," wrote Sir Walter Raleigh, "most gentle, loving, and faithful, void of all guile and treason, and such as live after the manner of the golden age."[64] In his poem, "To the Virginian Voyage" (1606), Michael Drayton referred to the Indians "To whose [sic], the golden age / Still nature's lawes doth give."

The evidence is overwhelming that pre–Civil War Englishmen were raised in the belief that the Indians were a peaceful and courteous people. In *A Brief and True Relation of the Discovery of the North Part of Virginia* (1602), John Brereton described the inhabitants as "exceeding courteous, gentle of disposition, and well-conditioned."[65] Others were no less enthusiastic in conveying news of the Americans:

They seemed all very civil and merry . . . a people of exceeding good invention, quick understanding, and ready capacity.[66]

The Indians, declared Sir Francis Drake, "are a loving, a very true and just dealing People."[67] "In all my life," Sir Walter Raleigh wrote in his *Discovery of Guiana*, "either in the Indies or in Europe, did I never behold a more goodly or better favoured people or a more manly."[68] The reports contained in Richard Hakluyt's *Principal Navigations Voyages Traffiques and Discoveries of the English Nation*, the most important encyclopedia of information about the New World in this period, are filled with such statements.[69] This is not to say that there were no reports or encounters with the Indians which contradicted this characterization, but it is still true that "throughout the late sixteenth and early seventeenth centuries, despite occasional reports of disasters, the public continued to believe that new Edens of infinite goodness would be discovered across the Atlantic."[70]

Thus, while the Indians were almost universally regarded by English-men as culturally inferior beings, they were not generally viewed as collections of politically hostile tribes. The "innocent and harmless Indians," Drake said, were ruled by many "petty kings . . . who live in great familiarity and friendship one with another."[71] Other voyagers confirmed his observation.[72] Although many travelers could not have been primarily interested in such things, the fact is that writers in the sixteenth and early seventeenth centuries went to great lengths to reconcile the reports from the New World with the cosmology they had inherited.[73] Believing that all men were created in the image of God, and that they were naturally sociable beings, it is hardly surprising that considerable efforts were made to integrate the Indians into a Christianized history of the world and a divinely instituted ontological hierarchy. In spite of "beastial" outbursts of violence, it was important to maintain the belief that even in the "barren and desolate wildernesse" of America, "the weak and glimmering light of nature" had not been extinguished.[74] In other words, to borrow the terminology of Thomas Kuhn, what was lacking was an alternative to the established paradigm, one which could be built on the anomalous evidence of hostility on the part of the Indians.[75] It is precisely for this reason that Hobbes' influence on the development of ideas in the seventeenth century deserves more careful attention than it has received.

In the most famous passage in the *Leviathan*, Hobbes wrote:

During the time men live without a common Power to keep them all in awe, they are in that condition which is called Warre; and such a warre, as is of every man, against every man. . . . In such condition, there is no place for Industry; because the fruit thereof is uncertain: and consequently no Culture of the Earth; no Navigation, nor use of the commodities that may be imported by Sea; no commodious Building; no Instruments of moving; . . . no Knowledge of the face of the Earth; no account of Time; no Arts; no Letters; no Society; and which is worst of all, continuall feare, and danger of violent death; and the life of man, solitary, poore, nasty, brutish, and short.

Immediately following this description of the state of nature, Hobbes declares that "the savage people in many places of *America*, except the government of small Families, the concord whereof dependeth on naturall lust, have no government at all; and live at this day in that brutish manner, as I said before."[76] Everything about this statement is interesting, but perhaps the first point to be emphasized is that it is not an isolated reference. In the first chapter of *De Cive*, entitled "Of the State of Men Without Civil Society," and again immediately following his description of "the natural state of men, before they entered into society . . . [as] a war of all men against all men," Hobbes proclaims, "They of America are examples hereof, even in this present age." And he goes on to picture the inhabitants of the New World as "fierce, short-lived, poor, nasty, and deprived of all that pleasure, and beauty of life, which peace and society are wont to bring with them."[77] In *De Corpore Politico*, the natural "estate of hostility and war" of men is sketched and said to be "known" from "the experience of savage nations that live at this day . . . where we find the people few, and short-lived, and without the ornaments and comforts of life."[78] Clearly, Hobbes' definition of the state of nature was explicitly intended by him to be associated with the "brutish" and "savage" life of the Indians.[79] Nor was this point overlooked by his opponents in their replies, as we shall see.

In a more general vein, Hobbes wrote that "in Nations not thoroughly civilized, severall numerous Families have lived in continuall hostility, and invaded one another with private force."[80] This, he believed, was the most accurate account of the origins of political society to be gained from reading history or from empirical observation.[81] Hobbes did not fail to draw the conclusion which followed from this assertion, namely, that "our ancestors" were no less brutish or savage at the founding of the British nation.[82] Indeed, the savages of the New World were important to Hobbes' argument precisely because he did not view them as exceptions, outside the framework of history or political theory. Having drawn a bestial portrait of man in general, the Indians naturally represented for Hobbes the primary living illustration of his redefinition of the traditional concept, the state of nature, as the condition of total war.

Thus, Hobbes rejected not only the basic precepts of Aristotelian cosmology, but also the accepted tenets of natural history and anthropology. It is not, however, his rejection of these two strands of seventeenth-century thought that is most significant, but rather his brilliant reformulation of orthodox ideas, now imbued with an almost totally opposite meaning. Of course, many of Hobbes' contemporaries recognized this and registered their strenuous protests. But, to borrow one of Hobbes' metaphors, they were like birds caught in lime twigs; the more they struggled to free themselves, the more they found themselves entrapped within the framework of the Hobbesian system.

III. The Structure of the Ideological Debate

Hobbes' contemporary critics are sometimes accused of having failed to understand his argument. Although I believe that there is a sense in which this is true, the "misunderstanding" was not due to a lack of intellectual acumen on their part, but rather to the ideological differences in their perception of political life. We are concerned here with only one aspect of Hobbesian political thought, but it must be recalled that Hobbes attacked orthodox opinions in many areas of intellectual life: theology, politics, philosophy, even mathematics and science. Hobbes, therefore, was an explosive phenomenon to be contained, and hundreds of seventeenth-century intellectuals formed a volunteer brigade and rushed into print their tracts, sermons, and books in a vain effort to extinguish his ideas. They fully appreciated the power of his genius, and if they did not make many concessions to his argument, it was because they found themselves in a life-and-death struggle to preserve what they regarded as the established orthodoxy. That they did not by any means agree among themselves on the nature of that orthodoxy accounts for the confusion of the debate when viewed as a whole, but it in no way affects the motivations of the participants.

Later, writers in the eighteenth and nineteenth centuries were inclined to discount both the motivations of Hobbes' critics and most of the issues raised in the debate. They did so largely on the grounds that the issues themselves were trivial. A more plausible and revealing explanation for their attitude, in my view, is that they themselves had already accepted many of Hobbes' ideas, having incorporated them into their political and religious belief systems. Hence, they no longer found Hobbesian ideas "charged" with the tension produced by system-shattering notions. I am suggesting, in other words, that Hobbes' contemporary critics failed to "understand" him because they found his ideas ideologically unacceptable, whereas many later writers failed to "understand" Hobbes because they accepted his ideological position and identified it with their own without recognizing that they had done so.

Having tried to indicate the major philosophical, anthropological, and political issues arising from Hobbes' definition of the "natural condition" of man, I want to examine the internal structure of his argument and some of the implications of his radical departure from tradition. I shall also consider in greater detail the reasoning employed by his critics in their defense of that tradition.

Aside from divine appointment, which receives little more than a metaphorical acknowledgement from Hobbes, the origins of government could be accounted for by seventeenth-century writers in one of three ways: force or conquest, patriarchal authority, or consent of the people. Hobbes, of course, maintained that government is based on consent. What is interesting, however, is that he does not set aside the alternative explanations; he merely *redefines* them in terms of consent, leaving intact the assumptions and framework of the theories themselves.[83] Although this tactic undoubtedly accounts for the floundering bewilderment of his contemporary critics, it also helps to explain the powerful purchase of Hobbes' argument.

Borrowing Hobbes' methodology, let us "resolve" his discussion of natural man into its component parts, considering men as animals, as members of families, and as subscribers to the "covenant" establishing political society. In this way we should be able to gain an appreciation of the respective roles that force, patriarchalism, and consent play in Hobbes' political thought.

Hobbes proposed to offer an account of the origins of political society without the benefit of support from Aristotelian or divine teleology. His critics accused him of achieving this goal by postulating a view of man that was "contrary to the Honor and Dignity of God." Hobbes' theory, they were convinced, overthrew the "order, beauty, and perfection of the world" as established by God.[84] Perhaps not everyone was willing to go as far as Bishop Bramhall in maintaining that "if God would have had men live like wild beasts, as lions, bears, or tigers, he would have armed them with horns, or tusks, or talons," but most of them shared his sense of theological outrage.[85] Since he denied men any knowledge of divine qualities, save God's *"irresistible power,"* Hobbes equated "order and beauty" with whatever exists in the universe.[86] And, to Bramhall's assertion that "Nature never intends the generation of a monster," he replied coolly that Nature has no "intention" whatsoever.[87]

Using similar arguments, but on a slightly different level, Hobbes' contemporaries criticized him for striking at the foundation of all systems of morality, which rested, they insisted, on the acceptance of "the noble condition of man as a rational creature" as a necessary starting premise.[88] Hobbes refused this gratuitous a priori statement and argued instead that men excel other beasts only in the art of "making rules" for themselves. Those who do so "deserve an honor above brute beasts," but those who do not are worse than beasts. "So that it is not merely the nature of man, that makes him worthier than other living creatures, but the knowledge that he acquires by meditation, and by the right use of reason in making good rules of his future actions."[89]

Hobbes' "debasement" of man was interpreted by some critics as a justification of force in the exercise of political power. Beasts which "are fierce, strong, and untameable," wrote Sir Matthew Hale, echoing the traditional view, "stand in need of some coercive power over them."[90] Since "rending lions" and "devouring Leviathans" do not observe the law of nature, but are rather guided by the use of force, Hobbes appeared to be arguing for that absolute tyranny which so often characterized political relationships in the animal kingdom.[91] In fact, the premise of his political theory, Hobbes steadfastly insisted, was the notion of consent. He agreed with virtually all previous political theorists that speech was the chief quality distinguishing men from other animals. Hobbes sometimes refers to the use of "method" or "names" or the ability to formulate "general rules" as defining characteristics of man, but all of these depend upon the use of speech.[92] The difference between Hobbes and Christianized Aristotelianism on this point turns on the former's emphasis on speech and reasoning as self-willed action rather than as a "property" or "faculty" natural to man. Hobbes asserts:

There is no other act of mans mind, that I can remember, naturally planted in him, so, as to need no other thing, to the exercise of it, but to be born a man, and live with the use of his five Senses. Those other Faculties, of which I shall speak by and by, and which seem proper to man onely, are required, and increased by study and industry; and of most men learned by instruction, and discipline; and proceed all from the invention of Words and Speech. For besides Sense, and Thoughts, and the Trayne of thoughts, the mind of man has no other motion; though by the help of Speech, and Method, the same Facultyes may be improved to such a height, as to distinguish men from all other living Creatures.[93]

In other words, men are not recognizably different from other animals by virtue of divine creation (which may leave them, as the "savages of America," still in the state of other animals, i.e., the state of war); they become different only because they themselves *create* a political society.[94] Since "it is impossible for a man . . . not to be in a perpetuall solicitude of the time to come," with "no repose, nor pause of his anxiety, but in sleep," man's position in the universe is hardly a fixed one.[95] He may easily sink beneath the level of beasts through his misuse of speech.[96] It is only his self-willed ability to "make rules" for himself that rescues him from that condition. Speaking of the differences between men and animals and their respective abilities to achieve a degree of harmony among themselves, Hobbes writes that "natural concord, such as is amongst those creatures, is the work of God by the way of nature; but concord amongst men is artificial, and by way of covenant." Whereas "bare natural inclination" is sufficient for animals "to preserve peace among them," this is not true for men, whose natural inclinations lead to hostilities.[97]

It should be stressed that Hobbes is *not* saying that animals are naturally social whereas men are naturally atomistic individuals. Rather, he argues that from the fact that men do not naturally desire solitude it does not follow that they are "naturally fit" for political society.[98] For the latter is not a "mere meeting" or "gathering," but the result of "faith and compacts." Hence, the difference between men and animals is not that the latter are social whereas the former are not, but that the natural "gatherings" of animals are generally sufficient to preserve peace among them, whereas those of men are not, without an additional action, namely, a covenant.[99] Outside the commonwealth, according to Hobbes, there might be "only a temporal league" which is "entered into by each man for his private interest, without any obligation of conscience." And he adds, "There are therefore almost at all times multitudes of lawless men," men, that is, who are still in the state of nature.[100] Even this "temporal league," however, represents a small advance for men over other animals. "The leaguing and societies of men," Hobbes argues, "are a greater power than the ungoverned strength of unruly beasts. In this it is that consisteth this dominion of man."[101] Men are capable of "banding" together, as other animals, but only the artificially instituted "bond" between them makes them human beings directed by laws. Yet, even prior to the creation of Leviathan, the "artificial animal," men in collectivities are superior to other animals.

After citing a passage from J. Bodin's *Six Books of the Commonwealth*, Hobbes attributes a number of misconceptions about politics to the failure to understand what is meant by the "body politic." That term, according to Hobbes, signifies "not the concord, but the union of many men." This distinction is sufficiently important to Hobbes' theory for him to insist that although it may be common practice to consider a corporation or a city "one person in law," neither, he maintains, is, properly speaking, a body politic.[102] It is not an exaggeration to say that for Hobbes everything depends upon recognizing that the social contract creates a *unity*, where before there was only a *collection* of men; that single action transforms individuals, whatever their previous condition, into citizens of a commonwealth. Elaborating on the "double signification" of the word "people," Hobbes explains that, in one sense, "people"

signifieth only a number of men, distinguished by the place of their habitation . . . which is no more, but the multitude of those particular persons that inhabit those regions, without consideration of any contracts or covenants amongst them. . . . In another sense, it signifieth a person civil, that is to say, either one man, or one council, in the will whereof, is included and involved the will of every one in particular.

If, therefore, the body politic is "dissolved," men become a "multitude" again, "*how well soever they agree, or concur, in opinions amongst themselves.*"[103]

In the light of Hobbes' view of men living in "leagues" outside the "bonds" of civil society, but still superior to animals, his example of the American Indians was well chosen. For, in the minds of most of his contemporaries, this was an accurate description of the Indians' condition. Still, clinging to the older notions, Hobbes' opponents could not surrender their belief in the created degrees of nature. They chose, rather, to "misunderstand" Hobbes' meaning.

Not only is it true that, by the middle of the seventeenth century, "a political philosopher . . . was addressing a public which knew about savages and expected a thinker to take account of them,"[104] but, as a more general commentary on the nature of ideological conflict, it is indicative of the ever expansive nature of that conflict that it draws into the center of controversy increasingly diverse kinds of issues and evidence. Much of the debate between Hobbes and his contemporaries on the separability of man from other animals, the natural sociability of the former, and the role of consent versus force in the establishment of political society is, as we have seen, a direct confrontation between two world views. But, following the Restoration, a much greater polemical use was made of empirical evidence gathered from the growing stockpile of travel literature.

One political writer, citing travel literature against Hobbes, maintained that "the most Rude and Barbarous Savages that late Voyages give any Account of, are never observed singly to wander the unfrequented Woods; nor to reside alone in the uninhabited Deserts; but are always found to live together in small Septs or Hords."[105] With a slightly different emphasis, Lord Clarendon wrote:

Nor will the instance he [Hobbes] gives of the inhabitants in *America*, be more to his purpose than the rest, since as far as we have any knowledge of them, the savage People there live under a most entire subjection and slavery to their several Princes.[106]

Similarly, Bishop Tenison quotes Hobbes' reference in the *Leviathan* to the "savage people" of America, and declares, "let it be supposed that many brutish Families" do exist in America. Still, because even these barbarous savages live in families, "you rather overthrow than prove your supposed state of Nature."[107]

None of these replies successfully met Hobbes' ideological argument. He did not have to assert that men had historically lived without religion or families, or that individuals wandered singly through the woods. He merely insisted that a proper or *civil* government was one established by consent, and that anything less than this—*whatever the form of their institutions*—was not a civil government.

Men in the intermediate stage between their existence as animals and as members of "civil society" are not only fragments of a "temporary multitude," they are also parts of a family grouping. Few writers in the seventeenth century, and Hobbes was not among them, questioned the notion that the family was the fundamental unit of human existence. Nevertheless, Hobbes was consistently attacked by his critics for having rejected the patriarchal theory of the origins of government. This misunderstanding reflected a disagreement not over the substantive tenets of the theory itself, but over the function that theory performed. That is, Hobbes granted a limited validity to patriarchalism as a historical explanation; most of his opponents, however, accepted it as a justification for the exercise of political authority.

To Hobbes "it is evident that . . . the beginning of all dominion amongst men was in families."[108] In the beginning of all countries, the people were "divided amongst an infinite number of little Lords, or Masters of Families," and these "joyned together" to form "a greater Monarchy."[109] Hence, a "great family" is "a little kingdom," and "a little kingdom a family."[110] This, of course, was thoroughly respectable and conventional doctrine.[111] To it, however, Hobbes added something that was not conventional. His picture of men living in small families lacked one crucial ingredient: security. In "all places, where men have lived by small Families," Hobbes observed, "to robbe and spoyl one another, has been a Trade."[112] He suggests that families "continually had wars one with another."[113] It is particularly true that "in Nations not thoroughly civilized, severall numerous Families have lived in continuall hostility, and invaded one another with private force."[114] So long as this is the "natural condition of mankind," the relations of small families to each other are those of the Hobbesian state of war.

In other words, Hobbes simply incorporated the theory of patriarchalism into his description of the state of nature. Men might possess greater strength than animals; they might band together in multitudes; they might be members of families in the state of nature; but they could not be truly human until they had left behind them the state of war by subscribing to a convenant and submitting themselves to a sovereign. Hobbes did not deny the divine creation of man, the Aristotelian proposition that speech is his chief characteristic, or the role of the family as the primary unit of human existence. But he did redefine these traditional assumptions in accordance with his own account of the origins of political society. Moreover, given his simplified and theologically unencumbered cosmology, Hobbes was able to make more effective use of anthropological evidence than his opponents.

Adversaries chided Hobbes for failing to cite a single instance from history of men's "covenanting" together, but they could hardly deny that there were historical precedents, especially in the New World, for something very close to the Hobbesian state of nature. Acosta, Hakluyt, and others had provided examples of "barbarous" men "without law, without king, and without any certain place of abode," living in "troops like savage beasts."[115] Such evidence posed some difficulties for the anti-Hobbists. In decrying Hobbesian man as a "pander to bestiality," or as an "affront" to the dignity of God, they could claim the orthodoxy of theology and Aristotelian ethics for their position. In opposing Hobbes' notion of the covenant with the patriarchal theory of authority, they appealed to Scripture and to history. But in refuting Hobbes' equation of the state of nature with the conditions of savagery, neither theology, nor Aristotle, nor history gave them much comfort, though, of course, they employed all these weapons as best they could.

Hobbes, Bishop Bramhall argued, "may search all the corners of America" and never find his state of nature. "There never was any such degenerate rabble of men in the world," he insisted, "that were without all religion, all government, all laws, natural and civil; no, not among the most barbarous Americans, who (except for some few criminal habits . . .) have more principles of natural piety, and honesty, and morality, than are readily to be found in his writings." Pressed by Hobbes, however, the bishop retreated slightly, admitting that "such barbarous thievish brigands" might "sometimes" have existed in history, and that it was true that in some "odd cases" there was evidence of the kind of "dispersed

rabble" as described by Hobbes.[116] Clarendon, who argued against
Hobbes on ethical and religious grounds, conceded that "the savage
People" in America did demonstrate a "hostility towards each other."[117]
James Tyrell was willing to give "considerable weight" to examples of
the behavior of inhabitants of "barbarous nations" in the argument against
the presence of innate ideas in men. But against "reasoned principles,"
examples of men living in "brutish and sensual Lusts" in "these ignorant
and barbarous Nations," he insisted, were of no avail.[118] "Let it be supposed," granted Bishop Tenison, "that many brutish Families in *America*"
do exist.[119]

Hobbes' opponents were willing to admit, however grudgingly, that
the inhabitants of the New World were "brutish," "barbarous," and "hostile." Hobbes' example of the American Indians as "natural men" was a
powerful one because, whatever else his critics believed, they did not
think the Indians civilized. The Indian in the seventeenth century was
"important for the English mind, not for what he was in and of himself,
but rather for what he showed civilized men they were not and must not
be."[120] It is true that Hobbes' discovery that, without the proper form of
government, "we are all still savages at heart" struck too deeply at the
conscious and unconscious barriers his contemporaries had raised against
the threat of savagery for them to admit openly its truth.[121] They objected,
in other words, not so much to Hobbes' references to the Indians, who
they were prepared to concede were wild and savage, as to the implication that civilized Englishmen without the proper form of government
were no better than savages. But, precisely because they did view the
Americans as inferior beings, Hobbes' equation of their existence with a
state of nature to be avoided fused his contemporaries' cultural prejudices
and their fear of a return to civil war and anarchy into an effective
ideological picture of anarchy as savagery.[122]

Hobbes' critics generally shared Grotius's view that "some nations are
so strange that no fair judgment of human nature can be formed from
them." Rather, our idea of man should be based upon an observation of
his life within the "civilized nations" of the world. To the extent that this
advice is heeded, one would not be inclined to conclude, as Hobbes had,
that man is "by nature, a wild unsociable creature."[123] Even if the Indians in America could be characterized by a "brutish way of living,
which is in too many Particulars practised by these Savage People,"
Tyrell asked, "ought the Practice of such Barbarous People to be of sufficient Authority to prove, that they live according to the true state of
Human Nature?"[124] In discussing political matters, one should not speak

"of the baser sort of men, who live little otherwise then beasts."[125] As the author of the *Vindiciae* observed, those "without restraint of laws" are inhabitants of the "barbarous nations," whereas "civilized people" reside in a "lawful condition."[126] The assumptions of a political theory, therefore, ought to be based on the general characteristics of the latter and not on the exceptional behavior of the former. Hobbes' violation of the accepted norms of political theory construction helps to explain the intensity of the censure directed at the *Leviathan*. Bishop Tenison rebukes Hobbes as a Christian for failing to uphold those standards of decency which separate "us" from "the barbarous will of that savage Man" Hobbes has taken for his model of natural man.[127] And Bishop Bramhall protests against "this savage opinion" of Hobbes, which "reflects too much upon the honour of mankind," meaning, of course, the honor of Christian English gentlemen. Since his ideas were unsuited to "our European climate," Hobbes had found "a fit place" for them "in America, among the savages."[128]

Hobbes' critics were inclined to identify "civilization" with Christianity, which had not yet fallen on the barren wasteland of America.[129] Hobbes, on the other hand, supposed civilization and religion to be secondary benefits of political society, which made it possible for him to imagine that Christians could be as uncivilized as other men. "Whatsoever distinguisheth the civility of Europe, from the barbarity of the American savages," he wrote, "is the workmanship of fancy, but guided by the precepts of true philosophy."[130] Philosophy and leisure, Hobbes explains, are products of civil society, arising within "great and flourishing *Cities*." The Indians, whatever their ethical, social, and scientific practices, remain outside the commonwealth as defined by Hobbes, and "are not therefore Philosophers."[131] If all our arts and sciences suddenly disappeared, as they do when the political order dissolves into a state of war, in what way, Hobbes asked, would "we differ from the wildest of the Indians" (that is, the "savage people as now inhabit divers places in America")?[132] Or, to put the matter in proper sequential importance, Hobbes believed that we could easily find ourselves "in that savage ignorance, which those men are in that have not, or have not long had laws and commonwealth, from whence proceedeth science and civility."[133] And, in his own history of the English Civil War, Hobbes spoke of the "warlike and savage natures" of the lords in Parliament,[134] a reference reflecting the "natural and savage" condition of men, "for the natural state hath the same proportion to the civil . . . which passion hath to reason, or a beast to a man."[135] The order of the world and the boundaries of civilization were, for Hobbes, extremely precarious; at any moment they might collapse, returning us to the "nasty" and "brutish" condition of savages. No geographical, religious, or cosmological principles could provide Englishmen with a guaranteed security against that misfortune. Only the fiction of a covenant and the Hobbesian Sovereign stood between them and "the wildest of the Indians." It was a truly terrifying thought that pierced the imaginations of Hobbes' contemporaries.

IV. Hobbes and Later Liberalism

Since the end of the seventeenth century, Locke has occupied center stage in every account of the development of liberalism. Yet, standing in the wings, unnoticed except by the actors themselves, is the ghostly figure of Hobbes. Even when they were engaged in denouncing his specter to the audience, later thinkers could not avoid echoing his lines. With surprising alacrity, liberalism consolidated its political gains, modified the sharpness of its rhetoric, and found a place of importance within its arsenal of defensive ideological weapons for Hobbesian man.[136]

The Glorious Revolution of 1688 revived once more the fundamental questions of seventeenth-century political theory: Were men returned, either by James II's "abdication" or William III's "invasion," to a state of nature? Was William a *de facto* or a *de jure* king? And if the latter, did the subject's obligation to obey the government derive from William's "conquest" or from the "consent" of the citizenry? In addressing themselves to these issues, contemporary writers frequently drew upon the works of an earlier generation, whose relevancy to the "settling" of a successful revolution could hardly have been ignored. One writer of inescapable notice with respect to these issues was Thomas Hobbes.

Referring to the Revolution, one author remarked ironically: "It is certain, there was a Dissolution of Government . . . so that here was a . . . pure State of Nature. How would the *Leviathan* have smiled, to have seen his *Chimæra* real?"[137] The natural "free" state of man, said another writer, was one of "universal chaos" where "rapines, violence, and murder were the chief ways of acquiring right." He then went on to justify the Glorious Revolution, building on the Hobbesian foundation he had laid.[138]

Despite the relative mildness of its phraseology, the oath of allegiance to William and Mary was refused by a number of clergy; and the issue of the subject's allegiance to the new government called forth a new spate of pamphlets imbued with Hobbesian language.[139] Allegiance was due the king, William Sherlock declared, because society would otherwise "dissolve into a *Mob*, or Mr. Hobbs's state of Nature."[140] Matthew Tindal advanced a similar argument in *An Essay Concerning Obedience to the Supreme Powers, and the Duty of Subjects in all Revolutions* (1694). If subjects refused to take the oath, "societies could not subsist, but must necessarily fall [into] a state of war and confusion."[141] From the other side, a post-Revolution writer complained that the "authority and the reasons" of Hobbes' political theory "are of a sudden so generally received, as if the doctrine were Apostolical."[142] And, whether or not Hobbes was referred to by name, by 1698 it had become a "commonplace" that the alternative to the existing government was a state in which "there can be no Peace, no Security, no quiet or comfortable Living, no Property, no calling anything one's own, and thence no honest Industry, nor none of the most ordinary Conveniencies of Life," in short, the Hobbesian state of war.[143]

For a radical Whig like Locke, unless the state of nature were viewed as a condition preferable to that of life under an absolute government, the justification for revolutionary action would be blunted. After the Revolution and with the establishment of William and Mary on the throne and the Whig party in power, however, Hobbes' idea of the state of nature might become a convenient addition to the latter's stock of political rhetoric. Even the Third Earl of Shaftesbury, Locke's tutee, could write that he wanted to "agree heartily" with the Hobbesian view that, apart from government, human nature should be viewed "under monstrous visages of dragons, Leviathans, and I know not what devouring creatures." And, he continued, if there is such a thing as a state of nature,

let it be a state of war, rapine, and injustice. Since 'tis unsocial, and let it even be as uncomfortable and as frightful as 'tis possible. To speak well of it is to render it inviting and tempt men to turn hermits. Let it, at least, be looked on as many degrees worse than the worst government in being. The greater dread we have of anarchy, the better countrymen we shall prove, and value more the laws and constitution under which we live.[144]

Thus, in the outcries of opponents to the Whigs throughout the period following the Glorious Revolution, the latter were denounced for reviving "this Monster" of "Hobbism," and reference was made specifically to the Whigs's reiteration of the Hobbesian state of nature.[145] On such a foundation could a stable liberal political order be erected.

By an extraordinary irony the absolutist argument was to be covertly revived by the "whigs" themselves, to take its place under heavy camouflage within the eighteenth-century Pantheon of Lockean liberalism.[146]

One of the results of the Glorious Revolution was an "end to ideology" period, during which men shifted their alliances in an effort to find a place in the new post-revolutionary order. Writers like Shaftesbury, Swift, and Mandeville could, in varying degrees, effect some combination of Lockean and Hobbesian ideas, as well as those of Locke and Filmer, minimizing the disagreements between them. There was very little difference, Bolingbroke argued, between Locke's and Hobbes' views of the state of nature.[147] The former's immoderate "excesses" could be dismissed as a circumstantial aberration, limited to his specific debate with Filmer during the exclusionist controversy.[148] Indeed, in his *Dissertation upon Parties* (1733–34), Bolingbroke minimized the differences between the Whigs and the Tories during the exclusion crisis and the Glorious Revolution.[149]

Still later in the century, reading the pages of ridicule heaped upon the idea of a "state of nature" in the writings of Hume, Bentham, and others, one could only ask, not whether Hobbes and Locke might actually have been in agreement with each other, but why they or anyone else had ever employed the concept in the first place. In eighteenth-century England—though not in France or America—the axis of political debate had shifted. "We are grown into a unanimity about principles of government," wrote Bolingbroke. Hence, party contests were fought over "power, not principle."[150] "The true rule of government," Hume proclaimed, "is the present established practice of the age."[151]

But if eighteenth-century liberalism, for its own purposes, "refined" Hobbesian man, it did not ignore the "savage" implications embedded in the original notion. The popularity of travel literature was running at high tide, and, despite a rebirth of the Noble Savage tradition, the Hobbesian portrait of the Indians had by no means been effaced. "Our relish or taste must of necessity grow barbarous," Shaftesbury complained, "whilst barbarian customs, savage manners, Indian wars, and wonders of the terra incognita, employ our leisure hours and are the chief materials to furnish out a library. These are in our present days what books of chivalry were in those of our forefathers." Nevertheless, Shaftesbury himself maintained that there was "a sort of hatred of mankind and society . . . peculiar to the more savage nations, and a plain characteristic of uncivilized manners and barbarity."[152]

The religious leader, John Wesley, could still describe the Indians as a people with "no letters, no religion, no laws, no civil government."[153] The state of nature, Hume observed, "is described as full of war, violence, and injustice."[154] And he goes on to refer to "that wretched and savage condition which is commonly represented as the state of nature."[155] One could find the "barbarous" condition of civil war "verified in the American tribes."[156] Thus, the link between the state of nature as a state of war, and its implication to the life of savagery, and specifically, to the American Indians, is preserved by Hume. In a candid disclosure of the kinds of actions that men holding such attitudes might take, Hume wrote:

> Were there a species of creatures intermingled with men, which, though rational, were possessed of such inferior strength, both of body and mind, that they were incapable of all resistance, and could never, upon the highest provocation, make us feel the effects of their resentment; the necessary consequence, I think, is that we should be bound by the laws of humanity to give gentle usage to these creatures, but should not, properly speaking, lie under any restraint of justice with regard to them, nor could they possess any right or property. . . . Our intercourse with them could not be called society, which supposes a degree of equality; but absolute command on the one side, and servile obedience on the other. . . . This is plainly the situation of men, with regard to animals; and . . . the great superiority of civilized Europeans above barbarous Indians, tempted us to imagine ourselves on the same footing with regard to them, and made us throw off all restraints of justice, and even of humanity, in our treatment of them.[157]

Civilization, John Stuart Mill proclaimed in an essay on the subject, is the opposite of what one would find among the "savage tribes" of America. For, "in savage life there is no commerce, no manufactures, no agriculture, . . . there is little or no law, or administration of justice; . . . every one trusts to his own strength or cunning, and where that fails, he is without resource."[158] Once more, the Hobbesian state of nature is but the relapse of "civilization," and for Mill, as for Hobbes, the threat of savagery was a constant one. There were always elements within society, as the French Revolution and Alexis de Tocqueville's study of America had made clear to him, which could thrust civilized society backward into that barbaric condition so aptly described in the *Leviathan*. For Mill, as for his later contemporary, Matthew Arnold, the choice between culture and anarchy was but another name for the choice between civilization and savagery.

Perhaps the most ironic twist, however, is that the Glorious Revolution itself came to be seen as the means by which the English nation had been spared a relapse into barbarism. Revolution in the past, that is, became the salvation from the evil in the present labeled "anarchy." As Thomas Macaulay phrased it:

And had we then [in the Glorious Revolution] at length risen up in some moment of wild excitement against our masters, what an outbreak would that have been! With what a crash, heard and felt to the farthest end of the world, would the whole vast fabric of society have fallen! How many thousands of exiles, once the most prosperous and the most refined members of this great community, would have begged their bread in Continental cities, or have sheltered their heads under huts of bark in the uncleared forests of America. . . . How many times should we have rushed wildly from extreme to extreme, sought refuge from anarchy in despotism, and been again driven by despotism into anarchy! . . . These calamities our Revolution averted.[159]

Macaulay then goes on to speak of the world situation in his own time, and his conviction of the superiority of English civilization is remarkable to behold:

All around us the world is convulsed by the agonies of great nations. Governments which lately seemed likely to stand during ages have been on a sudden shaken and overthrown. . . . Doctrines hostile to all sciences, to all arts, to all industry, to all domestic charities, doctrines which, if carried into effect, would, in thirty years, undo all that thirty centuries have done for mankind, and would make the fairest provinces of France and Germany as savage as Congo or Patagonia, have been avowed. . . . Europe has been threatened with subjugation by barbarians. . . . Meanwhile in our island the regular course of government has never been for a day interrupted.[160]

The irrepressible specter of Hobbes fills the pages of Macaulay's *History of England*. Those responsible for fomenting revolution, Hobbes wrote in his history of the Civil War, were wild fanatics, men of "savage" tempers who had returned a civilized society to a state of barbarism by their words and actions.

Thus, the Hobbesian state of nature as the opposite of civilized society and a persuasive against revolution, opposed by the defenders of the faith and by those who professed themselves liberals in Hobbes' lifetime, became within a very few years a convenient means for enforcing the Whig view of the Glorious Revolution, which, they asserted, had rescued men from the state of savagery. Indeed, so deeply did Hobbes' ideas become embedded within the later development of liberal political theory that revolution as an alternative to established liberalism necessarily evoked in response that particular concept of anarchy, the Hobbesian state of nature. In the *Leviathan*, Hobbes argues that the mark of sovereignty is the power to give "names" and to enforce "definitions"; the state is the great definer.[161] But, for all his perceptiveness and brilliance, not even Hobbes could have foreseen how convincing his definition of the rebel as a Wild Man, threatening to return civilization to the condition of savagery, would become to those who possessed the power to enforce it.

NOTES

1. See, for example, Sir Leslie Stephen, *Hobbes* (Ann Arbor, 1961), p. 67; Samuel Mintz, *The Hunting of Leviathan* (Cambridge, 1962), p. 147; and Sterling Lamprecht, "Hobbes and Hobbism," *American Political Science Review,* 34 (1940), 31–53. John Bowle places Hobbes "outside the main stream of English political thought in the seventeenth century"; *Hobbes and His Critics* (London, 1951), p. 13. The most extreme view is asserted by H. R. Trevor-Roper, who labels the *Leviathan* "an isolated phenomenon in English thought, without ancestry or posterity; crude, academic, and wrong" (*Historical Essays* [New York, 1966], pp. 236, 242–43).

2. See especially Quentin Skinner, "History and Ideology in the English Revolution," *The Historical Journal,* 8 (1965), 151–78; Skinner, "The Ideological Context of Hobbes's Political Thought," *The Historical Journal,* 9 (1966), 286–317; and J. A. W. Gunn, *Politics and the Public Interest in the Seventeenth Century* (London, 1969), pp. 55–108. Although I have placed Mintz above with those who emphasize the negative reaction to Hobbes, as his own work does, he does recognize that Hobbes' impact on others was a subtle one which forced even his opponents to adopt some of his ideas; p. viii.

3. Cited in Louis I. Bredvold, *The Intellectual Milieu of John Dryden* (Ann Arbor, 1956), p. 59.

4. Bredvold, *Intellectual Milieu,* p. 63.

5. Daniel Scargill renounced his "Hobbist" beliefs after being deprived of his studentship at Cambridge. A similar incident involving an Oxford student is mentioned by F. Tonnies; see Gunn, *Politics,* p. 87 n. Hobbes' books were condemned in a proclamation issued by Oxford University and were publicly burned on July 24, 1683. For George Lawson's views, see *An Examination of the Political Part of Mr. Hobbs his Leviathan* (London, 1657), preface. Richard Baxter likewise singled out "the younger sort of ingenious men" as the followers of Hobbes; Bredvold, *Intellectual Milieu,* p. 65.

6. Edward Hyde (Earl of Clarendon), *A Brief View and Survey of the . . . Leviathan* (Oxford, 1676), p. 2. For further on Hobbes' influence, see Skinner, "The Ideological Context," pp. 294–97.

7. Thomas Tenison, *The Creed of Mr. Hobbes Examined* (London, 1670), p. 2. My own examination of more than eighty library catalogs of seventeenth-century individuals lends support to Bishop Tenison's observation. Hobbes was the most widely owned English author in the survey, and most individuals owned more than one of his books. See my "John Locke's Library: Portrait of an Intellectual," *Cambridge Bibliographical Society Transactions,* 5 (1969), 47–60.

8. In advancing this cautionary advice, I am following the lead of Quentin Skinner, who has already done much to indicate the ideological importance of Hobbes' writings. See the articles cited in note 2.

9. The discussion of ideology here is based primarily on the work of Karl Mannheim, especially his *Ideology and Utopia*, trans. L. Wirth and E. Shils (New York, 1954).

10. Mintz, *Hunting of Leviathan*, p. viii.

11. Bramhall is cited in Bowle, *Hobbes and His Critics*, p. 126. Richard Allestree accused Hobbes of demolishing "the whole frame of Vertue," in *A Sermon Preached before the King at White Hall, on Sunday November 17, 1667* (London, 1667), p. 1. The phrase "ontological reductionism" is that of J. W. N. Watkins, *Hobbes's System of Ideas* (London, 1965), p. 46.

12. Not only clergymen, such as Bishops Bramhall and Tenison, and Cambridge Platonists, such as Ralph Cudworth (*True Intellectual System of the Universe*) and Nathaniel Culverwel (*Discourse of the Light of Nature*), but men as diverse as Sir Walter Raleigh (*The History of the World*), Sir Matthew Hale (*The Primitive Origination of Mankind*), Sir Thomas Browne (*Religio Medici*), John Locke (*Essay Concerning Human Understanding*), and the playwright Thomas Shadwell (*Psyche*) believed in the "great chain of being." Even Anthony Ascham (*Of Confusions and Revolutions of Governments*), who followed Hobbes on many points, defended Aristotelian cosmology. For a general discussion of the predominance of this idea, see Arthur O. Lovejoy, *The Great Chain of Being* (Cambridge, Mass., 1936), and W. H. Greenleaf, *Order, Empiricism and Politics* (London, 1964), pp. 14–56, 107–08.

13. John Calvin, *Institutes of the Christian Religion*, trans. F. L. Battles (London, 1960), I, 47 (bk. I, ch. iii, no. 3).

14. Calvin, I, 286 (bk. II, ch. ii, no. 26), 296 (II, iii, 5). See also bk. II, ch. iii, no. 8; ch. v., no. 1; and ch. viii, no. 1; bk. III, ch. iii, nos. 7, 8, and ch. xiv, no. 5; and bk. IV, ch. xv, no. 10.

15. Calvin, I, 604 (bk. III, ch. iii, no. 12).

16. Calvin, II, 1211 (bk. IV, ch. xi, no. 1). See also bk. IV, ch. x, no. 27. The purpose of the political order, Calvin states, is to provide an escape from "confusion, barbarity, obstinacy, turbulence, and dissension" (II, 1207 [bk. IV, ch. x, no. 29]). To be without civil government is to be in a state of "outrageous barbarity" (II, 1488 [bk. IV, ch. xx, no. 3]).

17. John Sharp, "The Profitableness of Godliness" (1675), in *Fifteen Sermons Preach'd on Various Occasions* (London, 1700), p. 81.

18. John Lightfoot, *Works* (London, 1684), II, 1062, 1308–09.

19. Cited in Ernest W. Talbert, "Lear the King," in *Medieval and Renaissance Studies*, ed. O. B. Hardison, Jr. (Chapel Hill, N.C., 1965), p. 98. For a general discussion of the Christian precedents for such a statement, see George Boas, *Essays on Primitivism and Related Ideas in the Middle Ages* (New York, 1966).

20. In *De Cive*, Hobbes refers to "the wicked disposition of the greatest part of men," and, a few pages later, to the "perverse desire" of most men; *De Cive: or, The Citizen*, ed. Sterling Lamprecht (New York, 1949), pp. 36, 55. Generally, commentators have denied that Hobbes ever employed such language, citing Hobbes' own denial that men must be labeled "wicked"; *De Cive*, p. 12. F. C. Hood rightly corrects this error, noting that Hobbes even appealed to the "Holy Writ" for support for his view; *The Divine Politics of Thomas Hobbes* (Oxford, 1964), p. 66. As a student in the early 1600s at Magdalen Hall, locus of Puritanism at Oxford, Hobbes would certainly have been thoroughly exposed to the language of Calvinism. Hobbes' rela-

tionship with Calvinism is given special emphasis by Phyllis Doyle in "The Contemporary Background of Hobbes' 'State of Nature,'" *Economica*, 7 (1927), 336–55. On the Puritan view of man without government, see Perry Miller, *The New England Mind: The Seventeenth Century* (Boston, 1961), pp. 417–22.

21. F. S. McNeilly has pointed out the change in terminology, and its importance, which occurred between the first edition of *De Cive* and the publication of *Leviathan;* see *The Anatomy of Leviathan* (New York, 1968), pp. 148–55. I agree with Professor Strauss that even in Hobbes' initial usage, human "wickedness" was intended to be understood as "the innocent wickedness of the brutes" (Leo Strauss, *The Political Philosophy of Hobbes* [Chicago, 1961], p. 14). Hobbes' argument required only that men and beasts be labeled "dangerous" or "noxious" rather than "evil."

22. Ralph Cudworth discusses the philosophical predecessors of Hobbes at great length, explicitly drawing the connections between them. See his *True Intellectual System of the Universe*, ed. Thomas Birch (Andover, Mass., 1839). Cf. Boas, *Essays on Primitivism*.

23. "Junius Brutus," *A Defense of Liberty Against Tyrants*, ed. H. J. Laski (London, 1924), p. 150. Without the observation of natural law, wrote Sir Walter Raleigh, "wee should remaine but in the state of brute beasts" (*The History of the World* [London, 1614], I, 288). Also, see Hugo Grotius, *The Rights of War and Peace*, trans. A. C. Campbell (London, 1901), pp. 86–89 (bk. II, ch. 2, no. 2).

24. Cited in Margaret T. Hodgen, *Early Anthropology in the Sixteenth and Seventeenth Centuries* (Philadelphia, 1964), pp. 197–98. Seventeenth-century writers believed that the period from Adam to the Flood encompassed 1,656 years. For a discussion of earlier conceptions of a state of nature similar to the one described by Hobbes, see Hodgen, pp. 1–107, and Boas, *Essays on Primitivism*. Sheldon Wolin remarks that Hobbes' state of nature is a "political version of Genesis, without sacral overtones and without sin" (*Politics and Vision* [Boston, 1960], p. 264). In a metaphorical sense, this is true; yet historical treatments of Genesis from a political viewpoint were a commonplace in seventeenth-century literature, and the *Leviathan* is not, on the whole, a contribution to this genre.

25. Walter Raleigh, *Three Discourses* (London, 1702), pp. 97–98. Although this essay was written in 1602, it was apparently first published in 1650.

26. Garcilaso de la Vega, *Royal Commentaries of the Incas*, trans. Clements R. Markham (London, 1869), I, 63; see also, I, 172, 174. Joseph de Acosta, *The Natural and Moral History of the Indies* (reprinted from the English translation by Edward Grimston in 1604), ed. C. Markham (London, 1880). Acosta reported that the earliest Indians lived "beastlike without any policy," without tilled lands, law, God, or reason; II, 450; see also I, 70, and II, 410, 426–27.

27. Louis Le Roy, cited in Hodgen, *Early Anthropology*, p. 199. Pierre d'Avity, whose work *The Estates, Empires, and Principalities of the World* was translated into English in 1615, similarly characterized the Indians; see Hodgen, pp. 201, 411.

28. *The Essays of Montaigne* (New York, 1946), p. 206. Although no systematic attempt has been made to collate references from literary sources, the obvious indebtedness of Shakespeare (*The Tempest*, act II, sc. 1) to Montaigne deserves mention. On the "tradition" of negative language to describe primitive society prior to Hobbes, see Hodgen, *Early Anthropology*, pp. 197–201.

29. Edward Topsel, *The History of Four-Footed Beasts and Serpents* (London,

1658), pp. 10–11. See Hodgen, *Early Anthropology,* pp. 362–65. The Indians, wrote one explorer, are "wilde people" who "live in the woods like Satyrs" (Richard Hakluyt, *The Principal Navigations Voyages Traffiques and Discoveries of the English Nation* [Glasgow, 1903–05], XI, 401 [hereafter cited as Hakluyt]).

30. Henry More, who attacked Hobbes, nevertheless praised "the excellency of his natural Wit and Parts" (*The Immortality of the Soul,* bk. 1, ch. 9, in *The Philosophical Writings of Henry More,* ed. Flora I. MacKinnon [New York, 1925], p. 87). Hobbes' wit, confessed Bishop Lucy, "*indeed is great (and it is a thousand pities he bestow'd it so ill)*" (*An Answer to Mr. Hobbes, His Leviathan,* Second Part [London, 1673], preface). Cf. Tenison, *Creed,* pp. 2, 108. For nearly a score of other testimonials to the "very great respect" and "very high esteem" conceded to Hobbes by his contemporaries, most of them critics, see Skinner, "Ideological Context," pp. 292–97.

31. See, for example, Howard Warrender, *The Political Philosophy of Hobbes* (Oxford, 1957); M. M. Goldsmith, *Hobbes's Science of Politics* (New York, 1966); Watkins, *Hobbes's System of Ideas;* McNeilly, *Anatomy of Leviathan;* David Gauthier, *The Logic of Leviathan* (Oxford, 1969); and several of the articles reprinted in Keith Brown, ed., *Hobbes Studies* (Oxford, 1965).

32. See Gauthier, *Logic of Leviathan,* pp. 118–19; Andrew Hacker. *Political Theory: Philosophy, Ideology, Science* (New York, 1961), p. 208; Hood, *Divine Politics,* pp. 74, 81, 177; and John Plamenatz, *The English Utilitarians,* 2d ed. (Oxford, 1958), p. 14. Wolin refers to it as "a timeless model" (*Politics and Vision,* p. 264). Cf. George H. Sabine, *A History of Political Theory,* 3d ed. (New York, 1961), p. 470 ("pure logical analysis").

33. Hood, *Divine Politics,* p. 81. Hobbes's state of nature "stood outside history" and was essentially "ahistorical" (Wolin, *Politics and Vision,* p. 264). Cf. Lamprecht, "Hobbes and Hobbism," pp. 41–42.

34. Sabine, *History of Political Theory,* p. 474. See also Sabine, p. 470; Hacker, *Political Theory,* p. 205; and Warrender, *Political Philosophy of Hobbes,* p. 143.

35. Warrender, *Political Philosophy of Hobbes,* p. 30 n, and pp. 239–40. Richard Peters asserts that Hobbes did not take the state of nature "seriously" as a historical hypothesis, although he did mention "in passing" the Indians in America; Richard Peters, *Hobbes* (London, 1956), p. 158. Leslie Stephen, although denying any historicity to Hobbes' argument, admits that Hobbes "is as ready as anybody to give an historical account of the origin of actual constitutions" (Stephen, *Hobbes,* p. 192–93). After insisting that it is "wholly independent of the historicity of a primitive state of nature," Hood acknowledges that the state of nature "is more than a fiction" and mentions Hobbes' references to the Indians. These, however, are merely "incidental and illustrative," and, so far as Hood is concerned, serve no important purpose in the exposition of Hobbes' thought; *Divine Politics,* pp. 81, 177.

36. On Hobbes's methodology, I have found the discussions in Watkins, *Hobbes's System of Ideas,* pp. 52–81, and McNeilly, *Anatomy of Leviathan,* pp. 59–91, the most helpful.

37. The best way to teach natural philosophy is to begin from "privation," "that is, from feigning the world to be annihilated" (Hobbes, *Body, Man and Citizen* [New York, 1962], p. 93 [hereafter cited as *B. M. C.*]). So, too, we must examine political societies "as if they were dissolved" (*The English Works of Thomas Hobbes of*

Malmesbury, ed. William Molesworth [London, 1839–45], II, xiv [hereafter cited as *E. W.*]). See Hood, *Divine Politics,* p. 74.

38. Sabine, *History of Political Theory,* p. 475. Otto Gierke, *Natural Law and the Theory of Society, 1500–1800,* trans. Ernest Barker (Boston, 1960), p. 61; Goldsmith, *Hobbes's Science of Politics,* pp. 129, 138; and J. W. N. Watkins, "Philosophy and Politics in Hobbes," in Brown, *Hobbes Studies,* pp. 237–62, esp. pp. 256, 261.

39. Lamprecht, "Hobbes and Hobbism," p. 43 n.

40. Gordon J. Schochet, "Thomas Hobbes on the Family and the State of Nature," *Political Science Quarterly,* 82 (1967), 427–45; R. W. K. Hinton, "Husbands, Fathers and Conquerors," *Political Studies,* 16 (1968), 55–67.

41. See especially C. B. Macpherson, *The Political Theory of Possessive Individualism: Hobbes to Locke* (Oxford, 1962). Macpherson was preceded in the emphasis on the historical sources of Hobbesian thought by Leo Strauss, though the latter approached the issue from a different direction. Strauss is one of the few writers to defend Hobbes' use of history against the misdirected attacks of eighteenth- and nineteenth-century critics; *Political Philosophy of Hobbes,* pp. 102–07. Cf. Keith Thomas, "The Social Origins of Hobbes's Political Thought," in Brown, *Hobbes Studies,* pp. 185–236.

42. See, for example, Nathaniel Culverwel, *An Elegant and Learned Discourse Of the Light of Nature, With several other Treatises* (London, 1652) (quotations from works other than the *Discourse* cited hereafter as *Treatises*), *Discourse,* pp. 38–39; Sir Matthew Hale, *The Primitive Origination of Mankind* (London, 1677), pp. 228, 369; Raleigh, *History,* p. 288; and Grotius, *Rights,* p. 23 (bk. I, ch. 1, no. 11). In support of his opinion, Grotius cites Hesiod, Cicero, Plutarch, Lactantius, and Polybius. John Locke maintained in his lectures on natural law at Oxford (1663–64) that it was not binding on animals, although nothing more than the title of this specific lecture was ever written; see *Essays on the Law of Nature,* ed. W. von Leyden (Oxford, 1954), p. 188 n. In his note, von Leyden adds John Selden (*De Jure Naturali et Gentium . . .*) as well as canon law to the list. Bishop Bramhall stated that beasts were in rebellion against man and God; cited in *E. W.,* V, 166. For Hobbes' assertion that animals are not subject to the law of nature, see *Leviathan,* ed. W. G. Pogson Smith (Oxford, 1965), pp. 208, 275 (bk. II, chs. 26, 31).

43. "There is a natural sense of God impressed upon the Minds of Men, Principles born and bred up with us." Without these innate principles, men "would be immediately hurried into disorder and a *Chaos,* and Mankind become like a Forrest of wild Beasts, equally savage, and mutually destructive of one another" (William Cave, *A Sermon Preached before the King at White-Hall, January 23, 1675/6* [London, 1676], pp. 8–10). Cf. John Wilkins, *A Sermon Preached Before the King, upon the Twenty-seventh of February, 1669/70* (London, 1670), p. 21; John Goad, *A Sermon Treating of the Tryall of all things by the Holy Scripture . . . Delivered . . . Nov. 8* (London, 1664), p. 10; Thomas Sprat, *A Sermon Preach'd before the Lord Mayor . . . on the 29th of January, 1681/2* (London, 1682), p. 14; Bishop William Lucy, *Observations, Censures and Confutations of Notorious Errours in Mr. Hobbes his Leviathan, and Other his Bookes* (London, 1663), p. 91; Bishop Bramhall, in *E. W.,* IV, 286; George Savile, *The Character of a Trimmer,* in *Seventeenth-Century Prose and Poetry,* ed. Alexander M. Witherspoon and Frank J. Warnke (New York, 1963),

p. 676; and William Strachey, *The History of Travel into Virginia Britannia* (1612) (London, 1849), pp. 18, 46–47.

44. It is Christianity that "tames mens brutish affections"; without it, they would be "Wolves and Lions still" (Lightfoot, *Works*, II, 1062). See also Edward Stillingfleet, *A Sermon Preached November V, 1673* (London, 1674), p. 3; Acosta, *Natural and Moral History*, II, 531–32; and Garcilaso de la Vega, *Royal Commentaries*, I, 44–45.

45. Lightfoot, *Works*, II, 1181.

46. Christopher Love, *The Naturall Mans Case Stated* (London, 1658), p. 24. An unconverted man is "a sepulchre full of corruption and rottenness . . . a loathsome carcas" in a worse condition than the beasts. He is "a morsel for that devouring *Leviathan*." It is "the common misery of all the unsanctified, that the Devil is their God" (Joseph Alleine, *A Sure Guide to Heaven* [London, 1688], pp. 51–52, 100 ff., 152, 155). According to Sir Thomas Gates, governor of the Virginia colony in 1609, the Indians were "chayned under the bond of Deathe unto the Divell" (cited in Roy Harvey Pearce, *The Savages of America* [Baltimore, 1953], p. 9; see also pp. 13, 15, 22).

47. See Acosta, *Natural and Moral History*, II, 299, 344; Culverwel, *Treatises*, pp. 40–41, 141; Perry Miller, *Errand Into the Wilderness* (Cambridge, Mass., 1956), ch. 6, "Religion and Society in the Early Literature of Virginia"; and Hakluyt, IX, 386, and XI, 333.

48. For a discussion of the polemical use to which voyagers' reports of the Indians' devil worship were put, see R. W. Frantz, *The English Traveller and the Movement of Ideas, 1660–1732* (Lincoln, Nebr., 1967), pp. 72–99, 146–53.

49. The existence of savages in America "shook Adamite theories of mankind to their foundation" (John L. Myres, *The Influence of Anthropology on the Course of Political Science* [Berkeley, 1916], p. 12). Cf. Greenleaf, *Order, Empiricism and Politics*, pp. 148, 198; Hodgen, *Early Anthropology*, pp. 405 ff.

50. Men are distinguishable from beasts, Grotius maintained, because of the latter's propensity for "doing wilful hurt" to each other; *Rights*, p. 23 (bk. I, ch. 2, no. 11). Hobbes, however, spoke of the "natural proclivity of men, to hurt each other" (Lamprecht, ed., *De Cive*, p. 29). On men's equal ability to kill one another, see Smith, ed., *Leviathan*, p. 94 (bk. I, ch. 13) and p. 118 (bk. I, ch. 15). "They are equals who can do equal things one against the other" (*De Cive*, p. 25).

51. *E. W.*, II, ii.

52. *E. W.*, IV, 153, 253. See also *E. W.*, V, 152; Lamprecht, ed., *De Cive*, p. 104; and *B. M. C.*, p. 333.

53. Cited in *E. W.*, IV, 284.

54. Bramhall, in *E. W.*, IV, 288, and Lucy, *Observations*, p. 142. See also Wilkins, *Sermon*, p. 19; Tenison, *Creed*, p. 110; Cudworth, *Intellectual System*, II, 350–51; Clarendon, *View and Survey*, p. 28; Lawson, *Examination*, p. 81; Bowle, *Hobbes and His Critics*, pp. 29, 80, 121; and Alexander Ross, *Leviathan Drawn Out with a Hook* (London, 1653), p. 17.

55. Acosta, *Natural and Moral History*, I, 31, and II, 449–55.

56. Garcilaso de la Vega, *Royal Commentaries*, I, 47, 66. See also pp. 50, 54, 57–58, 61, 63, 89, 102, 172, 224.

57. Cited in Pearce, *Savages of America*, p. 10; see also pp. 5–6.

58. Cited in Frantz, *English Traveller*, p. 101. The Indians have "little of Humanitie but shape" (Samuel Purchas, cited in Pearce, *Savages of America*, p. 7). They

have only "the shape and countenance" of men (Acosta, *Natural and Moral History,* I, 70). "These shadowes of men, howsoever wilde and savage" (Purchas, cited in Hodgen, *Early Anthropology,* p. 443).

59. Frantz, *English Traveller,* p. 104.

60. Hakluyt, XI, 297.

61. Sir Francis Drake, *The World Encompassed* (London, 1652), p. 53. Sir Walter Raleigh referred to the Indians as "a poor and harmless people" (cited in Christopher Hill, *Intellectual Origins of the English Revolution* [Oxford, 1965], p. 156). See Milton as cited in Christopher Hill, *Puritanism and Revolution* (New York, 1964), p. 149, and Strachey, *History of Travel,* p. 16.

62. Cited in Louis B. Wright, ed., *The Elizabethans' America* (Cambridge, Mass., 1965), p. 56; see also p. 114. The Indians, it was believed, despite their "Barbarous natures," would come "to a liking and a mutuall societie" with Englishmen if the latter showed them kindness; Hakluyt, VIII, 99. Several writers have confused the terms "beastial" and "rude" with "evil" or "hostile." The first set of terms expressed a cultural attitude so common that they invariably appear in any discussion of the Indians. The second set of terms, however, refer to a particular attitude of certain men, and, in the general literature on the Indians during this period, appear infrequently.

63. Montaigne, *Essays,* pp. 176–77.

64. Cited in Hill, *Intellectual Origins,* p. 172; cf. Hodgen, *Early Anthropology,* pp. 370–72. The most famous such report, of course, was that of Columbus.

65. Wright, *Elizabethans' America,* p. 143.

66. Wright, *Elizabethans' America,* p. 149. The people of Florida are "good and of a gentle and amyable nature" (*The Original Writings and Correspondence of the Two Richard Hakluyts* [London, 1935], II, 223, 254–55). The people of Virginia are "of a mylde and tractable disposition" (*Writings and Correspondence of Hakluyts,* II, 339, 347; Robert R. Cawley, *The Voyagers and Elizabethan Drama* [London, 1938], pp. 344–46).

67. Drake, *World Encompassed,* p. 107.

68. In Hakluyt, X, 383.

69. See, for example, Hakluyt, VIII, 147, 200–01, 219, 232, 300, 319–20, 432, 457–58; IX, 127, 132, 244, 430; X, 28–29, 165, 205, 208; and XI, 6, 8, 13, 130, 235, 281–82.

70. Wright, *Elizabethans' America,* p. 15. Sidney Lee, "The American Indian in Elizabethan England," in *Elizabethan and Other Essays,* ed. Frederick S. Boas (Oxford, 1929), pp. 263–301.

71. Drake, *World Encompassed,* p. 106.

72. Acosta, *Natural and Moral History,* II, 426–27. The Indians in Virginia are "divided into pety kingdoms" (*Writings and Correspondence of Hakluyts,* II, 328); see Pearce, *Savages of America,* pp. 13–15, and Wright, *Elizabethans' America,* p. 215.

73. Some explanations of Indian violence, of course, were not at all elaborate. Raleigh, Drake, and many other Englishmen attributed it to the cruelty and corrupt manner of living the Spanish had brought with them to America; see Drake, *World Encompassed,* pp. 28, 48; for Raleigh, see Hill, *Intellectual Origins,* p. 156. For other English opinion, see Hill, *Puritanism and Revolution,* p. 149; and Frantz, *English Traveller,* p. 79. On a more abstract level, it was argued (*pace* Montaigne) in a tract

on Virginia (1609) that "it is not the nature of men, but the education of men, which made them barbarous and uncivill" (cited in Pearce, *Savages of America,* p. 10). Many early settlers, but especially the Puritans, had little difficulty in seeing Indian wars as the scourge of the Almighty, to be suffered as any other divinely inflicted calamity; Roy Harvey Pearce, "The 'Ruines of Mankind': The Indian and the Puritan Mind," *Journal of the History of Ideas,* 13 (1952), 200–17, esp. 201–07. Or, conversely, in justifying the extermination of the inveterately "cruel and savage" Indians, it was asserted that "the will of God is, that good and civill men should inhabite fruitfull countries" (Hakluyt, XI, 257).

Two further points should be noted. First, there was from the beginning a distinction made between the savages in Africa and those in America, which had a great deal to do with the differential treatment of the natives. It was much more difficult to discover "humanity" in the Africans, but since there was comparatively little travel literature pertaining to that continent during this period, these "difficulties" did not become important until much later. Second, some effort was made to isolate cannibals from other Indians in the New World. In the century following the appearance of Montaigne's essay, the praise he had lavished on the cannibals was applied to the Indians generally, whereas the former were placed in a different, though hardly well-defined, category. Thus, Raleigh, who tended to wax ecstatic on the Indians generally, saw the cannibals as "inhumaine" (Hakluyt, X, 422). For the views of others on the cannibals, see Hakluyt, IX, 397; X, 18; and XI, 300. Christians, it was urged, ought to help the savages in their wars against the cannibals, the latter "being a cruell kinde of people" (Hakluyt, VIII, 100, 120). This advice made perfectly clear sense on the practical level; its intellectual premises, however, were much more obscure.

74. Culverwel, *Treatises,* pp. 40–41. See also Culverwel, *Discourse,* p. 84; and Wright, *Elizabethans' America,* p. 209.

75. Thomas Kuhn, *The Structure of Scientific Revolutions* (Chicago, 1962).

76. Smith, ed., *Leviathan,* pp. 96–97 (bk. I, ch. 13).

77. Lamprecht, ed., *De Cive,* p. 29.

78. E. W., IV, 84–85.

79. Later in the *Leviathan,* when Hobbes again refers to the state of nature, he cites the example of the social customs of the Amazons in support of his position; Smith, ed., p. 154 (bk. II, ch. 20).

80. Smith, ed., *Leviathan,* p. 154 (bk. II, ch. 22). In "all places, where men have lived by small Families, to robbe and spoyle one another, has been a Trade" (p. 128 [bk. II, ch. 17]).

81. In ancient Germany, "as all other countries in their beginnings," the people were "divided amongst an infinite number of little Lords, or Masters of Families, that continually had wars with one another" Smith, ed., *Leviathan,* p. 72 (bk. I, ch. 10). See also E. W., VI, 152–53, 259. As America is now, "other nations have been in former ages" (Lamprecht, ed., *De Cive,* p. 29).

82. The state of war we "know" from "the experience of savage nations that live at this day" and from "the histories of our ancestors the old inhabitants of Germany" (E. W., IV, 85).

83. Strauss speaks of Hobbesian political theory as "the union of two opposed traditions," i.e., patriarchalism and consent; *Political Philosophy of Hobbes,* p. 65. "While leaving the outer shell of the orthodox structure to all appearance unaltered,"

Hobbes "is really at work rebuilding the interior with entirely new materials" (Basil Willey, *The Seventeenth Century Background* [New York, 1955], p. 117).

84. Clarendon, *View and Survey*, p. 28. Hobbes makes God into "a hater of mankind" (Bishop Bramhall, cited in *E. W.*, V, 202, 222). See also Cudworth, *Intellectual System*, II, 56; Culverwel, *Discourse*, pp. 124–25; and Lucy, *Observations*, pp. 59–60, 115–16, 234–35.

85. Bramhall, in *E. W.*, V, 164–65. In his English version of Richard Cumberland's treatise on natural laws, James Tyrell makes the same argument; *A Brief Disquisition of the Law of Nature* (London, 1692), p. 76. See also John Eachard, *Mr. Hobbs's State of Nature Considered*, ed. Peter Ure (Liverpool, 1958).

86. See, for example, *E. W.*, II, 12, 13, 206–07; III, 345–46; IV, 249–50; and V, 225.

87. *E. W.*, V, 231, 237.

88. Lawson, *Examination*, p. 71. Hobbes debases "the Nobility of our Natures, to the condition of Brute Creatures" (Wilkins, *Sermon*, p. 19). See also Cudworth, *Intellectual System*, II, 250–51; Clarendon, *View and Survey*, p. 28; Bramhall, in *E. W.*, IV, 288, and V, 111; and Eachard, *State of Nature*, passim.

89. *E. W.*, V, 186. See also Smith, ed., *Leviathan*, p. 35 (bk. I, ch. 5).

90. Hale, *Primitive Origination of Mankind*, p. 369.

91. Culverwel, *Discourse*, p. 38.

92. Smith, ed., *Leviathan*, pp. 13–38 (bk. I, chs. 2–5); *B. M. C.*, p. 198; *E. W.*, V, 186.

93. Smith, ed., *Leviathan*, p. 22 (bk. I, ch. 3). Cf. Goldsmith, *Hobbes's Science of Politics*, pp. 48–49.

94. As Richard Peters has noted, Hobbes regarded speech as an "artificial construction" of men and not as the product of a teleologically natural growth. Speech, that is, is the result of arbitrary creation, not of "natural necessity." Hence, it was possible that human shapes without speech might be discovered. This treatment of speech, along with Hobbes' identification of reason with "reckoning," moved his view away from the notion of divinely created degrees separating men from animals; *Hobbes*, pp. 119–20.

95. Smith, ed., *Leviathan*, p. 82 (bk. I, ch. 12).

96. *B. M. C.*, p. 201. For Hobbes' comparison of men and animals to the disadvantage of the former, see *B. M. C.*, pp. 308–09; Smith, ed., *Leviathan*, pp. 128–32 (bk. II, ch. 17); and *E. W.*, IV, 120. Cf. Goldsmith, *Hobbes's Science of Politics*, pp. 48–49, 61–63.

97. *E. W.*, IV, 121; Smith, ed., *Leviathan*, pp. 128–32 (bk. II, ch. 17); *B. M. C.*, pp. 308–09.

98. Lamprecht, ed., *De Cive*, pp. 21–22 n.

99. Hobbes does not deny, as is commonly supposed, that there is in men an "aptnesse to Society" (Smith, ed., *Leviathan*, p. 116 [bk. I, ch. 15]). Moreover, we "are carried by nature, that is, by those passions which are incident to *all* creatures" into society; Lamprecht, ed., *De Cive*, p. 23 (italics added). But animals do not show "envy and hatred" toward each other as men do, and whereas animals "aim every one at peace and food common to them all; men aim at dominion, superiority, and private wealth." Hence, "irrational creatures" are able to "govern themselves in multitude," whereas men are not; *E. W.*, IV, 120.

100. *E. W.*, V, 184. Hobbes speaks of "the absolute necessity of leagues and contracts" among men; *E. W.*, II, vii.

101. *E. W.*, V, 187.

102. *E. W.*, IV, 207.

103. *E. W.*, IV, 145–46 (italics added). See also *E. W.*, II, 158; and Smith, ed., *Leviathan*, pp. 66–74 (bk. I, ch. 10). People are "disposed to take for the action of the people, that which is a multitude of actions done by a multitude of men" (*Leviathan*, p. 79 [bk. I, ch. 11]). Thus, the Saxons were not one united commonwealth, "but only a league of divers petty German lords" (*E. W.*, VI, 259). For a discussion of Hobbes' distinction between "people" and "multitude," see Warrender, *The Political Philosophy of Hobbes*, pp. 126–27; Gierke, *Natural Law*, pp. 267–68; Gunn, *Politics and Public Interest*, pp. 64–65; and John Laird, *Hobbes* (London, 1934), pp. 69, 198–99.

104. Myres, *Influence of Anthropology*, p. 28.

105. Peter Paxton, *Civil Polity* (1703), cited in Frantz, *English Traveller*, p. 156. For other uses of travel literature against Hobbes, see pp. 153–58.

106. Clarendon, *View and Survey*, p. 30.

107. Tenison, *Creed*, p. 134.

108. *E. W.*, VI, 147. In *De Cive*, Hobbes argues that "a son cannot be understood to be at any time in the state of nature" since he is always subject to parental authority; i.e., men have always lived in families; Lamprecht, ed., p. 28 n.

109. Smith, ed., *Leviathan*, pp. 72–73 (bk. I, ch. 10); see also bk. II, ch. 20. Prior to the institution of the Commonwealth, fathers were "absolute Sovereigns in their own Families" (*Leviathan*, p. 180 [bk. II, ch. 22]); see also bk. II, ch. 30. "Before the constitution of civil societies," mankind was "dispersed by families" (Lamprecht, ed., *De Cive*, p. 150). "Great monarchies have proceeded from small families" (*E. W.*, VI, 150).

110. Lamprecht, ed., *De Cive*, p. 100. See also *De Cive*, pp. 110–11; *B. M. C.*, p. 337; and Smith, ed., *Leviathan*, bk. II, chs. 17, 20; and bk. III, ch. 42. Nevertheless, "to govern well a family, and a kingdome, are not different degrees of Prudence; but different sorts of businesse." Only the former is a matter of prudence; to govern a kingdom, "science" is necessary; *Leviathan*, pp. 55–56 (bk. I, ch. 8).

111. See Schochet, "Thomas Hobbes," and Hinton, "Husbands."

112. Smith, ed., *Leviathan*, p. 128 (bk. II, ch. 17). The joining together of men in small numbers in the state of nature does not provide them with security; see bk. II, chs. 17, 20.

113. *Leviathan*, p. 72 (bk. I, ch. 10).

114. *Leviathan*, p. 182 (bk. II, ch. 22).

115. Acosta, *Natural and Moral History*, I, 70; and II, 410, 426–27, 454–55; Vega, *Royal Commentaries*, I, 63, 172; and Hakluyt, VIII, 100; IX, 191, 410; and X, 18. One traveler reflected after seeing the Indians: "For as government is the onely bond of common societie: so to men lawlesse, that each one to another are. Omnes hoc jure molesti, quo fortes." Such men "live in dayly tumultes, feares, doubets, suspitions, barbarous cruelties . . . wanting discipline, justice and good order" (Hakluyt, X, 473).

116. Bramhall, *Works* (Oxford, 1842–45), IV, 95, 567, 593.

117. Clarendon, *View and Survey*. p. 30.

118. Tyrell, *Law of Nature*, pp. 209–10. In fairness to Tyrell, he does go on to argue against Hobbes, and he is one of the few critics to cite actual evidence from the travel literature to support his argument. He concludes that although "these People [Indians] have often Wars with their Neighbours, yet it is not with all, but only some particular Nations, with whom they have constant Wars" (p. 330).

119. Tenison, *Creed*, p. 134.

120. Pearce, *Savages of America*, p. 5.

121. The words quoted are those of A. E. Taylor, in *Thomas Hobbes* (London, 1908), p. 68.

122. Speaking of the relationship between Hobbes' view of the state of nature and later primitivistic attitudes, M. T. Hodgen suggests that "Hobbes's influence upon subsequent thought was immense" (*Early Anthropology*, p. 490). See the list of eighteenth-century authors cited there. Also, R. W. Frantz notes that increasingly in the post–Civil War period of the seventeenth century the warlike nature of the Indians came to be emphasized; *English Traveller*, pp. 36–37, 101 ff. And although, obviously, this change in attitudes may have been due to factors operating quite independently of Hobbes' influence—the Indian massacres of the 1620s, 1640s, and 1670s are of immediate relevance—still, it was at least "convenient" to have available a widely publicized theory which saw in the actions of the Indians the hostility of natural men rather than the scourge of an angry Deity. Guiltless genocidal retaliation flourishes much better under the former than under the latter explanation of human behavior.

123. Grotius, *Rights*, p. 24 (bk. I, ch. 1, no. 12).

124. Tyrell, *Law of Nature*, p. 328. Cf. "Would any man in his right wits," Bishop Bramhall exclaimed, make the condition of American savages "to be the universal condition of mankind?" (Bramhall, *Works*, IV, 593).

125. Lucy, *Observations*, p. 238.

126. "Junius Brutus," p. 146; Savile, *Character of a Trimmer*, p. 669.

127. Tenison, *Creed*, p. 110.

128. Bramhall, *Works*, IV, 335, 596–97; cf. Lucy, *Observations*, p. 318.

129. "If we take Righteousness out of the heart of a man, we leave nothing there of the image of God . . . [the world would be] inhabited only by rapine, and violence. . . . Thus whatever increase of Civil Arts, whatever flourishing of populous Nations, whatever intercourse between people and people has been practis'd to supply the necessities, conveniences, and Ornaments of humane life: they were all at first founded on Righteousness" (Sprat, *Sermon*, pp. 14–15). If it is not the grace of Christianity, Culverwel asked, "how then comes a Christian to be neerer to the King-dome of Heaven then an Indian?" (*Discourse*, p. 209). To Bramhall, who raised a variant of the same question, Hobbes replied that fortunately for the English the Scriptures "were made law to us here, by the authority of the commonwealth." If, on the other hand, "they were laws in their own nature, then were they laws over all the world, and men were obliged to obey them in America" as soon as the gospel was preached to them—a telling point against the failure of a century of missionary work to "Christianize" the Indians; *E. W.*, IV, 368–70. What the Americans needed was not the gospel, which they had heard and rejected, but a Hobbesian sovereign who, incidentally, was a Christian.

130. *E. W.*, IV, 449–50.

131. Smith, ed., *Leviathan*, pp. 519–20 (bk. IV, ch. 46).

132. *E. W.*, IV, 72.

133. *E. W.*, V, 304.

134. These words do not appear in some editions of *Behemoth*. Cf. Strauss, *Political Philosophy of Hobbes*, p. 121, n. 1.

135. Lamprecht, ed., *De Cive*, p. 99.

136. The suddenness of the Whigs's volte-face has been emphasized by J. H. Plumb, *The Growth of Political Stability: England 1675–1725* (London, 1967). After the Glorious Revolution, the Whig party adopted a "whiggism which, abhoring revolutionary methods, seems now . . . almost indistinguishable from conservatism itself" (Herbert Butterfield, *The Englishman and His History* [Cambridge, 1945], p. 92). See also Caroline Robbins, *The Eighteenth-Century Commonwealthman* (Cambridge, Mass., 1959), pp. 133, 379.

137. *Reasons why the Rector of P--- took the Oath of Allegiance to King William and Queen Mary*, in *Somers Tracts* (London, 1748), V, 445.

138. *An Essay upon the Original and Design of Magistracy*, in *The Harleian Miscellany* (London, 1808–11), I, 4.

139. For a discussion of the use of Hobbesian theory in this controversy, see G. L. Cherry, "The Legal and Philosophical Position of the Jacobites, 1688–1689," *Journal of Modern History*, 22 (1950), 309–21; Skinner, "Ideological Context," p. 295 ff., and "History and Ideology," pp. 172–76. On the oath controversy and the position of the nonjurors generally, see Charles F. Mullet, "Religion, Politics, and Oaths in the Glorious Revolution," *Review of Politics*, 10 (1948), 462–74; Gerald Straka, *Anglican Reaction to the Revolution of 1688* (Madison, Wis., 1962); Gerald Straka, "The Final Phase of Divine Right Theory in England, 1688–1702," *English Historical Review*, 77 (1962), 638–58; L. M. Hawkins, *Allegiance in Church and State* (London, 1928); and Thomas Lathbury, *A History of the Nonjurors* (London, 1845).

140. William Sherlock, *The Case of the Allegiance Due to Sovereign Powers . . .* (London, 1691), p. 38. For Sherlock's description of the state of nature in rather Hobbesian terms, see *A Vindication of the Case of Allegiance . . .* (London, 1691), p. 14. Another writer, echoing Sherlock's defense of oath-taking, wrote: "When the Government is fixed, obedience becomes necessarie to it, and conscience obleiges privat persons to yield obedience, as well as prudence and safety to prevent anarchy, and the rable from spoilinge and robbinge the noble and wealthy" (cited in Straka, "Final Phase," *EHR*, p. 656 n).

141. Cited in Gunn, *Politics*, p. 309.

142. Skinner, "Ideological Context," p. 295.

143. Samuel Barton, *A Sermon Preach'd before . . . The Lord Mayor . . . On the Feast of St. Michael, 1698* (London, 1698), p. 13.

144. Anthony Ashley Cooper, Third Earl of Shaftesbury, *Characteristics of Men, Manners, Opinions, Times*, 2 vols. (Indianapolis, 1964), II, 83. The cautiousness of James Tyrell, one of Locke's closest friends, after the Revolution "was typical of many who supported the Revolution" (Robbins, *The Eighteenth Century Commonwealth*, p. 75). On John Shute, another of Locke's Whig associates, see Gunn, *Politics*, pp. 202 ff.

145. Skinner, "History and Ideology," pp. 173–74.

146. Skinner, "History and Ideology," p. 171.

147. Isaac Kramnick, *Bolingbroke and His Circle* (Cambridge, Mass., 1968), p. 97. See also pp. 84–110. On Shaftesbury's confused treatment of the state of nature, see *Characteristics*, II, 78 ff; for Bernard Mandeville, see *The Fable of the Bees* (New York, 1962), pp. 191–203. "Defoe was strongly influenced by the two main streams of political thought in England during the latter half of the seventeenth century" (i.e., Hobbes and his opponents) and "it was typical of Defoe's contemporaries to attempt a synthesis of these two views" (Maximillian E. Novak, *Defoe and the Nature of Man* [Oxford, 1963], pp. 14 ff.).

148. Kramnick, *Bolingbroke and His Circle*, p. 98.

149. Kramnick, *Bolingbroke and His Circle*, p. 26.

150. Kramnick, *Bolingbroke and His Circle*, p. 256, n. 56. For others who stress the same point, see Plumb, *Political Stability*, passim; and Robbins, *Eighteenth-Century Commonwealth*, p. 120. The author of *Faults on Both Sides* attributes political conflict to the "sinister Designs" of men in both parties; in *Somers Tracts*, fourth collection (London, 1751), III, 291, 296.

151. David Hume, *Essays*, cited in John B. Stewart, *The Moral and Political Philosophy of David Hume* (New York, 1963), p. 235.

152. Shaftesbury, *Characteristics*, I, 221–22, 332. The traveler proceeds from stories about "monstrous brutes" to those about "yet more monstrous men" (p. 223). "Monsters and monster-lands were never more in request" (p. 225).

153. Hodgen, *Early Anthropology*, p. 366.

154. David Hume, *A Treatise of Human Nature*, in *Hume's Moral and Political Philosophy*, ed. Henry D. Aiken (New York, 1948), p. 62.

155. *Hume's Moral and Political Philosophy*, p. 97.

156. *Hume's Moral and Political Philosophy*, pp. 102–23. Richard Price found in the American Indians "a love of domination, a desire of conquest, and a thirst for grandeur and glory" which led them to "plunder and massacre" (*A Discourse on the Love of Our Country* [London, 1790], p. 5).

157. David Hume, *An Enquiry Concerning the Principles of Morals* (La Salle, Ill., 1953), pp. 23–24.

158. John Stuart Mill, *Essays on Politics and Culture*, ed. Gertrude Himmelfarb (Garden City, N.Y., 1962), p. 46.

159. Thomas B. Macaulay, *The History of England, from the Accession of James II* (New York, n.d.), II, 517.

160. Macaulay, *History*, II, 522.

161. Cf. Wolin, *Politics and Vision*, pp. 259–62.

The Wild Man Comes to Tea

MAXIMILLIAN E. NOVAK

During a visit to London in 1726, Jonathan Swift set about the business of arranging for the publication of *Gulliver's Travels*, visited with his old friends, Pope, Gay, Congreve, and Arbuthnot and even chatted with his old enemy, the Prime Minister, Sir Robert Walpole. On the sixteenth of April, in the first letter extant after his arrival. he wrote to Thomas Tickell about another event that must have held considerable interest for the creator of the Yahoos and the Houyhnhnms:

This night I saw the wild Boy, whose arrivall here hath been the subject of half our Talk this fortnight[.] He is in the Keeping of Dr. Arbuthnot, but the King and Court were so entertained with him, that the Princess could not get him till now. I can hardly think him wild in the Sense they report him.[1]

Later in that year occurred an even more sensational event—the suppositious birth of rabbits to Mary Toft, but if Peter, the wild boy, ceased to be the talk of the town, speculative interest in him continued throughout the century. From the very beginning, he became the focal point for discussions of three closely related archetypes: Wild Man, natural man, and what might for want of a better name be called philosophic natural man—the ideal of the wise man living close to nature that was particularly dear to the hearts of the Stoics. In this essay I want to use these categories to discuss the works connected with Peter in particular, and more broadly, to focus on eighteenth-century attitudes toward those beings who were outside the pale of European society or the society of those noble barbarians—Incas, Aztecs, wise Chinese—and who constituted a problem in definition for philosophers and wits of the Enlightenment. Finally, I want to return to Swift and *Gulliver's Travels* for the purpose of examining this work in the light of contemporary theories about man and his savage counterpart.

I. Civilize Him Into Man

According to Joseph Friedrich Blumenbach, the anthropologist who attempted to destroy the legend of Peter and the concept of *Homo sapiens ferus* which had been accepted by scientists like Linnaeus and Buffon, Peter was first discovered near Hamelin on 27 July 1724.[2] He was naked, inarticulate, and brutish, and was quickly recognized as the long-sought specimen of man in a state of nature. He was transferred first to a hospital at Zell in October 1725, then to Hanover, and finally in March 1726 to London. Blumenbach was to bring some evidence that Peter was actually the mute and retarded son of a widower named Kruger, who had been thrust out into the woods by Kruger's second wife. But here we are concerned with what was a myth for the Enlightenment rather than with ascertaining the truth or falsehood of what is still an interesting problem for modern psychology—the condition of children reared in isolation.

James Burnett, Lord Monboddo, who was in the opposite camp from Blumenbach, sought out Peter when he was an old man, living with a farmer in Hertfordshire, and attempted to collect some of the reports about him that were published before his arrival; but the literature on Peter was more considerable than Monboddo realized.[3] The first accounts published in English newspapers were translated, with some variations, from the foreign press:

Hanover, Dec. 11, 1725. The Intendant of the House of Correction at Zell has brought a Boy hither, suppos'd to be about 15 Years of Age, who was catch'd some time ago in a Forest or Wood near *Hamelen*, where he walk'd upon his Hands and Feet, run up Trees as naturally as a Squirrel, and fed upon Grass and the Moss of Trees. By what strange Fate he came into the Wood is not known, because he cannot speak. He was presented to his Majesty at *Herenhausen* while at Dinner, when the King made him taste of all the several Sorts of Dishes that were serv'd up at Table, in order to bring him by Degrees to human Diet. His Majesty has given special Command that he may have such Provision as he likes best, and that he may have all the Instruction possible to fit him for human Society.[4]

Later reports followed his further actions, his escape into a tree to hide, his arrival in London, his being given to Dr. Arbuthnot "in order to try if he can be brought to the use of speech, and made a sociable creature," and his baptism. Swift's claim that he was the general subject of conversation during April is borne out by a comment in *The Country Gentleman* that "how he supported himself in that uncomfortable solitude is at present what takes up the conversation of the learned."[5]

His arrival produced a number of pamphlets, a sermon, a book-length satire by Daniel Defoe, and at least one poem. The last appeared in a well-known miscellany of 1726, edited by David Lewis, and was appropriately enough entitled "The Savage":

> Ye Courtiers, who the Blessings know
> From sweet Society that flow,
> Adorn'd with each politer Grace
> Above the rest of human Race;
> Receive this Youth unform'd, untaught,
> From solitary Desarts brought,
> To brutish Converse long confin'd,
> Wild, and a Stranger to his Kind:
> Receive him, and with tender Care,
> For Reason's Use his Mind prepare;
> Shew him in Words his Thoughts to dress,
> To think, and what he thinks express;
> His Manners form, his Conduct plan,
> And civilize him into Man.
> But with false alluring Smile
> If you teach him to beguile;
> If with Language soft and fair
> You instruct him to ensnare,
> If to foul and brutal Vice,
> Envy, Pride, or Avarice,
> Tend the Precepts you impart;
> If you taint his spotless Heart;
> Speechless send him back agen
> To the Woods of *Hamelen*;
> Still in Desarts let him stray,
> As his Choice directs his Way;
> Let him still a Rover be,
> Still be innocent and free.
> He, whose lustful lawless Mind
> Is to Reason's Guidance blind,
> Ever slavish to obey
> Each imperious Passion's Sway,
> Smooth and Courtly tho' he be,
> He's the Savage, only He.[6]

The most obvious component of this poem may be found in what we have come to call primitivism. But as Lovejoy and Boas suggested long ago, primitivism is a complex of ideas rather than a clear body of thought.[7]

The poet is intent on contrasting the outward polish and sophistication of eighteenth-century society with its potentiality for inner corruption. Without language, and therefore without the ability to reason and think as a human being, Peter is described as a creature in what might be called a prehuman condition. The poet never questions the idea that to "civilize him into Man" would be to improve his condition, but he does ask whether this process would be worth the price if by teaching Peter "Language soft and fair" he would also be taught to deceive and to commit evil. Under such conditions, the "innocence" and "freedom" of the forest might be better after all.

The poem ends with a paradox—a paradox not very different from that posed by the modern French anthropologist Claude Lévi-Strauss. Speaking of the myths and symbols of primitive man, which have been destroyed in the names of science and progress, Lévi-Strauss remarks that "knowledge in the scientific sense is merely the sharpened edge of this other knowledge. More penetrating it may be, because its edge has been sharpened on the hard stone of fact, but this penetration has been acquired at the price of a great loss of substance."[8] Like Lévi-Strauss, the author of "The Savage" sees true savagery in the hearts of civilized man rather than in Peter or that other heart of darkness—the natural wilderness which harbored him; but with the moderate optimism of his age, he still hopes reason can lead to virtue as well as to civilization. It was a note often struck by writers on Peter and other wild men, but as we shall see, there were other themes and variations.

II. Peter as Wild Man

During the seventeenth century the mythic Wild Man of folklore and literature began to attract the attention of writers on philosophical and anthropological subjects. The tale of Valentine and Orson was still a popular work of fiction into the eighteenth century, and A Most Pleasant Comedy of Mucedorus, with its Wild Man, Bremo, was reprinted numerous times during the Restoration.[9] When Defoe turned his mind to an example of a Wild Man comparable to Peter, Orson was the first to come into his mind, for Orson had been carried off by a bear which had supplied him with her milk and raised him with her cubs.[10] As a consequence of this nurture, Orson became "all rough and covered with hair, like a bear, leading the life of a beast."[11] Possessed with enormous strength, Orson is incapable of speech, but when Valentine invites him to enter "Humane Society" and wear clothes, he agrees at once. The Wild Man,

Orson suckled by a bear. From *Valentine and Orson: The Two Sonnes of the Emperour of Greece* (London, 1649).

Focas, in Calderón's play, *En Esta Vida Todo Es Verdad y Todo Mentira* (In this life all is true and all is a lie), grows up on the milk of wolves and, having absorbed the force of nature, is so much like a beast that even nature herself could not tell whether he was actually a man.[12] Almost all the qualities of the Wild Man, so well described by Richard Bernheimer in his *Wild Men in the Middle Ages*, are present in the Wild Man, Bremo, who is temporarily tamed, not by violence but by the sight of a beautiful woman.[13]

Behind these versions of the myth lay a certain kind of cultural primitivism, which had both its positive and negative aspects. Mucedorus sees in Bremo the state of man before he progressed to civilization:

> In time of yore, when men like brutish beasts
> Did lead their lives in loathsom Cells and Woods,
> And wholly gave themselves to witless will:
> A rude unruly root, then man to man became

A present pray; then might prevailed
The weakest went to walls;
Right was unknown, for wrong was all in all.
As men thus lived in their great outrage.[14]

This vision of the primitive life, which Panofsky has described so well as
an element in the paintings of Piero di Cosimo had some attraction for
an age rediscovering Lucretius and forming some of his thoughts into a
libertine philosophy.[15] The description of the young libertines of the
Restoration by Dryden as not so much wild in the woods, as "wild within
Doors, in Chambers, And in Closets,"[16] suggests the blending of the myth
of the Wild Man with that of the contemporary libertine. Today the cartoons of *Playboy* still feature ancient satyrs chasing nymphs as well as
their modern counterparts.

Such jests reveal a decline of the myth into folklore, but tales of wild
men were finding a new home in discussions of numerous voyagers. The
story of Pedro Serrano, who supposedly had reverted to an animal state
and grown hair over his body, was frequently quoted as part of a new
myth of regression.[17] Most voyagers, however, were interested in those
beings, like the Hottentot, who seemed to be only doubtfully human.
An English clergyman, who visited the Cape of Good Hope in 1615, gave a
graphic description of the Hottentot which shows that he saw them
through the myth of the animal man. He suggested that they were "beasts
in the skins of men, rather than men in the skins of beasts, as may
appear by their ignorance, habit, language, diet." This observer then
described their language as "an articulate noise rather than Language,
like the clucking of Hens, or gabling of Turkies." He compared their
movements to geese and remarked on their tendency to devour the guts
of cows raw, "when you may conceive their mouths full of sweet green
sauce." On these grounds he thought they must lack both the sense of
smell and taste. And yet he noted that when one of them, Cooree, was
taken to London, he preferred to return to his life in Africa.[18]

Thomas Herbert's *Some Yeares Travels unto Africa and Asia*, published
in 1665, reported much the same thing. He noted that their "language is
rather apishly than articulately sounded," and with that he attempts to
establish them as beings halfway between man and ape, remarking that
they have

a voice 'twixt humane and beast, makes that supposition to be of more credit,
that they have a beastly copulation or conjuncture. So as considering the
resemblance they bear with Baboons, which I could observe kept frequent

company with the Women, their speech (not unlike the *Semi-cani* neighboring the *Massagets* mentioned by *Apolonius* in his *Argo-nauts*) rather agreeing with beasts then men; their savage life, diet, exercise, and the like, these may be said to be the discent of Satyrs, if any such ever were; and probably 'twas one of these that appeared to *Anthony* the Hermite, in his life mentioned.[19]

Herbert then comments on the likelihood that the Hottentot women were in the habit of copulating with monkeys. As his final evidence that they were not men, he quotes Aristotle on the idea that the worship of God was universal and states emphatically that Hottentots have no religion whatsoever.

Herbert's quotations from Apolonius and Saint Anthony suggest that he was seeing his experience through a kaleidoscope of earlier myths. The same is true of the anatomist, Edward Tyson, whose *Orang-Outang, sive Homo Sylvestris,* written in 1699, blended accurate descriptions of the anatomy of what was probably a chimpanzee with a repetition of all the myths about wild men. Tyson connects the story of Pedro Serrano with that of Nebuchadnezzar, to explain how man might grow hairy in a state of nature. He speaks of the passions of apes for "fair *Women*" and repeats a story which must have delighted Swift, if he read it, of one "which grew so amorous of one of the *Maids* of *Honour,* who was a celebrated Beauty, that no Chains, nor Confinement, nor Beating, could keep him within Bounds; so that the *Lady* was forced to petition to have him banished [from] the Court." Tyson also suggested that apes had the same physical capacity for speech as men and remarks: "The *Ancients* were fond of making *Brutes* to be *Men:* on the contrary now, most unphilosophically, the *Humour* is, to make *Men* but meer *Brutes* and *Matter.* Whereas in truth *Man* is part a *Brute,* part an *Angel;* and is that *Link* in the *Creation,* that joyns them both together."[20]

In a special section Tyson rehearses all the ancient myths about satyrs and pygmies, concluding that most of the reports actually referred to various types of apes. He quotes the report of Ctesias on wild men who lacked language, and from Aelian and Cardan he takes examples of wild men who may have lost their speech by living in the woods, "just" wild men who live to the age of two hundred, and diminutive wild men small enough to be carried in a parrot's cage.[21]

Tyson helped to propagate another myth—that of the gentle and sentimental orangutan. The authors of the *Lay-Monk,* writing in 1713, argued that had apes the power of speech they might well be as entitled to the "Rank and Dignity of the human Race, as the Savage *Hotentot,* or stupid

Native of *Nova Zembla*." For the orangutan, they claimed a position just below mankind:

The most perfect of this Order of Beings, the *Orang Outang*, as he is call'd by the Natives of *Angola*, that is, the Wild Man, or Man of the Woods, has the Honour of bearing the nearest Resemblance to Human Nature, tho' all that Species have some Agreement with us in our Features, . . . yet this has the greatest Likeness, not only in his Countenance, but in the Structure of his Body, his Ability to walk upright, as well as on all fours; his Organs of Speech, his ready Apprehension, and his gentle and tender Passions, which are not found in any of the Ape Kind, and in various other Respects.[22]

The orangutan of "tender Passions" may refer to Le Comte's account of orangutans so loving that "to shew their Affections to Persons they know and love, they embrace them, and kiss them with transports that surprize a man."[23] When William Congreve remarked, "I could never look long upon a Monkey, without very Mortifying Reflections, thô I never heard of any thing to the Contrary, why that Creature is not Originally of a Distinct *Species*," the playwright was not speaking as a wise predecessor of Darwin, as one of his biographers believed, but merely as a man of his age.[24]

While the Wild Man of the woods was being explained away in anthropological terms that looked backward to ancient satyrs and fauns as being actually various kinds of apes,[25] the myth of the Wild Man reared by wolf or bear continued to find advocates. In 1697 Bern Connor reported several incidents of this nature in Poland. Connor describes one of these wild men in graphic terms as of "a hideous Countenance, and had neither the use of Reason, nor Speech: He went upon all four, and had nothing in him like a Man, except his Human Structure: But seeing he resembled a Rational creature, he was admitted to the Font, and christen'd; yet still he was restless and uneasy, and often inclin'd to flight." After being brought to a state "indifferently tame," and being even able to express himself "with a hoarse and inhuman Tone," he could remember nothing of his savage life.[26]

That Peter had been nurtured by a bear and somehow absorbed the vigor of nature was a suggestion offered seriously by only one brief pamphlet, *An Enquiry How the Wild Youth, Lately taken in the Woods near Hanover, (and now brought over to England) could be there left, and by what Creature he could be suckled, nursed, and brought up*. This little piece has a tripart illustration showing, in the center, Peter dressed as a civilized eighteenth-century man holding acorns. On the left he is

Bear suckling human child. From Bern Connor,
The History of Poland (London, 1967).

shown as an infant sucking milk from a bear and on the right in a branch
of a tree. The writer associates Peter with Romulus and Remus and
Orson and suggests, "It is not impossible, that some She-Bear, somehow or
other deprived of her Cubs, finding this Infant, and being full of a suckling, nursing, tender Temper, finding it a Living-thing, laid her self down
to it, and suckled it and brought it up 'til it could shift for it self." This
pamphlet is careful to point out that Peter "is strait and upright, & not
Hairy, except a bushy Head of dark brown Hair," and that he frequently

laughs. The author concludes that "'tis not improbable, that if a Bear was brought to him, he would discover by some Action or other, that

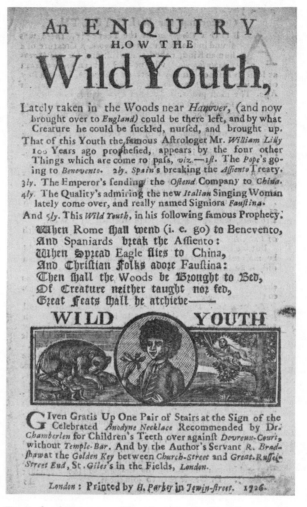

An ENQUIRY
HOW THE
Wild Youth,

Lately taken in the Woods near *Hanover*, (and now brought over to *England*) could be there left, and by what Creature he could be suckled, nursed, and brought up. That of this Youth the famous Aftrologer Mr. *William Lilly* 100 Years ago prophesied, appears by the four other Things which are come to pass, *viz.*—1ſt. The *Pope's* going to *Benevento*. 2*ly.* *Spain's* breaking the *Affiento* Treaty. 3*ly.* The Emperor's fending the *Oſtend* Company to *China*. 4*ly.* The Quality's admiring the new *Italian* Singing Woman lately come over, and really named Signiora *Fauſtina*.
And 5*ly.* This *Wild Youth*, in his following famous Prophecy.

When Rome ſhall wend (i. e. go) to Benevento,
And Spaniards break the Affiento:
When Spread Eagle flies to China,
And Chriſtian Folks adore Fauſtina:
Then ſhall the Woods be Brought to Bed,
Of Creature neither taught nor fed,
Great Feats ſhall he atchieve——

WILD   YOUTH

GIven Gratis Up One Pair of Stairs at the Sign of the Celebrated *Anodyne Necklace* Recommended by Dr. *Chamberlen* for Children's Teeth over againſt *Devreux-Couri*, without *Temple-Bar*. And by the Author's Servant R. *Bradſhaw* at the *Golden Key* between *Church-Street* and *Great-Ruſſel-Street End*, St. *Giles's* in the Fields, *London*.

London : Printed by H. Parker in Jewin-ſtreet. 1726.

Triptych of Peter as wild and civilized. (London, 1726).

might naturally break out that that Creature had been no Stranger to him, and would confirm the Opinion of his being brought up by that Creature, rather than any other."[27]

Such an invitation could hardly be resisted by the wits of the time. *It Cannot Rain but It Pours,* a work sometimes attributed to Swift and sometimes to Arbuthnot, proceeds much like the *Enquiry,* seeing Peter as the fulfillment of a prophecy, associating him with Romulus and Remus and Orson, and suggesting that he was *"nursed in the Woods* of Germany *by a Wild beast."*[28] But from this point on it becomes, like so many of the writings on Peter, a satire on contemporary life. More sustained is *The Most Wonderful Wonder,* which tells how a Dutchman, Veteranus, goes back to the woods to capture the bear that nursed Peter.[29] He finds another wild infant being nursed by a bear and, eventually, Peter's mother. Peter embraces his mother when she is brought to England and engages in a dialogue with her in the tradition of Montaigne's "Apology for Raimond Sebond" and of European animalitarianism that he influenced. According to Montaigne, man is inferior to the beast. The beasts act by instinct, "whilst us she abandons to chance and fortune, and forces us to seek by art the things necessary for our preservation; at the same time denying us the means of attaining, by any education or mental effort, to the natural skill of the animals. So that their brutish stupidity surpasses in all their contrivances everything we are able to do with our divine intelligence."[30] Thus Montaigne, and thus those who followed him: Charron, Gracián, Rochester.

Peter and his mother cannot conceive why such a vile animal as man should deprive them of their liberty. They conclude that the only possible reason is that men want to admire creatures superior to them. Peter complains of his clothes and of being forced to stand upright. To the bear's question concerning mankind's right to imprison them, Peter states that man's only right is "power":

The Beast call'd Man, has the Vanity to imagine himself the Head of the Creation; that every other Creature is subservient to him, and made by the Sun for his Use; and that he alone has the Benefit of Reason and Expression.

Bear. I find he is but a very silly Animal. Let him consult Experience (for Reason I suppose he has none) and see which has most Claim to Superiority, the Two leg'd, or the Four-leg'd Beast. Turn a Man loose to me, to a Tiger, or a Lion, and let him shew his Excellence. He seems to me the most imperfect Piece of the Creation; for the Sun has given him neither Hair to cover him, nor teeth nor Claws to defend him. Has he a Scent to find out his necessary Food?[31]

Though he is human, Peter has had the opportunity to observe man critically from an outside view. Peter states that men have pride and courage only when wearing clothes made from the fur and skins of other animals. (This was the presynthetics age.) Abstract words, such as "Justice, Honour, Religion, Truth, Friendship, Loyalty, Piety, Charity, Mercy, Publick Good," have no *"Idea"* attached to them. They worship gold as their God.[32]

Although this pamphlet contains the best statement of animalitarianism among the works on Peter, there is some of that type of thought in almost all the pamphlets. In one he is seen as speaking all the languages of animals and as taking particular delight in the conversation of horses. And in *The Manifesto of Lord Peter* he declares himself free of all civilization and government, not as a natural man but as a wild animal.[33] But nothing published in 1726, whether in jest or in earnest, exalted Peter's wild state as much as the writings of the man who discovered Peter just a decade before he died an old man in 1785—James Burnett, Lord Monboddo.

Monboddo is perhaps best known from a conversation recorded by Boswell. Dr. Johnson plucked Monboddo's name out of the air as a man who "talked a great deal of . . . nonsense." "Why, Sir," said Johnson, "a man who talks nonsense so well, must know that he is talking nonsense. But I am afraid, (chuckling and laughing), Monboddo does *not* know that he is talking nonsense."[34] Monboddo's insistence that the orangutan was actually an example of man in prehuman state was actually only a small part of his statements on language and human society, but it achieved great notoriety. In fact, as we shall see, Monboddo was more concerned with the savage state, but to describe man's progress from the brutal state to a condition in which he used language, Monboddo focused on two beings—the orangutan and Peter, the wild boy.

Monboddo's theory was not a complicated one. He was an evolutionist, believing that man had progressed, evolved, and, therefore, could degenerate. As an example of degeneration, he used the model for Robinson Crusoe, Alexander Selkirk, who was reported to have almost lost the use of language after three years on his island.[35] For Monboddo, Peter represented the animal-man. John Locke had asked whether we would call a parrot with human reason a man or whether we would so classify a being with human form but without reason. The answer was obvious—we identify man by his outward form, not by his degree of rationality.[36] Monboddo posed the question somewhat differently. "The case of the Orang Outang," wrote Monboddo after describing some new examples of the precocity of that animal, "I think, it is impossible to distinguish from the case of Peter the Wild Boy; for, if Mr. Buffon's Orang Outang was not a man, because he had not learned to speak at the age of *two*, it is impossible to believe that Peter, who, at the age of *seventy*, and, after having been above fifty years in England, has learned to articulate but a few words, is a man."[37] And the humanity of Peter, Monboddo reminded his readers, was never questioned.

Peter as an old man. From Johann Friedrich Blumenbach, *Beyträge zur Naturgeschichte* (Göttingen, 1806).

That Monboddo was somewhat gullible, that he believed that there were men in Borneo with tails and that some orangutans could speak, is undeniable. And his argument that language was not natural to man may ignore the very quality that separates man from the brutes.[38] But he was not trying to argue for returning mankind to a brute life or that orangutans were happier than men. Monboddo thought Peter an "extraordinary Phaenomenon." And indeed he was. Between the time of his arrival in England in 1726 and Monboddo's insistence in 1784 that Peter was indeed "a living example of the state of Nature,"[39] English thought was to travel from regarding natural law as a law of reason back to an older view of man as a higher animal, sharing a system of natural laws with his fellow brutes.

III. Peter as Natural Man

After some satirical reflections on the idea that Peter could possibly be like the mythic Wild Man, a being reared by a wild animal, Daniel Defoe nevertheless concluded that the discovery of Peter was indeed an important event:

He is now, as I have said, in a State of Meer Nature, and that, indeed, in the literal Sense of it. Let us delineate his Condition, if we can: He seems to be the very Creature which the learned World have, for many Years past, pretended to wish for, *viz.* one that being kept entirely from human Society, so as never to have heard any one speak, must therefore either not speak at all, or, if he did form any Speech to himself, then they should know what Language Nature would first form for Mankind.[40]

The questions that arose in Defoe's mind, and which he put down in what was the longest treatise on Peter written at the time, involved matters of language, cognition, perception, and natural man. That these should be the concerns of the author of *Robinson Crusoe* is hardly surprising. Unlike Orson, Crusoe does not grow a pelt, but his connection with the state of nature is indicated by his shaggy garment of goatskins. And Crusoe does have to undergo an education that involves throwing off civilized ways of thinking and acting in order to rediscover the way man had lived in a natural environment.

Like the author of "The Savage," Defoe wonders whether Peter will have to absorb knowledge of evil as well as knowledge of good in his new state, and whether his education will bring along with it the passions that he seemed to lack. The notice in *The Annual Register* of 1785 reporting Peter's death was careful to state that he did indeed have the ordinary passions,[41] but in 1726 this was not at all apparent. Remarking on the possibility that Peter might lack such passions, Defoe noted that were he to be regarded as an animal like a horse, there could be no question about passions. Regarded as natural man, however, Peter becomes a more complicated and important problem:

But speaking of a human Species, the Case alters, and there, I confess, to act as a Man, and to have no Pride, no Ambition, no Avarice, no Rancour or Malice, no ungovern'd Passions, no unbounded Desires, how infinitely more happy is he than Thousands of his more inform'd and better-taught Fellow Brutes in human Shape, who are every Day raging with Envy, gnawing their own Flesh, that they are not rich, great, and cloath'd with Honours and Places as such-and-such, studying to supplant, suppress, remove, and displace those above them, and even to slander, accuse, murder, and destroy them to get into their Places? Had Nature been beneficent to him, in bestowing something more upon him other ways, and yet kept his Soul lock'd up as to these Things, how had be been the happiest of all the Race of Rationals in the World?[42]

Such a picture of Peter has led to one line of interest in natural man— man as a Lockean *tabula rasa*, or as Defoe puts it, a "Lump of soft Wax, which is always ready to receive any Impression."[43] Defoe remarked that to give form to this shapeless lump takes infinite pains, and borrowing another image from Locke, he argued that "Mere Nature receives the vivifying Influence in Generation, but requires the Help of Art to bring it to Perfection of living: The Soul is plac'd in the Body like a rough Diamond, which requires the Wheel and Knife, and all the other Arts of the Cutter, to shape it, and polish it, and bring it to shew the perfect Water of a true *Brilliant*."[44]

Defoe's conclusions were those of an "extreme environmentalist."[45] He argued that without instruction, every man would be a Peter, "In a Word, the Man would be little more than a Man-Brute, as we see this Youth to be." Defoe then turned to the problem of language and ideas with some reflection on the deaf. The problem he raised was how human beings can conceive of ideas without words:

Words are to us, the Medium of Thought; we cannot conceive of Things, but by their Names, and in the very Use of their Names; we cannot conceive of God, or of the Attributes of God, of Heaven, and of the Inhabitants there, but by agitating the Word God, and the Words Infinite, Eternal, Holiness, Wisdom, Knowledge, Goodness, Etc. as Attributes; . . . we cannot muse, contrive, imagine, design, resolve, or reject; nay, we cannot love or hate, but in acting upon those Passions in the very Form of Words; nay, if we dream 'tis in Words, we speak every thing to our selves, and we know not how to think, or act, or intend to act, but in the Form of Words.[46]

If such concerns seem somewhat quaint today, the reader might consult Eric H. Lenneberg's "The Natural History of Language,"[47] published in 1966, or R. W. Brown's *Words and Things* (1958), in which the specters of Peter and other wolf children stalk through pages filled with graphs and statistical data concerning children reared in isolation or victims of parental neglect. Perhaps Lévi-Strauss is correct in suggesting that this is not the path to follow in searching for man's natural state.[48] But anyone interested in the way children learn to speak or, more broadly, the way man comes to know his environment will eventually find himself turning over the cases of feral man collected by Singh and Zingg in 1942.[49]

Rousseau, who used the case of Peter and other examples of feral man to illustrate his theories of nature and the savage, would have understood precisely what Defoe meant in remarking on how eager the world had been to discover Peter. "The philosophers, who have inquired into the foundations of society," wrote Rousseau, "have all felt the necessity of going back to a state of nature," and he noted ironically that "not one of them has arrived there."[50] Rousseau regarded Peter and other wild men as a possible argument for natural man as a quadruped. He eventually rejected such an idea as a general state for man, but he did believe that the solitary savage would not necessarily have language and that he would be extraordinarily healthy and strong—if not as powerful as the mythical Wild Man, still drawing health from the same natural source.[51]

Similar ideas were raised with the arrival of Peter in England. "I am told," wrote the author of It Cannot Rain but It Pours, "that the new Sect of Herb-eaters intend to follow him into Fields, or to beg him for a Clerk of their Kitchen; And that there are many of them now thinking of turning their Children into Woods to Graze with the Cattle, in hopes to raise a healthy and moral Race, refin'd from the Corruptions of this Luxurious World."[52] Almost everyone pointed to his obvious connection with the natural man of politics, who was independent of all control. On this basis, Peter, in his Manifesto, proclaims his freedom to choose a wife for himself and sets the conditons for her. She must be chosen from savage races; Hottentots, "wild Americans," or Arabians. He wants her to have sound teeth and be free from the weaknesses found in many civilized girls, yet as this satire proceeds, it appears more and more obvious that what he is demanding is the product of permissive education—Rousseau and John Dewey, Georgian style. Thus he insists on "One who has never been thwarted in her Humour, but treated with the utmost tenderness by some indulgent Mother, untam'd, and left to her own generous Passions and Inclinations, and who has given early proofs of her impatience of subjection to any sort of Government whatsoever." In demanding a young woman who is accustomed to conversing with beasts ("Cats, Dogs, Monkeys"), who uses her teeth and nails on all who come near her, who tends to nudity in wearing high skirts, who dances wildly, spells badly, spends lavishly (thereby showing contempt for money, "the Corrupter of the Morals of Tame Men"), and ignores time, Peter is actually asking for the worst product of civilized womanhood—the wild woman behind the civilized one.[53]

In much of this playful satire there was clearly an important motif for the age, and though primitivism is usually associated with the second half of the eighteenth century, there are signs enough that it was a flourishing theme in England long before 1726. For if a traveler like Thomas Herbert could pronounce the Hottentots subhuman, he could easily change his tone when speaking of the natives of Madagascar and the way they were

delighted with sports and novelties; hunting, hawking, fishing (of which, the Isle affords variety) and dancing; in *Maeanders* winding, beating and clapping their breasts and hands, their feet spurning the yielding sands, forcing the spectators further of; during which the women with savage harmony, modulating with hands and eyes, observing measure, equal if not exceed the men in their laborious treadings.[54]

And he excuses their ignorance of writing and arithmetic with an evolutionary view of human society. "And albeit this Character renders these people no other than savage," Herbert writes, "let us not condemn them over much, seeing that the most civilized Nations amongst us have in their infancy been no less incultured, as some render our Ancestors the *Britains*." Shortly after, he describes their nakedness as *"Adams* garb" and finds in the nakedness of the savages of America more purity than the "libidinous" European women with all their "immodest fashions and loose inventions."[55]

Similarly, in a collection of some of the works of John Toland published in the same year that Peter arrived, appeared a letter from a Frenchman in Carolina, purportedly written in 1688, which idealized the Indians as "Man in a state of pure nature . . . without a mask." These savages are described as living according to the gospel without any knowledge of Christ:

Never lying, never taking away from another what belongs to him; no ways dissolute, luxurious or debauched; the marry'd women being modest and vertuous, as to every thing that looks like gallantry, as well as the unmarry'd; civil and obedient to their husbands, according to the advice of St. Paul: all of them courteous, affable, and obliging towards strangers, no ways savage nor morose, no ways ungrateful, and never forgetting a good office; valiant and proud in war, tractable and mild in peace, hating thieves, robbers, lyars, and all such as break their word. This is the true Character of the Indians, with whom I conversed most.[56]

When the writer asked them concerning the possibility of their being converted to Christianity, the savage points out that the Christian convert merely assumes the vices of Christians:

You would . . . have us become Christians? well, to what end and purpose? Is it to make us better than really we are, or is it not rather to make us as wicked and vicious as your selves, to render us Adulterers, Whore-masters, Lyars, Murtherers, Robbers, without faith, honor, or honesty, minding nothing but how to deceive one another, and to destroy you upon pretense of Justice? Is this a party to choose, and to oblige us to renounce the simplicity of our manner of life, and the sweet tranquillity of mind we now enjoy?[57]

The wild boy easily lent himself to such idealizations of the savage life, but for writers like Monboddo and Rousseau, Peter was a very real and important creature—the missing link between the savage and the orangutan. "Man," wrote Monboddo, "is in this life in a state of progression from the mere Animal to the Intellectual Creature, of greater or less perfection, and a progression not to end in this life."[58] If he was led to absurd comparisons—such as whether Achilles could outrun an orangutan or Wild Man, he nevertheless expounded seriously a doctrine of evolution and of the importance of throwing off what civilization may have done to destroy the naturally good things in our environment.[59] In attempting to return with Rousseau to the true, natural state of man, Monboddo hoped that he would be able to restore man to a state of physical health that might have enabled men like Peter to survive cold and heat without the benefit of clothing:

The object, for example, of the physician's art, must be to restore, as far as possible, the body to that natural state, which must therefore be the standard of the perfection of his art. The political philosopher, in like manner, in forming his plans of polity, will study to preserve the natural strength and vigour of the animal, (human art can do it,) by proper diet, exercise, and manner of life, and to prevent, as much as possible, the indulgence of ease and bodily pleasure, by which the race of civilized men, in all nations, has been constantly declining from the earliest times, (while the animals living in the natural state continue invariably the same), and by which, not only families have been and are daily extinguished, but whole tribes and nations. And, *lastly*, every private man . . . will, if he knows this natural state, and is wise, endeavor to bring himself back to it as much as is consistent with the state of society in which we live.[60]

This is one reason why, even if he viewed Peter as somewhat below the condition of the orangutan in the progress of the human race, Monboddo still regarded him as "one of the greatest curiosities in the world . . . more extraordinary . . . than if we were to discover 30,000 more fixed stars."[61]

IV. Peter as Philosophic Natural Man

Monboddo's concern over the corruptions that the luxury of modern life had worked on the health of mankind has been shared by the Stoics, who had advised their followers to wear either animal skins or light, simple garments to demonstrate their allegiance to the laws of nature and their freedom from the unnatural luxuries of civilization. And although Monboddo might dismiss the possibility that any of his contemporaries could achieve stoic virtue, he did conceive that such an exalted state would be possible in the future:

And, with respect to the mind, it is impossible to say how far science and philosophy may carry it. The Stoics pretended, in that way, to make a *god* of a *man*; and there is no doubt but the human nature may, by such culture, be so exalted, as to come near to what we conceive of superior natures, and perhaps even to possess the rank of such as are immediately above us in the chain of being.[62]

The main source for such attitudes is probably Seneca's moral epistle, "On the Part Played by Philosophy in the Progress of Man." Seneca viewed man as being in a state of degeneration and urged his disciples to live close to nature. Looking back to a golden age, he praised nature in a classic passage of chronological primitivism: "Nature was not so hostile to man that, when she gave all the other animals an easy rôle in life, she made it impossible for him alone to live without all these artifices. . . . Houses, shelter, creature comforts, food, and all that has now become the source of vast trouble, were ready at hand, free to all and obtainable for trifling pains."[63] For the Stoics the true philosopher was he who had learned to live according to an inner wisdom rather than through material goods.

The process by which the hirsute Wild Man might be transformed into his philosophic counterpart is obvious enough. Clothed in skins, not because they are part of his savage culture but because they are symbolic of his scorn for luxury, the philosopher of nature is free to pursue virtue. It is not surprising that both the Houyhnhnms and Peter (in one pamphlet) are mystified by clothing, and Peter offers the explanation that these coverings are the products of corrupt human passions. To the Neo-Stoics of the seventeenth and eighteenth centuries, the true state of nature could only be achieved by subduing the passions, which they regarded as excrescences of civilization. And whereas with Wild Man and natural man, as Bernheimer suggests, "this abstention from all that enriches life materially shields primitive man from the vices of avarice and trickery and bellicosity,"[64] with the philosopher of nature, it is his initial and voluntary renunciation of civilization that enables him to understand the truth about the universe.

Probably no one was more influential in spreading this doctrine than

Pierre Charron, whose *Sagesse,* published originally in 1601, went into numerous editions and translations. He stated that his main aim was to make men hate the passions and, like his master, Montaigne, he argued that the passions put man below the brutes from whom he might learn "by reforming and reducing himself to that Innocence, Simplicty, Liberty, Meekness, and Gentleness of Temper, which Nature had originally implanted both in Us and Them: And, which in Brutes is still very conspicuous, but in Us is decay'd, chang'd, and utterly corrupted."[65] From Seneca, Charron quoted what even he called "a sort of Stoical Rant," on the possibilities of the mind's expanding itself to such an extent that man might become a god:

The Mind of Man (*says* Seneca) is a great and generous Being, and is bounded no otherwise than the Divinity it self. The Wise Man is not confined to the same narrow compass with the rest of the World. No Age, no Time, no Place limit his Thoughts, but he penetrates and passes beyond them all. How agreeable is it to Nature for a Man to stretch his Mind infinitely? For Nature hath formed him to this very purpose, that he should emulate the Gods, and like Them fill his own Infinite Space.[66]

While this *locus classicus* of stoic pride was frequently attacked during the Enlightenment, works like Antoine Le Grand's *Man without Passion: or, The Wise Stoick* continued to propagate the doctrine that the passions were "poison and venemous things" and that "Reason is . . . Man's only benefit: he must use it to climbe Heaven, he must consult it to govern his Life, and if he do but hearken unto her, he shall be vertuous, and tame the most insolent of his *Passions.*"[67]

Whether stoic or not, the thrust of most works about the awakening of the Wild Man to knowledge and wisdom went invariably in the direction of elevating the powers of reason over those of the passions and sensuality. Perhaps the paradigm of this type of work might be discovered in a work written in the twelfth century, but which was not translated into Latin until 1671 and into English until 1708. This was, in its English title, *The Improvement of Human Reason,* by Abū Bakr ibn al-Tufail. The subtitle, *Philosophus Autodidactus,* the self-taught philosopher, is inscribed on the frontispiece, which illustrates the ascent of the hero, Hai ibn Yokdhan, with his companion Asal, toward the temple of God. Yokdhan is naked except for the skin of some animal, the bestial hoof which hangs significantly from his shoulders in most of the illustrations.

Tufail informs us that though some have thought that Yokdhan was born through the natural force of the sun, actually he was cast adrift on the sea and floated to an island at the equator. He is nurtured by a roe and learns the language of the animals. Seeing that he alone of all the beasts is naked, he covers himself with leaves, then with feathers, and finally, with his animal skin. When the roe dies, he opens her body and learns the secrets of the soul, of life and death. Gradually he comes to understand his environment and the perfection of God. By his intellectual and spiritual voyage through the stars and the universe, he learns the

Hai ibn Yokdhan learning the secrets of the universe. From Abū Bakr ibn al-Tufail, *The Improvement of Human Reason*, trans. Simon Ockley (London, 1708).

way God conducts the world and eventually attains a vision of the Deity. When Yokdhan encounters Asal, the first man to come to his island, he fears that his meditations and his rational, ordered life will be disturbed. Asal teaches him to speak and discovers that through the knowledge gained from nature alone, Yokdhan has arrived at the same knowledge of God that he might have gained from a study of the Koran.[68]

This work has much in common with the numerous imaginary voyages and utopias written in Europe between the sixteenth and eighteenth centuries. For example, like so many dwellers in utopia, from the wise men of More to the deistic Hermaphrodites and Sevarites of Foigny and Veiras, Yokdhan reproves Western man for his avarice and pride. But unlike these works, *The Improvement of Human Reason* is mainly about education, closer to Rousseau's *Emile* than to an *Oceana* or even a *Telemachus*. On the surface, it resembles Gracián's *El Criticón;* and Paul Rycaut, who translated this work as *The Critick* in 1681, remarked on the similarity. "The design of both," he wrote, "is almost the same, being only to show how far the Spiritual and Immortal Soul of Man, is able in its natural capacity, and by its own reflex acts to consider its proper being, and the existence of something above it; and by degrees, and steps of exteriour Objects to proceed unto Rules for conservation of its own well-being, and that of others."[69] The name of Gracián's hero, Andrenio, was even combined with that of Yokdhan as a single archetypal character by a later writer.[70]

But there are vast differences between the two works. Perhaps the fact that Andrenio is not dressed in animal skins, as was his counterpart, signifies something of the direction of the two writers. Andrenio has been raised in a cave, with animals, entirely isolated from mankind. He is "a person void of Speech," but after Critilo teaches him to speak, he tells how, although he was raised by brutes, one day knowledge burst upon him.[71] He also explains, in what appears in Rycaut's translation as a Cartesian rhapsody, his realization of the differences between him and his brute companions:

What is this, said I? am I, or am I not? for since I live, and know, and observe, I must have a Being: But if I am, Who am I? and who hath given me this Being? And to what end hath he given it me? If it be to remain here, it were a high Infelicity! Am I a Brute like these? No, for I observe most apparent differences between us; for they are covered with Hair, but I, as less favoured of him, who gave me this Being, am Naked, and uncloathed; besides, I observed my whole Body otherwise proportioned than theirs; I laugh, and weep, they howl, and cry. I walk strait, raising my Face upwards, when they move bending with their Heads towards the Earth.[72]

Like Yokdhan, after escaping from his cave, Andrenio comes to admire the God who created nature, and Critilo, whose doctrines bear some resemblance to those of Shaftesbury at the end of the century, observes: "Nor is there any Nation so barbarously ignorant, in whom the Light of Nature hath not infused the awe, and reverence of a Deity, sufficient to curb the most audacious profaneness, and convince them of the Divine Essence, Omnipresence."[73] But all of this is merely an introduction to Andrenio's journey into life and his discovery that deceit is the central

Frontispiece from Daniel Defoe, *Robinson Crusoe* (London, 1719).

fact of human existence. The rest of the work is what one would expect of the writer of a manual on worldly prudence and an opponent of "Stoick stupidity."[74] Yokdhan, too, makes his voyage into the world, but only to discover that the world has nothing to teach him; Gracián's Wild Man does almost all his learning in the world itself.

At one time I argued that the story of Yokdhan, "so far from being the 'idea' of *Robinson Crusoe* as one writer has suggested, . . . is almost the complete reverse."[75] What I had in mind was the difference between Yokdhan's explorative attitude toward his environment as opposed to Crusoe's trepidation. I pointed out that Montesquieu had used Peter the wild boy to indicate the timorousness of man in the state of nature and suggested that Crusoe had some of the same qualities as Peter.[76] Allowing for this obvious difference between the two protagonists, it would nevertheless be absurd to deny a general similarity. Crusoe gradually loses his European clothing and puts on the skins of the beasts he has shot and tamed. He undergoes an education similar to that of Yokdhan, both religious and practical. Yokdhan has to learn the most basic things about his world, from the nature of extension and fire to the concepts of burial and horseback riding. Crusoe undergoes the same kind of training, learning to tame the wild goats into domestic animals and coming to an understanding of God:

What is this Earth and Sea of which I have seen so much, Whence is it pro-duc'd, And what am I, and all the other Creatures, wild and tame, human and brutal, whence are we?

Sure we are all made by some secret Power, who form'd the Earth and Sea, the Air and Sky; and who is that?

Then it follow'd most naturally, it is God that has made it all; Well, but then it came on strangely, if God has made all these Things, He guides and governs them all, and all Things that concern them; for the Power that could make all Things, must certainly have Power to guide and direct them.

If so, nothing can happen in the great Circuit of his Works, either without his Knowledge or Appointment.

And if nothing happens without his Knowledge, he knows that I am here, and am in this dreadful Condition; and if nothing happens without his Appoint-ment, he has appointed all this to befal me.[77]

The awareness of sin may smack more of spiritual autobiography than the archetypal story of the Wild Man as autodidact, but the degree to which the elements of isolation and self-instruction pervade *Robinson Crusoe* is not to be ignored. Crusoe is civilized man placed in the role of natural man for the purpose of having him rediscover nature and the God of nature. He thanks God often enough for the freedom from temptation

Alexander Selkirk dancing with his goats. From Isaac James, *Providence Displayed* (Bristol, Eng., 1800).

that the island provides. And if Gracián's Andrenio leaves his nakedness and the reminders of the natural life behind him in order to discover the deceit underlying civilization, Crusoe is an unwilling traveler back to the natural state where he is cured of that very civilized disease—discontent. Perhaps the very real story of Alexander Selkirk, who not only dressed himself in the skins of his goats but danced with them, and, according to a fascinating if doubtful legend, almost lost his human voice, may have lent a factual air to Defoe's work. But behind all the realistic technique that Defoe brought to the novel lies a wealth of suggestive symbols. Seen in the light of the legend of the Wild Man, Crusoe's gradual change from the helpless, timid solitary to "King" of his island and its inhabitants reveals something more profound than merely a parody on the evolution of government. If Crusoe does not return to the world with a prophetic message, he has at least gained an inner peace through an understanding of the teleological scheme of the universe and his place in it. If much of his knowledge seems rather more practical than that sought by Yokdhan, at least he has an insatiable curiosity and a longing after distant lands and new experiences. Of course, Crusoe regards his restlessness as a sin, but perhaps that quality suggests something about Defoe and his age— an age of men in quest of something indefinable, unsatisfied by the endless exhortations of divines and poets that they could find happiness by staying in one place.

All these works were written before Peter was brought to England, but one of peculiar interest, which appeared in 1747, drew upon the theme of the philosophic Wild Man in a way that showed familiarity not only with the three works we have been discussing but also with the debate over feral man, which Peter's arrival in England had done so much to provoke. This was John Kirkby's *Capacity and Extent of the Human Understanding*, commonly known by the name of its hero, Automathes.[78] The work begins with the now commonplace fictional convention of a journal found floating in the sea. The journal was written by a priest who had been shipwrecked in the vicinity of what is now Fort Bragg, California, but which, in Kirkby's work, is called the land of Soteria. Although the state of California has boasted of its system of education, many of its citizens might find the theories of Soteria a bit radical, for that people believed "all that, which is necessary to distinguish Men outwardly from mere Brutes in human Shape, was wholly owing to Education."[79]

This doctrine is restated by the bishop, Automathes, who suggests that this lesson has been learned by observing some of the children who had survived their parents' efforts to destroy them by abandoning them in the woods: "Several of these have been taken up at ten, twenty, and even thirty Years of Age; but all of them were found as void of Reason as the Brutes their Companions, only with this Difference, that the older they were, still the more uncapable of being brought to Reason afterwards."[80] We learn that Automathes underwent a similar childhood, with the exception of a brief period of education in his first two years of life. But it is only because of his dim memory of his parents and the knowledge they gave him that when he is discovered, after nineteen years, he "was found, in all respects, abating the Use of Speech, to be more like a Philosopher, than a Savage."[81]

After this brief description, we have Automathes' own narrative, a combination robinsonade and philosophic tale. His mother actually nursed him before she and her husband were shipwrecked on an island paradise, where they lived on herbs and roots, drinking the pure water of the streams. After the death of his mother, from the severity of life on the island, Automathes sucks the milk of an old tame hind. One day, Eugenius, his father, is accidentally caught in a tide that carries him away to another island. When Eugenius is rescued, he returns to the first island to rediscover his son, an "ignorant . . . being as destitute of all Language, as the brute Beasts," but a being who has actually learned a great deal about his world, both the physical universe and the Deity who rules it:

I seemed to them to have convinced myself of the Manner of my own Original, from that of other Creatures; and, from the Works of the Creation, to have inferred the Being of the Creator. The utter Incapacity of Thought in Matter, as such, seemed to have instructed me in the Independence of these one upon another; and from hence I appeared to have gathered the natural Incorruptibility of the thinking Principle.[82]

Automathes even comes to understand the concept of a fallen world through the accidental fire he starts that burns the island, destroys animals and vegetation, and gives him a sense of guilt. At the end Automathes restates his conviction that education is "supernatural in its Original" and that without education man lives as a beast.

Automathes may live in nature, but his orientation is toward civilization. He learns to play with the artifacts left on the island by his father and mother, to listen to harmonies from a music box, and to use the tools for cultivating a garden. Naked rather than draped, like a Wild Man or savage, in the skins of beasts, he is a vegetarian and is easily shocked by seeing men come to his island to slaughter the deer. And so far from idealizing the solitary life, Kirkby continually underscores the social nature of mankind. In short, with Automathes the brutish Wild Man has become a being who would seem more at home in a pastoral setting than in the wilderness. On Automathes' island nature is like "the Paradise of our first Parents, an universal Peace reigning through the whole Animal Creation."[83] Locke's influence pervades Kirkby's work, and Rousseau had not yet written his *Discours sur les Origines de l'Inégalité* to revive interest in the savage and what the primitive life could offer Western civilization. Thus if Automathes succeeds in educating himself, it is only by doing this that he succeeds in living a truly human life. For if education is natural to man, as Kirkby thought, the legendary Wild Man would have to be conceived as a creature living in a manner contrary to the true, indeed the natural, bent of mankind.[84]

The lesson of Automathes was not very different from that read by Defoe on Peter the wild boy:

Education seems to me to be the only specifick Remedy for all the Imperfections of Nature; . . . all the Difference in Souls, or the greatest Part at least, that is to say, between the Dull and the Bright, the Sensible and Insensible, the

Active and the Indolent, the Capable and the Incapable, are owing to, and derive from this one Article: That the Man is a Rational, or a Stupid, just as he is handled by his Teachers; and that as he can neither speak, read, write, dance, swim, fence, or perform some of the best and most necessary Actions of Life without being taught, so neither can he know, think, retain, judge, discern, distinguish, determine, or any of those Operations, in which the Soul is wholly the Operator, without the Guidance of an Instructor.[85]

And although this emphasis on educating the Wild Man was what has had the most practical application to theories of educational psychology, the wits of the time were not without point in suggesting that it was Peter who should be the teacher.

In fact, *The Manifesto of Lord Peter* pretends to reveal him as the son of a philosopher:

This Great Man, from a deep Sense of the Miseries brought upon Mankind by being civiliz'd, condescended to dedicate his only Son to an Experiment, by which he did not doubt but he should convince the World, how much a nobler Creature a Wild Man was than a Tame one. A Curse (quoth he) on all those whimsical Coxcombs, who by Fiddling, Singing, Drinking and Dancing, have erected Governments, built Cities, and spoil'd the noblest Animal of the Creation.[86]

The message of this work is naturalistic, but even Defoe indulged in the speculation that if one did allow Peter rational choice, it "would indeed be a terrible Satyr upon the present inspir'd Age" if "he should see it reasonable to chuse to continue silent and mute, to live and converse with the Quadrupeds of the Forest, and retire again from human Society, rather than dwell among the inform'd Part of Mankind."[87] And at least one piece, *Vivitur Ingenio,* pretended to be a series of wise speculations on manners and morals written by the father of the wild boy.[88]

But these were rare. It was Voltaire who spoke for the mainstream of the Enlightenment when he rejected the idea of the noble, solitary Wild Man, asserting what Blumenbach was to attempt to prove scientifically many decades later:

Men in general have ever been what they now are: by this I would not mean to say that they always had fine cities, cannon that were twenty-four-pounders, comic operas, and religious convents; but man always had the same instinct, which prompted him to love himself, in the companion of his pleasures, in his children, in his grandchildren, in the works of his hands.

This is immutable all over the universe. The foundation of society ever existing, there has therefore ever been some society, and we were consequently not made to live like bears.

Voltaire maintained that the discovery of a few children like Peter proved nothing. And with the faith of his age he asserted that man's true quality could be discovered in the reason given to him by God—a reason that "subsists in despite of all the passions which oppose it, in despite of those tyrants who would drown it in blood, in despite of those impostors who would annihilate it by superstition."[89]

V. Gulliver Meets the Wild Man

Probably the most important work connected with the various transmutations of the Wild Man is *Gulliver's Travels*. Even before we come upon the Yahoos, we find, in the materials associated with the Wild Man, numerous works from which Swift might have taken hints, from the men so small that they could be carried about in cages to the tales of wild

Gulliver attacked by the Yahoos. From Jonathan Swift, *Gulliver's Travels* (London, 1755).

men and their encounters with giants.[90] But it is particularly when we meet the Yahoos in the fourth part that we encounter a version of the Wild Man myth. In so many ways they represent what was reported of orangutans and sometimes of the Hottentot. Like Tyson's orangutan, they are capable of going on their hind legs, though they generally travel on all fours;[91] like the traditional Wild Man, they are hairy. The female Yahoo who attacks Gulliver resembles those lascivious male anthropoids who were so fond of women, and the long dugs of the females that hang down to the ground recall the Hottentot women who would throw their breasts over their shoulders to feed their children. As was sometimes reported of the Hottentots, the Yahoos are incapable of language and merely howl, grin, or chatter. D'Aubignac had discussed a type of ape or "Satyr," who, like the most lascivious of the Yahoos, was covered with red hair.[92] As did Monboddo, D'Aubignac believed reports of apes that were capable of speaking a few words, but whatever the capacity of apes to articulate a word or two, the most important distinction between man and both Wild Man and orangutan remained language, and here the credentials of the Yahoos are impeccable enough.

And yet everything is wrong. The vileness of the Yahoos is unmatched even in the most horrible descriptions of the Hottentot. The question is how nature could produce such a creature. In one late work on Peter the wild boy, Peter is depicted as having learned enough evil from the beasts he met in the forest to qualify for a modern politician:

> And thus the Mountains did produce
> Something, that's neither Man nor Mouse,
> In Soul and Body a poor Creature,
> The falsest, meanest Thing in Nature
> To no one single Virtue prone,
> But ev'ry Vice he made his own.[93]

Yet this is a minor indictment against nature compared with the picture of degenerated man in the Yahoos. There can be no doubt that the Yahoos are wild men, but whereas the treatment of Peter almost always tends to idealize the virtues that he may have absorbed from nature, Swift portrays man as the one creature that perverts nature—a being detestable to everything else in the creation. Like Hai ibn Yokdhan, the Yahoos are associated with a myth of spontaneous generation from the action of the sun, but there is considerable difference. The Yahoos may have been produced by the action of the sun on "corrupted Mud and Slime, or from the Ooze and Froth of the Sea,"[94] whereas Hai ibn Yokdhan was sometimes thought to have been produced by a direct act of God infusing a spirit into matter through the sun's power. The fact is that although the word "civilized" is used by Gulliver to describe his and his European compatriots' superiority over the Yahoo, yet Gulliver's master remarks that man has made no use of his reason other "than to improve and multiply those Vices, whereof their Brethren in this Country had only the Share that Nature allotted them."[95] Thus the cry to "civilize" Peter into man would seem futile in Swift's context. It would merely amount to improving his capacity to destroy his fellowman without changing his basic nature.

The only glimpse we get of natural man comes toward the end, when Gulliver encounters some natives, "stark naked, Men, Women and Children round a Fire." They discover Gulliver and wound him with an arrow, but Gulliver prefers "rather to trust my self among these *Barbarians,* than live with *European Yahoos.*"[96] The statement is significant, for if the Yahoo and the European are identified, such is not the case with the savage. The savages attack him to protect their wives and children, and Gulliver apparently does not feel the same kind of animus toward them that he shows toward his "civilized" Yahoos. This reaction is reflected in his condemnation of what he ironically calls a *"modern Colony,"* founded upon the conquest of a "harmless People" who may have treated them with kindness. Swift regretted that his idea of viewing Europe through the eyes of a savage had been appropriated from him by a number of *The Spectator,* and in *Gulliver's Travels* the natural man is treated with considerable generosity, considering the context.[97] Apparently between the corrupted Wild Man as Yahoo and the civilized Yahoo European there exists, for Swift, a possible middle ground of natural humanity, which is still discoverable in the rare example of a good civilized man—Pedro de Mendez, who rescues Gulliver and treats him well.

But Swift leaves us little to go on here. What is more evident is the parody on the Wild Man as philosopher. Professor Carnochan, in his excellent study of Gulliver, has repeated the idea that the Houyhnhnms are not Stoics. We might put this aside for the moment and merely assert that Gulliver's imitation of the Houyhnhnms is questionably modeled on the Stoics' idea of the Philosophic man's return to the state of nature to pursue a life of reason.[98] What I am suggesting, in short, is that too much emphasis has been put on the Houyhnhnms themselves and not enough on Gulliver's imitation of them.

We should be able to recognize the pattern well enough by this time. Gulliver's clothes gradually decay, and he assumes the garb of Crusoe and Yokdhan—the animal skin. His shoes too are replaced by the skin of a

Yahoo. He devotes himself to the task of self-improvement and laments: "I had also sometimes the Honour of attending my Master in his Visits to others. I never presumed to speak, except in answer to a Question; and then I did it with inward Regret, because it was a Loss of so much Time for improving my self."[99] And within this society, which lacks all but the simplest inventions and which has not searched into the bowels of the earth to find iron or bothered with the invention of writing, Gulliver can approximate the life that should prepare him for the life of a philosopher:

No Man could more verify the Truth of these two Maxims, *That, Nature is very easily satisfied*; and, *That, Necessity is the Mother of Invention*. I enjoyed perfect Health of Body, and Tranquility of Mind; I did not feel the Treachery or Inconstancy of a Friend, nor the Injuries of a secret or open Enemy. I had no Occasion of bribing, flattering or pimping, to procure the Favour of any great Man, or of his Minion. . . . No Pride, Vanity or Affectation: No Fops, Bullies, Drunkards, strolling Whores, or Poxes: No ranting, lewd, expensive Wives: No stupid, proud Pedants: No importunate, overbearing, quarrelsome, noisy, roaring, empty, conceited, swearing Companions: No Scoundrels raised from the Dust upon the Merit of their Vices; or Nobility thrown into it on account of their Virtues: No Lords, Fidlers, Judges or Dancing-masters.[100]

Gulliver is speaking of a world which has avoided the products of human passions.

The Houyhnhnms, of course, are not entirely without emotions. We are told, for example, that "their Language expressed the Passions very well," but these are rational passions, or "good affections," which the Stoics allowed to men of wisdom and virtue.[101] Gulliver continues to display elements of pride and vanity, but he believes that by avoiding the outward show of passions he can somehow become a better being. It is he, not the Houyhnhnms, who is guilty of stoic pride. Hence after the Houyhnhnms banish him, he searches for a Crusoe-like existence.

My Design was, if possible, to discover some small Island uninhabited, yet sufficient by my Labour to furnish me with Necessaries of Life, which I would have thought a greater Happiness than to be first Minister in the politest Court of *Europe*; so horrible was the Idea I conceived to returning to live in the Society and under the Government of *Yahoos*. For in such a Solitude as I desired, I could at least enjoy my own Thoughts, and reflect with Delight on the Virtues of those inimitable *Houyhnhnms*, without any Opportunity of degenerating into the Vices and Corruptions of my own Species.[102]

It takes all the persuasion of Pedro de Mendez to convince Gulliver that such an island is not to be found.

As for the Houyhnhnms, they are, as Gulliver suggests, "inimitable."

That is one of the reasons that Gulliver's attempt to imitate them might seem a form of madness—madness, at least, to the ordinary civilized man. They belong to the long tradition of the rational animal,[103] and more particularly, the dialogue between Ulysses, Circe, and Gryllus in Plutarch's *Moralia*. Gryllus, now converted into an animal, informs Ulysses of his newfound hatred for gold and silver: "Our Manner of living is accustom'd to necessary Pleasures and Desires; and as for those Pleasures which are not necessary, but only natural, we make such a Use of them as is neither without Order nor Moderation."[104] At the end of this dialogue, Ulysses warns Gryllus that it is not right that animals which lack a knowledge of the Deity should have reason, and the very fact that the Houyhnhnms are only creatures who have reached the height of rationality rather than ideal Christian beings should not be forgotten. But the satire is directed at man, not at the Houyhnhnms themselves. And if they are comic animals, it is only because of the human analogy. The ability of the sorrel nag to thread a needle may seem comic enough, but it is Gulliver who asks her to perform this act. The Houyhnhnms themselves have no use for needles because they do not wear clothes.

Defoe complained that some of the stories about Peter were "Romantick." If there was an effort to make him into a potential Houyhnhnm, it was because those writers saw him in terms of one form of Western utopia. If Gulliver succumbs to it himself, he is merely following the illusory philosophic ideal of his society. And the moral is clear enough. Society is a human product, and man would do well to reform himself within his own limitations rather than striving, like the Stoics, for an ideal beyond human limitations. Gulliver's master finds that, with the exception of sexual perversion, almost every vicious quality in civilized man about which Gulliver tells him is incipient in the *wild men* of his country—the Yahoos. Man, then, is less likely to raise himself to the level of the Houyhnhnms, who are physically equipped with reason and moderate affections, than to degenerate into the condition of the Yahoos.[105]

Lévi-Strauss speaks at one point of his desire "to pursue 'the primitive' [in man] to its furthest point," though it is hardly surprising that when he feels he encountered the quintessential "primitive" in a section of *Tristes Tropiques* appropriately called "Crusoe Country," he discovers no means of communicating with the members of a strange and savage tribe who seem to represent the ideal he has been searching for.[106] Lévi-Strauss does not draw any conclusions from this episode, but it is enlightening for the student of eighteenth-century primitivism. In searching for the Wild Man in Peter, they were actually searching for that mythical creature in their own psyche, but as Gulliver discovered, man's mirror image can often be unflattering—so unflattering that we turn away and search outside ourselves for a purity that the mirror did not show but that we continue to believe is there.

NOTES

1. *Correspondence,* ed. Harold Williams (Oxford, 1963), III, 128.

2. J. F. Blumenbach, *Contributions to Natural History, Part II,* in *Anthropological Treatises,* trans. Thomas Bendyshe (London, 1865), p. 329.

3. See *Ancient Metaphysics* (London, 1784), III, 57–64, 367–75. Monboddo had previously discussed Peter's case in *Of the Origin and Progress of Language,* 2d ed. (Edinburgh, 1774), I, 186–87.

4. In *Mere Nature Delineated,* by Daniel Defoe (London, 1726), p. 10; *St. James's Evening Post,* 14 December 1725; *British Journal,* 18 December 1725; and *Mist's Journal,* 18 December 1725.

5. *Ancient Metaphysics,* III, 59, 61.

6. *Miscellaneous Poems by Several Hands,* ed. David Lewis (London, 1726), I, 305–06.

7. Arthur O. Lovejoy and George Boas, *A Documentary History of Primitivism and Related Ideas,* I (Baltimore, 1935), 1–22.

8. Claude Lévi-Strauss, *Tristes Tropiques,* trans. John Russell (New York, 1964), p. 127.

9. William van Lennep reports fourteen editions of *Mucedorus* between 1660 and 1700 alone. See *The London Stage, 1660–1800; Part I: 1660–1700,* ed. William van Lennep et al. (Carbondale, Ill., 1965), p. cxxii. For a list of English editions of *Valentine and Orson,* see W. Seelman, "Valentine and Namelos," *Niederdeutsche Denkmaler* (1884), IV, 33–36.

10. *Mere Nature Delineated,* p. 8.

11. *The History of Valentine and Orson* [London, 1700 ?], pp. 39, 50.

12. Pedro Calderón de la Barca, *Obras Completas,* ed. A. Valbuena Briones (Madrid, 1966), I, 1110.

13. See *A Most Pleasant Comedy of Mucedorus* (London, 1668), sigs. D2–E1, and Richard Bernheimer, *Wild Men in the Middle Ages* (Cambridge, Mass., 1952), pp. 55, 124–25, illustration no. 35.

14. Sigs. E1ᵛ–E2.

15. Erwin Panofsky, *Studies in Iconology* (New York, 1939), pp. 33–67.

16. John Dryden, *The Tempest; Dramatic Works,* ed. Montague Summers (London, 1932), II, 180.

17. Garcilaso de la Vega, *The Royal Commentaries of the Yncas,* trans. Clements Markham (London, 1869), I, 41–45. For an example of a writer using Serrano's tall story to demonstrate regression to an animal state, see Edward Tyson, *Orang-Outang sive Homo Sylvestris or, the Anatomy of a Pygmie,* ed. M. F. Ashley Montagu (1699; rpt. London, 1966), pp. 8–9.

18. *A Voyage to East-India* in *The Travels of Sig. Pietro della Valle, a Noble Roman, into East-India and Arabia Deserta* (London, 1665), p. 331.

19. (London, 1665), p. 19. For a similar comment see "A Relation of Three Years Sufferings of Robert Everard," in *A Collection of Voyage and Travels*, ed. Awnsham Churchill, 3d ed. (London, 1732), VI, 278. John Locke accused his adversary, Bishop Stillingfleet, of reading the Hottentots out of the human race. See *Mr. Locke's Reply to the Bishop of Worcester's Answer to His Second Letter*, in *Works* (London, 1824), III, 494–97.

20. Tyson, *Orang-Outang*, pp. 8, 42, 55.

21. "A Philological Essay . . . ," bound with Tyson, *Orang-Outang*, pp. 9, 19, 42–43.

22. Richard Blackmore and John Hughes, *The Lay-Monk*, 25 November 1713.

23. Louis Le Comte, *Memoirs and Remarks . . . Made in Above Ten Years Travels through the Empire of China* (1697) (London, 1737), p. 510. It has also been suggested, convincingly enough, that Le Comte is describing a gibbon, but he also reports stories about an animal similar to an orangutan. See Ramona and Desmond Morris, *Men and Apes* (London, 1966), p. 150.

24. William Congreve, *Letters and Documents*, ed. John Hodges (New York, 1964), p. 178.

25. See Francois Hédelin D'Aubignac, *Des Satyres, Brutes, Monstres et Demons* (1627, rpt. Paris, 1888), pp. 64–66.

26. *The History of Poland* (London, 1698), I, 342–43.

27. (London, 1726), pp. 2–3.

28. (London, 1726), title page.

29. *The Most Wonderful Wonder that Ever Appeared to the Wonder of the British Nation* (London, 1726), pp. 4–5.

30. *Essays*, trans. E. J. Trenchman (Oxford, 1927), I, 447.

31. *Most Wonderful Wonder*, p. 8.

32. *Most Wonderful Wonder*, pp. 10–11.

33. *Manifesto of Lord Peter* (London, 1726), p. 6.

34. James Boswell, *Life of Samuel Johnson*, ed. George Birkbeck Hill, rev. L. F. Powell (Oxford, 1934–50), II, 74.

35. *Origin and Progress of Language*, I, 198. That Selkirk was almost inarticulate when rescued has been denied by his biographer; see John Howell, *The Life and Adventures of Alexander Selkirk*, in *The Life and Adventures of Robinson Crusoe*, by Daniel Defoe (Edinburgh, 1847), p. 510.

36. *An Essay Concerning Human Understanding*, ed. Alexander Fraser (New York, 1959), I, 444–48. For Lord Monboddo's remarks on Locke's parrot, see *Origin and Progress of Language*, I, 147.

37. *Ancient Metaphysics*, III, 367.

38. Some investigators have argued that they have detected a language among chimpanzees; see Roger Brown, *Words and Things* (Glencoe, Ill., 1958), pp. 156–72, 179.

39. *Ancient Metaphysics*, III, 67.

40. *Mere Nature Delineated*, p. 17.

41. (London, 1787), p. 44. That Peter died relatively old was a source of embarrassment for myth-makers. In César de Saussure's account of Peter, which included a

description of the savage at court, he reported that the wild boy "pined away and died about two months after his arrival in England, and just as he was learning to say a word or two" (*A Foreign View of England in the Reigns of George I and George II*, trans. Van Muyden [London, 1902], p. 150).

42. *Mere Nature Delineated*, p. 43.

43. *Mere Nature Delineated*, p. 61.

44. *Mere Nature Delineated*, p. 61.

45. I borrow this phrase from Roger Brown; see Brown, *Words and Things*, p. 188.

46. *Mere Nature Delineated*, p. 38.

47. In *The Genesis of Language: A Psycholinguistic Approach*, ed. Frank Smith and George Miller (Cambridge, Mass., 1966), pp. 234–35.

48. Claude Lévi-Strauss, *Les Structures Elémentaires de la Parenté* (Paris, 1949), pp. 2–5.

49. J. A. L. Singh and Robert Zingg, *Wolf-Children and Feral Man* (London, 1942).

50. Jean-Jacques Rousseau, *Discours sur les Origines de l'Inégalité* (1754), in *The Political Writings*, ed. C. E. Vaughan (Cambridge, 1915), I, 140.

51. Rousseau, *Discours*, I, 198 (n. c). The question of whether man might be more naturally a quadruped was raised in *Hudibras*, in Samuel Butler's inimitable mocking manner:

> For some philosophers of Late here,
> Write, men have four legs by nature,
> And that 'tis custom makes them go
> Erroneously upon but two;
> B' a boy that lost himself in a wood,
> And growing down t' a man, was wont
> With wolves upon all four to hunt.   (II, i, 725–32)

In his notes to the passage, Butler's eighteenth-century editor, Zachary Grey, listed Peter alongside that hairy quadruped, the wild boy of Liege, and the wolf boy of Hesse.

52. P. 8. The "Herb-eaters" were probably followers of Dr. George Cheyne, whose *Essay of Health and Long Life* (London, 1725) recommended eating vegetables, restrictions on meat and drink, and taking cold baths in winter.

53. *Manifesto of Lord Peter*, pp. 5, 7–9.

54. *Some Yeares Travels into Africa & Asia* (London, 1665), p. 23. For a discussion of these alternations between contempt and admiration for the savage, see R. W. Frantz, *The English Traveler and the Movement of Ideas, 1660–1732* (Lincoln, Nebr., 1967), pp. 104, 112, 115, 117.

55. *Some Yeares Travels*, pp. 23, 29, 122.

56. John Toland, *A Collection of Several Pieces* (London, 1726), II, 424. Toland's savage is remarkably like the old Tahitian who bids farewell to Bougainville in Diderot's famous *Supplément au Voyage de Bougainville*, telling the explorer that Western civilization can offer nothing to his people; see Denis Diderot, *Oeuvres*, ed. André Billy (Paris, 1951), pp. 969–74.

57. Toland, *Collection*, II, 427. A recent work has tended to suggest that, compared with the Negroes, the Indians were idealized. Although there is some truth in this,

some case could be made for the opposite viewpoint; cf. Roy Harvey Pearce, *The Savages of America* (Baltimore, 1953), pp. 5–31, and Winthrop Jordan, *White Over Black* (Baltimore, 1968), pp. 89–91. See also George Warren's criticism of the cruel treatment of black slaves and his praise of their fortitude in facing torture and death when they are caught attempting to escape. Warren's work, which formed an important source for Aphra Behn's *Oroonoko*, described the Indians as "a People Cowardly and Treacherous" (*An Impartial Description of Surinam* [London, 1667], pp. 19, 23).

58. *Ancient Metaphysics*, III, 69. See also Rousseau, *Discours*, I, 207–12 (n. j).

59. If the comparison of an orangutan with Achilles seems ludicrous to the modern reader, it should be pointed out that the much admired Giambattista Vico, who wrote a few decades before Monboddo, maintained that the men of the heroic age lacked articulate speech; see *The New Science of Giambattista Vico*, trans. Thomas Bergin and Max Fisch (Ithaca, 1948), p. 179 (sec. 560).

60. *Origin and Progress of Language*, I, ii–iii. See also Arthur O. Lovejoy, "Monboddo and Rousseau," *Modern Philology*, 30 (1933), 275–96. It is certainly true that wild men like the wild boy of Aveyron and Ishi seemed to have been healthier in the woods than in civilization.

61. *Ancient Metaphysics*, III, 57–62.

62. *Origin and Progress of Language*, I, 22–23.

63. *Ad Lucilium Epistulae Morales*, trans. Richard Gummere, Loeb Library ed. (London, 1920), II, 407–09 (epistle 90).

64. Bernheimer, *Wild Men in the Middle Ages*, p. 103.

65. Pierre Charron, *Of Wisdom*, trans. George Stanhope (London, 1707), I, 177, 263.

66. *Of Wisdom*, II, 31.

67. Antoine Le Grand, *Man Without Passion: or, The Wise Stoick* (London, 1675), p. 27. The emblematic illustration before English versions of Charron's work shows wisdom as a naked woman on a pedestal to which four other women—Passion, Opinion, Superstition, and Pedantic Science—are chained.

68. The translator, Simon Ockley, regarded the idea that men might "without any external Means, attain to the Knowledge of all things necessary to Salvation, and even to the Beatifick Vision it self, whilst in this State," as a dangerous doctrine. Like Defoe, who thought Peter's condition disproved the thesis that religion was an innate principle, Ockley attacked all "Quietists," "Mysticks," and "Enthusiasts" who wished a direct communication with God. See *The Improvement of Human Reason* (London, 1708), pp. 168–75.

69. Gracián, *The Critick*, trans. Paul Rycaut (London, 1681), sig. A8.

70. See *Memoirs for the Curious* (London, 1701), I, 47.

71. *The Critick*, pp. 4–6.

72. *The Critick*, p. 9.

73. *The Critick*, p. 39.

74. *The Critick*, p. 158.

75. *Defoe and the Nature of Man* (Oxford, 1963), p. 25. A work entitled *The Idea of Robinson Crusoe* (Watford, Eng., 1930), by A. C. R. Pastor, is entirely devoted to Tufail's book, with little more than a beginning paragraph to suggest any comparison between the two solitaries.

76. *Spirit of Laws,* trans. Thomas Nugent (Cincinnati, 1886), I, 4.

77. Daniel Defoe, *The Life and Strange Surprizing Adventures of Robinson Crusoe* (Oxford, 1927), I, 105–06.

78. Large sections were taken from an earlier work, *The History of Autonous* (1736), but it was Kirkby's hero, Automathes, who attracted attention.

79. *The Capacity and Extent of the Human Understanding* (London, 1747), pp. 21–22 (hereafter cited as *Automathes*). The study of wild men was eventually to have a direct influence on educational methods. Jean-Marc-Gaspard Itard, whose attempt at training the wild boy of Aveyron has been the subject of a recent movie by Truffaut, influenced Madame Montessori and her teaching methods. See George Humphrey, ed., *The Wild Boy of Aveyron,* by Jean-Marc-Gaspard Itard (New York, 1962), pp. xvi–xvii.

80. *Automathes,* p. 41.

81. *Automathes,* p. 43.

82. *Automathes,* pp. 76–77.

83. *Automathes,* p. 53. Hoxie Fairchild argued that the myth of the Noble Savage was distinct from pastoral. There is some truth in this, though it was surely no accident that John Gay moved from a Newgate pastoral, *The Beggar's Opera,* to a tale of noble savages in his sequel, *Polly.* Gay was trying to find an ideal virtue by which his thieves, now turned pirates, might be judged, and unable to find such a standard in the confines of Western civilization, he went outside, to the savages of America. This says less for the distinction between pastoral and the Noble Savage than it does for the growing uneasiness about the artificiality of pastoral as a literary mode; see *The Noble Savage* (New York, 1928), pp. 3, 336.

84. Kirkby's ideas might find some support in modern theories about speech as a motor function rather than as something learned. Contrary to many cases of feral man, there is one case on record of a child brought up in isolation who learned to speak with amazing rapidity and ease. As Ashley Montagu observed, the anthropologist abandons stories of wolf children "regretfully," since they fit so well "into the general theory of personal social development," however unscientific they may be. See Lenneberg, "The Natural History of Language," in *Genesis of Language,* pp. 219–33; Brown, *Words and Things,* pp. 121–92; and M. F. Ashley Montagu, *Anthropology and Human Nature* (Boston, 1957), p. 241.

85. *Mere Nature Delineated,* pp. 61–62.

86. *Manifesto of Lord Peter,* p. 3.

87. *Mere Nature Delineated,* p. 22.

88. (London, 1726).

89. Voltaire, *The Philosophy of History* (New York, 1965), pp. 29–32. For similar attitudes, see Itard, *Wild Boy of Aveyron,* pp. 49–50.

90. See, for example, T. S. Gueulette, "The Adventures of Kolao, the wild Man," *Chinese Tales,* trans. Thomas Stackhouse (London, 1726), II, 20–33, and Tyson, "A Philological Essay," p. 19. Gulliver's experience with a giant monkey in the land of the Brobdingnags is connected with a well-known incident of a monkey that took up a human child, cared for it, and punished the nurse who neglected the baby; see James Wood, "Gulliver and the Monkey of Tralee," *Studies in English Literature,* 9 (1969), 415–26.

91. Tyson, *Orang-Outang,* p. 80. In one satire Peter remarks, "We our selves have

often found it necessary and useful, to employ our Hands as Assistants to our Feet in walking" (*Manifesto of Lord Peter*, p. 10).

92. *De Satyres, Brutes, Monstres, et Demons* (1627; rpt. Paris, 1888), p. 65. It has been noted that the illustrations of the orangutan in Tyson's study depicted him as a "rather dissipated lascivious looking adult"; see M. F. Ashley Montagu, *Edward Tyson* (Philadelphia, 1943), p. 252.

93. *Peter. A Tale* (London, 1744), p. 7.

94. Jonathan Swift, *Gulliver's Travels*, ed. Herbert Davis (Oxford, 1959), p. 271.

95. *Gulliver's Travels*, p. 278.

96. *Gulliver's Travels*, pp. 284–85.

97. *Journal to Stella*, ed. Harold Williams (Oxford, 1948), I, 244. Swift had apparently suggested the idea to Steele as a number of *The Tatler*. Steele may have passed it on to Addison, who wrote *The Spectator*, no. 50, but unless Swift remarked some particular hint as his, there is little reason to believe that Addison would not have been capable of some variations on what was already a fairly common literary device.

98. W. B. Carnochan, *Lemuel Gulliver's Mirror for Man* (Berkeley, 1968), p. 70.

99. *Gulliver's Travels*, p. 277. The Hermaphrodites of Gabriel Foigny's mythical Australia, who resemble the Houyhnhnms in going naked, refusing to recognize man as a rational creature, and in practicing a perfect virtue "purely by their Natural Light," kept an animal much like the Yahoo as a kind of pet, and that is the best description of Gulliver's relation to his master; see *A New Discovery of Terra Incognita Australia, or the Southern World*, trans. John Dunton (London, 1693), pp. 66–71, 78, 104, 124. For some other parallels, see Kathleen Williams, *Jonathan Swift and the Age of Compromise* (Lawrence, Kans., 1968), pp. 180–86.

100. *Gulliver's Travels*, pp. 276–77.

101. *Gulliver's Travels*, p. 226. For a discussion of the Stoics' attitudes toward "good affections," see E. Vernon Arnold, *Roman Stoicism* (Cambridge, 1911), pp. 323–25, 340–41, 354. Swift's description of Houyhnhnm language is similar to what was sometimes thought to be the original language of man. Rousseau wrote that such a language "would be sung rather than spoken. Most of the root words would be imitative sounds or accents of passion, or effects of sense objects" (Rousseau and Herder, *On the Origin of Language*, trans. John Moran and Alexander Gore [New York, 1966], p. 15).

102. *Gulliver's Travels*, p. 283.

103. See John Monteverde, "The Rational Animal in English Literature 1603–1735." Diss. University of California, Los Angeles 1956, pp. 292, 334, 336, and R. S. Crane, "The Houyhnhnms, the Yahoos, and the History of Ideas," *Reason and the Imagination*, ed. Joseph Mazzeo (New York, 1962), pp. 231–53.

104. Plutarch, *Morals*, trans. Sir A. J. (London, 1718), V, 211.

105. Gulliver's master believes in the theory of degeneration, and Tyson quotes Aelian as his authority for a tribe of wild men who "for want of Education . . . and by their living wild in the Woods . . . lost their Learning and their Speech" ("A Philological Essay," p. 43).

106. P. 326.

The Wild Man's Return:
The Enclosed Vision
of Rousseau's Discourses

 GEOFFREY SYMCOX

Our reflexes have been conditioned with such Pavlovian precision that Rousseau's name always evokes the same association: the Noble Savage. To us Rousseau is still the high priest of the cult of primitivism, who shocked the jaded sensibilities of the Age of Reason by extolling a factitious age of lost innocence and unspoiled virtue, embodied in the person of the Noble Savage, whom he supposedly invented and popularized. Rousseau's Savage stands at the center of his political theory, and as a touchstone for measuring the artificiality of existing society, marks one of the points of departure for the revolution of Sensibility. The Noble Savage seems to bear a close resemblance to Jean-Jacques himself and to reflect his social attitudes: his unease in a world of salons and *beaux esprits;* his rejection, in the name of a higher vision of man's goodness, of a society which he felt instinctively to be too rationalistic, too formalistic. Rousseau's Savage supposedly connotes the supremacy of feeling over reason, and the uncritical rejection of European culture in favor of a better life, closer to nature, in which man's innate goodness would finally be liberated. In other words, the argument goes, Rousseau's Savage can be dismissed as a projection of his own social insecurity and simplistic idealism. Generations of hostile scholarship have helped form our image of Rousseau, compounded equally of neurosis and naïveté, and have linked him to the cult of the Noble Savage, which he supposedly fathered and then foisted onto the minds of his time. The purpose of this essay will be to use recent work on Rousseau and his Savage in order to show that the latter already had a long and distinguished career before Jean-Jacques adopted him; that he had largely superseded his ancestor, the Wild Man, and had gained general acceptance by the early eighteenth century; and that the originality of Rousseau's use of this stock figure lay in his rediscovering certain attributes of the Wild Man, and incorporating them in a new and improved version of the Noble Savage. Close examination will reveal that Rousseau's Noble Savage is a very sophisticated creature, radically different from the prosaic figures of standardized virtue used by Rousseau's contemporaries. Our task will therefore be to trace how the crude and mysterious figure of the Wild Man was disciplined and domesticated, emerging in the eighteenth century as the refined and rational Savage, and then to see how Rousseau turned back to the Wild Man in search of what the Savage lacked: emotions.

Over the last couple of generations there has been a tendency to debunk the popular myths about Rousseau and to suggest that his ideas were not so naïve after all.[1] Nor were they so original. In many ways Rousseau is typical of the general movement of ideas which was taking place around the middle of the eighteenth century. This was a crucial period, when developments in the natural sciences and a growing awareness of other cultures were beginning to revolutionize European social and political thought. This was the period which saw the origins of modern sociology, anthropology, ethnography, linguistics, and historiography, and Rousseau occupies a central place in this movement. The older view of the Enlightenment as a period of shared assumptions and homogeneity of thought is being abandoned; it was a period of great intellectual diversity, beset by crosscurrents and contradictions. Rousseau's thought evolves out of the intellectual milieu of the time, with all its variety: the same atmosphere that produced the Encyclopedists and the *philosophes*, his supposed enemies. He does not represent a clear-cut reaction against the prevailing currents of thought of the mid-eighteenth century; he is part of them, and the concept of opposition between him and his more "rationalist" contemporaries must be abandoned. Such opposition as there was came later and was the product more of personal than of intellectual differences. This essay will concentrate on the period when Rousseau was still very much a part of the intellectual world he was later to reject, and it will examine the chief productions of this period, the *First* and *Second Discourses*, to show that he was drawing on a common stock of ideas and reaching conclusions similar in many ways to those of his contemporaries. He was not the only thinker of the time to be preoccupied by the question of the Noble Savage, which was in a wider sense the whole problem of the origins and true nature of human society.[2]

Rousseau's fascination with primitive cultures was shared by his age and was soon to be intensified by the great series of discoveries in the Pacific which began in the 1760s. But Rousseau's study of primitive cultures and hypothetical early men,was to take him farther than his contemporaries in criticizing society as he found it: he would urge not just the modification of existing social forms, but their total renewal. This should not obscure the fact that he and the other theorists of his time were starting from the same point and working within a well-established tradition of political criticism, based on a belief in the innate goodness—or at least variety, mutability, or educability—of human nature. Since the discoveries of the fifteenth century, Europeans had been turning to alien cultures in search of a profounder understanding of their own, and in the process had projected their own views of human nature and society onto the unsuspecting indigenes. The Wild Man who symbolized the newly discovered cultures soon became the source of a movement of cultural relativism and political criticism, a mirror to hold up to the depravity of European morals and institutions. Under the influence of Jesuit solicitude and Cartesian orderliness, he was then purged of his grosser attributes, without losing his moral and political implications. He merely changed his name to the Noble Savage and remained at the center of a tradition of social criticism which continued from Montaigne through Fénelon to Rousseau and Diderot. A brief account of this transformation is necessary if we are to see Rousseau's Noble Savage in proper perspective.

From the early sixteenth century, travel literature enjoyed a wide vogue in France; late medieval romances vied with "true accounts" of Renaissance discoveries; Sir John Mandeville and Amerigo Vespucci rubbed shoulders in happy confusion.[3] In time the tales of Palestine and of feats of arms against the Turk gave way to reports of the Indies, Africa, and farther Asia. Meanwhile a whole new genre of travel fiction appeared, appealing to the same public, using the same material, and equally influential in forming popular notions of foreign lands. This literature of real or imagined voyages soon came to be associated with political and social criticism: comparison with European cultural norms was inevitable and often invidious. Utopias were customarily located in a mythical land whose wise inhabitants and subtly balanced institutions were to serve as a model for the wayward states of Europe. Much of the travel literature available in France dealt with the Spanish Empire in the Americas, whose exotic peoples provided ample material for comparison with the customs of the Old World. The figure of the Wild Man at this time was composed largely of characteristics drawn from the Caribs or Indians whom the Spaniards had found and subjugated, and much of the contradiction within the idea

of the Wild Man can be traced to the diversity of the peoples on which
he was based. Evidence was available for views of the non-European
as either barbaric or enlightened, primitive or sophisticated, agelessly
wise or childishly simple. Faced with this ambiguity in the Wild Man's
personality, and overwhelmed by the strangeness of cultures so different
from their own, early French travel writers would adopt one of two stand-
points. Either they would praise the wisdom and uncorrupted virtue of
the indigenes, or they would damn them for their cannibalism, idolatry,
and other reprehensible practices. A writer's attitude usually depended
upon his religion: A Catholic would dwell on the barbarity of the native
peoples and infer that the Spanish conquest had been a blessing, bringing
the benefits of civilization and the true religion. A Huguenot naturally
stressed the primitive virtues of the conquered peoples and glossed over
their nastier habits, in order to show that the bigoted and rapacious Spaniards were enslaving their moral superiors.

But the mere existence of these alien civilizations opened new perspectives which were apparent to every writer, regardless of the religious ax
he chose to grind. Obviously, the fact that whole nations had managed
to survive and prosper without the benefit of Holy Writ posed interesting
questions for orthodox theology, whether Catholic or Protestant. The
problem of how these peoples were to be governed gave enormous impetus to the development of the theory of natural law. It was evident that
whole cultures existed, and in some instances had attained very high
levels of development, without the trappings that Europeans had hitherto
considered indispensable. Furthermore, it had to be admitted that some
at least of their customs were better and wiser than those of Europe, and
that European practices did not necessarily constitute the ultimate standard on which judgment could be based. Montaigne observed in a famous
passage:

Everyone terms barbarity, whatever is not of his own customs; in truth it seems
that we have no view of what is true and reasonable, except the example and
idea of the customs and practices of the country in which we live.

We may call them barbarians then, if we are judging by the rules of reason,
but not if we are judging by comparison with ourselves, who surpass them in
every sort of barbarity.[4]

Acquaintance with the Wild Man soon led to skepticism and cultural
relativism.

With the foundation of New France in the early seventeenth century, a
new, distinctively French travel literature began to appear. From 1632

the Jesuits became the driving force in the missions to Canada, and to stimulate interest at home they published regular *Relations* describing their work among the Indians. This vast corpus of evidence focused the attention of French thinkers on the North American Indian, so that he became the definitive figure on whom concepts of the Wild Man were based. Soon he became the prototype of the Noble Savage, against whom civilized values were to be judged. His progress from ambivalent primitiveness to nobility was largely due to the artful presentation of his virtues by the Jesuits. The cruder aspects of the Wild Man now quietly dropped away; ambiguity was resolved by discarding his more obviously disturbing features. Jesuit theology encouraged the adoption of an optimistic view of human nature and led the missionaries to paint a favorable—not to say rosy—picture of the natives of Canada. Their information came mainly from their knowledge of the more friendly and peaceable tribes, such as the Huron, but even the fierce and warlike Iroquois could not completely dampen the enthusiasm of the Jesuit fathers.[5] Individual variations apart, the general picture of the North American Indian presented in the Jesuit *Relations* was one of uncorrupted virtue and innate nobility. Some of the bolder missionaries even speculated that the Indians might be free from original sin. A tradition of French literature was established which was to persist through Fénelon and Voltaire to Châteaubriand, and in this tradition Rousseau takes his place.

At first sight it may seem odd that the Jesuits reported so favorably on the Indians, who after all were idolaters liable to frequent lapses, and who did not always take kindly to the settled way of life prescribed for them. But the Jesuits believed in the goodness of man and held that no sinner was ultimately irredeemable. In any case, the Indians lacked many of the vices which the Jesuits were accustomed to encounter in Europe, and this led the authors of the *Relations* to dwell upon the truthfulness, innocence, and strong moral sense of their charges. The Indians thus became representative figures of simple virtue, superior in every way to Europeans save in their ignorance of revelation, and this defect would soon be made good by the labors of the missionaries. The work of evangelization was supported by private benefactors, for whom the *Relations* were primarily intended, so that there was a further reason for presenting potential converts in a favorable light: funds contributed to the missions would accomplish the worthy task of bringing these already noble savages to the final stage of earthly perfection by teaching them the true religion. Outside Canada the Jesuits took a similarly benevolent view of the people they evangelized. Their communities in Paraguay isolated the

Indians there from corrupting contact with Europeans and sought as far as possible to maintain the primitive simplicity of their way of life. Jesuit missionaries to the Orient reported in glowing terms on the ancient wisdom and innate virtue of the Chinese, who also seemed to escape complete perfection only through their lack of the true faith. The eighteenth century took over these Jesuit accounts of China and made them the basis of a cult extolling all things Chinese, contrasting Confucian wisdom with Christian bigotry.[6] The Jesuit missionaries were godfathers to the Noble Savage.

Under the urbane and benign influence of the Jesuits, the ambiguous and intractable Wild Man became reasonable and unequivocally virtuous. Another influence may also have been at work to hasten this transformation. The suppression of the animal qualities of spontaneity and naturalness, of lust and violence, hitherto displayed by the Wild Man, parallels the seventeenth century's search for order and rationality. The increasing discipline which Europeans were imposing on their own spirits was projected onto the Wild Man, tempering his passions with Cartesian restraint. The ideal form of virtue became rational rather than natural—the ideal of the *honnête homme*. Reason and scientific progress would not permit the continued existence of a disorderly figure like the Wild Man.[7]

The emergent figure of the Noble Savage soon produced its effect on travel literature, particularly in that genre of imaginary voyages which had long been popular, and which had always contained an undertone of social criticism. In these seventeenth-century "fantastic voyages,"[8] utopian political theory masqueraded as authentic travel reportage. Details culled from real voyages were used to lend conviction to the political message. By far the most influential of these imaginary voyages was Fénelon's *Télémaque*, written originally as a didactic entertainment for the Duke of Burgundy, heir to the French throne, and published in 1699.[9] It differs from other works of its type only in that its setting is ancient Greece rather than a lost island in the Indies or the fabulous Austral continent. Under the guidance of Mentor (personified wisdom), Telemachus travels to a variety of strange lands, each of which has lessons for him. The book can be read as a sequel to *The Odyssey*, but it was in fact a critique of Louis XIV's government, to which Fénelon was bitterly hostile on moral and political grounds. Fénelon believed that man's inherent goodness would permit him to build a society which need not be repressive, as he felt France had become under Louis XIV, and in the mythical land of La Bétique (book VI) he described such a community for the edification of Telemachus and the young Duke of Burgundy. Here the inhabitants were wise and happy because they lived in harmony with nature, tilling the soil, and avoiding the corrupting influence of city life and wealth. Their pattern of existence bears more than a passing resemblance to that of the Indians described in the Jesuit *Relations*. "Here in 1699 are the fullblown 'good savages' of the 18th century and the poetic, nomadic Indians of Châteaubriand."[10] Here too, it may be noted, is another guiding theme of eighteenth-century social criticism which emerges in a modified form in Rousseau: the return to nature. Fénelon's literary ability made *Télémaque* a success whereas other, less elegant imaginary voyages had failed. It reached a wide public and maintained its popularity through the eighteenth century. Rousseau apparently admired it, for in *Emile* he prescribed *Télémaque* as suitable reading for the young girl Sophie, whereas Emile himself was to read *Robinson Crusoe*.[11]

Fénelon's noble Greeks—or thinly disguised Hurons—were only a small part of the crowd of exotic figures who by the end of the seventeenth century were holding European manners and institutions up to criticism and even ridicule. It is no accident that Paul Hazard chose to start his great study of the shift in European consciousness during this period with a study of these literary figures, for they played a central role in the new direction of ideas.[12] The Noble Savage had by this time assumed a bewildering range of disguises; he might appear as a subtle Persian, a sardonic Turk living at Paris and reporting on the curious customs of the natives, an agelessly wise Chinese, or a simple and upright Huron. But his message was always the same: man could live justly and well even without the benefit of European culture and religion, if only he practiced what was natural for him. Regardless of their different cultural backgrounds, these wise lay-figures all agreed that the secret of man's happiness was within himself; by obeying the rule of reason and thus living in harmony with the laws of nature, man could achieve justice and contentment. But first he must rid himself of the restrictions imposed upon him by his artificial way of life, to allow free play to his innate goodness and reasonableness. True ethics were rooted not in the commandments of religion but in human nature, and in fact the subversive Bayle was to go so far as to suggest that a society of atheists could be every bit as moral as a society of Christians, if not more so.[13]

The cult of the Noble Savage, with all its political overtones, was thus fully formed by the beginning of the eighteenth century. A belief in the natural goodness of man, coupled with a critique of European cultural assumptions, made its appearance long before Rousseau. Seventeenth-century travel literature formed the foundation of these revolutionary ideas which were to gather momentum steadily in the next century and become the common property of nearly every political critic.

In the early eighteenth century, the great flood of travel books began to ebb a little. Exploration and discovery slowed down, hampered by the colonial rivalries of the great powers, and did not really resume until after 1763, when the emergence of England as the dominant colonial power abated these struggles for a time. Not until the expeditions of Bougainville and Cook opened the Pacific to Western eyes in the 1760s and 1770s did Europeans again make contact with unknown cultures. In the intervening period only a few expeditions took place, and such voyages as were made produced little impact in Europe. In the first years of the eighteenth century, French traders began to reach the Pacific; Vitus Bering explored parts of the northern Pacific for Peter the Great; Roggeveen and Anson circumnavigated the globe and made a few minor discoveries; the dilettante mathematician La Condamine wandered down the Amazon. From a scientific point of view, the most important voyages were those of William Dampier, buccaneer and scientist, undertaken at the turn of the century and recorded in two famous works which were soon translated into the principal European languages.[14]

Eighteenth-century travel literature therefore tended for a long time to take the form of collections of early voyages rather than of accounts of new ones, although there were now signs of a more scientific spirit at work in them. This new and more systematic approach affected both the way in which explorations were conducted and the deductions that were made from their findings. Information about non-European cultures was treated more rigorously in an attempt to throw light on the whole question of the origins of society. It was felt that the Noble Savage was the key to understanding the motives which had originally led men to form their social groupings. What was needed, therefore, was more precise information about the true condition of the Savage. In other words, anthropological data were to be used to solve the historical problem of the origin and development of cultures. Much could be learned about the earliest forms of society by studying cultures which still remained in a primitive stage of development in remote parts of the world, just as speculation about fossils was beginning to feed early conceptions of evolution. In fact, germinating ideas of biological evolution were being applied to society: a static model was being abandoned in favor of one which would allow for change and gradual development. An idea of progress, partly based upon extrapolation from the natural sciences, now began to dominate the study of human cultures. It was accepted that the laws governing the

development of societies were everywhere the same; like individual biological species, they evolved under the influence of environmental factors
such as geography and climate.[15] Study of the Huron or of the Hottentot
would therefore lead to an understanding of the early forms of European
culture, and political theorists scanned the travel literature for evidence
to support their contentions.

The ultimate outcome of the acceptance of an evolutionary model of
society was to render obsolete the traditional, contractual form of political theory. Rousseau's *Social Contract* was to be the last in a great line
of political treatises of this type. The conception of sudden transition, by
means of a contract, from the state of nature to that of political society
was incompatible with the new idea of gradual social evolution. But even
before the publication of the *Social Contract*, Rousseau had joined the
growing number of writers who were adopting the evolutionary model in
their investigations of society. About the middle of the century there was
a large crop of works owing something to this new conception. In 1746
Condillac published his *Essai sur l'origine des connaissances humaines;*
two years later it was followed by the most famous comparative study of
the century, Montesquieu's *Esprit des lois.* The next year the first volume
of Buffon's *Histoire Naturelle* was published, offering suggestive evidence
in favor of an evolutionary view of biology. Among the first parts of the
Histoire Naturelle was a *Histoire particulière de l'homme,* which treated
man as part of a general developmental scheme. In 1750, the year in
which Rousseau's *Discours sur les sciences et les arts* won the prize
offered by the Dijon Academy, the young Turgot was writing his *Plan
de deux discours sur l'histoire universelle,* one of the most important examples of the new method. Rousseau began work on his *Discours sur l'origine
et les fondements de l'inégalité* in 1753 and published it in 1755. It was
followed a year later by the completed version of Voltaire's *Essai sur les
moeurs,* which had been in preparation for over a decade.[16] Rousseau's
interest in the origins of human society was thus part of a general intellectual movement, but he was more aware than most of his contemporaries of the limitations of a method which relied on existing information
about primitive peoples for its basic assumptions. He therefore adopted
a rather different approach to the problem, supplementing the data gathered from travel literature by his own reflection and introspection.

Rousseau and several of his comtemporaries felt the need of more exact
information about primitive cultures; the old anecdotes of sea captains
and missionaries were no longer sufficient. The new systematic outlook
began to communicate itself to geographers and writers of travel litera-

ture. In 1751 Maupertuis brought out his *Lettre sur le progrès des sciences*, in which he outlined—among other projects—a plan for exploring the great continent which he believed to exist in the South Pacific. This continent might well be inhabited by a race of savages or wild men who would be of the greatest interest to science:

It is in the islands of that sea [the Pacific] that voyagers assure us they have seen wild men covered with hair and having tails, a species half-way between ourselves and the monkeys. I would rather spend an hour in conversation with one of them than with the greatest *bel esprit* in Europe.[17]

This passage was soon to attract the formidable mockery of Voltaire, who as the reigning *bel esprit* of Europe no doubt felt slighted by the comparison. But it is instructive to see how Maupertuis took the old stories of wild men with hair and simian characteristics, which go back to the Middle Ages, if not to Herodotus, and began to integrate them into a rudimentary idea of human evolution, making them possibly the earliest version of the "Missing Link." His interest also extended to the fabled giants of Patagonia; he seems to have believed in their existence and advocated an expedition to search them out for the benefit of science. Maupertuis's belief in the great southern continent was shared by the most thorough geographer of the time, the Président de Brosses, who published his *Histoire des navigations aux terres australes* in 1756. This authoritative work summarized and subjected to scrutiny the accounts of earlier travelers and was to exercise an important influence on the Pacific explorers of the next decade. Meanwhile the Abbé Prévost was turning out successive volumes of his *Histoire générale des voyages*, the most significant collection of travel literature of the century. Volume XI, dealing with the Pacific, appeared in 1753 and provided a summary of existing information which de Brosses feared for a moment might render his own work redundant.[18]

Both Bougainville and Cook used the work of de Brosses, and it helped to determine their objectives and methods.[19] Now really for the first time exploration began to be conducted systematically, in a spirit of scientific curiosity, with ethnographers, naturalists, astronomers, and geologists replacing the missionaries and adventurers of earlier days. The expeditions of the later eighteenth century were to provide a vast amount of new information about primitive cultures, many of which were totally unknown to Europeans until that time. The careful reports of the new generation of explorers gradually changed the whole concept of "the state of nature" and its inhabitant—the Noble Savage. The work of Rousseau and his contemporaries, written before this new information became available, was soon to be superseded by writers drawing on fresh material. Later writers, ignoring their debt to the pioneer work of thinkers like Rousseau, and overlooking the insight which allowed him to transcend the limitations of his sources, regarded him as the exponent of an uncritical primitivism discredited by more up-to-date "facts." Rousseau was not scientific enough for the next generation of ethnographers.

Rousseau's interest in primitive man was thus part of a general preoccupation of the mid-eighteenth century which produced the first scientific attempts to examine primitive societies and apply the lessons drawn from them to the problem of the development of human culture. Rousseau was one of the first social thinkers to place the figure of the Noble Savage within a scheme of historical development, to locate him in the dimension of time. A generation before, Vico had suggested that there might be similarities between the way of life of primitive peoples as they were then known and that of the earliest societies recorded in history. He was proposing a concept of historical parallelism which occurs with increasing frequency as the eighteenth century advances, even though there is little to suggest a direct influence from Vico to later proponents of this idea. The *Nuova Scienza* remained almost unknown, and there is no indication that Rousseau had heard of it. A more likely source for the concept of historical parallelism which appears in Rousseau's *Second Discourse* is to be found in the work of some early eighteenth-century Jesuits—Lafitau, Charlevoix, and Buffier—who were in many ways continuers of the dominant themes of the *Relations* of the previous century.[20] Lafitau's work, published in 1724 and known to Rousseau, bears the significant title, *The Customs of the American Savages Compared with the Customs of the Earliest Times.* These Jesuit writers tended to idealize the Indians and to assimilate them to the heroes of Homer and Plutarch, or to the biblical patriarchs. They were using their knowledge of primitive societies to provide a model for the first stage of development of human culture as a whole, as Rousseau was to do a little later, although his analysis was more sophisticated than that of his Jesuit precursors.

One reason for this greater insight lies in Rousseau's method of inquiry. His Savage was not merely an external, stock figure, borrowed from the intellectual baggage of his time; the Savage, for Rousseau, was essentially the Savage within. Nor was he just the traditional Savage, the paragon of ideal virtues operating on a lofty plane of reason. Rousseau's Savage in fact harks back to the older, more passionate figure of the Wild Man. Introspection and the use of imagination rather than pure reason led

Rousseau to rejuvenate the bloodless figure of the Noble Savage by reen-
dowing him with the passions he had lost. The truth, he remarked at the
end of the *First Discourse,* is written in every heart and reposes within
the conscience of each of us.[21] Consciously or unconsciously, Rousseau
was reverting to an older tradition which, although largely submerged by
the newer ideal of rational virtue, had never entirely disappeared. He
internalized the Wild Man and recognized his presence within himself, a
presence which he felt was good and necessary. He came to realize that
the Wild Man exists within us all, even though we may prefer to regard
ourselves as noble savages: below the civilized overlay of reason and
balance lies a deeper substratum of feeling inherited from a primitive
past. Rousseau's rediscovery of the Wild Man was the uncovering and
rehabilitation of the realm of feeling, which he instinctively felt was
essential to an understanding of man and society, and without which
social life could not be tolerable or fulfilling. This recognition of the role
of the emotions was a revolutionary departure which accounts for the
divergence between Rousseau and the other thinkers who operated
within what is apparently the same tradition.

Rousseau's different Noble Savage could be put to different uses. By
restoring his lost emotions, Rousseau made him into a more serviceable
vehicle for explaining the problem of social development which preoccupied his time. Neither the Wild Man nor the Noble Savage, taken separately, could provide an adequate explanation of why social evolution took
place. The complementary forces of reason and passion embodied in the
two figures, if combined, would go much farther toward creating a
dynamic model of human nature which, interacting with exogenous factors like climate and geography (as in Buffon or Montesquieu) could
provide the motive power of development. If man were really rational,
serious doubts could be raised about his motives for entering into civil
society, which might well seem superfluous to a rational and self-sufficient
being. And if man were indeed the child of reason, how had he managed
to create a society which was in so many ways unjust and irrational? The
Noble Savage alone could not adequately explain the formation and later
development of human society. The Wild Man too had serious drawbacks.
His animal gregariousness provided a more satisfactory motive for the
original association in civil society. But his unruly passions would tend—
as in Hobbes—to turn that society into a mechanism for checking and
repressing them. A careful blending of the two principles offered a way
out of this impasse, though it must be admitted that the solution, as

offered in the *Second Discourse,* is still not entirely satisfactory: the problem of the underlying dynamic of social evolution is only partially solved.

There is little need to emphasize how Rousseau's choice of his intuitive method was dictated by his own personal experience and by factors within his own psychology. His sense of the validity of his own emotional responses combined with a feeling of disenchantment to produce his unique vision of a commonplace problem. The epigraph to the *Discourse on the Sciences and the Arts* was a line from Ovid expressing the theme of personal alienation, which was so powerful a force in Rousseau's work: "Here I am the barbarian, for I am not understood by others." Rousseau found the role of social critic highly congenial, and the *First Discourse* is sprinkled with personal asides suggesting that he lives in a corrupt society which can only reward those who sparkle superficially, rather than the practitioners of true philosophy and austere virtue.[22] Once he had achieved fame, Rousseau began to affect the conspicuous simplicity of a Spartan elder or biblical patriarch, and to style himself "citizen of Geneva," adopting a manner of gruff independence in keeping with his newfound republican virtue. His social criticism reveals a strong moralistic streak, which probably originated in his upbringing in Calvinist Geneva and survived the rejection of his formal religious training. A strong admiration for the stern heroes of classical antiquity may also be traced to his early years; one of his first books was his father's Plutarch. There is a strong element of classically derived primitivism in Rousseau's thought; Tacitus and Seneca, as well as Plutarch, contributed to his ideal of unflinching republican virtue. This type of primitivism was not new: Rousseau shared it with many of his precursors, and his Savage, like theirs, would have been equally at home in the Sparta of Lycurgus, the Rome of Cincinnatus, or Tacitus's idealized Germany.

Rousseau's version of the Noble Savage is thus a new variation on a well-known theme. His intensely personal approach transformed the stock figure and gave it revolutionary implications. This is probably why Rousseau has become so closely identified with the concept of the Noble Savage: he revitalized an old idea and overshadowed others working in the same tradition. The main source for his conception of primitivism is the *Discourse on the Origins of Inequality.* In this work he set out to write a history of the origins of society. He was not trying to write a factual account of this development, but what he called "hypothetical history," for he was well aware of the problems involved in such an approach. The materials did not exist for writing the history of man's emergence from the state of nature: all was in the realm of the imagination, and the state of nature was "a state which no longer exists, which perhaps never existed at all, which will probably never exist in the future, but of which we must have an accurate idea in order to judge our present condition."[23] Such a state could only be recreated by imaginative deduction from what was known of present primitive societies; the "facts" could never be known. When this is borne in mind, Rousseau's famous injunction to "lay aside all the facts [meaning particularly Scripture] since they do not concern the question" appears less arbitrary than has often been claimed. The answer to the problem lay within, not in any external evidence.

We should be careful not to dismiss this admittedly nonempirical process of reasoning, and so to deny the validity of what Rousseau had to say on the grounds that it was merely an outgrowth of his various neuroses and personal maladjustment. What he offered was a sophisticated and closely reasoned social critique, not mere fantasy. If he began by discarding the facts in order to formulate his main hypotheses, he soon returned to them for corroboration. He documented his ideas from a wide range of reading, from earlier political theorists like Grotius, Pufendorf, Hobbes, and Locke, as well as from a number of travel works and collections of voyages, including Prévost and various Jesuits.[24] He evaluated this evidence with care and showed himself keenly aware of the limitations of material collected unsystematically by untrained observers, noting that the testimony of merchants and missionaries was no substitute for the informed observations of a Diderot or a Montesquieu.[25] Such information as he had, therefore, was to be interpreted in the light of his intuition of what had really happened.

Out of these diverse sources emerged a new vision of early man and society. By locating his primitive man—or "wild man" as he often called him—within a coherent scheme of social and historical development which relied on more than mere rationalism for its underlying system of causation, Rousseau avoided the pitfalls of the uncritical primitivism so typical of his age. His primitive men are far more satisfactory creatures than Voltaire's philosophical Indians or Diderot's happy Tahitians. Around the figure of this first man Rousseau marshals the questions which are to recur throughout his work. The *Social Contract* and *Emile* may be read as answers to the problems posed in the *Discourses:* How are the damaging effects of social life on man to be avoided or repaired? Assuming that man must live in society, how is he to retain the good qualities of his primitive self and yet reap the benefits of communal life, which until then, Rousseau felt, had only stifled or perverted him? The *Social Contract* provides the political framework which Rousseau felt would allow men to combine the advantages of social existence without too great a sacrifice of their spiritual qualities, whereas *Emile* describes a system of education which would preserve man's innately good traits in order to fit him for social life. Emile is in fact the Noble Savage in another guise, and Rousseau specifically describes him as such: "Emile is not a savage to be left in the deserts; he is a savage made to live in cities."

The *Discourse on the Origins of Inequality* was Rousseau's entry for the essay competition set by the Dijon Academy late in 1753. As soon as he saw the title which had been set for the competition, he realized that it would offer him the chance to pursue many of the ideas which had been preoccupying him since his *Discourse on the Sciences and the Arts* won the Dijon Academy's prize in 1750.[26] In his *Confessions* Rousseau describes the intellectual and spiritual turmoil which accompanied the composition of both the *First* and *Second Discourses*. But whereas the first had been a rhetorical denunciation of the evils of civilized life, the second was to be a far more profound and tightly reasoned piece of work, though ironically it did not win the prize as its predecessor had done. In between the composition of the two *Discourses*, Rousseau had evidently been reading a good deal of natural history, political theory, and travel literature, and the influence of all these sources is far more marked in the *Second Discourse:* Buffon is particularly important. Using an evolutionary scheme which seems to derive mainly from Buffon, Rousseau sketches out a plan of man's prehistory down to the establishment of political institutions.

In a penetrating study of Rousseau's "supposed primitivism," Arthur O. Lovejoy has pointed out that his scheme of human evolution involves several distinct stages, only one of which is truly beneficent.[27] Each of the four stages represents a different "state of nature," passing from a purely animal form of existence, through small family groupings and larger "nations" (as Rousseau terms them), to a final stage which witnesses the emergence of differences based on property and something close to a concept of social class. Social inequality is created by this process of evolution from one state of nature to another, setting up stresses which can be met only by the creation of political institutions. At the same time Rousseau also traces the development of man's mental faculties. His account of the earliest periods of animal or near-animal existence draws heavily on the concept of the Wild Man, giving way in the later stages to a figure closer to the idea of the Noble Savage.

Man's first condition—the only true "state of nature"—was purely animal. Here the influence of Buffon and of the accounts of wild men and primates in the travel literature is at once apparent. This first stage could only be called human because man possessed the potentiality of humanity, and no more. To all intents and purposes his life was that of an animal. He lived as a part of the natural order, not divorced from it by any process of reflection or thought; his only activities involved the satisfaction of his physical needs; his only mental processes were those of perception and feeling.[28] He lived off the fruits of the earth and the forest, which provided an inexhaustible supply of food. He was strong and hardy, inured to intemperate weather, skilled in defending himself against other wild beasts, for even if he was weaker and less agile than they, he was still more intelligent and resourceful. His life was lived in a state of immediacy with nature. The conditions under which he lived, although by no means comfortable or secure, were by no means intolerable. Since man did not think, he had no desires or expectations outside his immediate physical needs. Although he was subject to diseases which might be less prevalent in a civilized state, he was nonetheless spared many of the maladies which arise in society and was not plagued by the attentions of doctors, which Rousseau knew only too well. Like other animals, man in his first stage of development was neither good nor bad; he had no moral feelings. On balance, he was probably more timid than aggressive. "Above all, let us not conclude with Hobbes that because he had no idea of goodness, man was of necessity bad."[29]

Man at this earliest stage was thus truly wild. Rousseau's description of this initial state shares many of the traditional characteristics of the accounts of wild men. Man's salient features were his spontaneity, his nonrationality, his improvidence, his close kinship with the rest of the animal kingdom. Sexually he partook of many of the traditional ways of the Wild Man. He led a solitary existence, mating and parting at hazard, unconcerned by the responsibility of rearing children, who would follow the mother until old enough to fend for themselves and assume the solitary roving life which was their lot. Rousseau was also concerned by the question of how close man was to the rest of the animal kingdom; were wild men actually men, or some species of animal, or an intermediate species between the two? Rousseau did not accept the idea of man's evolution from the lower animals. Like Linnaeus, he seems to have regarded man and the great apes as a separate species, unconnected with the other orders of animals, and to have accepted the concept of the fixity of species. But the problem of the relation of man to the apes remained. Rousseau held that the great apes and orangutans could conceivably represent a survival of this earliest form of mankind that he described at the beginning of the *Discourse on the Origins of Inequality*. Within the human race there was great diversity; this led him to suggest that the great apes, and such wild men as turned up from time to time, might be members of the same species. The line between species was hard to draw. The great apes seemed to lack the basic human quality of "perfectibility" (to be discussed in a moment), but this could have been the result of biased or slipshod observation. Rousseau noted that the wild boy found at Hanover in 1725 might well have been considered nonhuman by an inexpert observer. In other words, the great apes might be living fossils left over from the first stage of human evolution; close examination might reveal their kinship to man, and their possession of certain characteristics hitherto thought to be distinctively human, like the faculty of speech. They might in fact be our ancestors, the original wild men. This speculation on the humanity of the great apes and their possible identity as the archetypal wild men was to start a long and energetic debate.[30] It also prefigures the work of modern animal behaviorists who seek to understand human behavior through study of the primates.

What distinguished man from the rest of the animal kingdom was his potentiality for change both as an individual and as a species. This potential faculty only began to reveal itself under the pressure of events which obliged man to adapt to gradual changes in his environment. Throughout the *Second Discourse*, Rousseau insists on the slowness of the changes he is describing and stresses the importance of even very small factors if they operate over a long period to time.[31] Here his affinity with dawning ideas of evolution is apparent. As man's surroundings changed, the distinctive quality which Rousseau termed "perfectibility" began to act, permitting man to adapt and so overcome the adverse conditions created by changes of climate and natural catastrophes. The result was the gradual development of man's intelligence and his passing to the second stage of development.

This faculty of perfectibility needs close examination, since it forms the key to Rousseau's scheme of human development. By perfectibility Rousseau did not mean an automatic tendency to improvement and progress; he was not such an uncritical devotee of the idea of progress. His concept of perfectibility can best be defined as an innate ability to adapt or learn. All animals possess this in early life, but soon lose it and thereafter learn no more; only man retains this infantile capacity into adult life.[32] Rousseau's concept of perfectibility has a modern parallel in the idea of neoteny, the capacity to prolong infantile traits—notably learning—into later life, and thereby adapt more rapidly and successfully to environmental changes.[33] Perhaps it might be better to paraphrase Rousseau's term and call it adaptability, for perfectibility has the implication that perfection has been or can be achieved, and this is not what Rousseau meant; the mere possession of the power to change did not guarantee man against changing in the wrong way, and Rousseau felt that many of the changes which had occurred during man's development had been for the worse. "Perfectibility" was merely the ability to change, for better or for worse. Rousseau describes it as

that faculty which, aided by circumstances, develops all the others in succession. . . . It is sad to have to recognize that this distinctive and almost limitless power is the source of all man's unhappiness; it is this power which takes him, in the course of time, away from his original condition, in which his days passed calmly and innocently; it is this power which unfolds over the centuries his talents and his errors, his virtues and his vices, and which at length makes him a tyrant over himself and Nature.[34]

Clearly Rousseau did not regard this quality as automatically beneficial. But it was this power to change which made man unique, and in his earliest stage of development, before this potentiality began to realize itself, there was nothing to distinguish him from his fellow animals. Since man was in fact an animal, this first stage of his development could not be termed human, and was therefore not to be regretted; Rousseau did not hanker after this particular state of nature.

Imperceptibly, man began to move beyond this initial, animal stage. His surroundings changed and forced him to adapt; in response, his intelligence developed as the faculty of perfectibility took over. He began to develop rudimentary skills, including that of language, and started to live in small family groups. The main impetus in this stage of social life was man's emotion, rather than the ability to reason, which was still hardly more than mere instinctual response. The basis of family life was to be found in man's tendency, shared with other animals, to associate with others of the same species. Language evolved out of the natural cries denoting fear or pleasure, which gradually became a sophisticated system of communication, and without which family life would not have been practicable.[35] It will be observed that the passions—the basic characteristic of the Wild Man—play the predominant role in Rousseau's account of man's early development as a social being. Another characteristic of the Wild Man, his amorality, also dominates this early phase. Rousseau felt that man was still the morally neutral creature he had been in his earliest days. He was not bad, since his fatal quality of *amour-propre*, or self-esteem, had not yet developed; this faculty, which was to divide man from his fellows, did not develop until man's reasoning powers were stronger. But Rousseau did not idealize his early man: he may not have been bad at this stage, but neither was he particularly good or noble. The basis of his feelings was the animal instinct of sympathy or pity for his fellows, which led him to adopt as a general rule of conduct, "Do what is good for yourself, with the least harm to others."[36] This second epoch of man's development was therefore marked by defects almost as great as those of the first stage; man was still largely unformed and lacking in the qualities which would make him truly human. He was a savage of the most rudimentary kind, in no way noble. Rousseau evinced little nostalgia for this second stage of development.

It was the third stage of development outlined in the *Second Discourse* which Rousseau found most attractive, and whose passing he may have regretted. This was the period which saw the full emergence of man's mental powers and of the characteristics which now made him truly human for the first time. Yet his emergent reason was still balanced by his animal instincts of sympathy. Only at this point did man become a social being, and therefore fully human. The reasons for his gradual progress, according to Rousseau, were not merely changes in the environment, but also pressures and opportunities arising out of social life. Speaking of the previous stage of development, he had noted:

In this new condition of simple and solitary life, with very limited needs, and the instruments which they had invented to fulfil them, men enjoyed a great deal of leisure and employed it to procure themselves various amenities which their fathers had never known; this was the first yoke which they imposed upon themselves without realizing it, and the first cause of all the ills which beset their descendants.[37]

Rousseau's mechanism for change thus appears as the interaction of man's developing intelligence with the new opportunities created by shifts in his social or physical environment. Out of the primitive family groups larger "nations" coalesced, often separated from their fellow men by the action of floods or earthquakes (again the influence of Buffon is apparent) and gradually adopting distinctive social characteristics, such as language and diet.[38] Man by now had the basic skills to protect and feed himself and to support himself in larger groups than the family. But the groups in which he lived were still small enough to allow him to retain his sense of identity, while his feeling of solidarity with the group, inherited from his animal past, had not been overcome by his dawning *amour-*

propre. This stage of human evolution saw the appearance of the earliest arts—poetry and music. The origin of art, as of language, was to be found in the emotions: "Singing and dancing, the true children of love and leisure, became the amusement or rather the occupation of men and women congregated together with time on their hands."[39] If there was any stage of human development whose passing should be regarded with a sense of loss, this was it. Man's intelligence had developed sufficiently to give him a reasonably secure and fulfilled life; he had become fully social and therefore fully human; yet he retained enough of his original animal sentiment to keep him from seeking to dominate his fellows.

But this happy period of balance could not last; inequality began to appear, as intelligence and reason developed. In the passage from the third period of development to the final stage of social inequality and conflict, Rousseau is in a sense secularizing and historicizing the myth of the Fall. Close association in society led to emulation, and soon to invidious comparison. Man desired to excel at the expense of his neighbors in order to gratify his *amour-propre.* As reason developed, so did self-consciousness, and the desire of the individual to distinguish himself at the expense of his fellows. This was the problem which afflicted man in Rousseau's fourth and final stage of primitive society, and which became insuperable because it gradually took the form of self-aggrandizement through the acquisition of property. Rivalry among men was sharpened by technological advances. With the beginnings of agriculture and metallurgy the concept of property was born, and inequality became the rule. The way was now open for the domination of the poor by the rich. The ensuing conflicts could ultimately be resolved only by the creation of political institutions which could guarantee peace, order, and property. Rousseau's final stage of social development closely resembles Hobbes' original state of nature; inequality led to conflict, and conflict to the erection of repressive institutions. As Rousseau observed, man had been enslaved by grain and iron.

This final period contrasts unfavorably with the stage which preceded it. It is significant that the model for this earlier and more pleasant social condition was drawn from accounts of the life of the North American Indians, the prototype noble savages. Rousseau's main reason for choosing them seems to have been that they had no concept of private property, and hence were not subject to political oppression.[40] To some extent, therefore, Rousseau may be criticized for falling into the traditional pitfall of idealizing a primitive people on the basis of scanty information. But it should be remembered that neither the Savage nor the society in which he lived was presented as wholly admirable and flawless. Rousseau was ready to admit that even the state of nature which he regarded as least objectionable had serious faults, and in any case was doomed by the irreversible progress of man's intelligence; the clock could not be turned back. Rousseau was only suggesting that this third stage of social development might have certain lessons which could render civilized life more tolerable. Notably this meant the tempering of reason and its associated quality of *amour-propre* by the more generous emotions inherited from an earlier time. Rousseau's cry of "back to nature" was by no means as simplistic as is usually assumed. He realized that civilization was here to stay.[41] The question was not to destroy it—he did not want to "go to live in the woods like a bear"—but to improve it by resurrecting certain human qualities which had been submerged in the onward march of intellectual and material progress. Rousseau was presenting the model of an earlier and a happier time in an effort to humanize the society in which he lived.

The *Second Discourse* thus poses the problem squarely: Given that European man has chosen a form of society based upon inequalities of property, how can the harmful effects of this choice be remedied or palliated? Can earlier forms of social organization, or primitive cultures still existing, offer any help in arriving at a solution to the problem? Rousseau had answered the question posed by the Dijon Academy and suggested a "hypothetical history" of how human inequality had developed. The answer to the problem of inequality was to be found in his later works. What is particularly noticeable, for the purposes of this essay, is the use which he made of traditional information about primitive society to achieve a greater understanding of man's earliest development. In the *Second Discourse* Rousseau reveals a far deeper sympathy for the early types of society which he is describing, and a far more penetrating insight into the development of social and political institutions than any of his contemporaries working in the same line of inquiry, with the possible exception of Turgot. His primitivism is not the uncritical adulation of the Noble Savage which appears in Diderot's *Supplément au voyage de Bougainville,* or in the Abbé Raynal. His insight into the primitive mind gives his work a validity which is lacking in that of his contemporaries, who were too much the prisoners of their own myths, and makes him one of the founders of modern anthropology and prehistory. It is Rousseau's understanding of the primitive mind which makes him worth reading today, and which has led his great admirer, Lévi-Strauss, to call him "the most ethnographically-minded of all the *philosophes*" and the real father and inspirer of anthropological studies.[42] Rousseau's "ethnographic-mindedness" did not come from the possession of better information. He used the same materials as his contemporaries and never traveled outside Europe. It was his unique character and genius which gave him his insight into the workings of primitive society and allowed him to transcend the limits of his sources.

Rousseau's study of primitive man was not an idealization of his subject, but it was nonetheless an indictment of the overelaborate society in which he lived. Although Rousseau adopted the evolutionary plan of social development then becoming fashionable, this did not lead him into a facile acceptance of the myth of progress which had captivated so many of his fellow *philosophes*. Progress there might be; evolution seemed to be unquestionable. But was it always for the better? And since it was irreversible, there was no point in trying to return to a supposedly lost age of innocence. What had to be done was to understand other social and political organizations in order to improve those under which European man now lived. The Noble Savage and his society were not to be idealized, but examined for what they could teach modern European man. The answer which the stock figure of the Noble Savage presented— the rule of reason, obedience to some "law of nature"—was not enough. The arid rationalism represented by the Savage had to be supplemented by some of the passion of his earlier avatar, the Wild Man.

NOTES

1. See, for instance, Albert Schinz, *Etat présent des travaux sur Jean-Jacques Rousseau* (New York, 1941), and Ernst Cassirer, *The Question of Jean-Jacques Rousseau,* trans. and ed. Peter Gay (New York, 1954). Gay's introduction gives a useful survey of the history of Rousseau scholarship.

2. A parallel to the impact of ideas about primitive society on the eighteenth century can be seen in the current rethinking of social and political theories under the influence of new discoveries in animal behavior (Konrad Lorenz's work, for instance) or in paleontology (the work of Louis B. Leakey); see Robert Ardrey, *African Genesis* (New York, 1961), for a discussion of this. A different view of the implications of these discoveries is in Ashley Montagu, *The Human Revolution* (Cleveland, 1965).

3. Geoffrey Atkinson, *La littérature géographique française de la Renaissance: répertoire bibliographique* (Paris, 1927), and the same author's *Supplément* to it (Paris, 1936).

4. Michel de Montaigne, *Essais*, bk. I, ch. 31 ("Des Cannibales"). The influence of Montaigne on Rousseau is evident from references scattered throughout the *Discourse on the Origins of Inequality*.

5. On the Jesuit literature, see John H. Kennedy, *Jesuit and Savage in New France* (New Haven, 1950); and Gilbert Chinard, *L'Amérique et le rêve exotique dans la*

littérature française au XVIIe et au XVIIIe siècle (Paris, 1934), pp. 122–50. On the ambiguity of the figure of the Wild Man, and the confusion between benevolent and malevolent images of the New World, see David B. Davis, *The Problem of Slavery in Western Culture* (Ithaca, N.Y., 1966), pp. 5–8.

6. On the Jesuits in Paraguay, see John H. Parry, *The Spanish Seaborne Empire* (London, 1966), pp. 170–71. On China, see Virgile Pinot, *La Chine et la formation de l'esprit philosophique en France, 1640–1740* (Paris, 1932).

7. The advance of rationalism at the expense of more disorderly states of mind is described by Michel Foucault, *Histoire de la folie dans l'âge classique* (Paris, 1961), trans. R. Howard as *Madness and Civilization* (New York, 1965).

8. Geoffrey Atkinson, *The Extraordinary Voyage in French Literature before 1700* (New York, 1920), and *The Extraordinary Voyage in French Literature from 1700 to 1720* (Paris, 1922).

9. On the background to *Télémaque,* see Lionel Rothkrug, *Opposition to Louis XIV: The Political and Social Origins of the French Enlightenment* (Princeton, 1965), pp. 249–86.

10. Atkinson, *Extraordinary Voyage before 1700,* p. 150; see also Chinard, *L'Amérique,* p. 218.

11. For the influence of Fénelon on Rousseau, see Frederick C. Green, *Jean-Jacques Rousseau: A Critical Study of his Life and Writings* (Cambridge, 1955), pp. 198, 260.

12. Paul Hazard, *La crise de la conscience européenne* (Paris, 1935), translated as *The European Mind, 1680–1715* (Cleveland, 1963). See especially ch. 1 of the English version, and also p. xx: "The door had been opened to anarchy by those who held up to contrast the virtues of the primitive, untutored savage on the one hand, and the errors and crimes of civilization on the other."

13. See Hazard, *European Mind,* ch. 5.

14. For the background to Pacific exploration, see John Dunmore, *French Explorers in the Pacific,* vol. I, *The Eighteenth Century* (Oxford, 1965); Andrew Sharp, *The Discovery of the Pacific Islands* (Oxford, 1960); and John C. Beaglehole, *The Exploration of the Pacific,* 3d ed. (Stanford, 1966). On Dampier, see Joseph C. Shipman, *William Dampier, Seaman-Scientist* (Lawrence, Kans., 1962).

15. On the development of evolutionary views of society, see Marvin Harris, *The Rise of Anthropological Theory* (New York, 1968). For early exponents of biological evolution, see Jacques Barzun, *Darwin, Marx, Wagner,* 2d ed. (Garden City, N.Y., 1958), pt. 1, ch. 2; Loren Eiseley, *Darwin's Century* (Garden City, N.Y., 1958), ch. 2; and Gertrude Himmelfarb, *Darwin and the Darwinian Revolution* (Garden City, N.Y., 1959), ch. 5. See also Arthur O. Lovejoy, *The Great Chain of Being* (New York, 1936), chs. 6–9. As an example of the direct influence of biological concepts on social thinking, we may point to the use of several biological images by Turgot in his *Discours sur l'histoire universelle* (ca. 1751). The whole relationship between the new views of primitive man and political theory is discussed briefly by John L. Myres, *The Influence of Anthropology on the Course of Political Science* (Berkeley, 1916), esp. p. 7. Jan de Vries, *The Study of Religion: A Historical Approach,* trans. Kees W. Bolle (New York, 1967), notes that a similar approach is discernible in the study of religion. Here too the Jesuit *Relations* were of great importance in opening the way for comparative study and the idea of parallel evolutionary development,

according to laws operating similarly in every culture. De Vries notes that Fontenelle concludes in his *Discours sur l'origine des fables* "that all peoples have the same spiritual disposition . . . [and that] the red Indians could have reached the high level of Greek culture if they had had a chance for development without external hindrance" (p. 31).

16. This period also produced several studies of the kindred problem of the development of language: for example, Turgot's *Réflexions sur les langues* (ca. 1751); Maupertuis' *Réflexions philosophiques sur l'origine des langues et la signification des mots* (before 1759); and Rousseau's *Essai sur l'origine des langues* (1761).

17. *Lettre sur le progrès des sciences*, in *Oeuvres de Maupertuis*, new ed. (Lyons, 1768), II, 382.

18. Alan C. Taylor, *Le Président de Brosses et l'Australie* (Paris, 1937), p. 46.

19. For the influence of de Brosses on Bougainville, see J.-E. Martin-Allanic, *Bougainville navigateur et les découvertes de son temps* (Paris, 1964), I, ch. 2. For Cook, see Beaglehole, *Exploration of the Pacific*, p. 235, and James A. Williamson, *Cook and the Opening of the Pacific* (New York, 1948), esp. p. 114.

20. On these eighteenth-century Jesuits, see Chinard, *L'Amérique*, pp. 313 ff. Chinard calls Rousseau "un continuateur des missionaires jésuites." See also J. Poirier, *Histoire de l'ethnologie* (Paris, 1968), p. 16: "En fait, ce protestant doit beaucoup aux jésuites"; and W. E. Muhlmann, *Geschichte der Anthropologie* (Frankfurt am Main, 1968), pp. 44–45.

21. J.-J. Rousseau, *Oeuvres complètes*, vol. III, *Du contrat social, écrits politiques*, ed. R. Derathé et al. (Paris, 1966), p. 30. Subsequent references to this volume will be cited *Ecrits politiques*. Translations are by the author.

22. *Ecrits politiques*, pp. 21, 25–26.

23. *Ecrits politiques*, p. 123.

24. Chinard, *L'Amérique*, pp. 345 ff.; G. Pire, "Jean-Jacques Rousseau et les relations de voyages," in *Revue d'histoire littéraire de la France*, 56 (1956), 355–78; and Jean Morel, "Des sources du *Discours sur l'Inégalité*," in *Annales de la Société J.-J. Rousseau*, 5 (1909), 120–98.

25. Rousseau's own note X to the *Discourse on The Origins of Inequality*, in *Ecrits politiques*, pp. 208–14.

26. On the Dijon Academy, see M. Bouchard, *L'académie de Dijon et le premier Discours de Rousseau* (Paris, 1950). Buffon and de Brosses were soon to join the Academy, although at the time of the two competitions in which Rousseau took part they had not done so.

27. Arthur O. Lovejoy, "The Supposed Primitivism of Rousseau's *Discourse on Inequality*," in *Essays in the History of Ideas* (New York, 1960), see esp. 14–16.

28. Rousseau's note VI to the *Discourse on Inequality*, in *Ecrits politiques*, p. 199.

29. *Ecrits politiques*, p. 153; see also p. 136.

30. Rousseau's views on the humanity of the apes, and on the allied question of wild men, are summarized in his note X to the *Discourse on Inequality; Ecrits politiques*, pp. 208–14, where he gave qualified acceptance to the possible existence of a race of wild men. In general he seems to have regarded apes and wild men as survivors of the original condition of mankind. The model for his first stage of development is thus based on information about orangutans and wild men, including the wild boy from Hanover. But he did not believe that man had once walked on all

fours, and so might be assumed to have evolved from the lower animals; see his note III, *Ecrits politiques,* p. 196. For the debate on the humanity of the great apes and the possibility that they might be taught to speak, see Arthur O. Lovejoy, "Monboddo and Rousseau," *Essays in the History of Ideas,* pp. 38–61. For a full discussion of the wild boy found near Hanover, see Novak's essay (pp. 183–221).

31. *Ecrits politiques,* p. 162: "la puissance surprenante des causes très-légères lorsqu'elles agissent sans relâche."

32. *Ecrits politiques,* p. 142.

33. For a discussion of the concept of neoteny and its evolutionary implications, see Montagu, *Human Revolution,* pp. 126–38; and Desmond Morris, *The Naked Ape* (London, 1968), pp. 30–31.

34. *Ecrits politiques,* p. 142.

35. *Ecrits politiques,* p. 147. Rousseau pursued the question further in his *Essai sur l'origine des langues* (1761), which presents the same basic argument of the nonrational development of language. This concept of linguistic development is in direct contrast to the more orthodox, rationalistic arguments of Maupertuis. Morel, "Des sources," p. 145, points to the influence of Condillac on Rousseau's scheme of intellectual development. Cf. Rousseau's *Confessions,* ed. Jacques Voisine (Paris, 1964), pp. 409–10, for his close association with Condillac at the time of writing the *Discourses.* Rousseau's ideas are more convincing than those of Maupertuis, who tried to deduce the development of language from an innate propensity toward a sort of mathematical reason; see his *Réflexions philosophiques sur l'origine des langues et la signification des mots,* in *Oeuvres,* I, 253–85, esp. 259 ff.

36. *Ecrits politiques,* p. 152; see also p. 156.

37. *Ecrits politiques,* p. 168.

38. *Ecrits politiques,* p. 169.

39. *Ecrits politiques,* p. 169.

40. *Ecrits politiques,* p. 172. One should remember that the sedentary tribes of the southwestern United States were still unknown in Europe; the image of the Indian was that of the nomads and hunters of the east. Rousseau's view that the real beginning of social organization, with its accompaniment of class differentiation, only comes with the development of agriculture and metallurgy is an interesting anticipation of modern prehistorians such as V. Gordon Childe and their idea of the "neolithic revolution."

41. *Ecrits politiques,* p. 207 (Rousseau's note IX); see also *Discourse on the Sciences and the Arts,* in *Ecrits politiques,* p. 8, in which Rousseau rejects the idea that man was better off in the state of nature.

42. Claude Lévi-Strauss, *Tristes Tropiques* (Paris, 1955), p. 421. Various other laudatory references to Rousseau occur in this and other works by Lévi-Strauss.

Papageno: The Unenlightened Wild Man in Eighteenth-Century Germany

✑ EHRHARD BAHR

The Wild Man occupies a position of considerable prominence not only in German folklore but also in early German literature; for instance, a number of Shrovetide plays of the sixteenth century center on the Wild Man. In art, too, the Wild Man and his followers are prominent figures, as can be seen, for example, in fifteenth-century tapestries and in sixteenth-century woodcuts and sculptures.[1] At first sight, therefore, it would seem surprising that in the eighteenth century the Wild Man has almost completely disappeared from the German literary scene. The only types which come close to the Wild Man are the "noble savages," hermits, and outcasts of society who live in forests, for example, highwaymen, charcoal burners, and gypsies.

A Wild Man fountain stands opposite Schiller's birthplace, at Marbach in Swabia, but apparently it left no impression on the dramatist. The men in his plays become outcasts and indulge in some wild behavior, like the characters in *Die Räuber,* but they are certainly no wild men. Not even Wilhem Tell qualifies as a Wild Man. Definite traces of the Wild Man tradition are noticeable in Goethe's satirical short play *Satyros* (1773), but classical influences, as shown by the title, are predominant. Only in *Faust: Part Two* does one find some genuine German giants who announce in chorus:

> Die wilden Männer sind s' genannt,
> Am Harzgebirge wohlbekannt;
> Natürlich nackt in aller Kraft,
> Sie kommen sämtlich riesenhaft.
> Den Fichtenstamm in rechter Hand
> Und um den Leib ein wulstig Band,

> Den derben Schurz von Zweig und Blatt,
> Leibwache, wie der Papst nicht hat. $(5864-71)^2$

These giants are still part of the sixteenth- and seventeenth-centuries Shrovetide dance and drama tradition, and it is no coincidence that they appear in Goethe's *Faust* only once, during the carnival masque at the emperor's court; they do not take part in the dramatic action of the tragedy of Faust.

However, the vanishing of the Wild Man in eighteenth-century German literature becomes quite plausible when seen in the context of the Enlightenment and German Classicism. In fact, the only outstanding example of a clearly identifiable Wild Man figure of the period—Papageno in *Die Zauberflöte (The Magic Flute)* (1791)—is conceived as a contrasting character and foil to the ideal representatives of the Enlightenment. The opera by Mozart and Emanuel Schikaneder deals with the mythological cosmic conflict between light and darkness which has given the concept of Enlightenment its very meaning. In the opera this conflict is at the same time a mythological battle between the male and the female principals. Sarastro, priest of the realm of wisdom and virtue and of the sun, wards off the machinations of the Queen of the Night, who tries to reach beyond her sphere of influence. These mythological conflicts are linked to the ideas of the Enlightenment and to Free Masonry, which embraces the same ideas (*Die Zauberflöte* includes a rite of initiation not unlike that of the Free Masons).[3]

Papageno, the amiable "bird man," a strange and colorfully appealing mixture of man and animal, is one of the pawns in these conflicts. The other pawns are Prince Tamino and Pamina, daughter of the Queen of the Night, both in search of enlightenment and in love with each other. Details of the plot are deliberately omitted here since, in W. H. Auden's words, "even the most ardent opera fans . . . are apt to find the libretto of [*Die Zauberflöte*] hard to swallow, and with some justification."[4] Tamino and Pamina pass successfully all the tests imposed by Sarastro and are finally initiated into the Society of the Enlightened.

On the other hand, Papageno, the charming failure, remains quite unenlightened. His survival is due only to his artistic creators' genial and more tolerant Austrian nature. According to one of the representatives of Sarastro's realm, Papageno would have deserved "auf immer in finstern Klüften der Erde zu wandern" (II, 23).[5] However, Schikaneder and Mozart wanted to show that there is also room on earth for people of Papageno's kind.

Interpretations of Papageno are innumerable and diverse. He has been identified as the somewhat disreputable but highly entertaining clown (*Hanswurst, Kasperle*) of the old Viennese theater who once populated the stages all over Germany, to the delight of the groundlings in the pit. But during the first half of the eighteenth century the clown was banished from the German stage by J. C. Gottsched's reforms. These reforms aimed at bringing enlightenment to the theater and at abolishing absurd and obscene gestures and plots. But they did not reach so far as the southern parts of Germany, and so the clown found refuge and flourished in one of his original habitats, the Austro-Bavarian regions—areas in which also the wild men of folklore thrive. To this day the clown has not had a successful comeback on the North German stage.

In *Enten-Eller*, Kierkegaard considers Papageno the second stage of the erotic or the musical erotic, a prefiguration of Don Juan, whom he regards as the final stage. For Kierkegaard, Papageno represents desire as a quest, not as a conquest. In *Die Zauberflöte* the emphasis, he says, lies on the "journey of discovery": "Papageno udseer, Don Juan nyder."[6]

W. H. Auden, who translated *Die Zauberflöte* for a 1956 production of the NBC Opera Theater, calls Papageno "the uncorrupted child of Nature" and "a Noble Savage": "He enjoys a happiness and self-assurance which Tamino, and even Sarastro, cannot share; one might even say that he is the unlettered aristocrat, they but learned clerks."[7]

Alfons Rosenberg perceptively considers Papageno a phallic figure related to fertility cults. Furthermore, he sees in him a descendant of the seraphim of the Bible and of the sirens of Greek mythology.[8]

All these interpretations have validity in terms of the libretto. What has escaped attention so far is the fact that Papageno is also a Wild Man. He fits the description and definition. Dressed in feathers, he carries a panpipe in his hand, and he is master of the animals as he sings,

> Drum kann ich froh und lustig sein,
> Denn alle Vögel sind ja mein. (I, 2)[9]

Papageno's character as a Wild Man becomes fully exposed when contrasted to Prince Tamino, the representative of civilization who is striving not so much for Pamina, daughter of the Queen of the Night, as for wisdom, virtue, and enlightenment.[10] The first encounter between Papageno and Tamino is in the form of the classical tradition of the Wild Man theme, highly reminiscent of the encounter between the knight Calogrenant and the Wild Man in Chrétien de Troyes' *Yvain* and in Hartmann von Aue's *Iwein*. In this medieval courtly romance, the knight meets a

Wild Man dressed in hides, who is the master of the beasts of the forest, providing a foil for the ideal knight and the values of courtly society.[11] Prince Tamino meets Papageno in similar fashion. He introduces himself as a man of noble birth, but Papageno answers that noble blood does not mean anything to him, and he asks for further explanations. Tamino obliges with the statement: "Mein Vater ist Fürst, der über viele Länder und Menschen herrscht; darum nennt man mich Prinz." But lands, people, princes do not mean anything to Papageno either. He is surprised to hear that there are other human beings and lands beyond his own habitat. He does not know where he lives other than "zwischen Tälern und Bergen." Nor does he know the name of the land or who the ruler is. He cannot answer that question any more than he can tell how he happened to come into this world. Tamino begins to wonder whether Papageno is a human being or not, considering also the feathers covering him. He comes closer to him, saying: "Nach deinen Federn, die dich bedecken, halt' ich dich—." "Doch für keinen Vogel?" Papageno parries quickly this somewhat aggressive approach. And he boasts of having the strength of a Wild Man: "Bleib zurück, sag ich, und traue mir nicht, denn ich habe Riesenkraft, wenn ich jemand packe." But alas, he protests too much. Papageno is probably the meekest in the family of wild men. He cannot hide his close relationship to *Hanswurst*, the clown of the Viennese stage. In an aside he admits: "Wenn er sich nicht bald von mir schrecken läßt, so lauf' ich davon." He tries to bluff Tamino into believing that he had rescued him from a ferocious serpent which was about to kill him. Here again Papageno follows the tradition of the Wild Man who in Chrétien's *Yvain* subdues wild bulls with the sheer strength of his hands. Papageno pretends to have choked the serpent with his own hands: "Bei mir ist ein starker Druck mit der Hand mehr als Waffen" (I, 2).[12] But unfortunately for him the Three Ladies, attendants of the Queen of the Night, expose Papageno's lies and shut him up by locking his mouth with a padlock so that he is reduced to humming pitifully and contritely (I, 3).

The animal side of Papageno's nature is comically revealed when he is afraid that Sarastro will pluck his feathers and fry him like a chicken (I, 8). This comical fear and cowardice, a characteristic of Papageno, is also part of the *Hanswurst* tradition. Papageno accompanies Tamino on his quest for wisdom, virtue, enlightenment—and also for Pamina, but he fails the tests of virtue and wisdom which Tamino passes; he falls victim to the fear which Tamino overcomes: fighting is not exactly in his line, as Papageno says, and he does not need any wisdom either: "Ich bin so ein Naturmensch, der sich mit Schlaf, Speis' und Trank begnügt; und wenn es ja sein könnte, daß ich mir einmal ein schönes Weibchen fange—" (II, 3).[13] It becomes evident here how Papageno as a Wild Man figure is the eighteenth-century symbol of man in the state of nature. In his essay, "Was ist Aufklärung?" (1784) Kant enumerates two qualities— cowardice and laziness—which he holds responsible for the fact that a large part of mankind is still unenlightened and, in fact, enjoys remaining intellectually immature. "Es ist so bequem, unmündig zu sein," he adds.[14] The *Hanswurst* motif and the Wild Man tradition meet here in Kant's diagnosis of the state of Enlightenment in the eighteenth century.

Tamino, on the other hand, is the man who matures during the course of the opera. He is able to follow Kant's exhortation: "*Sapere aude!* Habe Mut, dich deines eigenen Verstandes zu bedienen!*"[15] In the beginning Tamino is full of maudlin emotions and of fear—his first words: "Zu Hilfe! Zu Hilfe!" (I, 1)[16]—and of class prejudices. Peter Ustinov calls Tamino, at his first appearance, a typically Austrain *fils à papa* who constantly talks about his father, the king, and who is shocked that Papageno does not know who his parents are.[17] But soon Tamino is ready, in Kant's terms, "sich aus der . . . Unmündigkeit herauszuarbeiten." He takes the courage "allein zu gehen," and he pursues "einen sicheren Gang" (both the opera and Kant's essay abound with road imagery).[18] Tamino has the moral support of Sarastro's society, which consists, in Kant's terms, of "Selbstdenkende," of the people who think for themselves. Tamino proves that he is not only a prince, but "noch mehr—er ist Mensch!" (II, 1).[19] Finally Tamino succeeds in escaping from immaturity, as the chorus sings:

> Es siegte die Stärke
> Und krönet zum Lohn
> Die Schönheit und Weisheit
> Mit ewiger Kron'! (II, 30)[20]

So Tamino demonstrates that enlightenment is not only possible but "beinahe unausbleiblich," as Kant says.[21] But not for Papageno. It is interesting to follow the same Kantian images and ideas outlining Tamino's enlightened character as they apply negatively to Papageno. He clearly considers "den Schritt zur Mündigkeit, außer dem daß er beschwerlich ist, auch für sehr gefährlich," to quote Kant's reference to the majority of men.[22] Terrified at the prospect of a journey with Tamino through unknown terrain to the castle of a "villainous magician," he does all he can to extricate himself until he is finally forced into it by the Queen of the Night. During his journey with Tamino through strange regions the stage echoes with his cries of fear. He lives in constant terror at the

thought that Tamino might desert him and that he might have to face
the world on his own. Not even the prospect of catching "ein schönes
Weibchen" can persuade him into any feat of courage or daring: "Ich
bleibe ledig," he swears (II, 3).[23] "Wenn mir ja die Götter eine Papagena
bestimmten, warum denn mit soviel Gefahren sie erringen? . . . Bei so
einer ewigen Wanderschaft möcht' einem wohl die Liebe auf immer
vergehen" (II, 6).[24] When told that he will never experience "das himm-
lische Vergnügen der Eingeweihten," Papageno is not worried in the
least: "Ja nun, es gibt ja noch mehr Leute meinesgleichen. Mir wäre jetzt
ein gut Glas Wein das größte Vergnügen" (II, 23).[25]

His wish is granted, and in the end the feathered Wild Man also gets
his feathered wild woman—after his one and only gesture of valor and
defiance, and a rather comical one, performed under the spell of the
pretty girl's presence (II, 25). In their final love duet we are assured of
the happy perpetuation of the species in linguistic and musical imitations
of the reproductive process: "Pa-Pa-Pa-Pa-Pa-Pa-Papageno/Papagena!"
The duet continues:

> Welche Freude wird das sein,
> Wenn die Götter uns bedenken,
> Unsrer Liebe Kinder schenken,
> So liebe kleine Kinderlein,

ending the fertility chant with:

PAPAGENO:	Erst einen kleinen Papageno!
WEIB:	Dann eine kleine Papagena!
PAPAGENO:	Dann wieder einen Papageno!
WEIB:	Dann wieder eine Papagena!
BEIDE:	Papagena! Papageno! Papagena!
	Es ist das höchste der Gefühle,
	Wenn viele, viele, viele, viele
	Pa-Pa-Pa-Pa-geno,
	Pa-Pa-Pa-Pa-gena,
	Der Eltern Segen werden sein, (II, 29)[26]

thus making sure that Kant's "größter Teil der Menschheit" will survive
in an unenlightened state of nature.[27]

Although it is very doubtful that Mozart or Schikaneder ever read
Kant's essay, the analogies of ideas and images are quite startling, demonstrating the great impact of the Enlightenment on eighteenth-century
German culture, however temporary its effect may have been viewed
from a long-term perspective. Yet there is one basic and important dif-

ference in the two concepts: Kant truly believed that man is able to develop freely and that "die Hindernisse der allgmeinen Aufklärung oder des Ausganges aus ihrer selbstverschuldeten Unmündigkeit allmählich weniger werden."[28] *Die Zauberflöte*, on the other hand, presents a different vision in the final scene, when mankind is shown on two levels: on the top level is the world of the enlightened; and on a lower level, the world of Papageno and Papagena, the Wild Man with his wild woman. In true folklore tradition, Mozart and Schikaneder use the Wild Man figure as a colorful contrast to their personifications of Reason and Enlightenment. In the two bird people they project the joyful, pleasure-seeking elements of society and the earthy, phallic part of life. Civilization, however highly developed, depends for its survival on this basic essence of life, which is symbolized so aptly in the figure of the Wild Man.

NOTES

1. See Oswald A. Erich and Richard Beitl, eds., *Wörterbuch der deutschen Volkskunde*, 2d ed. (Stuttgart, 1955), pp. 890–91; Alexander H. Krappe, *The Science of Folklore* (New York, 1964), pp. 91 ff.; Lutz Röhrich, *Sage* (Stuttgart, 1966), pp. 18–20, 45–46; Leopold Schmidt, *Das Deutsche Volksschauspiel* (Berlin, 1962), pp. 49, 70, 96, 97, 148, 150, 208, 209, 213, 214, 244, 246, 263, 292, 294, 323, 338.

2. The wild men come, and such their name,
Hartz Mountain Heights know well their fame,
As stark as Nature, naked, strong,
And each a giant in that throng,
With pine-tree bole in huge right hand,
And round the waist a studded band,
With apron rough, twigs, leaves entwined,
Such body-guard no pope could find.

(Goethe, *Faust: Part Two*, trans. Philip Wayne [Baltimore, 1959], p. 64)

Goethe had planned to write a continuation to *The Magic Flute*, in which a daughter of Papageno and Papagena was to appear. By not doing so he deprived us of another literary instance of wild people in the eighteenth century. See Hans-Albrecht Koch, "Goethes Fortsetzung der Schikanederschen Zauberflöte: Ein Beitrag zur Deutung des Fragments und zur Rekonstruktion des Schlusses," *Jahrbuch des Freien Deutschen Hochstifts* (1969), pp. 121–63.

3. See Joseph Szövérffy, "Zauberflöte und Welttheater," *Archiv für Kulturgeschichte*, 48 (1966), 262–77; Moriz Enzinger, "Randbemerkungen zum Textbuch der Zauberflöte," *Sprachkunst als Weltgestaltung: Festschrift für Herbert Seidler*, ed. Adolf Haslinger (Salzburg, 1966), pp. 49–74. Hans-Albrecht Koch, "Das Textbuch der Zauberflöte: Zur Entstehung, Form und Gehalt der Dichtung Emanuel Schikaneders," *Jahrbuch des Freien Deutschen Hochstifts* (1969), pp. 76–120; Lieselotte Dieckmann, "Zum Bild des Menschen im achtzehnten Jahrhundert: Nathan der Weise,

Iphigenie, Die Zauberflöte," *Festschrift für Detlev W. Schumann zum 70. Geburtstag,* ed. Albert R. Schmitt (Munich, 1970), pp. 89–96.

4. *The Magic Flute: An Opera in Two Acts,* music by W. A. Mozart. *English version after the libretto of Schikaneder and Giesecke by W. H. Auden and Chester Kallman* (London, 1957), p. 9.

5. "To wander forever in the dark abyss of the earth." Wolfgang Amadeus Mozart, *Die Zauberflöte: Oper in zwei Aufzügen, Dichtung von Emanuel Schikaneder* (Stuttgart, 1966). All quotations in the text are cited by act and scene. Translations are from the English version by Ruth and Thomas Martin (New York, 1941), except when a verbatim rendering was preferable.

6. *Samlede Værker,* eds. A. B. Drachmann, J. L. Heiberg, H. O. Lange, 2 (Copenhagen, 1962), p. 78. "Papageno selects, Don Juan enjoys," *Either-Or,* trans. David S. and Lillian M. Swenson (Princeton, 1946), p. 65.

7. *The Magic Flute,* trans. W. H. Auden and Chester Kallman, pp. 13–15. The Marxist philosopher Ernst Bloch also calls Papageno a child of nature; "Die Zauberflöte und Symbole von heute," *Verfremdungen I* (Frankfurt am Main, 1963), p. 101.

8. *Die Zauberflöte: Geschichte und Deutung von Mozarts Oper* (Munich, 1964), pp. 212–20.

9. "Therefore I can be happy and gay / Because all birds are mine."

10. Szöverffy, "Zauberflöte und Welttheater," p. 267.

11. See Franz H. Bäuml, *Medieval Civilization in Germany 800–1273* (London, 1969), pp. 132–36.

12. "My father is a king who rules over many lands and people. That is why they call me Prince." "Between valleys and mountains." "According to the feathers that cover you, I take you for—." "Not a bird, by any chance?" "Stay away from me, I tell you, and don't trust me, because I have the strength of a giant." "If he does not begin to be afraid of me soon, I shall have to run for it." "With me, a good squeeze of the hand is more than weapons."

13. "I am just a child of nature, who is satisfied with sleep, food and drink. And if I once catch a pretty little wife—."

14. Immanuel Kant, *Ausgewählte kleine Schriften* (Hamburg, 1965), p. 1. "It is so comfortable to be immature." All translations are from *The Philosophy of Kant: Immanuel Kant's Moral and Political Writings,* ed. Carl J. Friedrich (New York, 1949), pp. 132–39.

15. *Ausgewählte kleine Schriften,* p. 1. "Sapere aude! Have the courage to use your own intelligence!" (*The Philosophy of Kant,* p. 132).

16. "O help me, protect me!"

17. *Program Notes,* State Opera, Hamburg, December 1968.

18. *Ausgewählte kleine Schriften,* p. 2. "To work himself out of the state of immaturity." "To walk alone." "A firm path." (*The Philosophy of Kant,* p. 133) .

19. "More than that—he is a human being."

20. Thus courage has triumphed,
and virtue will rise,
The laurels of wisdom
receiving as prize.

21. *Ausgewählte kleine Schriften,* p. 2. "Even inescapable" (*The Philosophy of Kant,* p. 133).

22. *Ausgewählte kleine Schriften,* p. 1. "The step into maturity not only as difficult but as very dangerous" (*The Philosophy of Kant,* p. 133).

23. "A pretty little wife." "I remain single."

24. "If the gods really have selected a Papagena for me, why do I have to exert myself so hard to win her? . . . With such eternal wanderings, one really feels like giving up love forever."

25. "The heavenly pleasures of the [Enlightened]." "I don't care a fig about the [Enlightened]. At the moment, to me the greatest pleasure would be a glass of wine."

26. What a joy for us is near
When the gods, their bounty showing,
And their grace on us bestowing,
Will send us tiny children dear.
First we will have a Papageno.
Then we will have a Papagena.
Then come another Papageno(a),
Papageno(a), Papageno(a)!
It is the greatest joy of any
When many, many
Pa-pa-pa-pa-pa-pa-pa-pageno(a)s
Upon their parents blessing bring.

27. *Ausgewählte kleine Schriften,* p. 1. "The largest part of mankind." *The Philosophy of Kant,* p. 133.

28. *Ausgewählte kleine Schriften,* p. 7. "The hindrances preventing a general enlightenment and an escape from . . . immaturity [are gradually reduced]" (*The Philosophy of Kant,* p. 138).

The Wild Man's Pedigree: Scientific Method and Racial Anthropology

✑ J O H N G . B U R K E

The eminent historian of science, George Sarton, once described science as "the endless struggle against errors, innocent or wilful, against superstitions and spiritual crimes."[1] Science, he declared, is "a civilizing and liberating power" and "the only development in human experience which is truly cumulative and progressive." In viewing science as an "increasing knowledge of the world and of ourselves," Sarton emphasized the rationality and the logic which the scientific method brings to bear on the mysteries of nature. Scientists attempt to catalog, to classify, to measure, to quantify, and thereby to erect a firm structure of positive knowledge about the universe.

In this process, however, scientists may fall into error; a fact, incidentally, of which Sarton was keenly aware. First, they may postulate an incorrect theory from imprecise or hasty observations and fail to test it thoroughly. Second, they may reify abstract concepts; that is, seize upon a pure creation of the mind and regard it as something concrete and real. Third, in their attempts to achieve mathematical precision, they may be seduced into a fallacy by excessive reliance on statistics. Let me illustrate each of these paths to error.

First, with respect to theory: The pseudoscience of astrology is based upon the assumption that the positions of the sun, moon, and planets against the background of the so-called fixed stars, in particular the constellations within the band of the zodiac, either at the time of conception or of birth determine a person's character, disposition, good or ill fortune, and ultimately his fate. Recognizing phenomenonologically that the sun and moon bear a relationship to the occurrence of a few earthly happenings such as the seasons of the year or the tides, astrologers long ago

259

inferred that heavenly bodies not only cause but determine all earthly events. Numerous scientists, from Ptolemy to Kepler, were astrologers, and over centuries astrological theory became further elaborated. Although it ceased to be taken seriously by scientists after the sixteenth century, astrology still has its devotees; and stocks and bonds are sold on Wall Street on the basis of astrological predictions.

Second, with respect to the reification of concepts: A good example is the belief in the existence of an ether, an idea that dominated physics in the last half of the nineteenth century. The ether was postulated initially as the medium which served to transmit forces across space, and more particularly the waves of light from the sun and the stars to the earth. There was general agreement among scientists that there had to be an ether; otherwise light waves could not be transmitted, just as the waves in a pond created by a pebble being dropped into it could not appear without the presence of water. Consequently, scientists gave this mental abstraction an independent reality, even in the face of a gross contradiction. On the one hand, calculations demonstrated that in order to transmit light waves at the known velocity of light, the ether would have to be more than a million times denser than steel. But despite this unbelievable density, the ether did not diminish in the slightest the velocity of the planets as they moved through it, and further the ether could not be seen, felt, smelled, tasted, or weighed. Only when precise experimentation over a period of years failed to detect the presence of the ether was the concept restored to its rightful role as a mental abstraction and its reality denied.

Another example of the reification of concepts, more germane to our central subject, is in the area of the social sciences. Karl Popper writes that one theory of the role of the social sciences is as the

study of behaviour of social wholes, such as groups, nations, classes, societies, civilizations, etc. These social wholes are conceived as the empirical objects which the social sciences study in the same way in which biology studies animals or plants.

This view must be rejected as naive. It completely overlooks the fact that these so-called social wholes are very largely postulates of popular social theories rather than empirical objects. . . . What they stand for is a kind of ideal object whose existence depends upon theoretical assumptions. Accordingly, the belief in the empirical existence of social wholes . . . has to be replaced by the demand that social phenomena, including collectives, should be analysed in terms of individuals and their actions and relations.[2]

Popper, then, points out the fallacy of the reification of any kind of social group by scientists, but in practice his stricture has not been heeded.

A third path to error is the excessive dependence upon and belief in the validity of quantitative techniques in describing natural phenomena. A good example involves a theory of the earth proposed by a French scientist, Dortous de Mairan. In 1765 Mairan published a lengthy article in the *Mémoires de l'Académie Royale des Sciences* in which he employed extraordinary mathematical legerdemain to prove that the sun was responsible for only a tiny amount of the heat of the soil and the atmosphere of the earth, and he asserted that this heat, in fact, resulted from the emanations of a huge central fire at the earth's core. Owing primarily to its mathematical exposition, Mairan's theory held sway for well over a half century, until the so-called greenhouse effect of the atmosphere began to be investigated; and it was not completely discredited until the discovery of radioactivity.

Such blunders may be serious obstacles to the progress of science, and I intend to demonstrate how scientists, from the eighteenth century on consistently erred in these ways in their studies of man. In my view, however, these fallacies pale into insignificance in comparison with the possible effects of the values or the prejudices in the mind of a scientist which he unconsciously or consciously holds when addressing himself to his subject matter. Both Sir Francis Bacon and René Descartes in the era of the scientific revolution recognized and warned against this danger to scientific objectivity. Bacon included such mental biases among his famous "idols," those four impediments in the path of rational understanding. Descartes, in his *Discourse on Method*, declared that he resolved to "accept nothing as true which [he] did not evidently know to be such, that is to say, scrupulously to avoid precipitance and prejudice."[3]

Despite such admonitions, scientists, in practice, have not been uniformly successful in attaining objectivity. Particularly in the development of the sciences of man we can observe that theories were colored by religious dogma and ancient beliefs. Also, it is obvious that these sciences were conditioned by psychological factors: that is, by innate fear, distrust, or distaste for the strange or alien, and by a compulsion to rationalize uneasiness through excessive emphasis on the superiority of one's own group in every conceivable respect.

Perhaps the well-known lines from John Keats's poem "On First Looking into Chapman's Homer" will be illustrative:

> Then felt I like some watcher of the skies
> When a new planet swims into his ken;

> Or like stout Cortez when with eagle eyes
>   He star'd at the Pacific—and all his men
> Look'd at each other with wild surmise—
>   Silent, upon a peak in Darien.

Here Keats has eloquently and trenchantly expressed the impact on the human psyche when it is confronted by a vast unknown and recognizes it as such. Unfortunately, no poet has so succinctly described the feelings of civilized Europeans when they faced the savages of newly discovered lands during their voyages of exploration. We know that their feelings must have been mixed. There existed surprise, curiosity, and lust, together with fear, a sense of superiority, and disgust. That the chronicles of the explorers over centuries did little to temper the shock of an initial meeting is attested to by the words of the young Charles Darwin when he reported his impressions of the Patagonians at Tierra del Fuego in 1832. "Viewing such men," he wrote in his journal, "one can hardly make oneself believe that they are fellow-creatures and inhabitants of the same world."[4] It is worth emphasis that popular opinions concerning race, not only in the nineteenth but also in the twentieth century, were heavily influenced by scientific theories, which, as I have remarked, were in turn conditioned by religious views and psychological factors.

I

Steeped in religious tradition, the explorers must have been amazed when they found savage men in newly discovered lands. In *The City of God*, Augustine had categorically denied the possibility of men's inhabiting the far reaches of the earth. He declared:

But as to the fable that there are Antipodes, that is to say, men on the opposite side of the earth, where the sun rises when it sets to us, men who walk with their feet opposite ours, that is on no ground credible. And, indeed, it is not affirmed that this has been learned by historical knowledge, but by scientific conjecture, on the ground that the earth is suspended within the concavity of the sky, and that it has as much room on the one side of it as on the other: hence they say that the part which is beneath must also be inhabited. But they do not remark that, although it be supposed or scientifically demonstrated that the world is of a round and spherical form yet it does not follow that the other side of the earth is bare of water; nor even, though it be bare, does it immediately follow that it is peopled. For Scripture, which proves the truth of its historical statements by the accomplishment of its prophecies, gives no false information; and it is too absurd to say, that some men might have taken ship and traversed the whole wide ocean, and crossed from this side of the world to the other, and that thus even the inhabitants of that distant region are descended from that one first man.[5]

The surprise of the explorers in encountering savages and in determining whether they were indeed fellow humans was undoubtedly compounded by the popular lore of the Middle Ages. Greek and Roman chroniclers, such as Diodorus Siculus and Pliny the Elder, had passed on tales of headless men whose eyes and mouths were located in their breasts; men with one, three, or four eyes; men with such large ears that they slept wrapped in them; men with feet growing from the backs instead of the fronts of their legs; men with feet shaped like those of geese; men with no mouths who survived solely by smell; and men with hairy bodies and dogs' faces. These fictions were recorded and illustrated in various encyclopedias and compendiums of the Middle Ages and the Renaissance, and they had wide popular appeal.

One such thirteenth-century encyclopedia, compiled by Thomas of Cantimpré, entitled *On the Nature of Things*, provoked scholastic discussion that illustrated the difficulty involved in framing a distinct definition of the necessary attributes of a human being. Thomas repeated the stories from Herodotus, Aristotle, and Pliny concerning pygmies and dwarfs, and his tales prompted two scholars, Albert of Saxony and Peter of Alvernia, to attempt to answer these questions: first, Do pygmies exist? and second, Are they men? On the basis of the evidence, both declared that the existence of pygmies was credible; but both denied that they were men, although for different reasons. Peter asserted that the pygmies' lack of reason, of critical judgment, and of capability to achieve morality and to avoid evil prevented their inclusion in the human species. Albert compared pygmies to morons, incapable of culture, and ignorant of science and art. In his view they were wild, in a state midway between man and the ape. To illustrate his point, Albert related one of the first of many stories concerning mental defectives or other unfortunates found in the state of nature apart from but close to civilization. His tale concerned a wild couple who were tracked by hunters and attacked by their dogs. The woman did not survive the ordeal, but the man was cornered and captured. Thereafter, Albert wrote, the man was taught to stand erect but could learn only a few words and obviously did not possess reason. Pygmies, in Albert's view were similar to such wild men. Combining the views of both Scholastics, then, a man to be considered human must not only be rational but also civilized.[6]

However, in the enthnocentric culture of western Europe, being rational and civilized rather than wild was also associated with being a Christian. Thus, from the beginning, the savages of the newly discovered lands were viewed as the devil's creation; their religions were considered as the devil's service; and their gods as various forms of the devil.[7] Although the bull of Pope Paul II of July 2, 1537, declared that the inhabitants of North and South America were true men, it qualified this statement by adding that their membership in the human race through Christianization was a clearly recognizable *possibility*.[8] With this attitude it is small wonder that between fifteen and twenty million Indians were killed or died during the half-century following the Spanish colonization of the Americas, the loss to be repaired later by the importation of black slaves from Africa.[9] Furthermore, the distinction between human being and Wild Man persisted among the explorers. In the first decade of the eighteenth century an Englishman, Captain Rogers, visited California and wrote that since the natives were naked, ignorant of European customs, and understood no word of Spanish, they must be wild.[10]

II

As it became more evident that the newly discovered men were capable of civilization and also amenable to conversion to Christianity, a new dilemma arose. What were the origins of these various savage groups, and how had they come to populate distant and widely separated lands? The first to voice a polygenist theory—the creation of a plurality of races—was Theophrastus Paracelsus, in 1520. Paracelsus declared:

I cannot abstain . . . from making mention of those who have been found in the out-of-the-way islands, and still remain, and are to be met with there. No one will easily believe that they are the posterity of Adam and Eve, for the sons of Adam by no means departed into out-of-the-way islands. It is most probable that they are descended from another Adam.[11]

In another passage he said:

It cannot be proved that those men who inhabit the hidden countries are descended from Adam; but it is credible that they were born there after the deluge, and perhaps they have no souls. In speech they are like parrots, and have no souls, unless God be pleased to join them in the bonds of matrimony with those who have souls. [12]

The speculations of Paracelsus were subsequently reinforced by other considerations, which not only shaped the polygenist theory in later centuries but also contributed to the eventual discarding of the biblical account of Creation. Against the earnest advice of friends, Isaac de la Peyrère, in 1655, published a work entitled *Pre-Adamitae*, wherein he attempted to prove that Adam and Eve were not the first human beings on earth. Peyrère based his theory on an obscure biblical passage: verses 12–14, chapter 5, of Paul's Epistle to the Romans. The first creation, Peyrère postulated, occurred several thousands of years before the time of Adam, thus explaining the origin of the Gentiles. The peoples of the New World, Peyrère asserted, were undoubtedly descendants of these pre-Adamites. Peyrère's book, published in Amsterdam, was condemned and burned at Paris, which created widespread public interest in it and a subsequent substantial rise in its price. In 1658, Peyrère, however, was forced to abjure his theory as well as his Calvinist beliefs.[13]

Some seventeenth-century scholars, notably R. Brerewood and Matthew Hale, hoping to save the biblical account, voiced the hypothesis that the American Indians had probably come from Siberia by way of Alaska. Although somewhat in agreement with this idea, Robert Hooke, noting that the Indians did not possess the wheel, concluded that they had either migrated before its invention or were not of Tartar origin.[14]

Nevertheless, the polygenist theory grew in popularity. Two anonymous essays published in London in 1695 declared that the postulation of a former land bridge between Asia and North America, subsequently destroyed by earthquakes or inundations, merely begged the question. The writer pointed out that the vast number of Indian languages were totally different from European languages. He added that the bitter northern climate would preclude migration from northern Asia and that navigation from China would have been impossible because of unfavorable winds, unseaworthy ships, and ignorance of the compass in ancient times. He admitted that sailing from the west coast of Africa was a better possibility, but he contended that the people of Africa and America differed completely, that the natives must not have brought any of the animals known to be useful in the Old World, and further that there were many animal species in America never found in Europe or Africa. The author concluded:

As many difficulties lye against the Mosaick system, of confining all species of living terrestrial creatures within the Asiatick, or primaeval Paradise, and afterwards to Noah's ark; so more seem to arise against the propagation of all mankind out of one single male and female, unless all posterity, both blacks and whites, separated by vast seas, were all included actually in form within Adam and Eve.[15]

To many, then, the vast distances and the perilous seas separating the continents and the island archipelagos, the differences of color, of head and body conformation, of language, and of customs among the human inhabitants of the earth militated against the belief in a single genesis of mankind at a specific time. And, as the number of known, diverse animal species multiplied, the story of Noah and his ark came increasingly under suspicion.

III

The eighteenth century was the period par excellence for classification in the sciences. It was at this time that the great naturalists, Linnaeus and Buffon, flourished. Cultured nobles and rich merchants vied to assemble the most complete cabinets of minerals, plants, and fossils. But display for instruction and illumination required a type of rational ordering process; classification was necessary to detect similarities and to accentuate differences among the collected materials. Man was not excluded from this classification procedure, and it was at this time that the modern concept of race began to emerge.

It is instructive to follow the development of the thought of Linnaeus with respect to the classification of man. In the first edition of the *Systema Naturae,* published in 1735, Linnaeus considered man as a quadruped animal, placing him in the same class as the ape and the sloth. Appended to this class, as an anomaly, he listed the orangutan, described as "tailed, hairy, bearded, with a human body, much given to gesticulations, extremely lascivious," and a species of ape. "The *tailed man,*" Linnaeus continued, "of whom modern travellers relate so much, is of the same genus."[16]

In 1740, in the second edition, Linnaeus distinguished four varieties of man, based on geography and color: the white European, the red American, the dark Asiatic, and the black African. He continued this classification until 1758, although in 1748 he eliminated the anomaly listed above. Linnaeus's tenth edition, in 1758, represents his mature and most complete classification of Homo sapiens. He included six varieties: wild, American, European, Asiatic, African, and monster. An abbreviated version of his description is as follows:

    a. Wild—shaggy hair, mute, four-footed.
    b. American—red, choleric, erect; thick, straight, black hair; distended

nostrils; freckled face; beardless chin; obstinate, gay, free. He paints himself with variegated, red lines. He is ruled by custom.

c. European—white, sanguine, muscular; long, blond hair; blue eyes; gentle, most intelligent; a discoverer. He covers himself with clothing suitable to the northern climate. He is ruled by religious custom.

d. Asiatic—yellow, melancholy, rigid; dark hair; dark eyes; austere, arrogant, greedy. He covers himself with loose clothing. He is ruled by opinion.

e. African—black, phlegmatic, lax; black, curly hair; silky skin, apelike nose; swollen lips; the bosoms of the women are distended; their breasts give milk copiously; crafty, slothful, careless. He smears himself with fat. He is ruled by authority.

f. Monster—divided into two groups: those so by nature as dwarfs and giants; and those so by custom as eunuchs, and peoples with compressed or elongated heads.[17]

Leaving aside monsters and wild men for the moment, we see that Linnaeus's classification is founded on contrasts. In addition to his previous distinctions based on geography and color, he now includes the ancient theory of the four humors in his classification, as well as supposed racial personality traits, facial and bodily features, wearing apparel or the lack of it, and customs. His bias in favor of the European is apparent, a prejudice that has continued to the present among a number of anthropologists and psychologists.

But the disparities between the views of Linnaeus and of later systematizers should also be highlighted. As his classification showed, he did not clearly distinguish between apes and those humans later recognized as mental defectives or lacking one or more of the senses. As proof that there were wild men, Linnaeus referred under this division to stories about boys and girls living in a wild state among bears, wolves, or other animals. One such example was the so-called *juvenis ovinus Hibernus,* or Irish sheep boy, who had been described by the Dutch writer, Tulpius, and whose account Linnaeus accepted at face value.[18] Such stories, Linnaeus declared, were in agreement on these points: that those so found could not speak at all; that they all were hairy; and that they ran about on their hands and feet and could climb trees in a moment. He concluded that it was extremely difficult to distinguish between these wild men and apes.

Similarly, Linnaeus did not differentiate from apes those men later characterized as albinos. In an essay entitled "Anthropomorpha," published in 1760, Linnaeus summarized stories concerned with ape-men, commonly known as troglodytes:

These children of darkness, who turn day into night and night into day, seem to me to be most nearly related to us. . . . They are not much larger than a boy of nine years old; white in colour, and not sunburnt, because they always go about at night; they walk erect like ourselves; the hair of their head is short, and curly by nature, like that of the Mauritanians, but at the same time is white. Their eyes are orbiculated; the pupil and iris golden, a thing which deserves particular attention. Their eyebrows hang down in front, so that their vision is oblique and lateral; under the upper eyelid they have the membrana nictitans, like bears and owls, and other animals which go about by night, and this is the principal mark by which they are distinguished from us. . . . They lurk in their caves during the day, and are nearly blind, before they are caught by men and accustomed to the light. . . . They have a language of their own which they speak in a whistle, so difficult, that scarce any one can learn it except by long association with them. . . . In many places of the East Indies they are caught and made use of in houses as servants to do the lighter domestic work, as to carry water, lay the table, and take away the plates. . . . And it would be no small gain to a philosopher, if he could spend some days with one of these animals, and investigate how far the power of the human mind surpasses theirs, and what is the real difference between the brute and the rational being.[19]

Here Linnaeus employed a similar criteria to distinguish a human as did the Scholastics, Albert of Saxony and Peter of Alvernia; that is, lack of reason, of critical judgment, and inarticulate speech. From this time forward, however, close observation of anatomical features and attempts to measure or quantify differences among men became characteristic of the method employed by scientists concerned with humans.

In many respects Johann Friedrich Blumenbach was the most important figure in eighteenth-century anthropology. In his early writings Blumenbach followed Linnaeus with respect to dividing men into four races on the basis of geography and color. But he refuted Linnaeus's ideas concerning the troglodytes, maintaining that they were men afflicted with a disease that affected both the skin and the eyes simultaneously. He also discounted the story of the Irish sheep boy, pointing out that no wild sheep were to be found in Ireland. Further, Blumenbach made a painstaking investigation of another of Linnaeus's prime examples of a Wild Man, the so-called *puer Hannoveranus,* proving that the youth, found in a wild state, was a mute mental defective who had been driven away from his home by a new stepmother.[20]

Blumenbach's most important conclusions were based on craniology. He studied many human skulls and believed that skull conformation could be employed to distinguish five races of mankind: the Caucasian, the Mongolian, the Ethiopian, the American, and the Malay. The Caucasian skull, Blumenbach thought, had the most perfect form. He was particularly impressed by the exquisite symmetry of the skull of a female from Georgia in the Caucasus region, and he considered the Caucasian to be the primeval race from which others had diverged over time. He was reinforced in this opinion by color. The Caucasian race was white, and as he said:

We may fairly assume [white] to have been the primitive color of mankind, since . . . it is very easy for [white] to degenerate into brown, but very much more difficult for dark to become white, when the secretion and precipitation of this carbonaceous pigment . . . has once deeply struck root.[21]

Blumenbach, in fact, believed and taught that the four other races had resulted from the degeneration of the Caucasian; in one direction through the American Indian to the Mongolian; and in the other through the Malay to the Ethiopian. The degeneration, he declared, was the effect of "turning aside" of the "formative force" by such influences as climate, diet, and mode of life, acting long and continuously through many series of generations.[22]

Blumenbach, however, did not reify the concept of race; that is, he did not make race an empirical object as later ethnologists were to do. There were innumerable varieties of mankind, he asserted, and they merge into each other in insensible degrees. He stressed the fact that the races he had delineated were merely the five principal varieties. Further, Blumenbach did not use the term "degeneration" in any pejorative sense. In one of his early works, he did describe the inhabitants of China and Korea as "distinguished for depravity and perfidiousness of spirit and manners," but at the time he was strongly influenced by Linnaeus.[23] Later, however, he was particularly critical of those of his contemporaries who considered the black to be either an inferior race or a separate species. "There is no single character," Blumenbach argued, "so peculiar and so universal among the Ethiopians, but what it may be observed . . . everywhere in other varieties of men."[24] He attributed good disposition and natural tenderness to blacks; and he declared that they had the capacity for learning mathematical and physical sciences, medicine, poetry, and literature; the capability of producing fine handiwork; and that they possessed a noted gift for music. In short, Blumenbach was convinced that the mental faculties and talents of blacks were just as perfectible as those of the members of the other large divisions of mankind.

The virulently racist theories of the nineteenth and twentieth centuries, however, were anticipated in Blumenbach's time by such men as Samuel T. Soemmering and Christoph Meiners. Soemmering compared all the external bodily features of blacks and Europeans and concluded that the black stood much closer to the ape than did the European. Inasmuch as the black was barely separated racially from the ape, he declared, the fact that they walked in an upright fashion as other humans did should not be used as an argument for the abolition of slavery.[25] Meiners, overwhelmed by the repulsive appearance of the greater part of humanity, set forth an extremely simple classificatory system containing only two categories: the beautiful, namely the white race; and the ugly, including all other races. The European peoples, excluding the Slavs, Meiners thought, were mentally and physically superior to all other races. These other races, he asserted, possessed a sickly irritability, from which arose such traits as extraordinary agility, inherited despair, convulsions, torpidity, impotence, and a high probability of suicide. Further symptoms of their innate inferiority were imitativeness, good recollection of words, timidity and slyness coupled with stupidity and falsehood.[26]

Meiners's thinking, in fact, presaged the highly influential work of Count Arthur de Gobineau, whose *Essai sur l'inégalité des races humaines,* was published between 1853 and 1855. In it Gobineau summarized the theories of his predecessors as follows:

Such is the lesson of history. It shows that all civilizations derive from the white race, that none can exist without its help, and that a society is great and brilliant only so far as it preserves the blood of the noble group that created it, provided that this group itself belongs to the most illustrious branch of our species.[27]

With Gobineau the myth of the Aryan master race gained popularity, and his work became the bible of its later adherents, most notably the Nazis and their führer, Adolf Hitler.

IV

Such were the results of those eighteenth-century hypotheses concerning race that rested on a qualitative approach to anthropology, that is, the study of gross anatomy or the social and cultural characteristics of various peoples. In the late eighteenth century, however, there was a concurrent effort to delineate the differences among men quantitatively: by measurements of a variety of bodily features. One of the first to employ this method was Peter Camper, of Holland, an older contemporary of Blumenbach. Camper's interest in ethnology derived from his desire to introduce realism into painting. He was disturbed that such masters as Rubens had portrayed the Eastern Magi as Negroes but had not truly represented the skull conformation and features of blacks. In order to encourage the accurate delineation of facial characteristics in portraiture, Camper devised a method of distinguishing various human crania by mathematical means. His two most important measurements were the breadth of the skull and the facial angle which, he taught, varied from 70° to 100° in man. In Camper's system the Kalmuck had the broadest skull and the black the narrowest. The facial angle of the black was the most acute, being approximately 70°, while that of the statues of Greek antiquity was about 100°. The facial angles of the other races ranged in between these two extremes.[28]

Camper's initial attempt to determine the differences among men by mathematical means has, of course, persisted to the present. Another early finding concerned the ratio of the length of the forearm to that of the upper arm. According to Charles White, of Manchester, if the length of the upper arm is taken as 100, the forearm in the chimpanzee is 94, in the inhabitant of Tierra del Fuego 81.9, in the black 77.7, and in the European 73.4.[29] The smaller ratio found in the European supposedly indicated a higher development or an innate superiority.

In the nineteenth century such measurements were extended to include the capacities of the crania of various human types and the weights of brains. In these studies a central assumption was that there was a distinct correlation between mental ability and cranial volume or brain weight. This was a curious echo of the ancient and medieval belief that rationality was the criterion which differentiated the human species from all others. Now it was thought that a way had been found to measure or quantify rationality. The practice was in vogue during most of the century, and proslavery writers in the United States used the findings of ethnologists engaged in such research to justify the degraded status of the black man. The most publicized study was that of Samuel George Morton, of Philadelphia, a physician, naturalist, and ethnologist, who, at his death, was president of the American Academy of Natural Sciences.

Morton collected human skulls from all over the world, cataloged them according to race or racial subgroup, and measured the volumes of the crania. He determined that the mean volume of the crania of African-born and American-born blacks was 83 cubic inches, that of the crania of Germans, English, and Anglo-Americans 92 cubic inches, and those of other racial groups in between these two extremes. Morton offered these mean values as evidence of the innate mental inferiority of the black race, and he concluded that since the black was by nature mentally inferior to the white, he would forever remain in that condition.[30]

The substance of Morton's ideas, considered as the irrefutable teachings of contemporary science, was repeated in the pages of such periodicals as the *Southern Literary Messenger* of Richmond and *De Bow's Commercial Review* of New Orleans.[31] Most of the criticism leveled at Morton's theory was of a theological nature; for example, it was argued that the simultaneous creation of a plurality of races contradicted the teachings of the Bible.[32] A few voices were raised to question the scientific validity of Morton's conclusion that blacks were mentally inferior. For example, one transplanted northern preacher wrote in an 1845 issue of Charleston's *Southern Quarterly Review*:

It is readily granted that the average size and weight of the brain is less in the Ethiopian than in the European, but so long as cases are frequently found in the former race, which attain and overreach the average of the latter, we must conclude that the former are susceptible of change, and that their inferiority may be and probably is the effect of degradation.[33]

This was solid criticism, inasmuch as Morton's published table showed that the largest cranial volume among the Anglo-Americans was 97 cubic inches compared with one of 99 cubic inches among those of native Africans. In like manner, the smallest among the crania of Germans was 70 cubic inches, whereas the smallest cranial volume among native-born blacks was 73 cubic inches. Convinced of the power of his statistical method, however, Morton neglected to explain these anomalies among the individual crania and only superficially considered such variables as age and sex.

Hardly any scientists questioned the bases of Morton's theory: the conviction that the race concept was a physical reality, and the assumption that cranial volume was a valid indication of human mental power or intelligence. Rather, Morton's views were grasped by contemporary scientists. They were incorporated in a book written in 1854 by the ethnologist, Josiah Clark Nott, and a former diplomat, George R. Gliddon, entitled *Types of Mankind*. This work went through ten editions, and it frankly stated the mental superiority of the white as a scientific fact. The book included a letter from the noted Swiss scientist, Prof. Louis

Agassiz, of Harvard, who supported this view without qualification.[34] Contemporary science, then, accepted the thesis that there were distinct races of mankind, and that owing to their innate mentality, the Malay, Mongolian, American, and particularly the Negro races must resign themselves to unalterable and eternal inferiority. The Negro, Nott asserted, could not exist alongside the white race except as a tributary either in name or in fact.

After the Civil War, in 1869, another study of the weights of brains produced some curious conclusions. Sanford B. Hunt, in cooperation with Surgeon Ira Russell of the Eleventh Massachusetts Volunteer Regiment, examined the brains of over four hundred white, racially mixed, and black soldiers. Hunt found again that the average weight of the brains of blacks was less than that of the brains of whites, but also determined that as the percentage of white blood increased there was a corresponding increase in the weight of the brain of the black. Assuming again that brain weight was the essential condition of intellectual prowess, Hunt estimated that the competitive advantage of the white over the black was 9.5 percent. Hunt's study, however, turned up another peculiar statistic. He compared his data with those published previously in various European journals and to his amazement discovered that the average weight of the brains of the white Americans he had measured was greater than that of white Europeans. Sliding easily from the concept of the reality of race to that of the reality of national character and cultural conditions, Hunt concluded that the brains of whites had enlarged under the free republican institutions of America; that is, on the average, Americans were currently more intelligent than Europeans. Further, Hunt declared, it was completely logical to conclude that the intelligence of black would profit similarly from their newly granted freedom. However, Hunt admitted that his sample of twenty-four brains of white Americans was probably not large enough to support his generalizations and called for further research on the subject.[35]

Hunt's speculations that American political and social institutions might have the effect of enlarging the brain provoked an immediate and negative response on the other side of the Atlantic. J. Barnard Davis, a Fellow of the Royal Society of London, seriously questioned Hunt's methods How had the brains been weighed? Had they been divested of membranes and drained of fluids? Were the medullae oblongatae considered to be portions of the brains and weighed along with them? Hunt's results, in Davis's opinion, were inexact, just as the prior observations of Morton were crude and unworthy of serious consideration because of discrepancies and omissions. The size, stature, and weight of the individual, as well as his or her age or sex, Davis believed, had not been thoroughly taken into account in studies of brain weight. All these factors, Davis argued, must be given attention before any worthwhile scientific conclusions could be made. But, reflecting the general climate of scientific thought, Davis emphasized that the weight of the brain was a characteristic of race, appertaining exclusively to a race. He denied emphatically that the weight of the brain could, under any circumstances, be considered a national idiosyncrasy.[36]

Davis's strictures concerning the methodology of investigations of the weights of human brains imposed severe restrictions on this line of research. Although such studies continued, it became increasingly apparent that while the mean brain weight of various races or ethnic groups did vary, the range of variation within a particular group far exceeded the mean variation between races or groups. Such findings defied explanation; consequently, late in the nineteenth century scientists adopted what appeared to be a more promising approach to the question of rationality and race.

The new trend was stimulated primarily by Sir Francis Galton's studies of heredity. Galton's basic hypothesis was that intellectual ability evolved over a considerable period of time, that it gradually became innate, and that is finally was transmitted as an inherited characteristic. He attempted to substantiate his theory by gathering data on generations of men from the upper classes of England and demonstrating that success in the professions, politics, or business tended to be limited to the members of certain families. Such success, Galton thought, should constitute an outward indication of the degree of intelligence possessed by a person.[37]

Galton's work had two results: First, the concept of intelligence now became reified just as the concept of race had been previously. Second, it led scientists to the belief that intelligence could be completely defined from a behavioristic point of view and that it could be treated mathematically in the same manner that physicists dealt with mass or velocity. One could not clearly distinguish the pedigrees of various human types by describing their members qualitatively, nor could any sense be made of the differences in skull size or brain weights. But surely, the innate differences, *known* to exist, should be amenable to discrimination by "objective" tests in which ability to answer correctly a variety of questions could be measured.

Consequently, during the early twentieth century, work in this direction resulted in the construction of several psychological- or psychometric-type intelligence tests. A number of such tests were administered to small, selected groups of both whites and blacks prior to the First World War, but to the unconcealed delight of psychologists, mass tests on about 81,000 native-born American whites, 12,000 foreign-born whites, and 23,000 blacks were authorized to be administered in U.S. Army training camps after America's entry into the war. The basic examination was known as the Alpha test, and in addition, another, the Beta test, was given to illiterates and to soldiers who were unable to understand the questions asked them on the Alpha test. One major conclusion drawn from this study was that the black recruits had markedly lower mental ratings than the whites. Statistically, the black overlap in these tests was about 13 percent, which meant that about seven-eighths of the black recruits were below the average of the whites.[38] It was only a short time after these results were published in 1920 that their social implications were clearly spelled out. In 1921, Prof. G. O. Ferguson, of the University of Virginia, wrote:

The mental difference between whites and Negroes in general indicates that there should be a difference in the organization of the schools of the two races. . . . The psychological backwardness of colored children is everywhere paralleled by their educational backwardness.[39]

C. C. Brigham, one of the principal investigators, completed a comprehensive work on the army tests in 1923, entitled *A Study of American Intelligence*. In it Brigham examined the charge that the army tests merely showed differences in environment and education and vigorously denied this inference. He stated: "Our educational institutions are themselves a part of our race heritage. The average Negro child cannot advance through an educational curriculum adapted to the Anglo-Saxon in step with that child."[40] Further, Brigham concluded that the average intelligence of immigrants to the United States had been declining, owing to the increased immigration of Alpine and Mediterranean races, which, he believed, were intellectually inferior to the Nordic race. The blending of the four races—Nordic, Alpine, Mediterranean, and black— would, he asserted, cause the future racially-mixed American to be far less intelligent than the present native-born white American. Brigham warned:

The decline of American intelligence will be more rapid than the decline of the intelligence of European national groups owing to the presence here of the Negro. These are the plain, if somewhat ugly, facts that our study shows. The deterioration of American intelligence is not inevitable, however, if public action can be aroused to prevent it. There is no reason why steps should not be taken which will insure a continuously progressive upward evolution. The steps that should be taken to preserve or increase our present intellectual capacity must, of course, be dictated by science and not by political expediency.[41]

Just what Brigham was hinting at in the last sentence is not clear. It might have been a strengthening of laws against mixed marriages between races or possibly a eugenics program. In any case, the passage of stricter immigration laws within a few years reflected this type of thinking.

Brigham's conception of race and group intelligence as independent realities or empirical objects is manifest, as is his conviction that his statistical findings were valid measures of the true state of affairs. Such questions as these had been asked on the Army Alpha test:

The Knight engine is used in (a) the Packard (b)the Lozier (c) the Stearns (d) the Pierce Arrow. Joseph Choate was (a) a merchant (b) an engineer (c) a lawyer (d) a scientist.

The recruit was requested to select the proper answer from among the multiple choices. At the time, Brigham could not accept the objection that this type of question was primarily a test of information acquired through the agency of the environment. In other words, there was confusion among test psychologists between ignorance and stupidity.

V

But in the same period that Brigham was writing, some men in both the physical and social sciences were beginning to reject as empirical objects those mental abstractions which had been previously attributed a concrete reality. As mentioned earlier in this essay, the ether was one of the first to be discarded, and then with Einstein's theories of relativity, the conceptions of absolute space and absolute time. In 1929, Brigham himself made a courageous retraction of his earlier views. He finally came to the conclusion that separately the army Alpha and Beta tests had a low reliability, that the attitudes of the persons taking the tests could materially affect the test scores, and that for the purpose of comparing individuals and groups, tests in the vernacular had to be used only with individuals having equal opportunities to acquire the vernacular of the tests; in other words, that persons had to have equal developmental and educational environments before they could be compared with such tests. But even more important, Brigham pointed out that psychologists had been guilty of a "naming fallacy" which enabled them to slide mysteriously from the score in the test to the hypothetical faculty suggested by the name given to the test, for example, sensory discrimination, perception, memory, and intelligence, whereas the reference was to a certain objective test situation. He concluded:

This review has summarized some of the more recent test findings which show that comparative studies of various national and racial groups may not be made with existing tests, and which show, in particular, that one of the most pretentious of these comparative racial studies—the writer's own—was without foundation.[42]

Meanwhile, anthropologists attempted to clarify the concept of race. Ernest A. Hooten defined a race as "a great division of mankind, the members of which, though individually varying, are characterized as a group by a certain combination of morphological and metrical features, principally nonadaptive, which have been derived from their common descent."[43] In addition, Hooten returned to the position of Blumenbach, when he stated that no single bodily characteristic exhibited a sufficient range of variation to enable anthropologists to assign to each of the large human groups a distinct and exclusive development of that feature. Similarly, Franz Boas spoke of race as a *concept,* which was lacking in clarity, and he asserted that a great error was committed by assuming that people who look alike in some respects must be alike in all respects.[44] The behaviorist psychologist, John B. Watson, denied claims that slight anatomical differences affected the formation of habits, and he stressed the great influence of the environment in human development. In Watson's judgment, intelligence tests were in no respect tests of intelligence, but only more or less random samplings of the organization of individuals at a given age.[45]

Thus, gradually, race and intelligence were restored to their rightful roles in science, as useful concepts rather than as concrete realities. Racial divisions could be valuable as a research tool, but there was among many scientists an increasing understanding that one could not legitimately extend generalizations derived from this model to the individual or to his social situation. Similarly, it was perceived that a wealth of personality factors of an environmental nature could contribute to the so-called success or failure on intelligence tests. Measurement and quantification which merely attempted to prove invalid theoretical assumptions was, by and large, recognized to be unintelligent and fruitless.

Yet, it appears that a number of scientists are presently prostituting their mentalities to prove racist theory. They grasp at such findings as the presence of the Rh negative gene solely among northern Europeans, or the sickle-cell gene predominantly but not exclusively among blacks, as proof of the validity of the belief in race as an empirical object. Similarly, they continue to ascribe objective reality to the concept of intelligence as measured by intelligence tests. They seek to support their hypothesis of the mental inferiority of black people by reference to the apparently more rapid uterine development of the black, to the apparently smaller supragranular layer of the cortex of the brain of the black, or to electroencephalograph studies. Reversing the earlier position of Christoph Meiners, they now also claim that the lower suicide rate among black peoples than among whites demonstrates the mental inferiority of blacks.[46]

In the search for the pedigree of the Wild Man, of the pagan savages of Africa, of the Americas, and of the islands of the Pacific, scientists have left a dismal record and a heavy legacy. Their statements of unsubstantiated hypotheses, their reification of the conceptual models of race and intelligence, and their use of statistical nonsense to support fallacious assumptions united with their deep psychological biases to provide a seemingly rational scientific basis for the exploitation and destruction of millions of human beings. Humanity can no longer tolerate the perpetuation of such errors. As one noted anthropologist recently wrote: "It is time for the 19th century to come to a close in racial anthropology, even among amateurs."[47]

NOTES

1. George Sarton, *A Guide to the History of Science* (New York, 1952), p. 11.

2. Karl R. Popper, "Prediction and Prophecy in the Social Sciences," in *Theories of History*, ed. Patrick Gardiner (New York, 1959), p. 281.

3. Norman Kemp Smith, ed. and trans., *Descartes' Philosophical Writings* (London, 1952), p. 129.

4. Charles Darwin, *Journal of . . . the Beagle* (New York, 1952), p. 235.

5. Marcus Dods, trans., *The City of God*, in *Works of Augustine* (Edinburgh, 1934), II, 118–19 (bk. XVI, ch. 9).

6. Joseph Koch, "Sind die Pygmäen Menschen?" *Archiv für Geschichte der Philosophie*, 40 (1931), 194–213.

7. Wilhelm E. Mühlmann, *Methodik der Völkerkunde* (Stuttgart, 1938), p. 17 (hereafter cited as *Methodik*).

8. Wilhelm E. Mühlmann, *Geschichte der Anthropologie* (Frankfurt am Main, 1968), p. 35 (hereafter cited as *Geschichte*). For fuller commentary on this papal bull, see the discussion in Robe's essay (p. 47).

9. *Methodik*, p. 18.

10. *Methodik*, p. 18.

11. Thomas Bendyshe, "The History of Anthropology," *Memoirs of the Anthropological Society of London*, I (1863–64), 353 (hereafter cited as *History*).

12. *History*, p. 354.

13. *History*, pp. 355–56; *Geschichte*, p. 43.

14. J. S. Slotkin, *Readings in Early Anthropology* (Chicago, 1965), pp. 97, 99–100.

15. *History*, p. 370.

16. *History*, p. 422.

17. *History*, pp. 424–25.

18. Thomas Bendyshe, trans. and ed., *The Anthropological Treatises of Johann Friedrich Blumenbach* (London, 1865), pp. 165–66 (hereafter cited as *Blumenbach*).

19. *History*, pp. 455–57.

20. For a full account of *puer Hannoveranus*, see Novak's essay (pp. 183–221).

21. *Blumenbach*, p. 269.

22. *Blumenbach*, p. 194.

23. *Blumenbach*, p. 100 n.

24. *Blumenbach*, p. 270.

25. Samuel Thomas Soemmering, *Ueber die körperliche Verschiedenheit des Negers von Europäer* (Frankfurt am Main, 1785), trans. J. H. Guenebault as *Natural History of the Negro Race* (Charleston, S.C., 1837), pp. 54–88.

26. *Methodik*, pp. 30–38.

27. Arthur de Gobineau, *Essai sur l'inégalité des races humaines*, 5th ed. (Paris, 1853–55), I, 220.

28. D. J. Cunningham, "Anthropology in the Eighteenth Century," *Journal of the Royal Anthropological Institute*, 38 (1908), 16–20.

29. Cunningham, "Anthropology," pp. 20–22.

30. Samuel George Morton, *Crania Americana* (Philadelphia, 1839), p. 88; J. C. Nott and George R. Gliddon, *Types of Mankind* (Philadelphia, 1855), pp. 450–54; Samuel George Morton, "On the Size of the Brain in the Various Races of Man," *Proceedings, Philadelphia Academy of Natural Sciences*, 5 (1850), 122. See also William Stanton, *The Leopard's Spots: Scientific Attitudes Toward Race in America, 1815–59* (Chicago, 1960).

31. *Southern Literary Messenger*, 5 (1839), 616; *De Bow's Commercial Review*, II (1851), 184, 403, 630.

32. John Bachman, *The Doctrine of the Unity of the Human Race Examined on the Principles of Science* (Charleston, S.C., 1850); also Stanton, *Leopard's Spots*, passim.

33. *Southern Quarterly Review*, 7 (1845), 372.

34. Nott and Gliddon, *Types of Mankind*, pp. lxxv–lxxvi, 52, 79, 185, 260, 415.

35. Sanford B. Hunt, M.D., "The Negro as a Soldier," *The Anthropological Review*, 7 (1869), 40.

36. J. B. Davis, "The Brain in the Negro," *The Anthropological Review*, 7 (1869), 190. Also J. B. Davis, "Contributions toward Determining the Weight of the Brain in Different Races of Man," *Philosophical Transactions of the Royal Society*, 158 (1868), 505–27.

37. Sir Francis Galton, *Inquiries into the Human Faculty and Its Development* (London, 1883).

38. Clarence S. Yoakum and Robert M. Yerkes, eds., *Army Mental Tests* (New York, 1920), p. 130; C. C. Brigham, *A Study of American Intelligence* (Princeton, 1923), pp. 79, 190.

39. G. O. Ferguson, Jr., "The Mental Status of the American Negro," *Scientific Monthly*, 12 (1921), 542.

40. Brigham, *Study of American Intelligence*, p. 194.

41. Brigham, *Study of American Intelligence*, p. 197.

42. C. C. Brigham, "Intelligence Tests of Immigrant Groups," *Psychological Review*, 37 (1930), 165.

43. Ernest A. Hooten, "Methods of Racial Analysis," *Science*, 63 (1926), 76.

44. Franz Boas, *Aryan and Semite* (New York, 1934), p. 33.

45. John B. Watson, *The Ways of Behaviorism* (New York, 1928), pp. 36, 123.

46. Nathaniel Weyl, *The Negro in American Civilization* (Washington, D.C., 1960), pp. 143–55.

47. Morton H. Fried, *Science*, series 2, 146 (1964), 1526.

The Wild Man's Revenge

⟲ PETER L. THORSLEV, JR.

From the first one must concede that whatever revenge the Wild Man took in the nineteenth century—or still takes in the twentieth—is more metaphorical than real. With nineteenth-century imperialism, reinforced with more and more sophisticated and mechanized means of slaughter and enslavement, the Wild Man ceased to be a physical threat anywhere but on the farthest frontiers of the white man's civilization. Even there, one could rest assured that any physical revenge the Wild Man managed to take was avenged in turn tenfold: for every scalp raised on the Little Big Horn, or every British or Afrikaner life lost in a Zulu raid in the Transvaal, ten redskins or Zulus gave their lives in turn, and had their children oppressed or enslaved, even to the third and fourth generation. But from the first the Wild Man was more speculation and myth than red-blooded reality; like Voltaire's God, when he did not exist he was of necessity invented, to serve a psychological or a symbolic need. He must stand as the antithesis of culture and civilization, and therefore for whatever we have lost or have repressed in becoming civilized. In the nineteenth century the Wild Man as physical reality became a more and more rare breed, until the word itself came to have a rather archaic ring to it. Today Claude Lévi-Strauss must journey to the far reaches of the Amazon to find his vanishing likeness. But as myth the Wild Man is immortal: one might almost say that he flourishes the more, the fewer the facts are to support his existence.

This brings us to the first point to be made about the myth of the Wild Man in the nineteenth century: the shape which the myth takes, and therefore the character of the Wild Man himself, depends not so much upon facts and discoveries as upon the psychological needs and attitudes of the civilized white man who creates the myth. The eighteenth century saw the first really scientific voyages of discovery with some effort at anthropological investigation and contrastive study—the circumnavigations of Captain Cook, for instance. The century also saw, as has been noted, the beginnings of a more sophisticated theorizing, and attempts to catalog and categorize cultural and anthropological distinctions and to reduce them to science: Montesquieu's rather misguided theories on the determining effects of climate on a people's behavior, for instance, or the later theories on race and "organic" cultural history of German proto-Romantics like Herder. But these attempts at fact-finding and theorizing had only a peripheral, or at most a modifying, effect on the popular and literary myth of the Wild Man. The Noble Savage began as a redskin and evolved to include Africans and South Sea Islanders, Albanians and Scotch Highlanders, but he remained essentially the same in character: brave, loyal, stoic, aloof, and inclined to be sententious in his comparisons between native cultures and imported European civilizations. For the Wild Man's character is determined not by science but by changing cultural attitudes toward the natural and the primitive which he represents or symbolizes.

I. From Noble Savage to Dionysian Man

When nature, and especially human nature, is conceived, on the model of Newtonian physics and of the associationist and egalitarian psychologies which proceeded from it, as simple, uniform, dependable, and above all rational, as in the early years at least of the Enlightenment, the Wild Man becomes the Noble Savage.[1] With the demise of the concept of original sin, primitive man was conceived to be an innocent, and the world of nature unfallen and pure. This is not to say that progress of some sort is impossible, but there is the clear implication—evident long before Rousseau—that culture in refining man makes him effete, and that the artificialities of civilization sap a man's energies and moral fiber and make him prone to corruption. It is for this reason that from the first the Noble Savage could be used as a mouthpiece for satire on contemporary culture, as an "ideal" outside observer—as were the Indian "kings" in Addison's *Spectator* papers. This older Noble Savage is frequently sensitive, even sentimental; courageous, in the stoic manner, but also inclined to moralizing; and he can easily become a bore. Although born of the Enlightenment, he retained an honorable place in the Romantic Movement—as, for instance, the venerable and blind old sachem Chactas, who tells his tragic story, in Chateaubriand's *Atala*, and comforts and admonishes René, when the latter, a far more characteristic Romantic hero, is driven half-mad and to thoughts of suicide by the death of his incestuous love. Perhaps the last at all significant Noble Savage of this pure strain in English literature is Outalissi, the Oneida warrior and friend of the white man in Thomas Campbell's *Gertrude of Wyoming* (1809). In his valedictory "death song," which concludes the poem, Outalissi paraphrases the speech which Logan, the Mingo chief, delivered to the governor of Virginia.[2] It is fair to say that this Noble Savage reached his apogee by 1800; he is revived in some of the good Indians of Cooper's fiction, but he has lost much of his stoic dignity. In the twentieth century he survives in the westerns as the wise old medicine man who counsels the young warriors to patience and reason, and who is as invariably betrayed by the perfidious whites.

From the beginning of the Enlightenment, however, as Lovejoy has also pointed out, there existed a quite different conception of nature, and a conception that was ultimately, in the Romantic Movement, to prove radically subversive of the uniform order and common sense of the Age of Reason.[3] When nature is conceived as being not geometrically ordered, but infinitely fecund and varied, not subject to finite reason, but sublimely disruptive of it, then the Wild Man becomes Nature's Child. Chateaubriand's Atala and Chactas are prototypical children of nature, and they are American Indians, but the Child might also be brought up in the mountains of Wales or the Highlands of Scotland, as James Beattie's shepherd-boy Edwin was, in his popular poem *The Minstrel* (1771), and as Byron sometimes imagined himself to be. The Child of Nature does not reason, he feels; he does not preach, as does the Noble Savage, but he breaks spontaneously into poetry and song, especially when confronted by his mother nature in her wilder and sublimer moods. It is in this guise that the Wild Man became for a time dominant in the Romantic Movement, and he surely survives, even if in a debased form, into the twentieth century.

Nature was not all sweetness and light, however, even for the Romantics. Aldous Huxley once criticized Wordsworth for sentimentalizing nature in his assertion that

> One impulse from a vernal wood
> May teach you more of man,
> Of moral evil and of good,
> Than all the sages can.

Had Wordsworth been brought up in the jungles of Central America, Huxley suggested, he would not have entertained such benevolent thoughts about nature's moral impulses.[4] Nature can be "red in tooth and claw," as Tennyson suggested, and even such an apologist as Wordsworth was sometimes willing to admit it. There is not only the ministry of beauty in *The Prelude,* but also the ministry of fear. The disillusioned Solitary of book III of *The Excursion* is not merely a mouthpiece even for an older and conservative Wordsworth, but his search for the Noble Savage in the wilds of America is not untypical, even in Romantic literature. The Solitary has been first disillusioned with the United States, that "unknit Republic," as he calls it, and, deciding to leave her to "the scourge / Of her own passions," he will go to "regions"

> "Whose shades have never felt the encroaching axe,
> Or soil endured a transfer in the mart
> Of dire rapacity. There, Man abides,
> Primeval Nature's child. . . .
> More dignified, and stronger in himself;
> Whether to act, judge, suffer, or enjoy.
> True, the intelligence of social art
> Hath overpowered his forefathers, and soon
> Will sweep the remnant of his line away;
> But contemplations, worthier, nobler far
> Than her destructive energies, attend
> His independence, when along the side
> Of Mississippi, or that northern stream
> That spreads into successive seas, he walks."[5]

But when the skeptical but still hopeful Solitary actually travels "westward, tow'rd unviolated woods," in search of that "pure archetype of human greatness," the Noble Savage is nowhere to be found:

> "There, in his stead, appeared
> A creature, squalid, vengeful, and impure;
> Remorseless, and submissive to no law
> But superstitious fear, and abject sloth."[6]

There are, in other words and as Cooper demonstrated in his novels, good Indians and "bad Injuns," virtuous Chingachgooks and Uncases (Noble Savage and Child of Nature, respectively), and vicious Maguas, and the passing of the last of these Indians is a mixed blessing and a curse. Whether the Wild Man is taken to be the one or the other depends not upon facts but upon the symbolic purposes he is to serve when he appears. A nature that is benevolent and moral will produce the Noble Savage and the Child of Sensibility; a "Nature red in tooth and claw" will produce naked and rapacious brutes. Moreover, however incongruous the types may appear, they exist side by side in the popular and even the literary mind. Noble savages strutted upon the New York or Boston stages at the same time as their less domesticated and real-life brethren were scalping settlers in the western territories.

It is nevertheless probably true to say that the Noble Savage and the Child of Nature diminished steadily in importance as mythical figures—at least in first-rate works of literature—with the diminution of Romantic faith in nature, and with the rise of a Victorian faith in evolution, in progress, and in the benefits of a mercantile and industrial civilization. In a reply "To an Independent Preacher who preached that we should be 'in harmony with nature,'" Matthew Arnold voices a more representative Victorian sentiment:

> Know, man hath all which Nature hath, but more,
> And in that *more* lie all his hopes of good.
> Nature is cruel, man is sick of blood;
>
> . . . .
>
> Nature is fickle, man hath need of rest;
>
> . . . .
>
> Man must begin, know this, where Nature ends;
> Nature and man can never be fast friends.[7]

For Kipling, at the close of the century, the collective wild men of the far-flung Empire have become "the White Man's burden," the "lesser breeds without the Law." When the Noble Savage or the Child of Nature survives into our own century, it is in popular culture and subliterature: in dime novels and pulp fiction, in western motion pictures and popular songs. Tarzan of the Apes, as he appears on our television screens, is something of a cross between the sententious Noble Savage and the spontaneous Child of Nature, but his comments on civilized ways have been reduced to terse and subliterate pronouncements, and his poetic song to a cross between a Swiss yodel and the bellow of a bull elephant.

There is, however, a fourth conception of primitive nature which the Wild Man came to symbolize, a conception which also originated in the Romantic Movement, and which has been perhaps of more enduring significance than either the Noble Savage or the savage brute. Nature may be conceived not as rational, uniform, and ordered, nor as cruel and slothful, to be refined and overcome. As fecund, spontaneous, sublime, yes, but as more than that: as "mother mysterious," a dark and amoral force from under earth, thrusting up indifferently foul weeds or fragile flowers; a "blood-consciousness" ranged forever against sterile rational order and efficiency, and creative of all that is lustful, much that is destructive, and all that is beautiful. When nature is so conceived, then the Wild Man regains some of that mystery he had in the Renaissance and earlier, when he stood symbol for fallen nature and was blood brother to Satan and the dark angels. The rational Noble Savage is Apollonian, for all his sensibilities; this naked savage is Dionysian. He is Blake's fiery and hairy Orc; he is, from different viewpoints, Frankenstein's monster, or Nietzsche's hermit Zarathustra who descends to scourge the morality of slaves; among these savages "Mistah Kurtz" saw into the heart of darkness; D. H. Lawrence sought him out in Taos and in Mexico. It is an oversimplification to identify this Dionysian savage merely with the passions and lusts surrrounding sex, although this is certainly one of his dominant characteristics. He is a product of an earthward mysticism, a radical denial not only of rational order, but of all otherworldliness and transcendentalism. It is this savage on which Wallace Stevens' female persona meditates on a "Sunday Morning," when she has rejected all Christian mysteries and otherwordly Edens with their "insipid lutes":

> Supple and turbulent, a ring of men
> Shall chant in orgy on a summer morn
> Their boisterous devotion to the sun,
> Not as a god, but as a god might be,
> Naked among them, like a savage source.
> Their chant shall be a chant of paradise,
> Out of their blood, returning to the sky;
> And in their chant shall enter, voice by voice,
> The windy lake wherein their lord delights,
> The trees, like serafin, and echoing hills,
> That choir among themselves long afterward.
> They shall know well the heavenly fellowship
> Of men that perish and of summer morn.
> And whence they came and whither they shall go
> The dew upon their feet shall manifest.[8]

This Dionysian savage is the most enduring of them all, because he is quite immune to fact and to scientific voyages of discovery: he is on the one hand pure myth, on the other a universal psychological reality.

II. Some Representative Wild Men and What They Symbolize

The Wild Man, in whatever of these modern guises, takes his revenge on the civilized man of the nineteenth century by standing as a symbol for what we have lost or what we have repressed in becoming civilized. At the simplest level, then, he represents a nostalgia for a lost Eden, a life free of both ambitions and inhibitions, a mythical past which exists, if only in dreams, as a longed-for escape. On a somewhat more complex level he represents an actual and more immediate past, a sterner and more difficult life in the Scotch Highlands, for instance, but a life heartier without effete luxuries, and a life of manly virtues and simple loyalties. Finally, "internalized," the Wild Man comes to stand symbol for the Dionysian savage we have repressed within ourselves.

On the simplest level of a time before the curse of Cain doomed man to bring forth the fruits of the earth with the sweat of his brow, the myth of the Wild Man is of course related to the classic legend of a golden age. The first voyage of Cook around the Horn and the Cape of Good Hope, in 1768–71, provided a locus for this Wild Man myth which has never been surpassed. Cook was not particularly enthusiastic about the South Sea Islanders himself, as the nineteenth-century publication of his journals shows (1893, ed. Wharton), but his records and those of Sir Joseph Banks, the naturalist who accompanied him, were edited and doctored by John Hawkesworth, a director of the East India Company, and published in 1773 in a compilation generally known as *Hawkesworth's Voyages*. Hawkesworth relates most of the facts, but he also sentimentalizes and editorializes, and when he was finished the Tahitians were firmly established as children of nature. They live, of course, in a subtropical climate of blue skies, broad beaches, and palm trees; exotic fruits and fish are readily available; clothing and styles are no problem, since the natives largely forego them; and if their sexual habits seem a bit promiscuous, these Hawkesworth excuses with the suave indifference of cultural relativity: sexual mores are but custom, after all, he suggests, not natural law.

The breadfruit, which Cook did not find particularly appetizing, was also mythologized, and came appropriately enough to stand as a symbol for this Wild Man's emancipation from the curse of Cain. It also provided an economic and a historic occasion for the propagation of the South Sea myth, even into our own day. Certain West Indian planters, having heard of the South Pacific breadfruit and seeing it as an opportunity to provide cheap food for slave labor, commissioned a ship named the *Bounty*, with Lieutenant Bligh in charge, to take on a cargo of the trees and transport them to the West Indies. Lord Byron was one of the first to poeticize the famous mutiny in his last verse romance, entitled *The Island* (1823), and his panegyric on the breadfruit deserves quotation.[9] He is speaking of the mutinous sailors' landing on Tahiti and their reception there with

"The Cava feast, the Yam, the Cocoa's root, / Which bears at once the cup, and milk, and fruit," but his special praise is reserved for

> The Bread-tree, which, without the ploughshare, yields
> The unreaped harvest of unfurrowed fields,
> And bakes its unadulterated loaves
> Without a furnace in unpurchased groves,
> And flings off famine from its fertile breast,
> A priceless market for the gathering guest;—
> These, with the luxuries of seas and woods,
> The airy joys of social solitudes,
> Tamed each rude wanderer to the sympathies
> Of those who were more happy, if less wise,
> Did more than Europe's discipline had done,
> And civilised Civilisation's son![10]

Byron recognizes that these islanders are not all virtuous—indeed, he was never one to find morality in impulses from vernal woods—but he gives the traditional defense:

> True, they had vices—such are Nature's growth—
> But only the barbarian's—we have both;
> The sordor of civilisation, mixed
> With all the savage which Man's fall hath fixed.[11]

The morally more conventional Coleridge was less charitable; if the account of his friend Southey can be trusted, he once suggested that the islanders' breadfruit trees ought to be destroyed, in an effort to convert them to the virtues of hard work.[12] It is only to be expected that in the Victorian Age, with its veneration for frugality, industry, and progress, the "abject sloth" of the South Sea Islander and of savages in general would be looked upon with stern disapproval, if perhaps also with half-conscious envy. This surely accounts for the particular venom shown by Carlyle, the self-appointed first apostle of the "Gospel of Work," in his writings on the emancipation of the West Indian slaves. He is against the institution of slavery, he writes in the most notorious of these essays, entitled "The Nigger Question" (first published anonymously in 1849; the slaves had been freed in 1833), but he would not have been in so great a hurry to abolish it. Some means should first have been found to compel the slave, once free, "to do competent work for his living. This is the everlasting duty of all men, black or white . . . to labour honestly accord-ing to the ability given them; for that and for no other purpose was each one of us sent into this world."[13] The breadfruit tree, however, has been replaced in Carlyle's mythology with the West Indian pumpkin. "Where a Black man, by working about half-an-hour a-day . . . can supply himself, by aid of sun and soil, with as much pumpkin as will suffice, he is likely to be a little stiff to raise into hard work!" Carlyle paints an offensive portrait of the emancipated West Indian blacks, "sitting yonder with their beautiful muzzles up to the ears in pumpkins, imbibing sweet pulps and juices . . . while the sugar-crops rot round them uncut, because labour cannot be hired."[14]

Nevertheless, the thought of that plenitude of pumpkins or of breadfruit, under such warm and sunny skies as required a minimum of shelter and of clothing, must have continued to provide a mythical attraction at least for the Victorian poor, industrious or otherwise, just as visions of hula skirts and sex among the hibiscus blossoms has always provided an attractive myth for those haunted by "Victorian" inhibitions. Melville develops the South Sea Island myths in his first ambitious works, *Typee* and *Omoo* (1846–47), romanticized travelogues and tales of adventure of his four-year experience in the South Pacific on various whaling ships, merchant vessels, and warships, beginning in 1841. Melville does not idealize life among the savages to the degree that Byron does in *The Island*. Indeed, the Typee tribesmen are cannibals, even though they have the good grace not to eat the destitute white sailors. But in both books Melville made it plain, to the discomfort of many of his more conventional American readers, that civilized intruders, especially missionaries, Roman Catholic or Protestant, have worked far more harm than good; and even among the cannibal Typees Melville manages an affair of romantic love between the sailor Tom, or "Tommo," and the beautiful young Typee maiden Fayaway.

The sexual license of these islanders shocked Captain Cook—he had practical reasons also for disapproval, since it spread the white man's venereal disease, carried to the island by the earlier voyage of Bougainville, among his English sailors. It rather amused Sir Joseph Banks, the naturalist on Cook's voyage; and it was finally rationalized by Hawkesworth as a matter of relative customs and traditions. This same sexual freedom could also be idealized in a more traditional and literary manner, however, and be transformed into Romantic love—an outlawed relationship of the utmost loyalty, and of a rather etherialized passion, sanctioned not by law or custom but by natural feeling. The central episode in Byron's *The Island* is the tale of the love of Neuha, the island chief's daughter, for Torquil, one of the sailors, and of her rescuing him from the pursuit of the British naval vessel sent to seize the mutineers. There is a

certain irony in the fact that Romantic love, surely one of the most literary and sophisticated of human relationships, should also come to be
associated with the Wild Man. The association started early, of course,
with the Noble Savage Oroonoko at the close of the seventeenth century,
but it surely reached its climax in the story which epitomized Romantic
primitivism for generations of Europeans: Chateaubriand's *Atala*.

When published as a separate novelette in 1801, *Atala* was Chateaubriand's first great success. The work went through five editions in the
first year and was quickly translated into all the western European languages. It had been prepared for by Rousseau, and also by the natural
and sentimental effusions of Bernardin de St. Pierre, particularly in his
story of simple life and melancholy love, *Paul and Virginia,* set in the
tropical French colony of the Isle de France. Chateaubriand professed
to have based the description in his story on the experience of his five-
month trip to the United States in 1791, but it is no more accurate in
geographical or botanical detail than any of the other Noble Savage
stories, and in any case it seems clear that in his stay in America Chateaubriand never got south of Baltimore, and the story is set in the "Floridas,"
on the banks of the "Meschacebe" (the Mississippi) and the Ohio rivers.
Chactas, who as a blind old sachem is narrating the story of his youth to
the traveling Frenchman, René, was a son of Outalissi, a Natchez chief.
When a young warrior, Chactas had gone with his father on an expedition against the Muskogee Indians, north of Pensacola Bay. Outalissi
and most of his followers had been killed, and Chactas and the few
Natchez survivors took refuge with their allies, the Spanish. So it happens
that Chactas receives some rudiments of a white man's education,
although he refuses to the last to accept the white man's religion. Soon
he feels once more the call of the wild and leaves the civilized comforts
of St. Augustine to rejoin his tribe. Predictably, he is captured by his
Muskogee enemies, and, when he bravely confesses his identity as the
son of a Natchez chief, it is decided that he is to be burned alive at the
Muskogees' home village, in a kind of sacrificial rite. Chateaubriand does
not omit the more gruesome of savage customs, although he does of course
offer the traditional apologies: the Indians are but children, after all, and
in their wars and devastations Europeans are little better, in spite of their
Christian culture.

Fortunately, the tribal village is some moons distant, and along the
journey Chactas makes the acquaintance of the Muskogee chief's
daughter, Atala. She appears to him at first as the "Maiden of Last Love,"
sent to solace condemned prisoners of war, but she turns out to have had

a Christian education from her convert mother, and of course to have a soul of the deepest sensibility. The rest of the story is taken up with the lovers' escape and their wanderings, including a passionate love scene in a trackless swamp, with a forest fire approaching from one direction and a hurricane from another. They reach a haven at last in the Indian village of a hermit missionary, Father Aubrey, but their happiness is short-lived. Atala soon sickens and dies, and Chactas, after a funeral ceremony half Christian, half pagan, is left to continue the long pilgrimage of life which leaves him eventually as the blind old sachem, telling his story to an exiled Frenchman while on a beaver-hunting expedition on the banks of the Ohio.

The story of Atala was originally intended as an episode in Chateaubriand's projected epic of natural man, *The Natchez*, but during his exiled years in England, Chateaubriand underwent a reconversion to Roman Catholicism, and this story and its companion piece, *René*, were incorporated in his apology for Roman Catholicism, *The Genius of Christianity*. Published just after Napoleon's Concordat with the Vatican, this work gained the favor of the emperor, as well as the public in general, and launched Chateaubriand on a long diplomatic and literary career. *Atala* concludes, therefore, in a defense of simple or primitive Christianity, but the love scenes are more pagan than Christian, and it is at least ironically significant that Atala dies as a result of her mother's mistaken religious zeal. On her deathbed her mother had exacted a vow from her daughter that she would dedicate her life in chastity to God. When Atala finds herself so in love with the pagan Chactas that she can no longer keep her vow, she administers a slow-acting and fatal poison. In the protracted death scene, the good Father Aubrey rebukes her and her dead mother for their misguided zeal, but the fact remains that it is civilization and Christianity which precipitate the tragedy.

The immediate and overwhelming success of this melancholy tale of the redskin as Romantic lover was due in part, of course, to the fact that it appeared at so propitious a time, as Chateaubriand was himself canny enough to realize. The French reading public, particularly, seemed surfeited with an Age of Reason and the excesses of the Revolution, and was more than ready not only for a reconciliation with the Church, but for just such an orgy of primitive feeling and melancholy sentiment, sanctified with a whiff of incense, as Chateaubriand's story provided. The precedent once established, however, it has never died. Wild men all over the world fall prey to the white man's disease of Romantic and melancholy love. Even Southey, who probably knew more about actual wild men

than any other English poet before or since,[15] described something very
like the tenderness of Romantic love in two of his verse romances:
among the Aztecs, in *Madoc* (1805), and among the Paraguayan Indians,
in *A Tale of Paraguay* (1825). And of course in popular literature, the
love calls of Hiawathas and Minnehahas have echoed down through the
ages to our own.

The South Seas or the primeval Floridian savannas are rather exotic,
however, and breadfruit and *Liebestoden* may have seemed too remote
even for dreaming, to a nineteenth-century public so immersed in the
Victorian getting and spending, which was laying waste their imaginative
powers. Moreover, eating breadfruit and falling in love are passive preoc-
cupations: the Wild Man must also stand as a symbol for those manlier
virtues with which even a Carlyle could sympathize. And for the British
there were wild men nearer at hand and in a more immediate past: not
the Irish peasants, who had stood too long in the English mind for down-
trodden and papist stupidity, but the Highland Scot. For his hero in
The Island Byron had chosen from among the *Bounty* mutineers a wild
young Scot whom he renamed Torquil, and in his description of him he
emphasizes this primitive heritage:

> And who is he? the blue-eyed northern child
> Of isles more known to man, but scarce less wild;
> The fair-haired offspring of the Hebrides,
> Where roars the Pentland with its whirling seas;
> Rocked in his cradle by the roaring wind,
> The tempest-born in body and in mind.[16]

Byron also draws the obvious parallels, and in so doing he makes a kind
of catalog of the outlaw heroes of his other verse romances:

> Placed in the Arab's clime he would have been
> As bold a rover as the sands have seen,
> And braved their thirst with as enduring lip
> As Ishmael, wafted on his Desert-Ship;
> Fixed upon Chili's shore, a proud cacique;
> On Hellas' mountains, a rebellious Greek;
> Born in a tent, perhaps a Tamerlane;
> Bred to a throne, perhaps unfit to reign.[17]

As such, Torquil, "A soaring spirit, ever in the van, / A patriot hero or
despotic chief," is a fit "husband of the bride of Toobonai," Neuha, who
is, we are assured, "Of a long race, the valiant and the free, / The naked
knights of savage chivalry."[18]

But the true bard of the Wild Man of the Highlands was Sir Walter Scott, both in his narrative verse and in the Waverley novels, and Scott makes this Wild Man's symbolic significance rather more clear. Perhaps the most memorable of Scott's literary wild men is the legendary Rob Roy of the MacGregor clan, who gives one of the novels its title, even though he does not play its leading role. Scott was proud of his anti-quarian expertise, and in a long preface and a plethora of notes and appendixes he vouches for his character's authenticity, but he also points up the special features of Rob Roy's interest for a reader in the Romantic Age. He was a kind of eighteenth-century Robin Hood, Scott maintains, and the wonder is that

a character like his, blending the wild virtues, the subtle policy, and unre-strained license of an American Indian, was flourishing in Scotland during the Augustan Age of Queen Anne and George I. Addison, it is probable, or Pope, would have been considerably surprised if they had known that there existed in the same island with them a personage of Rob Roy's peculiar habits and profession. It is this strong contrast betwixt the civilized and cultivated mode of life on the one side of the Highland line, and the wild and lawless adventures . . . on the opposite side of that ideal boundary, which creates the interest attached to his name.[19]

The interest of this "ideal boundary" provides the theme of Scott's most important novels with an eighteenth-century background: a nostalgia for a simpler past, a hardy life for body and spirit, with clan and family loyal-ties, and where rule is by personal force and bravery, not established by law and politics. There is a certain amount of idealization in Scott's portraits of highland life, but his contrast is not so simplistic or so simple-minded as it is sometimes made out to be by his critics, and of course his loyalties were divided. He was quite willing to admit that Rob Roy could be obtuse in his dedication to lost causes, and that in his dealings with Scotch Lowlanders he was often "subtle" rather than straightforward or even honest. Moreover, the conditions of highland life were often not only hearty, but brutal: Baths were infrequent, at best; children went barefoot and with inadequate clothing and diet; and the cottages were drafty and cold—and these evils could not be laid entirely to oppression at the hands of the English establishment and their Scotch allies. The wave of the future lies with Georgian England, with industry, capitalism, and representative government, and Scott is on the whole resigned to it—and yet he maintains that we must be aware of what we are losing. So Scott's Wild Man of the Highlands comes to stand as the symbol not only for the personal savage virtues, but also for social virtues—organic ties of fellowship and leadership—and even for a sense of tribal and national identity. In founding the genre of the historical romance, Scott helped to make nineteenth-century readers aware of their national histories, and aware also of the part played in those histories by the wild men who were their ancestors.

Scott does not idealize his Highlanders or their way of life to the extent that romancers of the South Sea Islands idealized the Tahitians, perhaps because Scott had lived in the Highlands and had met the survivors of his wild heroes, and he was aware that whatever the virtues and beauties of the land, it was no second Eden, and Rob Roy was no second Adam. Yet Scott's Highlanders are never gratuitously cruel or wantonly destructive: they commit no battlefield atrocities. It is the Georgian English who do, and in describing such atrocities Scott had the authority of history on his side. After the Battle of Culloden, for instance, featured in the first of the novels, *Waverley,* the victorious Duke of Cumberland and his forces spent the next couple of days making sure that no wounded Highlander or prisoner of war lived to propagate further rebellion. As Scott points out in his notes and prefaces, both before and after Culloden, pogroms with government sanction were conducted against rebellious Highlanders, which included the systematic slaughter of whole families. Rob Roy's clan, the MacGregors, were for many years forbidden to use their clan name, under penalty of death.

Highland wild men were Christian, however, even if lawless; Muslim wild men need not be so inhibited, and they had the advantage of being exotic, but still within traveling distance for the peripatetic Englishman. Byron had never been to the South Pacific, but he had been to the Near East, and in canto II of *Childe Harold* he brought back an account of the Albanians and the Suliotes which added them to the roster of wild men:

> Fierce are Albania's children, yet they lack
>   Not virtues, were those virtues more mature.
>   Where is the foe that ever saw their back?
>   Who can so well the toil of War endure?
>   Their Native fastnesses not more secure
>   Than they in doubtful time of troublous need:
>   Their wrath how deadly! but their friendship sure,
>   When Gratitude or Valour bids them bleed,
> Unshaken rushing on where'er their Chief may lead.[20]

Here is the catalog of the virtues of the Noble Savage: valor, endurance, gratitude for favors, and hospitality. Their capricious and occasional

cruelties are apologized for on the basis of their being, after all, "immature" children of nature. Byron was proud of the fact that at the age of
twenty-one he was the first Englishman, aside from the resident British
consul, to have penetrated beyond the capital into the rugged interior of
Albania, a region which, as he notes that Gibbon had remarked, although
"within sight of Italy is less known than the interior of America."[21] It
was indeed a hazardous journey on which his life was threatened by
bandits, flash floods, and shipwreck, but he enjoyed the trip and carried
back with him as a souvenir an Albanian costume costing fifty guineas
in which he later posed for a portrait by Thomas Phillips. He also brought
back an Albanian war song with which he frightened Annabella Milbanke
in the carriage on their honeymoon, and with which he later entertained
the Shelleys on a windy moonlight night on Lake Geneva. Mary Shelley
rather unkindly remarked that it sounded like a "strange, wild howl."[22]

He was particularly impressed with the Ali Pasha, whom he calls a
"Mohammetan Buonaparte" in one of his letters, and whom he describes
as a kind of Albanian Rob Roy.[23] In a note on the passage in *Childe
Harold*, he extends the comparison of Albanians with Scotch wild men:

The . . . Albanese, struck me forcibly by their resemblance to the Highlanders
of Scotland, in dress, figure, and manner of living. Their very mountains
seemed Caledonian, with a kinder climate. The kilt, though white; the spare,
active form; their dialect, Celtic in its sound; and their hardy habits, all carried
me back to Morven [*i.e.*, Ossian].[24]

Byron does not, however, idealize their characters or omit their cruelties.
They are, he notes, "detested" by their hostile neighbors; they can be
treacherous thieves when not restrained by the laws of hospitality; and
the old Ali Pasha, who "has been a mighty warrior," is also "as barbarous
as he is successful, roasting rebels, etc."[25] The Albanians in general, and
the old Ali Pasha as Byron imagined him in his warrior youth, became
nevertheless models for a whole line of Byronic Heroes as noble outlaws,
bandits, and corsairs in his verse romances which followed on his return
to England. They are fierce in war and sometimes cruel to their enemies,
and the unquestioned leaders of small "organic" bands of loyal followers,
but they are also always tender in their regard for women—a Romantic
virtue which Byron did not find among his Muslim Albanians.

These, then, are a representative group of the more traditional or
mythic wild men of the Romantic Age: pagan Tahitians and Roman
Catholic Highlanders, American Indians and Muslim Albanians. They
range in character from fierce savage warriors to sentimentalized

children of nature; in their relations with women, from uninhibited promiscuity to the tenderest romantic love and loyalty. Together they represent what we have lost in becoming civilized, but there is very little in their presentation to indicate that they are our brothers under the skin. As a matter of fact, their exotic distance, in time or place, is a great part of their attraction; they have not been "internalized," and they are seldom psychologized. I believe these more traditional and literary figures reached their climax of popularity in the Romantic period, but they did not, of course, die with it, although they declined more and more into "popular" literature.

One such popular novelist, writing at almost the close of the century, illustrates this survival and also shows the extension of these types to include South African Negroes. H. Rider Haggard is remembered today, if at all, as the author of *King Solomon's Mines* and *She,* both African romances, but with little in the way of factual pretensions, both of which have survived into our own day as popular subjects for motion pictures. But Haggard was a prolific writer—his biographer lists some sixty volumes, largely novels and travelogues—and in many of them he attempted to exploit his personal knowledge of the natives of South Africa. In one representative novel, *Nada the Lily* (1888), Haggard undertook, for a time, to "forget his civilization, and think with the mind and speak with the voice of a Zulu of the old régime."[26] Indeed, no white man appears as a character in the novel, and the story is supposedly recorded from the dying lips of an old Zulu medicine man, Mopo or Umbopo by name. One cannot vouch for the authenticity of the language—it comes across as a vague blend of the Old Testament prophets, of Ossian, and of the stilted speech of bad translations from primitive tongues—but Haggard did make a genuine attempt to base his narrative on authentic historical detail, and he includes in it every one of the traditional wild men types which we have so far discussed. The major historical figure is the Zulu chieftain Chaka (died, 1828), the type of the savage as cruel tyrant, and Haggard compares him in the preface to Napoleon and Tiberius. He is credited in history and legend with the slaughter of upward of a million people in his rise to the dominion of most of native Southeast Africa, and Haggard makes no attempt to idealize his reign, although he admits that some of the "details" have been suppressed as being too horrible, even in "this polite age of melanite and torpedoes."[27] Mopo, the medicine man who survives to report the story to a white English traveler, is of course the aged and noble sachem: in one episode he disproves a charge of treason and proves his stoic endurance by holding his hand in the fire before the king until it is charred—becoming thereafter known as the man with the withered hand. The two young heroes of the story, Galazi and Umslopogaas (the latter is actually the son of Chaka, but only Mopo knows his true identity) are noble savages, brave in battle and yet sensitive of heart. They also hunt and go into battle with a pack of wolves, which they suppose to be the "grey ghosts" of their ancestors, and who are of course faithful to death to their human leaders. Haggard defends this alliance on the grounds that "similar beliefs and traditions are common in the records of primitive people"—although he concedes that the wolves would in truth have had to be hyenas, "for there are no true wolves in Zululand."[28] And, indeed, wolf-boys are common enough in legend and literature, but no Child of Nature was ever nurtured by a hyena. Through the narrative of hunt and slaughter there is woven a tender love story between Umslopogaas and Nada the Lily—and here we have the Wild Man as Romantic lover.[29] They grow up believing they are brother and sister—a theme of borderline incest so common in love stories of the Romantic Age as long before to have become cliché. Nada finally dies of thirst and starvation in a cave where she had been hidden for protection during a battle, reaching with her last strength through an aperture in the stones to hold the hand of Umslopogaas, who, severely wounded, is too weak to effect her rescue. When she speaks "for the last time of all," her voice comes "in a gasping whisper through the hole in the rock":

"Farewell, Umslopogaas, my husband and my brother, I thank you for your love, Umslopogaas. Ah! I die!"

Umslopogaas is too weak to make an answer, but he watches "the little hand" he holds: "Twice it opened, twice it closed upon his own, then it opened for the third time, turned grey, quivered, and was still forever!"[30] Even this last touching episode Haggard maintains "is a true Zulu tale," although it "has been considerably varied to suit the purposes of this romance"[31]—but the parallel with the tomb scene in *Aida* seems almost too close for coincidence.

Even though it could take advantage of the increased English interest in South Africa, with the Boer Wars, at the turn of the century, *Nada the Lily* was not a great success with the critics, but it was always one of Haggard's favorites, and the public obviously agreed, for, as his daughter puts it in her biography of her father, "*Nada* travelled down the years, selling steadily for more than half a century." Moreover, as she also points out, *Nada* had an even more popular offspring in one of the most famous

of modern children of nature, for it was the story of the wolf-warriors in
Nada which set Haggard's friend Kipling off on the train of thought that
led to his writing "a lot of wolf stories," as he put it, including, of course,
the story of Mowgli in *The Jungle Book*.[32] Still, for all his romanticizing
of the Zulus, Haggard had a genuine if rather old-fashioned respect for
them as noble savages:

> To serve their country in arms, to die for it, and for the king; such was their
> primitive ideal. If they were fierce they were loyal, and feared neither wounds
> nor doom; if they listened to the dark redes of the witch-doctors, the trumpet
> call of duty sounded still louder in their ears; if chanting their terrible 'Ingoma'
> at the king's bidding they went forth to slay unsparingly, at least they were
> not mean or vulgar. From those who continually must face the last great issues
> of life and death, meanness and vulgarity are far removed.[33]

If the Victorian *pro patria* theme sounds a bit dated, the sentiment in the
last clause sounds as modern as Hemingway's in *Death in the Afternoon*.

The Wild Man has come to stand as a symbol not only for what we
have lost in becoming civilized but also for what we have repressed. As
Professor Symcox points out in his essay (pp. 233–34), Rousseau was
the first to "internalize" the Wild Man, to suggest that he lives on in all
of us, that when we strip ourselves of the evils as well as of the refine-
ments of civilization, we find naked savages. So long as this naked savage
is also noble, the prospect is not unpleasant. This is not to say that Rousseau suggested that we should or even that we could so divest ourselves—
although this was most often what he was interpreted to have said[34]—but
at least he did not suggest that the soul of this primeval savage was
tainted with original sin or possessed of dark and mysterious powers. In
the nineteenth century, however, when the civilized man looked within
to discover his primitive unconscious, ever more frequently it was not
the brave and open face of the Noble Savage which greeted him, but the
dark face of Dionysus.

I believe this must be accounted for in the first place by the fact that
the Wild Man came to be thought of increasingly as black, and the black
man was in the white man's chains. Of course, there is a very long Christian tradition which associates black hearts and black skins with evil and
the ways of Satan, and there must surely have been some unconscious
vindication of slavery in this association. On the other hand, antislavery
literature has existed almost as long as has slavery, in English-speaking
countries at least, and a constant theme of this literature was the brother-
hood of black and white, and the concomitant theme, in view of the

black's less advanced civilization, of the black man's being a child, especially a Child of Nature—affectionate, spontaneous, with sometimes the capricious and somehow innocent cruelty of children.[35] To this must be added the high value which the Romantic generation placed on suffering as a source of wisdom: "Grief should be the instructor of the wise; / Sorrow is knowledge," as Byron writes in the opening soliloquy in *Manfred*, and Wordsworth concurs in his Gothic tragedy, *The Borderers*:

> Action is transitory—a step, a blow,
> The motion of a muscle—this way or that—
> 'Tis done, and in the after-vacancy
> We wonder at ourselves like men betrayed:
> Suffering is permanent, obscure and dark,
> And shares the nature of infinity.[36]

And of course if suffering of itself confers wisdom and even moral superiority, surely no one in 1800 was superior to the black slave. The white man's burden becomes above all a burden of inexpiable guilt. Emotional attitudes became tangled and complex: the black Wild Man stands as a symbol for the darker side of human nature, and therefore his chains are justified. On the other hand, he is our brother and perhaps the child in all of us, and in enslaving him we enslave ourselves. The chains of slavery become symbolic not only of the oppression of wildness by a mercantile civilization, but also symbolic of the repression of passion and spontaneity by the forces of reason; and the real or imagined fears of slave rebellion come to represent the fear of an irruption of the irrational within. Much has been made of this insight in recent times, as regards sex, at least, by critics like Leslie Fiedler, and by novelists and essayists like Norman Mailer and James Baldwin,[37] but their insight was anticipated by the Romantics in the development of the theme of the Wild Man.

As is the case with so many novel Romantic ideas, I believe these become apparent first in the symbolic system of William Blake. This is true to a certain extent even in that well-known "Song of Innocence," "The Little Black Boy." The poem is usually taken to be only another efflorescence of the antislavery movement, with the implicit moral that both black and white boy are alike in soul, under the skin, and that both will so appear, "round the tent of God," when they are free from the black and white "clouds" of their mortal bodies. But the last stanza contains an implication which shows the black boy's moral superiority:

> I'll shade him from the heat till he can bear,
> To lean in joy upon our fathers knee.

> And then I'll stand and stroke his silver hair,
> And be like him and he will then love me.[38]

The direct vision of God, represented in accord with tradition as the sun shedding light (wisdom) and heat (love), is more than the little white boy can bear; he must be shielded (shaded) by his black brother until he becomes strong enough. Not that the black boy argues or asserts this moral superiority or closeness to God: in an irony of which he is quite unaware, he intuits it, takes it for granted, and thinks only of the benefit of love which it can effect.

Blake's primeval Wild Man, however, born in blackness and associated now with the lost Atlantis sunk under the sea (Blake's vision of the golden age), now with Africa, the "heart-shaped continent," is Orc, the fiery, hairy spirit of revolution. His name is one of Blake's inventions or adaptations, as are the names of most of the "Giant Forms" in Blake's myth, and Blake draws upon a dozen literatures or myths to suggest his background and symbolic significance. The "Orc" (Lat., *orca*) is a South Sea whale or leviathan, mentioned in *Paradise Lost*.[39] Perhaps it is an anagram for *cor*, suggesting his fiery and rebellious heart. *Orcus* is also Latin for hell, and like Blake's tiger, Orc has the fierce beauty of a fallen angel. One ingenious critic has recently suggested that his name might be derived from the Greek *orchis*, for testicle—and certainly his association with sexual potency is apparent in many of the episodes in which he appears. He is hairy because he is also associated with Esau, the prototypical Old Testament Wild Man whom the wily Jacob cheated of his birthright, in what Blake believed to be an archetypal instance of the repression of wildness by the cunning of reason.[40] He is the first offspring of Los, the personification of imaginative vision, and Enitharmon, the spirit of earth and nature, and his natural home is in the south, the land of heat and passion. In his first major appearance in the early prophecy, *America*, he embraces the "Shadowy Female," and she gives birth to the American Revolution, and in *The Book of Urizen* he is chained to a rock and becomes emblematic, like Prometheus, of man's hubris and of his suffering spirit.

Above all, he epitomizes the Wild Man "internalized" and imperfectly repressed. His natural antagonist is Urizen, who stands as a symbol in Blake's system for analytic and repressive reason, and whom Blake believed to be the motive force behind not only Newtonian and materialistic science, but also behind all monarchies and tyrannies, and behind all established religions. Orc therefore represents above all youthful and rebellious energy, and he appears most often in the form of the serpent, that appropriately equivocal symbol, for the Romantic poets, of destructive lust and temptation on the one hand, and of creativity and fertility on the other. This is not to suggest that Blake's vision of Orc had any direct influence on the myths of the Wild Man in the nineteenth century: it is only in our own century that his "diabolic" reading of Scripture and myth has been finally decoded. He does, however, give us the first clear picture—and in works published even before 1800—of the Wild Man as Dionysian savage, a constant threat from within to civilization and to civility.

This final transformation of the myth of the Wild Man is his ultimate revenge: that as he gradually fades away as a physical reality, he reappears as a psychic reality. Aside from Blake's prophecies—and they are *sui generis*—I believe it is in what we.loosely call Gothic literature that this realization finally appears, or becomes inescapable. The stories of wild men which we have so far reviewed—even Chateaubriand's *Atala* and Byron's *The Island*—have some basis, however tenuous, in fact. In Gothic literature, on the other hand, the imagination was emancipated from fact, from natural law, and from social realities. The freedom is used at first playfully, in terror romances and in the early Gothic novels, but by the time of the Romantic Movement it was being put to serious symbolic use. One cannot, of course, do more than sketch in the outlines of the use of wild men in Gothic literature, but I should like to suggest two main lines of development: first, the frankly symbolic rather than narrative use of actual wild men, Indians, or Negroes; second, the symbolic use of imagined or mythic monsters.

There is not much use of wild men in English Gothic literature: terrors were located in a more familiar but almost equally mythic past—particularly a Roman Catholic and medieval past—the evidences of which were still around, in ruined castles, dungeons, and abbeys. Gothic villains, moreover, if not actually monks or priests, were perhaps bandits or pirates, but almost always with a secret past of fallen nobility. There was little or no use made of exotic races. "Monk" Lewis does include two Negro servants in his *Castle Spectre*, one of whom, at least, is savage enough to qualify, but when accused by his critics of anachronism, he frankly admits that he included them for the sake of some color on the stage (the pun is his, in the preface). The East Indian maid who appears in the later episodes of Maturin's *Melmoth the Wanderer* is an innocent, who belongs rather in the Child of Nature, lost Eden tradition. There are, of course, the Near Eastern mysteries of Beckford's *Vathek*, and there is a strong suggestion that they do indeed represent the dark forces

in his own psyche, the products of his neuroses, but the atmosphere in
the hall of Eblis is rather too opulent to be classified as primitive, however hellish. Similarly, the sinister Asians who haunt De Quincey's opium
dreams are related more closely to the nightmare terrors of drugs than
to naked savages.

In American Gothic, however, the story is different. Charles Brockden
Brown, the first American Gothic novelist, set out quite frankly to find
an American substitute for Europe's sinister past, for the ruined castles
of the Pyrenees or the Appenines and their Gothic inhabitants, and he
found the substitute in the American forests and the red man. "Puerile
superstition and exploded manners, Gothic castles and chimeras, are the
materials usually employed" in exciting the passions and sympathies of
the readers of romance, he proclaims, but "the incidents of Indian hostility, and the perils of the Western wilderness, are far more suitable; and
for a native of America to overlook these would admit of no apology."[41]
As Leslie Fiedler points out, "It is not the Indian as social victim that
appeals to Brown's imagination, but the Indian as projection of natural
evil and the id."[42] Brown's Indians are a rather taciturn lot, but like
the panthers with which they are associated (and one remembers that
Chateaubriand and Thomas Campbell also inhabited the American forests with panthers), they are not the less sinister for all that. Brown
therefore made the Wild Man a permanent fixture in American Gothic,
and the dreamlike quality of episode and character, and the incidence of
illusion and madness in his plots, make a psychological and symbolic
interpretation almost inevitable. The Indians in Cooper's novels are
another matter. They are by no means all noble savages—there are, as we
noted, good Indians and "bad Injuns"—but however much he may have
disliked being called a derivative American Scott, Cooper finally writes
more in the straightforward tradition of the historical romance and the
social novel than in the tradition of the Gothic.

Melville, on the other hand, is indeed in the Gothic tradition, and in
his later fiction the Wild Man becomes quite obviously a psychological
symbol. We have already noticed *Typee* and *Omoo,* works largely of
fact, which the public, as he noted with some pique, insisted on reading
as works of fiction. In *Mardi* he used the same South Sea Island territory
for a work frankly of fiction, which, as he said, he hoped that his readers
would take for fact. The long quest voyage which gives the novel its
structure is patently, not to say painfully, allegoric and didactic, and the
two wild women, both regal, the one blond and the other dark, represent
the dichotomy in human nature of the innocent and the pure and of the

sinister and experienced. The narrator loves the blond Yillah, rescues her from her native bondage, and marries her, only to lose her on their wedding night. In his frustrated pilgrimage in search of her he is continually pursued by messengers from Queen Hautia. When finally he gives up his search and joins the dark wild queen, there is the suggestion, at least, that Yillah's white purity may also be found in those hearts of darkness. There is a related psychological dichotomy in *Moby Dick,* with Queequeg, the cannibal tribesman who befriends, shelters, and even loves the boy Ishmael, standing for savage benevolence, and Fedallah, the Parsee who becomes Ahab's soothsayer and evil genius, standing for savage darkness and mystery.

In Melville's "Benito Cereno," however, the theme of psychological repression is once more combined with the physical oppression of slavery. The story had some basis in fact: Captain Amasa Delano, a true, trusting, salt-of-the-earth New England seaman, while anchored off an uninhabited island on the coast of Chile, comes across a mysterious Spanish colonial ship, in a sad state of repair, with a very mixed crew of Spaniards and Negro slaves. The captain, a nobleman by the name of Don Benito Cereno, acts very peculiarly indeed, but Captain Delano lays his actions to a combination of Old World arrogance and effeteness. It is only at the last perilous moment that Cereno manages to escape and to inform Delano that the ship has in fact been seized by the black slaves who have murdered or imprisoned the Spanish crew. The slave's leader, Babo, whom Delano had taken to be only a devoted valet and a "faithful fellow," has actually been holding Cereno captive, with threats of death to him and to the rest of the Spanish crew. Delano represents the sane and trusting analytic reason which struggles only to make sense of facts and appearances; Cereno, with his Old World sophistication and experience of radical evil, can see farther into the mystery. Not that he can therefore make sense of it, but he does at least acknowledge it. Even when things have been put to rights, when the Negroes are once more below decks and in irons, and Cereno is on his way toward home and recovery, he cannot regain his spirits, in spite of Delano's sensible admonitions: "But the past is past; why moralise upon it? Forget it." And again, "You are saved: what has cast such a shadow upon you?" "The Negro," Benito Cereno replies simply, and has no more to say.[43] So also with Kurtz in Conrad's story: "The horror, the horror"—for both have seen into the heart of darkness.

The last of our representative wild men is also in the Gothic tradition, but in a peculiar and distinctively modern form. He is quite frankly monstrous and purely imagined, although he has some basis in myth and a firm reality in mind. On the famous evening in Geneva when the Shelleys, Claire Claremont, Byron, and his physician Polidori sat around the fire and told ghost stories, Byron began one on a vampire which Polidori concluded and published over Byron's name, and Mary Shelley began her story of Dr. Frankenstein's monster. She initiated what was to become a new genre of science-fiction Gothic, with the stereotypes of the mad scientist and his monstrous creation, but the monster takes on all the characteristics of the Wild Man of tradition. Like the Noble Savage, he is capable of trenchant and laconic remarks about the evils of civilization, as these are embodied in the overweening ambition which created him. On the other hand, like the Child of Nature, he is also capable of eloquent rhapsodies, on birds and flowers and the woods in autumn, but especially on nature in her sublimer moods, as in the glaciers of Mont Blanc or Jura, where he finds refuge. He is, of course, fiercely cruel and destructive, capable again and again of wanton or vengeful murders, but this is only the perversion of a nature that is in essence gentle and affectionate, especially with children, as is evident in his reactions to the peasants in the family drama which he observes, unbeknown to them, through the chinks in the cottage walls while he is learning the language. He is, in a sense, the first pathetic monster in modern literature: his remorse at the close of the novel fills five closely printed pages of superlatives. The real evil exists not in the heart of the Wild Man but in the heart of the man who created him, Frankenstein, "the modern Prometheus," as Mary Shelley ironically calls him in the subtitle. As the remorseful monster explains, at the close of the narrative, his murders were the uncontrollable effects of a passion for revenge which was a direct result of an unending and unendurable loneliness, of the frustrations of his natural desires for companionship and love. Frankenstein had promised to create him a mate, and retired to the Orkneys to do so, but at the last moment, horrified at the thought of a whole race of monsters, Frankenstein reneges and destroys his female model.

"Sooner murder an infant in its cradle than nurse unacted desires," as Blake says in one of his "Proverbs of Hell," and the monster does literally murder infants in their cradles *because* of unacted desires. Frankenstein and his monster are split aspects of the same personality: in Blake's terms, they are Urizen and Orc. Frankenstein represents the will to dominate and control all of life by means of science and reason (this is the hubris implicit in Mary Shelley's reference to Prometheus); the monster represents those desires for human companionship and love which, in the process of fulfilling ambitions for power, are frustrated, repressed, and perverted.

In retrospect it seems that this is perhaps the end toward which the myth of the Wild Man has been tending all along. For centuries the Wild Man has stood as the civilized man's projection upon the outside world of his own desires and values: both those which he would not hesitate to acknowledge—a longing for lost innocence and uninhibited and oblivious love, for instance—and also those darker impulses which he attempts to suppress or hide. This projection or externalization serves both to give an objective and extra-personal sanction to the civilized man's values, and also to transform his evil desires into something physical and external which he can control or even enslave. The final revenge of the Wild Man comes when, as in the Gothic tradition, the myth becomes transparent, and civilized man is forced to recognize that the only source of evil, as well as the only sanction of value, is within himself.

In this last development of the Wild Man as the savage yet pathetic monster, *Frankenstein* has had a prodigious progeny, especially in pulp fiction and in motion pictures. The theme is still not dead, however, even for first-rate works of literature. The sixties in particular have seen a great variety of Orc-like rebellions against embattled Urizen, both in life and in art. Thom Gunn, an expatriate Englishman living in California, seemed particularly fascinated, in his early poetry, at least, with the theme of suppressed and resurgent violence, among the young especially: motorcyclists, the Hitler Jugend, nightwalkers in San Francisco. In one of his poems, "The Allegory of the Wolf Boy," he uses the werewolf motif to emphasize both the savagery and the pathos of these unconscious compulsions:

> he seeks the moon,
> Which, with the touch of its infertile light,
> Shall loose desires hoarded against his will
> By the long urging of the afternoon . . .
>
> White in the beam he stops, faces it square,
> And the same instant leaping from the ground
> Feels the familiar itch of close dark hair;
> Then, clean exception to the natural laws,
> Only to instinct and the moon being bound,
> Drops on four feet. Yet he has bleeding paws.[44]

NOTES

1. See Arthur O. Lovejoy, "The Parallelism of Deism and Classicism," in *Essays in the History of Ideas* (Baltimore, 1948), pp. 78–98. The standard study of the Noble Savage in English literature is still Hoxie Neale Fairchild, *The Noble Savage: A Study in Romantic Naturalism* (New York, 1928).

2. The Wyoming of Campbell's title was a settlement in Pennsylvania, desolated in an Indian raid of 1778. Campbell had never seen America, but in his notes he makes reference to many travels and histories, including the journals of the Lewis and Clark expedition, and Jefferson's *Notes on Virginia*, in which he read the story of Chief Logan.

3. See Lovejoy, "On the Discrimination of Romanticisms," in *Essays*, pp. 228–53.

4. The quotation from Wordsworth is in "The Tables Turned"; Aldous Huxley, "Wordsworth in the Tropics," in *Do What You Will* (New York, 1930), 123–39.

5. *The Excursion* in *Poetical Works*, ed. E. de Selincourt and Helen Darbishire (Oxford, 1940–49), V, 106–07 (bk. III, ll. 913–32) (hereafter cited as Wordsworth).

6. Wordsworth, V, 107 (ll. 944–55).

7. In *Poetical Works*, ed. C. B. Tinker and H. F. Lowry (London, 1950), p. 5.

8. *The Collected Poems of Wallace Stevens* (New York, 1954), pp. 69–70.

9. The mutiny had already been poeticized by Mary Russell Mitford (better known as the author of *Our Village*) in *Christina, the Maid of the South Seas, A Poem* (London, 1811). The story is supposedly told by the last English survivor among the mutineers on Pitcairn Island, and is replete with noble Tahitian savages.

10. In *Poetical Works*, ed. E. H. Coleridge (London, 1898–1904), V, 608–09 (canto II, ll. 258–71) (hereafter cited as Byron).

11. Byron, V, 602 (canto II, ll. 67–70).

12. Letter to John Rickman, December 23, 1803, in *The Life and Correspondence of Robert Southey*, ed. Charles Cuthbert Southey (London, 1849–50), II, 243.

13. Thomas Carlyle, "Occasional Discourse on the Nigger Question," in *Works* (New York, 1903–04), XXIX, 355.

14. Carlyle, "Occasional Discourse," pp. 350–52.

15. Southey wrote for a living, particularly in the reviews and quarterlies of the day. After 1800 he became something of a Wild Man buff and reviewed almost every book that appeared in England on savage lands, from scientific journals and voyagers' accounts to the diaries of missionaries. A list of some of the books he reviewed is appended to his *Life and Correspondence*, VI, 398–402.

16. Byron, V, 605–06 (canto II, ll. 163–69).

17. Byron, V, 606 (canto II, ll. 179–86). Byron took as his model for Torquil the mutineer George Stewart, who was indeed a son of the Hebrides, but who had a better education and a more "honorable" ancestry than Byron credits him with.

18. Byron, V, 607 (canto II, ll. 203–17).

19. Preface to *Rob Roy* (London, 1877), pp. 5–6.

20. Byron, II, 141 (canto II, st. 65).

21. *Childe Harold*, canto II (note 11); Byron, II, 174.

22. As cited in Leslie A. Marchand, *Byron: A Biography* (New York, 1957), II, 623.

23. *Letters and Journals*, ed. Rowland E. Prothero (London, 1898–1901), I, 252.

24. Byron, II, 174.

25. Byron, II, 174.

26. H. Rider Haggard, *Nada the Lily* (London, 1892), p. x.

27. *Nada the Lily*, p. x; in spite of his suppressions, Haggard was severely criticized in his day for being too fond of blood and cruelty.

28. *Nada the Lily*, p. xi.

29. Umslopogaas was indeed a historical figure, of royal blood of the Swazi nation. Haggard came to know him well when, as a very young man, he joined Sir Theophilus Shepstone on an expedition into the Transvaal. See Lilias Rider Haggard, *The Cloak that I Left: A Biography of the Author Henry Rider Haggard* (London, 1951), pp. 54 ff.

30. *Nada the Lily*, p. 287.

31. *Nada the Lily*, pp. x-xi.

32. Lilias Rider Haggard, *Cloak that I Left*, p. 147. She quotes from a letter of Kipling's to Haggard dated 1895.

33. From a draft dedication of the novel *Child of Storm*, cited in Lilias Rider Haggard, p. 54.

34. Lovejoy, in "The Supposed Primitivism of Rousseau's Discourses," in *Essays*, discusses the popular misconception of Rousseau's ideas. It began very early, however: all the English Romantics who mention Rousseau obviously share it, at least concerning the *Discourses*.

35. See Eva Beatrice Dykes, *The Negro in English Romantic Thought* (Washington, D.C., 1942).

36. Wordsworth, I, 188 (ll. 1539–44). Admittedly the lines are given to the villain of the drama, but Wordsworth repeats them, with some variation, as an epigraph to *The White Doe of Rylstone*.

37. Leslie Fiedler, *Love and Death in the American Novel* (New York, 1960); Norman Mailer, *The White Negro* (San Francisco, 1957); James Baldwin, *The Fire Next Time* (New York, 1963).

38. In *The Poetry and Prose of William Blake*, ed. David V. Erdman (New York, 1965), p. 9.

39. *Paradise Lost*, XI, 831. Orc appears as a whale from the South Seas in *America*, plates I and II.

40. The derivation from *orchis* and the association with Esau are suggested by Kathleen Raine, *Blake and Tradition* (Princeton, 1968), II, 377 ff.

41. Preface to *Edgar Huntley* (Port Washington, N.Y., 1963), p. 4.

42. Fiedler, *Love and Death*, p. 147.

43. Herman Melville, "Benito Cereno," in *Works* (London, 1923), X, 168, 169.

44. Thom Gunn, in *The Sense of Movement* (Chicago, 1957), p. 35. This book was originally published in London.

Conclusion:
Avatars of the Wild Man

The Wild Man, like an errant sun, stands at the core of his own constellation, attracting energies away from the traditional orderly universe conceived by the mind of man. He is the anti-Apollo, irrevocably opposed to existing hierarchies and the organizing force of intellects both human and divine. But he is not Dionysus, the celestial escape valve who was awarded his place among the gods as an excess-energy release to assure the smooth operation of the totality. The Wild Man has no such recognition and, more importantly, his energies are located outside the system. He is rather those forces not within any plan, an antiuniverse whose existence is not always suspected but whose intimate reality undermines the solidity of those structures by which man seeks to live. Whether far away or hidden in the seams of daily life, he is always a threat but not necessarily a destructive one. As a complex of energy whose organization or disorganization differs from the heavenly or worldly cities, he can never be absorbed into oblivion or given full citizenship in any government but his own. His history is as varied as his face and form. In the preceding studies he has been portrayed in many incarnations—savage, barbarian, giant, monster, hero, nemesis, savior, shadow, whipping post.

The full story of the Wild Man's avatars cannot be summed up here, but a pattern can be traced as we follow his journey through the consciousness of European civilization. Essentially he signals an evolution in both feeling and belief that eroded certain values and strengthened others. Institutional confidence grew on the basis of narrowly posited assumptions whereas personal and psychic confidence suffered a serious crisis. Europe prospered, but European man lost contact with the ancestral beliefs that had fostered his strength.

Hayden White's study excavates the basic philosophic and psychic predispositions of the classical world and of medieval Christendom. These attitudes, some conscious, some unconscious, have surfaced again and again in the modern era. For instance, the parallels between Augustine's City of God and the Secular City of Hobbes are rather striking. Both define their respective unities by saying what they are not; both consider wildness as the antipodes of their uniquely desirable redemptive states. But the Wild Man was to have a double life. Whereas for some he was the distant barbarian, for others he was an internal threat, within men and within civilization. He was the ego's shadow and the state's underground.

This double life is visible in the next two essays. Both Stanley Robe's study of the Spanish chroniclers and Gary Nash's analysis of the racial standoff in our own country focus on actual confrontations between Europeans and wild men, that is, with men not included in Europe's view of civilization. Significantly there were Europeans in the very first generation of explorers who opted for the "wild" condition. Yet the great imperial states, Spain and England, were united in a common purpose as they sought to organize the energies of the New World on the patterns of the Old. It was inevitable that the actions of these two peoples, Europe's shock troops in her confrontation with the barbarian, should shape subsequent thought and government. Thus we find that many developments in the fields of philosophy (ostensive self-definition in thought) and empire (ostensive self-definition in action) were outgrowths of the first steps taken in the wilderness.

The many conflicting feelings of civilized men faced with the Wild Man quite naturally find form and meaning in the writings of the two greatest artists of the age, Cervantes and Shakespeare. Cervantes' view of wildness, although not overly optimistic, does map out a possible means by which this uncontrollable energy can be integrated into a new totality. He portrays Cardenio, a young nobleman who distintegrates into a wild man, and then, with the help of Don Quijote, reconstitutes his humanity on a broader basis. The situation as Cervantes unravels the elements is edged with peril, but it contrasts with Shakespeare's pessimistic vision of unintegrated wildness in *The Tempest*. Caliban is only precariously restrained by the more noble forces of Prospero, and the polarity is not resolved at the play's end. Shakespeare's view of man is of essence tragic; Cervantes' is redemptive. Cervantes' masterpiece has been called the Spanish Bible— man will find both God and himself in the divine pilgrimage. Shakespeare, like the Greeks before him, sees man caught in an unresolvable struggle between demonic forces and the gods. European thought today is still divided into the two cosmic visions that found expression at the opening of the seventeenth century: the fatal dominance of instinctive passions portrayed in the works of Shakespeare and the triumphant transformation of will into reality exemplified in the figure of Don Quijote.

Later in the century Hobbes described a working synthesis of human affairs that owes something to each camp. Richard Ashcraft's study points out that Hobbes, like his fellow citizens, the Restoration dramatists, is concerned with governments for wild men. And he makes hard-line distinction between what he considers to be a true government and other organizations of society, or "wild societies," to call them what they became in his thought. Thus it was Hobbes who presented Whig imperialism with its *in hoc signo vinces,* and everything beyond Europe was marked off as fair game for colonial expansion. But his thought also shares something of the Spanish experience—perhaps his source was El Inca Garcilaso—in that he does not see wild men as of essence different from civilized men. He does not divide humankind into Prosperos and Calibans. Rather he sees that his wild men are different because of the structure of the societies in which they live. Colonial peoples were fated to join his secular pilgrimage just as Columbus had foreseen; they became servants. In this way he seemed to answer the bothersome question the seventeenth century continually asked: What can we do with the Wild Man?

The eighteenth century opened with a new kind of encounter and a new question concerning the Wild Man's reality. Maximillian Novak's essay "The Wild Man Comes to Tea" relates the celebrated case of Peter the wild boy, a mysterious child from the woods of Germany, who came to occupy a significant position vis-à-vis the intellectual life of Augustan England. In a sense the Wild Man did come to tea for the Enlightenment, which regarded wildness with a new kind of curiosity, the way one observes a spectacle. Ehrhard Bahr notes that Papageno did cavort in the gilded halls of Rococo palaces, and the Wild Man became an object of investigation and speculation. Diderot and the philosophes of the Encyclopedia shared this fascination with the Wild Man but at the same time utilized him in the polemics of the era as a means of criticizing civilization and ourselves. As Geoffrey Symcox shows, Jean-Jacques Rousseau alone has gone beyond this in his intuitive probings of the primitive mind.

John Burke's search for the Wild Man's origins focuses the basic question of eighteenth-century curiosity. Who is the Wild Man? In what way is he different from European man? The answers the scientists gave were just the ones Europe wanted: The Wild Man is different and inferior. And these judgments have prevailed, almost unchallenged, in many sectors of modern life until very recently.

In the final essay "The Wild Man's Revenge," Peter Thorslev finds that the nineteenth century was the restless heir to the categories that the eighteenth century had hardened into dogma. These polarities generated new passions transforming the Wild Man into a creature regarded with fear and longing. The strange appeal of the Byronic hero in the Romantic era was based on his forbidden wisdom. He had gazed on the face of the Wild Man within and had not flinched. This was the nature of his loathsome knowledge and his numinous attraction. And this came as close as the Romantics cared to come to answering their own unspoken question. If the baroque kings and saints had asked what to do with the Wild Man, and the philosophes had wondered who he was, the Romantics both feared and yearned to know who they would be if they released the hidden Wild Man in their own psyches. This fascination with the problem did not diminish throughout the century but led to scientific voyages into the uncivilized—and previously ignored—unconscious. This interiorization of the Wild Man coincided with the disappearance of the dark places of the planet, as Conrad called them in *Heart of Darkness*. Australia may still be remote enough to harbor a Kangaroo Woman (the "Nullarbor Nymph") as late as 1972, but the very last place of exclusion has turned out to be human nature itself.

This is why the entire concept continues to fascinate us and why François Truffaut's film, *The Wild Child* (L'Enfant Sauvage, 1970) is so appealing to the modern sensibility. Although Truffaut re-creates the late eighteenth-century milieu with extraordinary accuracy, the camera that observes the encounter between Jean-Marc Gaspard Itard and Victor, the Wild Child of Aveyron, gives us a modern focus. Itard, as we view him, is a product of the best in his age. He is a humane, rational, kindly man, but he is also a man who has never seriously examined the values of his civilization. After all, in his book on the wild child, Itard had argued that man's "moral superiority" was entirely a product of civilization, whereas the state of nature was a "state of nullity and barbarism." In Itard we see the limitations of civilized man. In the wild child we see the savage creature we might have been. We observe Victor hitting the back of his head against a tree the way infants do before they are told not to. We see him biting and snarling, insensitive to the sounds of civilization, yet moving alertly at the cracking of a nut. And at one instant, when it is raining, we watch him whirling about in the fields, dancing with delight, in perfect harmony with nature. At that moment Truffaut's camera suddenly moves the distant forest toward the viewer in such a way that the wilderness seems to be studying and measuring us.

Through the efforts of men like Itard, the Wild Man, along with all the other demonic forces of nature, has been officially demythologized. He is merely those energies which have previously evaded the organizing forces of the City of God or the City of Man. But in spite of his demythologization, the Wild Man has successfully resisted encroachments on his domain. Science has only managed a few exploratory probings and some tentative control measures. Even Carl Jung, the most optimistic of searchers, has declared the unconscious uneducable, and so the future of wildness seems assured.

The Wild Man's fate is now more than ever tied to the fate of mankind itself. Man will confront wildness in an uneasy and perilous Prospero-Caliban standoff, hoping that the finger of reason will not have to push the panic button. Or he will seek a more fruitful integration of the Wild Man—not a suppression of him but a new Don Quijote. We can learn to live with wildness and its burning energy only if we redeem ourselves. The question is still redemption or tragic destruction.

Biographical Notes
Index

Biographical Notes

RICHARD ASHCRAFT, Ph.D. (University of California at Berkeley) is Professor of Political Science at UCLA. He is primarily interested both as a teacher and as a research scholar in political theory. He has published many articles on Hobbes, Locke, and Marx, among which are "Hobbes' Natural Man: A Study in Ideology Formation," *Journal of Politics,* November 1971; and "Marx and Weber on Liberalism as Bourgeois Ideology," *Comparative Studies in Society and History,* April 1972.

EHRHARD BAHR, Ph.D. (University of California at Berkeley) is Professor of German at UCLA. His teaching and research interests include nineteenth- and twentieth-century German literature. Among his publications are *Die Ironi im Späpwerk Goethes* (Berlin, 1972); *Georg Lukács* (English translation: New York, 1972); and numerous articles.

JOHN G. BURKE, Ph.D. (Stanford University) is Professor of History at UCLA and Associate Dean of the Graduate School. His primary teaching interest is the history of science and technology. He is the author of *Origins of the Science of Crystals* (Berkeley and Los Angeles, 1966); he has edited *The New Technology and Human Values* (Belmont, Calif., 1966, 2d ed., 1972); and he has written numerous articles.

EDWARD DUDLEY, Ph.D. (University of Minnesota) is Professor of Hispanic and Comparative Literatures at the University of Pittsburgh. He is Chairman of the Department of Hispanic Studies and Co-Director of the Comparative Literature Program. His primary teaching and critical interests are Cervantes and the development of early novel forms. He is the coauthor of *El Cuento* (New York, 1966), has published various articles, and is one of the editors of the new *Latin American Literary Review.*

EARL MINER, Ph.D. (University of Minnesota) is Professor of English at Princeton University, and formerly Clark Professor at UCLA. His teaching and publishing interests include a broad area of seventeenth-century English studies as well as Japanese-Western literary relations. He has published numerous volumes including *The Metaphysical Mode from Donne to*

Cowley (Princeton, 1969); *Dryden's Poetry* (Bloomington, Ind., 1967); and *The Cavalier Mode from Jonson to Cotton* (Princeton, 1971). At present he is completing a three-volume study of seventeenth-century poetry from Donne to Dryden.

GARY B. NASH, Ph.D. (Princeton University) is Professor of History at UCLA. A Guggenheim fellow, 1969–70, Professor Nash teaches courses in the history of American race relations. He has published *Quakers and Politics: Pennsylvania 1681–1726* (Princeton, 1968); *Class and Society in Early America* (Englewood Cliffs, N.J., 1970); and has edited (with Richard Weiss) *The Great Fear; Race in the Mind of America* (New York, 1970).

MAXIMILLIAN E. NOVAK, Ph.D. (Oxford) has been chosen Clark Professor of English at UCLA (1973–74) and is Director of the Seventeenth and Eighteenth Centuries Study Group at the Clark Library. His teaching and criticism concentrate on the Restoration and Augustan periods. His publications include *Economics and the Fiction of Daniel Defoe* (Berkeley and Los Angeles, 1962); *Defoe and the Nature of Man* (Oxford, 1963); *William Congreve* (New York, 1971); an edition of Dryden's *Works* (Berkeley and Los Angeles, 1970); and numerous articles.

STANLEY L. ROBE, Ph.D. (University of North Carolina) is Professor of Spanish and Chairman of the Department of Spanish and Portuguese at UCLA. His teaching and research are oriented toward popular culture and speech in Hispanic America. His publications include *The Spanish of Rural Panama* (Berkeley and Los Angeles, 1960); *Mexican Tales and Legends from Los Altos* (Berkeley and Los Angeles, 1970); *Mexican Tales and Legends from Veracruz* (Berkeley and Los Angeles, 1971); and *Amapa Storytellers* (Berkeley and Los Angeles, 1972). His *Index of Mexican Folktales* is currently in press.

GEOFFREY SYMCOX, Ph.D. (University of California, Los Angeles) is Professor of History at UCLA. His current teaching and research concentrate on French and Italian history of the early modern period, with particular emphasis on diplomatic and military affairs during the reign of Louis XIV. He has published various articles as well as translations from the French, and his book, *War, Diplomacy and Imperialism 1618–1763*, is to be published soon.

PETER L. THORSLEV, JR., Ph.D. (University of Minnesota) is Professor of English at UCLA and was a Guggenheim Fellow (1966–67). His area of interest spans the themes, motifs, and the history of ideas in the Romantic Age.

His publications include *The Byronic Hero* (Minneapolis, 1962) and articles in various journals.

HAYDEN WHITE, Ph.D. (University of Michigan) is Professor of History at UCLA. He works primarily in the fields of cultural history, philosophy of history, and literary theory. He is co-author of *The Emergence of Liberal Humanism* (New York, 1966), editor of *The Uses of History* (Detroit, 1968), and coeditor of *Giambattista Vico* (Baltimore, 1969).

Index

Aarne, A.: cited, 53
Abrams, M. H.: cited, 110n
Abū Bakr ibn al-Tufail, 202–06, 219n
Accursedness: as attribute of Wild Man, 11, 16, 174n
Acosta, J. de: cited, 147, 161, 171n, 174n, 178n; quoted, 174–75n
Adair, J., 75, 77; cited, 84n, 85n, 86n
Addison, J.: cited, 221n
Aelianus, Claudius (Aelian): quoted, 221n
Africans, 79, 176n, 188, 218n, 264, 296–98
Agassiz, L., 272–73
Aguilar, J. de, 48–50
Aiken, H. D.: cited, 181n
Albanian Wild Man, 294–95
Albert of Saxony, 263, 268
Albinos, 267–68
Alleine, J.: cited, 174n
Allestree, R.: quoted, 170n
Amazons, 176n. *See also* Wild woman
Anarchy, 141–42, 245n
Anghiera, Pietro Martire d', 43–47 *passim*
Animalitarianism, 193–94
Animality: as antithesis to humanity, 4–5, 18–19, 150–52, 177n; of Wild Man, 18–19, 128–29, 132, 147, 171n, 174n, 181n, 186, 188, 216–17n, 228, 232
Anson, G. A., 230
Anzigues, 111n
Apes, 212, 238–39, 246–47n, 266–68 *passim. See also* Chimpanzees; Gibbons; Orangutans
Aquinas, Thomas: cited, 37n; on soul, 18–19
Arawaks, 42–46
Arber, E.: cited, 80n, 81n, 82–83n
Arbuthnot, J., 183–84, 193
Archaism, 25–27. *See also* Primitivism
Archer, G.: cited, 82n
Ardrey, R.: cited, 244n

Ariosto, L., 125–26
Aristotle, 263; cited, 20, 23–24, 37n, 47
Arnold, E. V.: cited, 221n
Arnold, M.: quoted, 285
Art: as concept, 4; as mirror, 87, 109–10; origins of, 242
Ascham, A.: cited, 170n
Ashcraft, R., 311; cited, 169n
Atkin, E.: cited, 85n, 86n; quoted, 76
Atkinson, G.: cited, 244n, 245n
Aubignac, F. H., abbé d': cited, 217n
Auden, W. H.: quoted, 250, 251, 256n
Aue, H. von: cited, 251–52
Auerbach, E.: cited, 11, 37n
Augustine, Saint, 137; on being, 8; cited, 36n, 37n, 310; on the impossibility of Antipodes, 262–63; quoted, 3, 16, 18; on sin, 17–18; on state of grace, 4
Avalle-Arce, J. B.: cited, 138n
Avity, P. d': cited, 171n
Aztecs, 292

Babcock, W. H.: cited, 80n
Bachman, J.: cited, 279n
Bacon, F.: cited, 261
Bahr, E., 311
Bailey, A. G.: cited, 86n
Baker, H.: cited, 113n
Baldwin, J., 299; cited, 307n
Banks, J.: cited, 287, 289
Barbarian: concepts of, 6–7, 10, 19–20, 30, 35, 152, 162–63, 226; distinction from Wild Man, 20-21
Barbarity, 226
Barbour, P.: cited, 82n, 83n, 85n
Baritz, L.: cited, 80n
Barlow, A.: quoted, 62
Bartolomé de las Casas. *See* Las Casas, Bartolomé de
Barton, S.: cited, 180n
Barzun, J.: cited, 245n
Baudet, H.: cited, 82n

321